||| | ||| ||||| | ||| | ||||||||| | | |||
W9-CTH-621

DATE DUE

			PRINTED IN U.S.A.

FOR REFERENCE

Do Not Take From This Room

Authors & Artists for Young Adults

ISSN 1040-5682

R

Authors & Artists for Young Adults

VOLUME 15

E. A. Des Chenes
Editor

Gale Research Inc.

An International Thomson Publishing Company

I(T)P

NEW YORK • LONDON • BONN • BOSTON • DETROIT • MADRID
MELBOURNE • MEXICO CITY • PARIS • SINGAPORE • TOKYO
TORONTO • WASHINGTON • ALBANY NY • BELMONT CA • CINCINNATI OH

Riverside Community College
Library
4800 Magnolia Avenue
Riverside, California 92506

JUL   '95

Ref
PN
1009
A1 A88

E. A. Des Chenes, *Editor*

Linda R. Andres, Shelly Andrews, Thomas F. McMahon, and Diane Telgen,
Associate Editors

Mindi Dickstein, David P. Johnson, Ronie-Richele Garcia-Johnson,
Marion C. Gonsior, Janet L. Hile, Laurie Collier Hillstrom, Michael Scott Joseph,
Tom Pendergast, Nancy E. Rampson, Megan Ratner, Susan M. Reicha,
Kenneth R. Sheperd, Tracy J. Sukraw, Sarah Verney, Barbara A. Withers,
Laura M. Zaidman, *Sketch Contributors*

Victoria B. Cariappa, *Research Manager*
Donna Melnychenko, *Project Coordinator*

Tamara C. Nott and Norma Sawaya, *Research Associates*
Alicia Noel Biggers, Maria E. Bryson, Julia C. Daniel, and Amy Beth Wieczorek,
Research Assistants

Margaret A. Chamberlain, *Picture Permissions Specialist*
Susan Brohman, Diane Cooper, Arlene Johnson, and Barbara A. Wallace,
Permissions Associates

Mary Beth Trimper, *Production Director*
Mary Kelley, *Production Associate*

Barbara J. Yarrow, *Graphic Services Supervisor*
Sherrell Hobbs, *Macintosh Artist*
Willie Mathis, *Camera Operator*
Pamela A. Hayes, *Photography Coordinator*

While every effort has been made to ensure the reliability of the information presented in this publication, Gale Research Inc. does not guarantee the accuracy of the data contained herein. Gale accepts no payment for listing; and inclusion in the publication of any organization, agency, institution, publication, service, or individual does not imply endorsement of the editors or publisher. Errors brought to the attention of the publisher and verified to the satisfaction of the publisher will be corrected in future editions.

∞™ The paper used in this publication meets the minimum requirements of
American National Standard for Information Sciences—Permanence Paper
for Printed Library Materials, ANSI Z39.48-1984.

This publication is a creative work fully protected by all applicable copyright laws, as well as by misappropriation, trade secret, unfair competition, and other applicable laws. The authors and editors of this work have added value to the underlying factual material herein through one or more of the following: unique and original selection, coordination, expression, arrangement, and classification of the information.

All rights to this publication will be vigorously defended.

Copyright (c) 1995 by Gale Research Inc.
835 Penobscot Building
Detroit, MI 48226-4094

All rights reserved including the right of reproduction in whole or in part in any form.

Library of Congress Catalog Card Number 89-641100
ISBN 0-8103-5731-3
ISSN 1040-5682

10 9 8 7 6 5 4 3 2 1

Printed in the United States of America

I(T)P™ Gale Research Inc., an International Thomson Publishing Company.
ITP logo is a trademark under license.

Authors and Artists for Young Adults

NATIONAL ADVISORY BOARD

A five-member board consisting of teachers, librarians, and other experts on young adult literature was consulted to help determine the contents of *Authors and Artists for Young Adults*. The members of the board for this volume include:

Jonathan Betz-Zall
Children's Librarian for the Sno-Isle Regional Library System in Edmonds, Washington, and book reviewer for *School Library Journal, Kirkus Reviews,* and *Multicultural Review*

Patricia Campbell
General Editor, Twayne's Young Adult Author Series, and author of columns "The Sand in the Oyster" for *Horn Book Magazine* and "Alternative Routes" for the *Wilson Library Bulletin*

Cathi Dunn MacRae
Librarian, young adult advisory board director at the Boulder Public Library in Colorado, and author of *Wilson Library Bulletin*'s "Young Adult Perplex" column

Pam Spencer
High school librarian and chair of the *School Library Journal* "Adult Books for Young Adults" column

Nancy Vogel
Professor of English at Fort Hays State University in Kanas and author of *Robert Frost, Teacher*

Authors and Artists for Young Adults

TEEN BOARD ADVISORS

A number of teen reading boards were consulted to help determine series' content. The teen board advisors for this volume include:

Barbara L. Blosveren
Head of Young Adult Services and advisor for the Youth Review Board at the Stratford Library in Connecticut

Dana Burton
Youth Services librarian and advisor for the Bloomington Teen Council at the Monroe County Public Library in Indiana

Cathi Dunn MacRae
Librarian, young adult advisory board director at the Boulder Public Library in Colorado, and author of *Wilson Library Bulletin*'s "Young Adult Perplex" column

Golda B. Jordan
Member of the Louisiana Teen-Age Librarians Association and librarian at the Patterson High School Library in Louisiana

Nancy Paul
Member of the Brandon Library Young Adult Advisory Committee and librarian at the Brandon Public Library in Wisconsin

Judith A. Sheriff
Youth Services librarian at the Duluth Public Library in Minnesota

Diane Tuccillo
Member of the Young Adult Advisory Council and Young Adult Services Supervisory librarian at the Mesa Public Library in Arizona

Jed Turner
Advisor to the Teen Advisory Board and Young Adult librarian at the Patchogue-Medford library in New York

Authors and Artists for Young Adults

TEEN BOARD

———

The staff of *Authors and Artists for Young Adults* wishes to thank the following young adult readers for their teen board participation:

Ginger Renee Alleman
Toby Anekwe
Noah Angeron
Chad Anslum
Hannah Arel
Coleen Bach
Mary Bailey
Allison Barrett
John-David Bechler
Debbie Berenz
Kimberly Bilke
Shane Adam Blanco
Brad Borden
Kit Borden
Heather Bosch
Samuel Boutte
Vanessa E. Bowler
Renee Nicole Broussard
Clarice A. Brown
Jason A. Brown
Alyssa Bryner
Ashley Burns
Dylan Burns
Kevin Cameron
David Carleton
Damon Cart
Regina Carter
Alexandra Chebat
Camille Coffey
Christa Cook
Lin Costello
John Darce
Carrie Dautel
Charles De Boer II
Hannah Dentiger
Jessica Donnelly
Alison Dougherty

Brian Downs
Malinda Dunckley
Lisa Ann Eaton
Casey Favors
Heather Foster
Laura L. Fournier
Alda Fox
Raymond Furchat
Damon Galinis
Tamika Haynes
Allen Heinecke
Zeke Henline
Chantal Holland
Chris Johnson
Tori Johnson
Tristan Jones
Sheila Keys
Jenny Kreag
Sara Krochko
John-Thomas Landry
Sara Lavender
Chrissyanne Lawson
Kristen Lindgren
Doug Lipari
Joey Lipari
Kent Lyman
Kathleen Maher
Aaron Manning
Travis McBride
Ryan McLaughlin
Michael Mezzo
AnnMarie Michaud
Betsy Michel
Angela Miller
Jennifer Moon
Larry Mosely
Evet Mouton

Chris Meyers
Jorge O'Campo
Leroy O'Gwin
Andy Packingham
Joseph Peacock
Shawn Pierce
Thomas Pierce
Annie Pettigrew
Carlene Pollmer
Anne Pizzi
Caryn Rasmussen
Paul Reed
David Rees
Linda Reling
Anna Salim
Heather Seal
Erica Sebeok
Amee Shelley
Kaveh Shoraki
Olivia Simantob
Dewana Span
Elizabeth Stern
Beth St. Romain
Lisa C. Sweeney
Jennifer Theriault
Alyson Hope Tiffany
Gregory Trupp
Ingrid Ulbrich
Dan Uznanski
Noel Vande Slunt
Matt Verret
Andy Wallace
Jenn Wilson
Cara Wittchow
Angela Yalteau

Contents

Introduction

Authors and Artists for Young Adults is a reference series designed to serve the needs of middle school, junior high, and high school students interested in creative artists. Originally inspired by the need to bridge the gap between Gale's *Something about the Author,* created for children, and *Contemporary Authors,* intended for older students and adults, *Authors and Artists for Young Adults* has been expanded to cover not only an international scope of authors, but also a wide variety of other artists.

Although the emphasis of the series remains on the writer for young adults, we recognize that these readers have diverse interests covering a wide range of reading levels. The series therefore contains not only those creative artists who are of high interest to young adults, including cartoonists, photographers, music composers, bestselling authors of adult novels, media directors, producers, and performers, but also literary and artistic figures studied in academic curricula, such as influential novelists, playwrights, poets, and painters. The goal of *Authors and Artists for Young Adults* is to present this great diversity of creative artists in a format that is entertaining, informative, and understandable to the young adult reader.

Entry Format

Each volume of *Authors and Artists for Young Adults* will furnish in-depth coverage of twenty to twenty-five authors and artists. The typical entry consists of:

—A detailed biographical section that includes date of birth, marriage, children, education, and addresses.

—A comprehensive bibliography or filmography including publishers, producers, and years.

—Adaptations into other media forms.

—Works in progress.

—A distinctive essay featuring comments on an artist's life, career, artistic intentions, world views, and controversies.

—References for further reading.

—Extensive illustrations, photographs, movie stills, cartoons, book covers, and other relevant visual material.

A cumulative index to featured authors and artists appears in each volume.

Compilation Methods

The editors of *Authors and Artists for Young Adults* make every effort to secure information directly from the authors and artists through personal correspondence and interviews. Sketches on living authors and artists are sent to the biographee for review prior to publication. Any sketches not personally reviewed by biographees or their representatives are marked with an asterisk (*).

Highlights of Forthcoming Volumes

Among the authors and artists planned for future volumes are:

Jeffrey Archer	Howard Fast	Janette Oke
Richard Adams	Keith Haring	Marsha Qualey
Sandy Asher	Stephen Herek	Conrad Richter
Patricia Beatty	David Hockney	Cindy Sherman
Malcolm Bosse	Magic Johnson	Dan Simmons
Ben Bova	Louis L'Amour	Yoshiko Uchida
James L. Brooks	Patricia MacLachlan	Jules Verne
Patricia D. Cornwell	Bernard Malamud	John Waters
Brian Doyle	Kevin Major	August Wilson
Linda Ellerbee	Carolyn Meyer	Stan Winston
M. C. Escher	Walter Mosley	Tobias Wolff
Alan Dean Foster	Tim O'Brien	Robert Zemeckis

The editors of *Authors and Artists for Young Adults* welcome any suggestions for additional biographees to be included in this series. Please write and give us your opinions and suggestions for making our series more helpful to you. Direct your comments to: Editors, *Authors and Artists for Young Adults*, Gale Research, Inc., 645 Griswold St., Suite 835, Penobscot Building, Detroit, MI 48226-4094.

Authors
& Artists
for Young
Adults

Chinua Achebe

■ Personal

Given name, Albert Chinualumogu Achebe; born November 16, 1930, in Ogidi, Nigeria; son of Isaiah Okafo (a Christian missionary teacher) and Janet N. (Iloegbunam) Achebe; married Christie Chinwe Okoli, September 10, 1961; children: Chinelo (daughter), Ikechukwu (son), Chidi (son), Nwando (daughter). *Hobbies and other interests:* Music. *Education:* Attended Government College, Umuahia, 1944–47; attended University College, Ibadan, 1948–53; London University, B.A., 1953; studied broadcasting at the British Broadcasting Corp., London, 1956.

■ Addresses

Home and office—Bard College, Box 5000, Annandale-on-Hudson, NY 12504.

■ Career

Nigerian Broadcasting Corp., Lagos, Nigeria, talks producer, 1954–57, controller of Eastern Region in Enugu, 1958–61, founder and director of Voice of Nigeria, 1961–66; served on diplomatic missions for Biafra during the Nigerian Civil War, 1967–69; University of Nigeria, Nsukka, senior research fellow, 1967–72, professor of English, 1976–81, professor emeritus, 1985—; University of Massachusetts, Amherst, visiting professor of English, 1972–75, professor, 1987–88; Anambra State University of Technology, Enugu, pro-chancellor and chairman of council, 1986–88; Bard College, Annandale-on-Hudson, NY, professor of English, 1991—; writer. Visiting professor and lecturer at universities in Nigeria and the United States, including University of Connecticut, 1975–76, and University of California, Los Angeles, 1984. Chairman, Citadel Books Ltd., Enugu, Nigeria, 1967; director, Heinemann Educational Books Ltd., Ibadan, Nigeria, 1970—; founder and publisher, *Uwa Ndi Igbo: A Bilingual Journal of Igbo Life and Arts,* since 1984. Member, University of Lagos Council, 1966, East Central State Library Board, 1971–72, Anambra State Arts Council, 1977–79, and National Festival Committee, 1983; director, Okike Arts Centre, Nsukka, 1984—; deputy national president of People's Redemption Party, 1983; governor, Newsconcern International Foundation, 1983; president of town union, Ogidi, Nigeria, 1986–92; speaker at events in numerous countries throughout the world. *Member:* International Social Prospects Academy (Geneva), Writers and Scholars International (London), Writers and Scholars Educational Trust (London), Commonwealth Arts Organization (member of executive committee, 1981—), Association of Nigerian Authors (founder, president, 1981–86), Ghana Association of Writers (fellow), Royal Society of Literature (London), Modern Language Association of America (honorary fellow), American Academy of Arts and Letters (honorary member).

■ Awards, Honors

Margaret Wrong Memorial Prize, 1959, for *Things Fall Apart;* Rockefeller travel fellowship to East and Central Africa, 1960; Nigerian National Trophy, 1961, for *No Longer at Ease;* UNESCO fellowship for creative artists for travel to United States and Brazil, 1963; Jock Campbell/New Statesman Award, 1965, for *Arrow of God;* D.Litt., Dartmouth College, 1972, University of Southampton, 1975, University of Ife, 1978, University of Nigeria, Nsukka, 1981, University of Kent, 1982, Mount Allison University, 1984, University of Guelph, 1984, and Franklin Pierce College, 1985; Commonwealth Poetry Prize, 1972, for *Beware, Soul-Brother, and Other Poems;* D.Univ., University of Stirling, 1975; Neil Gunn international fellow, Scottish Arts Council, 1975; Lotus Award for Afro-Asian Writers, 1975; LL.D., University of Prince Edward Island, 1976; D.H.L., University of Massachusetts, Amherst, 1977; Nigerian National Merit Award, 1979; named to the Order of the Federal Republic of Nigeria, 1979; Commonwealth Foundation senior visiting practitioner award, 1984; citation in Anthony Burgess's 1984 book *Ninety-nine Novels: The Best in English since 1939,* for *A Man of the People;* Booker Prize nomination, 1987, for *Anthills of the Savannah.*

■ Writings

NOVELS

Things Fall Apart, Heinemann, 1958.
No Longer at Ease, Heinemann, 1960.
Arrow of God, Heinemann, 1964.
A Man of the People, John Day, 1966.
Anthills of the Savannah, Anchor Books, 1988.

SHORT STORY COLLECTIONS

The Sacrificial Egg, and Other Stories, Etudo, 1962.
Girls at War, and Other Stories, Heinemann, 1973.

ESSAYS

Morning Yet on Creation Day, Doubleday, 1975.
The Trouble with Nigeria, Fourth Dimension Publishers, 1983.
Hopes and Impediments, Heinemann, 1988.

POETRY

Beware, Soul-Brother, and Other Poems, Nwankwo-Ifejika, 1971, Heinemann, 1972.
Christmas in Biafra, and Other Poems, Doubleday, 1973.

JUVENILE

Chike and the River, Cambridge University Press, 1966.
(With John Iroaganachi) *How the Leopard Got His Claws* (bound with "The Lament of the Deer" by Christopher Okigbo), Nwankwo-Ifejika, 1972, Third Press, 1973.
The Flute, Fourth Dimension Publishers, 1978.
The Drum, Fourth Dimension Publishers, 1978.

EDITOR

(With Dubem Okafor) *Don't Let Him Die: An Anthology of Memorial Poems for Christopher Okigbo,* Fourth Dimension Publishers, 1978.
(Coeditor) *Aka Weta: An Anthology of Igbo Poetry,* Okike, 1982.
(With C. L. Innes) *African Short Stories,* Heinemann, 1984.
(With Innes) *The Heinemann Book of Contemporary African Short Stories,* Heinemann, 1992.

OTHER

Founding editor, "African Writers Series," Heinemann, 1962–72; editor, *Okike: A Nigerian Journal of New Writing,* 1971—; editor, *Nsukkascope,* a campus magazine. Contributor to numerous anthologies, including *Modern African Stories, Through African Eyes, Africa Speaks: A Prose Anthology with Comprehension and Summary Passages,* and *Stories of War and Peace from Nigeria. Things Fall Apart* has been translated into forty-five languages.

■ Adaptations

Things Fall Apart was adapted for the stage and produced by Eldred Fiberesima in Lagos, Nigeria, adapted for radio and produced by the British Broadcasting Corp. in 1983, and adapted for television in English and Igbo and produced by the Nigerian Television Authority in 1985.

■ Sidelights

"Travellers with closed minds can tell us little except about themselves," the Nigerian writer Chinua Achebe put forth in his essay "An Image of Africa" in the collection *Hopes and Impediments.*

It's no wonder, then, that Achebe's Africa, as presented in his acclaimed novels, looks nothing like the Africa previously written about. For well into this century, virtually the only recognized African literature was not really African at all. It was written by Europeans and was more about their experiences of conquest than anything else. This colonialist perspective saw Africa as the dark opposite of civilization, peopled by savages who were the dark opposite of Europeans. Achebe's Africa, on the other hand, is a real place, full of real people, with real occupations and real voices, who live the legacy of a real history.

Achebe, whose writings include five novels, two short story collections, essays, poetry, and children's stories, is considered one of the most significant figures in contemporary African literature. Among the first to write authentically in English about African culture, Achebe is credited with not only helping to create a foundation for a new body of literature but also for adapting English to the needs of African culture. "I feel that the English language will be able to carry the weight of my African experience. But it will have to be a new English, still in full communion with its ancestral home but altered to suit its new African surroundings," Achebe told Jonathan Cott in *Pipers at the Gates of Dawn: The Wisdom of Children's Literature*. Achebe's five novels "form a continuum of time over some one hundred years of Igbo civilization . . . an imaginative history of a segment of a major group of people in what eventually became Nigeria, as seen from the perspective of a Christian Igboman," summarized G. D. Killam, writing in the *Dictionary of Literary Biography*. A theme in all of Achebe's novels is England's occupation and exploitation of Africa, beginning with the imposition of a foreign culture on the traditional one and the ongoing effects of colonization on individuals and on society. Because Achebe was born at a transitional time in the history of his people, he has had the rare opportunity to look both backward and forward at two different worlds. The view seems to be of both the tragic and the optimistic, which in his writing stand side by side.

Chinua Achebe was born to Christian parents in 1930 in the Igbo village of Ogidi in eastern Nigeria. His father was a missionary teacher for the Church Missionary Society, and the family read the Bible and attended church regularly. Yet, as Achebe explained to Patrick H. Samway in *America* magazine, ". . . there was also another part of the village that was not Christian. . . . So in my early years, I was exposed to both the Christian faith and the traditional religion of the Igbo people. When I look back, what was important to me then was that I was exposed to two different ways of seeing the world. Without knowing it, I was fascinated by the interplay between them." His given name, Albert Chinualumogu, reflects something of that duality, something of the Nigeria he was born into, a place irreversibly changed by and bearing the marks of English colonization, but where the traditional Igbo village culture of the past was still alive. Of his name, Achebe wrote in "Named for Victoria, Queen of England" in *Hopes and Impediments*, "I dropped the tribute to Victorian England when I went to the university . . . So if anyone asks you what Her Britannic Majesty Queen Victoria had in common with Chinua Achebe, the answer is: They both lost their Albert! As for the second name, which in the manner of my people is a full-length philosophical statement, I simply cut it in two, making it more businesslike without, I hope, losing the drift of its meaning." Chinua, then, Achebe explained, is a shortened way of saying, "May my chi [personal god] fight for me."

Through the philosophical significance of a name, an intricate way of using proverbs in conversation to circle around a difficult subject, or storytelling that instructs and delights while at the same time stoking the imagination of both teller and listener, Achebe makes clear throughout his writings the central importance of language in Igbo society. In his first novel, *Things Fall Apart*, he wrote of the Igbo: ". . . the art of conversation is regarded very highly, and proverbs are the palm-oil with which words are eaten." It is something Achebe seems to have understood from an early age. In "Named for Victoria" he explained: "I have always been fond of stories and intrigued by language—first Igbo, spoken with such eloquence by the old men of the village, and later English, which I began to learn at about the age of eight. I don't know for certain, but I have probably spoken more words in Igbo than English but I have definitely written more words in English than Igbo. Which I think makes me perfectly bilingual."

As a boy, Achebe loved hearing the stories that his mother and older sister told, which never sounded quite the same from one telling to the next. Achebe received his primary education at the Church Missionary Society's school in his village; then, at age fourteen, he was among a select group chosen to attend Government College in Umuahia for his secondary schooling. One of the best schools in West Africa, Government College was based on the British system and gave Achebe access to a good library at a time when books were still a rarity in African schools. "I remember the very strong impression made on me by the rows and rows of books in my school library when I first got there in 1944," Achebe wrote in his essay "What Do African Intellectuals Read?" in the essay collection *Morning Yet on Creation Day*. He continued, "In our time, literature was just another marvel that came with all the other wondrous things of civilization, like motor cars and airplanes, from far away. They had very little to do with us, or rather we had very little to do with them, except in the role of wide-eyed consumers. Today, in the realm of literature at least, such inhibiting non-identification is already a thing of the past."

Achebe began his undergraduate studies in English literature in 1948 at University College at Ibadan, where his course work followed the degree program of the University of London. While a student, he wrote stories and essays for the university magazine, the *University Herald* (some of those stories were published in 1973 in *Girls at War, and Other Stories*.) After receiving his bachelor's degree in 1953, Achebe began a professional broadcasting career with the Nigerian Broadcasting Corporation in Lagos. In 1961 he married Christie Chinwe Okoli and started a family that would grow to include two daughters and two sons. It was a near decade of beginnings for Achebe, for in 1958, amidst the advent of professional and family life, his first and most famous novel, *Things Fall Apart*, was published.

New Stories to Tell

"You can't explain why you become a writer, actually, in one word. But you can certainly show strands of the story. . . ." Achebe told Kay Bonetti in an interview in the *Missouri Review*. Among those strands was exactly the kind of non-identification Achebe himself felt with existing literature about Africa, which had been written by Europeans and was based on ignorant and racist stereotypes, "simple stories about good white people and sinister savages," as Achebe described the lit-

Achebe's first novel tells the story of a self-made man who kills himself rather than yield to a foreign threat.

erature to Samway in *America*. He went on in that interview to say that "it was when I realized the implications of these stories that I finally came to the conclusion that something had to be done. New stories had to be written; those of the white man and the savage were really not my story. And thus the genesis of my desire to tell my own story and the story of my people."

In *Things Fall Apart*, Achebe begins that story by looking back to his grandfather's generation, revealing for readers something of the Igbo people's long, rich history before colonial power overcame traditional society. In *The Growth of the African Novel*, Eustace Palmer wrote, "Chinua Achebe's *Things Fall Apart* . . . demonstrates a mastery of plot and structure, strength of characterization, competence in the manipulation of language and consistency and depth of thematic exploration which is rarely found in a first novel." Set in the village of Umuofia and its environs in the latter half of the nineteenth century, when white men had just begun their conquest of western Africa, *Things Fall Apart* is the story of Okonkwo, a self-made man who dies by his own hand rather than yield to foreign threat. G. D. Killam, in his *The Novels of Chinua Achebe*, described *Things Fall Apart* as a story "concerned with the passions of living people, with the validity of traditional religion, with property ownership, with the relations between the rich and the poor, with the arrangements of marriages and the celebrations of deaths. The conflict in the novel, vested in Okonkwo, derives from the series of crushing blows which are levelled at traditional values by an alien and more powerful culture causing, in the end, the traditional society to fall apart." Hence, Killam explains, the importance of the book's title, which comes from W. B. Yeats' poem "The Second Coming."

Things Fall Apart is a tragedy in the classical sense, the story of a flawed hero, Okonkwo, told in the context of the rituals and celebrations of day-to-day Igbo village life. Okonkwo is the son of the good-natured layabout Unoka, who loved wine and music to the extent that he left his family unprovided for. By the sheer force of hard work and an "inflexible will," Okonkwo raises himself above his lowly beginnings, becoming an accomplished wrestler, courageous warrior, wealthy farmer, and man of title and authority. Even so, as readers are told in the novel, Okonkwo's "whole life was dominated by fear, the fear of failure and weakness. . . . It was not external but lay deep within himself. It was the fear of himself, lest he should be found to resemble his father. . . . And so Okonkwo was ruled by one passion—to hate everything that his father Unoka had loved. One of those things was gentleness and another was idleness."

Achebe shows readers the extent of Okonkwo's fear of weakness in what has been cited as perhaps one of the most memorable and heart-wrenching scenes he has written: Okonkwo receives word from the village oracle that Ikemefuna, a boy who three years before had been won from a nearby village in a dispute, must be killed. And even though he has come to love the boy like a son, when the time comes, Okonkwo himself cuts the boy down with his machete rather than appear weak. This horrifying act is all the more forceful for the way Achebe juxtaposes it with Ikemefuna's brave innocence during his death walk: he is afraid at first but consoles himself with thoughts of returning home to an overjoyed mother:

> Then quite suddenly a thought came upon him. His mother might be dead. He tried in vain to force the thought out of his mind. Then he tried to settle the matter the way he used to settle such matters when he was a little boy. He still remembered the song. . . . He sang it in his mind and walked to its beat. If the song ended on his right foot, his mother was alive. If it ended on his left, she was dead. No, not dead, but ill. It ended on the right. She was alive and well. He sang the song again, and it ended on the left.

This event is the first signal of Okonkwo's impending doom. The second comes when Okonkwo accidentally shoots and kills a fellow villager and is banished for seven years to his mother's village. Killam, writing in the *Dictionary of Literary Biography*, described this as the period when "readers learn of the arrival of the white man and of the religion and colonial government gradually introduced into the area. The economy of Achebe's prose and his restraint in telling his story belie the complexity of the issues. Because the coming of the foreigners is gradual, the processes by which these new values are established are insidious." Villagers—including Okonkwo's son Nwoye—join the Christian church, and, according to Killam, "this, together with the establishment of a political-judicial system administered by Europeans (and supported by African police) and the introduction of a cash-based trading economy, causes things to change irreversibly. . . . The traditional balance is upset." The novel comes to its tragic close when, following Okonkwo's return to Umuofia, a clash with the Christians brings about a confrontation between villagers and government officers. Okonkwo, being the inflexible man he is, cannot back down and sees only one alternative: to fight. Okonkwo kills the white man's messenger, and then, rather than die at the hands of the white men, he hangs himself. It is a shameful death for a man determined to be shamed by no one, yet the tragedy will be no more than a brief anecdote in some district officer's memoirs.

Achebe turns to the modern Nigeria of mid-twentieth century—just before the country's independence from European rule—in his second novel, *No Longer at Ease*. The title comes from T. S. Eliot's poem "The Journey of the Magi." Achebe's novel tells the story of Okonkwo's grandson, Obi Okonkwo, a forward-looking young man educated in England who, despite being full of high ideals and moral purpose, comes up short in the end against traditional demands that conflict with modern life, against his country's vices, and against his own weakness. Much has happened to transform Nigeria and the distance between Obi and his kinsman Okonkwo seems wide indeed. Killam wrote in the *Dictionary of Literary Biography* that *No Longer at Ease* is both "the tragic story of a modern man" and a telling of "the tragedy of a modern state." Killam noted, "The novel reveals the changes to Nigerian society that result from foreign intervention—the extent to which things have fallen apart."

Obi Okonkwo returns from England convinced that the greed and corruption prevailing in Nigeria can be overcome and the country changed for the better by men like him: modern, moral, and educated. He lands a job as a civil servant and finds happiness in romance with Clara, a nurse he met on his return voyage. Yet for all Obi's good and moral intentions, when he faces social and moral difficulties created out of the conflict between the traditional and the modern, the ideal and the real, he finds that he is not as strong as the forces that are working against him. So begins his downfall.

The Umuofia Progressive Union, which represents his village and has financed his education, expects repayment; at the same time, Obi feels pressure to maintain an expensive lifestyle that reflects the success the Union has helped him achieve. He soon finds himself in over his head. And while Obi receives praise for his success as a modern man, he is expected to pay heed to certain traditional beliefs that he believes no longer have relevance. He plans to marry Clara, even though her ancestors were of a slave class that were forced to live apart from the rest of the village. Such a marriage is still considered taboo to Obi's parents, village elders, and friends. When Clara becomes pregnant and undergoes an unsafe abortion, Obi is unable to stand up for her and loses her. This loss, his mother's death, and his unsurmountable financial problems are too much for Obi. He gives

in, takes the bribes which he has resisted until now, is caught and convicted. Both Okonkwo and Obi Okonkwo meet with tragic endings wrought with irony: the former stands fast, the latter gives way. Both lose. Achebe puts forth his view of tragedy in *No Longer at Ease* when Obi indirectly contrasts his grandfather's fate with a foreshadowing of his own: "Real tragedy is never resolved. It goes on hopelessly for ever. Conventional tragedy is too easy. The hero dies and we feel a purging of the emotions. A real tragedy takes place in a corner, in an untidy spot, to quote W. H. Auden. The rest of the world is unaware of it."

Achebe originally conceived of *Things Fall Apart* and *No Longer at Ease* as the first and third parts of a trilogy documenting three generations of a family. However, he never wrote the story of Isaac Nwoye, Okonkwo's son and Obi Okonkwo's father. "The middle generation—when I got to it, I got stuck. It's very interesting, it's very strange. . . . I began to suspect that I did not know enough about this very, very strange generation, my father's generation, to be able to do justice to it in the novel. I didn't know enough about my father—why did he become a Christian? Why did people of the generation decide to abandon their religion and their faith? What was it? It's a good story, but I think that it probably isn't as simple as I imagined it originally," Achebe reflected in the Bonetti interview.

Power Struggles

Not that any of the stories Achebe *has* written are simple. Critics do, however, consistently cite the simple eloquence of Achebe's style and masterful economy of his storytelling. "In the earlier novels Achebe, with great literary skill, was supreme in making action convey to the reader the terrifying truths he exposed," wrote John Povey in *African Arts*. This is particularly true of *Arrow of God*, Achebe's third novel, which is perhaps his most complex in terms of the way it examines the processes that work together to bring down an individual of power and authority. In the book, readers are taken back to the early part of the twentieth century to a pre-modern village much like Okonkwo's, ". . . but more dynamic, in comprehensive detail, a world redolent of the complexities of daily domestic, social, political, and religious living but further complicated by the religious and political prescriptions the colonial force has introduced into Igbo society, rules that are

30023-4/U.S. $4.95

Chinua Achebe
Modern Africa's Most Celebrated Novelist
No Longer At Ease

The story of Okonkwo's family is continued in this 1960 work that charts the coming-of-age of European-educated Obi Okwonko.

now institutionalized," wrote Killam in the *Dictionary of Literary Biography.* As in *Things Fall Apart,* Achebe brings this past world to life with its sights and sounds, rituals and relationships, to an extent where it might be tempting to attribute these books' value to their documentation of a segment of traditional African society and culture. Yet, Killam, in *The Novels of Chinua Achebe,* pointed out, "So much has been written about the anthropological and sociological significance of *Things Fall Apart* and *Arrow of God*—their evocation of traditional nineteenth- and twentieth-century Igbo village life—so much about Achebe's attempt to write stories which have the components of Aristotelian tragedy, that the overall excellence of these

books as pieces of fiction, as works of art has been obscured."

Arrow of God is about Ezeulu, the chief priest of Umuaro, a coalition of six villages which joined together to better protect themselves against a common enemy. Ezeulu's god, Ulu, was chosen as Umuaro's principal deity, thus supplanting the gods worshipped by the individual villages and creating a power struggle between Ezeulu and the priest of a god which no longer has dominance. In addition to this tension is the suspicion and jealousy engendered among Ezeulu's family and neighbors when he decides to send his son, Oduche, to the white man's Christian church and school. This brings additional trouble to Ezeulu's compound when Oduche, in devotion to his new religion, commits the sacrilege of trying to kill a sacred python. And finally, Ezeulu defies a request by the British district officer and is imprisoned. Ezeulu punishes his people for not standing behind him by refusing to announce the beginning of the yam harvest at the usual time. This brings on a famine. In desperation, the people turn against Ezeulu and make their offerings to the Christian god in exchange for the Christians' promise of a protected harvest.

In a moving attempt to reclaim something of his father's good name, another of Ezeulu's sons, Obika, agrees to take on the persona of the night spirit ekwe-ogbazulobodo and runs a ritual funeral race, even though he is ill. Achebe conveys the intensity of Obika's undertaking through a stream of proverbs intertwined with Obika's struggling heart and breath. But after a noble run, Obika drops dead. Ezeulu, who convinced himself that he was the arrow of his god, acting on the deity's behalf, is struck down by the grief over his cumulative losses which "finally left a crack in Ezeulu's mind. . . . It allowed Ezeulu, in his last days, to live in the haughty splendor of a demented high priest and spared him knowledge of the final outcome."

"The novel is a meditation on the nature and uses of power, and on the responsibility of the person who wields it," wrote Killam in the *Dictionary of Literary Biography.* ". . . Ezeulu is forced to try to reconcile the contending impulses in his nature: to serve the needs of his people and to indulge his desire for greater personal power through pushing his authority to its limits. Out of the contending impulses his tragedy arises." Ezeulu, then,

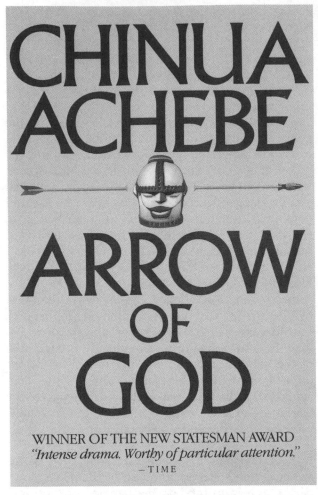

CHINUA ACHEBE

ARROW OF GOD

WINNER OF THE NEW STATESMAN AWARD
"Intense drama. Worthy of particular attention."
– T I M E

This 1964 work explores the processes that work together to bring down an individual of power and authority.

proves the Igbo proverb that one man, no matter how great, cannot win against all of his people. Achebe, in a preface to the second edition of *Arrow of God,* wrote: "Whenever people have asked me which among my novels is my favourite I have always evaded a direct answer, being strongly of the mind that in sheer invidiousness that question is fully comparable to asking a man to list his children in the order in which he loves them. A paterfamilias worth his salt will, if he must, speak about the peculiar attractiveness of each child. For *Arrow of God* that peculiar quality may lie in the fact that it is the novel which I am most likely to be caught sitting down to read again."

A Man of the People, Achebe's fourth novel, goes back to the future, so to speak, taking place in modern, postcolonial Africa, where "there is an atmosphere of unrestrained acquisitiveness in the midst of political corruption: there is no national voice but only a confusion of competing village voices, an atmosphere where it is every man for himself in acquiring as large a piece of the national financial cake as possible and by whatever means are the most effective," Killam explained in the *Dictionary of Literary Biography.* Achebe's protagonist is a young teacher, Odili Kamalu, who gets involved in politics after his associations with a charismatic but corrupt government official, Chief Nanga, bring him betrayal and disillusionment. Odili is like *No Longer at Ease*'s Obi Okonkwo in that he is full of moral purpose and youthful idealism. He is unlike Obi in that he is able to stand firm in his principles. Odili joins a fledgling political party and runs against Chief Nanga, whose party even Odili's father supports. Of course Odili cannot win against the wealthy, powerful, and unprincipled rival, and the rigged election results in Nanga claiming victory and Odili in the hospital after a humiliating and life-threatening beating by Nanga's men. This ending for Odili, however, is not altogether about loss, for through his struggle he keeps his principles, wins his father's respect, and gains the love of Nanga's fiancee. For the country, however, *A Man of the People* is less optimistic, ending with the murder of Odili's political ally, Max, and a military coup, signalling a violent and uncertain future devoid of leadership responsible to the will of the people.

A Man of the People was published in 1966 and has been called prophetic because just after its publication a military coup actually took place in Nigeria. The political climate became dangerous and resulted in acts of violence and murder against the Igbo people, primarily in northern Nigeria. The eastern region of the country, including Igboland, rebelled and formed a separatist state, Biafra. This led to a civil war that lasted for more than two years. Achebe left the Nigerian Broadcasting Corporation in 1966 and became a spokesman, at home and abroad, for the Biafran cause.

The Writer as Teacher

During this period of unrest, Achebe, with another writer, John Iroaganachi, published a children's story, *How the Leopard Got His Claws.* The experience gives an illustration of the power that stories can wield. Achebe and his friend Christopher

Okigbo had fled to Enugu where they had set up the Citadel Press. Iroaganachi had submitted a story called "How the Dog Became Domesticated," and Achebe had set to work editing it. As Achebe recounted to Cott in *Pipers*, ". . . it grew until it just turned into something else, it wasn't about the dog at all anymore but rather about the leopard. And it was now a parable about Nigeria—the common house that had been torn apart." As such, the book provides an accessible way to begin learning about a segment of Africa's political past.

The book was in the process of being printed when federal forces took Enugu and Achebe and his colleagues fled. A friend was able to save a copy of the story, and *How the Leopard Got His Claws* was eventually published, together with "The Lament of the Deer," a poem by Okigbo, who was killed in the Biafran struggle. Achebe continued in *Pipers*: "Now at the end of the war, we went back to the site of the publishing house, and it had been razed to the ground—it seemed to me that whoever did it didn't like publishing or at least this particular publishing house and perhaps this particular book. . . . Later on, one chap who was working as an intelligence officer with the federal troops said to me, 'You know, of all the things that came out of Biafra, that book was the most important.'" Clearly, as Achebe told Cott in *Pipers*, ". . . I really feel that stories are not just meant to make people smile, I think our life depends on them."

On writing for children, Achebe said in *Pipers*, "It's a challenge I like to take on now and again because it requires a different kind of mind from me when I'm doing it—I have to get into the mind of a child totally, and I find that very rewarding. I think . . . we should return to childhood again and again. And when you write for children it's not just a matter of putting yourself in the shoes of a child—I think you have to be a child for the duration." Achebe has written several other children's stories: *Chike and the River* (1966) and his version of two traditional folk tales, *The Flute* (1978) and *The Drum* (1978). *Chike* is a chapter book—often used as a reader in African schools—about a bright and adventuresome boy who leaves his village to live with his uncle in Onitsha, a market city. There he makes friends at school, gets in and out of trouble, and dreams of crossing the River Niger, which his mother has warned him against. He learns that hard work is

the only way to find reward and finally makes enough money for the ferry ride across the river. He catches some thieves while stranded on the far bank and comes home a hero. While readers may not know firsthand the worlds of Achebe's stories, certainly the minds of Achebe's fictional children are recognizable. Readers know about their songs and games and can relate to their giving of nicknames, making up after squabbles, writing in readers, contemplating new words and phrases they find in books and hear at school, fearing punishment, and longing for impossible things.

Achebe told Cott in *Pipers*, "The adult is someone who has seen it all, nothing is new to him. Such a man is to be pitied. The child, on the other hand, is new in the world, and everything is possible to him. His imagination hasn't been dulled by use and experience. Therefore, when you restory the adult, what you do is you give him back some of the child's energy and optimism, that ability to be open and to expect anything. The adult has become dull and routine, mechanical, he can't be lifted. It's as if he's weighted down by his experience and his possessions, all the junk he's assembled and accumulated. And the child can still fly, you see. Therefore the story belongs to the child, because the story's about flying."

Achebe's most recent novel, *Anthills of the Savannah*, was published in 1988, more than twenty years after *A Man of the People*. It was nominated for Britain's prestigious Booker Prize. "It is a strangely loving book. Achebe is a master neither of plot, which is rudimentary, nor narrative, which can be choppy, nor even—in the narrow sense of the word—of character. He is a master of the culture of which he writes . . . its reverence, its humor, its breathtaking practicality, its toughness, its fragility, and what I must call its loveliness. He is master, above all, of the comic, bewitching and agonizing shock of its collision with the blind forces of modernization," wrote Richard Eder in the *Los Angeles Times Book Review*. *Anthills* is an indictment of one-man government, as well as political corruption and moral decline. It takes place in an African country Achebe calls Kangan, and features three school friends, Sam, Chris, and Ikem who, as adults, become, respectively, a military dictator, a government information minister in his service, and a newspaper editor. When one province—Ikem's homeland—does not support his bid to become ruler-for-life, Sam becomes suspicious and has Ikem killed. Chris, who has supported Ikem, fears for his life and flees. The army then ousts and kills Sam. Chris, too, is killed by a soldier. The tale's optimism comes through its heroines, Beatrice, an administrator, and Elewa, a shop girl. As Achebe explained to Bonetti, "Traditionally when the men have tried and failed, then they have called in the women. The women have the insights for survival. . . . But it's not a guarantee. It's only a conditional source of hope."

In *Anthills,* Achebe uses a mixed manner of storytelling, which John Updike, writing in *The New Yorker,* notes as "voices [that] fitfully range from poems and myths to cocktail gossip, from almost unintelligible dialogue in West African patois . . to equally opaque flights of literarese. . . .

By the author of *Things Fall Apart*

CHINUA

ANTHILLS

O F

T H E

SAVANNAH

"*Anthills of the Savannah*...will prove hard to forget. It's a vision of social change that strikes us with the force of prophecy."—*USA Today*

ACHEBE

Nominated for the Booker Prize, this work is an indictment of one-man government, political corruption and moral decline.

In some sentences, the words accumulate like sandbags being piled by a weary worker. . . . Nevertheless, from the fractured telling a number of truths about Africa emerge." These truths have to do with failed leadership, which Achebe described in his 1983 book *The Trouble with Nigeria,* "There is nothing basically wrong with the Nigerian character. There is nothing wrong with the Nigerian land or climate or water or air or anything else. The Nigerian problem is the unwillingness or inability of its leaders to rise to the responsibility, to the challenge of personal example which are the hallmarks of true leadership."

Achebe believes a writer must do more than provide entertainment or create "art for art's sake." He must be a teacher, one who, for the good of others, passes on what he has gained for himself. In an essay devoted to this topic, "The Novelist as Teacher" in *Hopes and Impediments,* Achebe discusses the legacy of racial inferiority left to his people by colonialism and what he as a writer has tried to do about it. "It is too late in the day to get worked up about it or to blame others, much as they may deserve such blame and condemnation. What we need to do is to look back and try and find out where we went wrong, where the rain began to beat us." He goes on to tell of one of his wife's students who wrote about winter—a season he had never experienced—rather than the Harmattan, which is the dry, dusty wind that blows from November to March from inland Africa toward the Atlantic coast. When asked why he did not write about it, the boy said he feared he would be called a bushman if he had. "Now, you wouldn't have thought, would you, that there was something shameful in your weather? But apparently we do. How can this great blasphemy be purged? I think it is part of my business as a writer to teach that boy that there is nothing disgraceful about the African weather, that the palm tree is a fit subject for poetry. . . . I would be quite satisfied if my novels (especially the ones I set in the past) did no more than teach my readers that their past—with all its imperfections—was not one long night of savagery from which the first Europeans acting on God's behalf delivered them."

Looking to his future, Achebe sees himself carrying on with the work he has started. Even a terrible car accident in Nigeria in 1990, which left Achebe near death, has not stopped him. After months of surgeries and physical therapy, he came to the United States and took up a teaching post at Bard College in Annandale, New York. It is one more accomplishment to add to a career list of books, awards, some twenty honorary doctorates, and teaching posts in this country and in Nigeria. "The nature of my writing might change by what I have undergone, but I cannot predict exactly what will happen," Achebe told Samway. "I plan to continue with a novel I have in mind, but I am not sure how the details will develop. In addition, I hope to write my autobiography in the near future because so much has happened to me in the recent past. So, you see, my days will be full."

Where one thing stands, another stands beside it. This is an Igbo proverb often cited by Achebe which illustrates the duality of all things in life. Where Europe's stories about Africa have stood, now, due in large part to Achebe's work, a growing body of African literature stands beside it. Achebe's novels have much to say about reclaiming the past and taking personal responsibility within one's community, something that has national implications. Such messages are of great relevance for today's young Americans, who search for themselves amidst crumbling institutions and fallen heroes, whose lives bear the marks of violence and disunity, whose experiences are largely mediated by television. In "An Image of Africa" in *Hopes and Impediments,* Achebe recalled a letter he received from a high school student, who, having just read *Things Fall Apart,* was "particularly happy to learn about the customs and superstitions of an African tribe. . . . The young fellow . . . is obviously unaware that the life of his own tribesmen in Yonkers, New York, is full of odd customs and superstitions and, like everybody else in his culture, imagines that he needs a trip to Africa to encounter those things."

■ Works Cited

Achebe, Chinua, *Things Fall Apart,* Heinemann, 1958.

Achebe, Chinua, *No Longer at Ease,* Heinemann, 1960.

Achebe, Chinua, *Arrow of God,* Heinemann, 1964.

Achebe, Chinua, *Morning Yet on Creation Day,* Doubleday, 1975.

Achebe, Chinua, *The Trouble with Nigeria,* Fourth Dimension, 1983.

Achebe, Chinua, *Hopes and Impediments,* Heinemann, 1988.

Bonetti, Kay, interview with Chinua Achebe, *Missouri Review,* Vol. XII, No. 1, 1989.

Cott, Jonathan, *Pipers at the Gates of Dawn: The Wisdom of Children's Literature,* Random House, 1981, pp. 161–92.

Eder, Richard, "Peacocks on the Day of Reckoning," *Los Angeles Times Book Review,* February 28, 1988, pp. 3, 8.

Killam, G. D., *The Novels of Chinua Achebe,* Africana Publishing Corp., 1969.

Killam, G. D., "Chinua Achebe," in *Dictionary of Literary Biography, Volume 117: Twentieth-Century Caribbean and Black African Writers, First Series,* Gale, 1992, pp. 15–34.

Palmer, Eustace, *The Growth of the African Novel,* Heinemann, 1979.

Povey, John, review of *Anthills of the Savannah, African Arts,* August, 1988, pp. 21–3.

Samway, Patrick H., "An Interview with Chinua Achebe," *America,* June 29, 1991, pp. 684–86.

Updike, John, review of *Anthills of the Savannah, The New Yorker,* June 13, 1988, p. 114.

■ For More Information See

BOOKS

Contemporary Literary Criticism, Volume 75, Gale, 1993, pp. 1–31.

Children's Literature Review, Volume 20, Gale, 1990, pp. 1–9.

PERIODICALS

Los Angeles Times Book Review, December 24, 1989, p. 4; February 4, 1990, p. 14.

New York Times Book Review, November 12, 1989, p. 55.

Publishers Weekly, August 25, 1989, p. 53.

Times Literary Supplement, October 9, 1987, p. 1106.

Utne Reader, March/April, 1990, p. 36.

—*Sketch by Tracy J. Sukraw*

Ray Bradbury

Screenwriters Guild, Science Fiction and Fantasy Writers of America (president, 1951–53), Pacific Art Foundation.

■ Personal

Also writes as D. R. Banat, Leonard Douglas, William Elliott, Douglas Spaulding, Leonard Spaulding, and Brett Sterling. Born Ray Douglas Bradbury on August 22, 1920, in Waukegan, IL; son of Leonard Spaulding (a power lineman) and Esther (Moberg) Bradbury; married Marguerite Susan McClure, September 27, 1947; children: Susan, Ramona, Bettina, Alexandra. *Education:* Attended schools in Waukegan, IL, and Los Angeles, CA. *Politics:* Independent. *Religion:* Unitarian Universalist. *Hobbies and other interests:* Painting in oil and water colors; collecting Mexican artifacts.

■ Addresses

Home—10265 Cheviot Dr., Los Angeles, CA 90064. *Agent*—Don Congdon, 156 Fifth Ave., #625, New York, NY 10010.

■ Career

Writer, primarily of fantasy and science fiction, 1943—; lecturer; newsboy in Los Angeles, CA, 1939–42. *Member:* Writers Guild of America West,

■ Awards, Honors

O. Henry Prize, 1947, for short story "Homecoming," and third prize, 1948, for short story "Powerhouse"; Benjamin Franklin Award for best story of 1953–54 in an American magazine, for "Sun and Shadow" in *The Reporter;* Commonwealth Club of California gold medal, 1954, for *Fahrenheit 451;* award from National Institute of Arts and Letters, 1954, for contributions to American literature; Boys' Clubs of America Junior Book Award, 1956, for *Switch on the Night;* Golden Eagle Film Award, 1963, for *Icarus Montgolfier Wright* screenplay; Academy Award nomination for Best Animated Short Subject, 1963, for *Icarus Montgolfier Wright;* Mrs. Ann Radcliffe Award, Count Dracula Society, 1965, 1971; Valentine Davies Award from Writers Guild Award (with Philip Dunne), 1974, for work in cinema; World Fantasy Award, 1977, for lifetime achievement; D.Litt., Whittier College, 1979; Balrog Award, 1979, for Best Poet; Aviation and Space Writers Award, 1979, for television documentary "Infinite Space: Beyond Apollo"; Gandalf Award (Grand Master), World Science Fiction Society, 1980; George Foster Peabody Award from University of Georgia, Emmy Award nomination from Academy of Television Arts and Sciences, and American Film Festival Blue Ribbon, all 1982, all for "The Electric Grandmother"; Jules Verne Award, 1984; HBO Ace Award for writing in a dramatic series, 1985, for "Ray Bradbury Theater"; Body of Work Award, PEN, 1985; Los Angeles Drama Critics Circle Award (five) for "The Martian Chronicles"; Grand Masters Award, Nebula Science Fiction Writers of America, 1988.

■ Writings

YOUNG ADULT

Switch on the Night, Pantheon, 1955, Knopf, 1993.
R Is for Rocket (short stories), Doubleday, 1962, Bantam, 1990.
S Is for Space (short stories), Doubleday, 1966, Bantam, 1990.
The Halloween Tree, Knopf, 1972, 1988.
(With Gary Kelley) *The April Witch*, Creative Education, 1987.
(With Gary Kelley) *The Other Foot*, Creative Education, 1987.
The Foghorn, Creative Education, 1987.
(With Gary Kelley) *The Veldt*, Creative Education, 1987.
Fever Dream, St. Martin's, 1987.

NOVELS

The Martian Chronicles, Doubleday, 1950, revised edition published in England as *The Silver Locusts*, Hart-Davis, 1951, Buccaneer, 1991.
Fahrenheit 451, Ballantine, 1953, Simon & Schuster, 1993.
Dandelion Wine, Doubleday, 1957.
Something Wicked This Way Comes, Simon & Schuster, 1962.
Death Is a Lonely Business, Knopf, 1985.
A Graveyard for Lunatics, Knopf, 1990.
The Smile, Creative Education, 1991.

STORY COLLECTIONS

Dark Carnival, Arkham House, 1947, Buccaneer, 1994.
The Illustrated Man, Doubleday, 1951, Buccaneer, 1991.
The Golden Apples of the Sun, Doubleday, 1953, Bantam, 1990.
The October Country, Ballantine, 1955.
A Medicine for Melancholy, Doubleday, 1959, revised edition published in England as *The Day It Rained Forever*, Hart-Davis, 1959, Bantam, 1990.
The Small Assassin, Ace Books, 1962.
The Machineries of Joy, Simon & Schuster, 1964.
The Vintage Bradbury, Vintage Books, 1965.

The Autumn People, Ballantine, 1965.
Tomorrow Midnight, Ballantine, 1966.
I Sing the Body Electric!, Knopf, 1969.
(With Robert Bloch) *Bloch and Bradbury: Ten Masterpieces of Science Fiction*, Tower, 1969, published in England as *Fever Dreams and Other Fantasies*, Sphere, 1970.
(With Robert Bloch) *Whispers from Beyond*, Peacock Press, 1972.
Long After Midnight, Knopf, 1976.
The Best of Bradbury, Bantam, 1976.
The Mummies of Guanajuato, Abrams, 1978.
To Sing Strange Songs, Wheaton, 1979.
The Aquaduct, Squires, 1979.
The Stories of Ray Bradbury, Knopf, 1980.
The Last Circus and the Electrocution, Lord John, 1980.
Dinosaur Tales, Bantam, 1983.
A Memory of Murder, Dell, 1984.
The Toynbee Convector, Random House, 1988.

SELECTED PLAYS

The Anthem Sprinters and Other Antics, Dial, 1963.
The Day It Rained Forever (one-act), Samuel French, 1966.
The Pedestrian (one-act), Samuel French, 1966.
Dandelion Wine (music composed by Billy Goldenberg), first produced at Lincoln Center's Forum Theatre, 1967.
The Wonderful Ice-Cream Suit and Other Plays, Bantam, 1972, published in England as *The Wonderful Ice-Cream Suit and Other Plays for Today, Tomorrow, and Beyond Tomorrow*, Hart-Davis, 1973.
Pillars of Fire and Other Plays for Today, Tomorrow, and Beyond Tomorrow, Bantam, 1975.
The Martian Chronicles, first produced at the Colony Theatre, Los Angeles, 1977.
Fahrenheit 451, first produced at the Colony Theatre, Los Angeles, 1979.
A Device Out of Time, Dramatic Publishing, 1986.

Also author of other produced plays, musicals, and cantatas.

FILMS

It Came from Outer Space, Universal Pictures, 1953.
The Beast from 20,000 Fathoms (based on his story "The Foghorn"), Warner Bros., 1953.
(With John Huston) *Moby Dick*, Warner Bros., 1956.
(With George C. Johnson) *Icarus Montgolfier Wright*, Format Films, 1962.

Something Wicked this Way Comes, Walt Disney, 1983.

Also author of television scripts for various programs, including "Jane Wyman Theatre," "The Trouble Shooters," "Alfred Hitchcock Presents," "The Twilight Zone," and "Ray Bradbury Television Theatre."

POETRY

Old Ahab's Friend, and Friend to Noah, Speaks His Piece: A Celebration, Squires, 1971.

When Elephants Last in the Dooryard Bloomed: Celebrations for Almost Any Day in the Year, Knopf, 1973.

That Son of Richard III: A Birth Announcement, Squires, 1974.

Where Robot Mice and Robot Men Run Round in Robot Towns, Knopf, 1977.

Man Dead? Then God is Slain!, California State University—Northridge, 1977.

Twin Hieroglyphs That Swim the River Dust, Lord John, 1978.

The Bike Repairman, Lord John, 1978.

The Author Considers His Resources, Lord John, 1979.

Beyond 1984: A Remembrance of Things Future, Targ, 1979.

This Attic Where the Meadow Greens, Lord John, 1979.

The Ghosts of Forever, (five poems, a story, and an essay), Rizzoli, 1980.

Imagine, Lord John, 1981.

The Haunted Computer and the Android Pope, Knopf, 1981.

Then Is All Love? It Is, It Is!, Orange County Book Society, 1981.

The Complete Poems of Ray Bradbury, Ballantine, 1982.

The Love Affair, (two poems and a short story), Lord John, 1983.

America, Lord John, 1983.

To Ireland, Lord John, 1983.

The Last Good Kiss, California State University—Northridge, 1984.

Long After Ecclesiastes, Goldstein Press, 1985.

Death Has Lost Its Charm for Me, Lord John, 1987.

A Climate of Palettes, Lord John, 1988.

OTHER

(Editor and contributor) *The Circus of Dr. Lao and Other Improbable Stories,* Bantam, 1956.

The Ghoul Keepers, Pyramid Books, 1961.

Zen and the Art of Writing, Capra Press, 1973, 3d revised edition, Odell, 1993.

the Mummies of Guanajuato, Abrams, 1978.

Beyond 1984: Remembrance of Things Future, Targ, 1979.

Los Angeles, Skyline Press, 1984.

Orange County, Skyline Press, 1985.

(Editor) *A Day in the Life of Hollywood,* Collins, 1992.

Work is represented in over seven hundred anthologies. Contributor of short stories and articles, sometimes under pseudonyms, to *Playboy, Saturday Review, Weird Tales, Magazine of Fantasy and Science Fiction, Omni, Life,* and other publications.

■ Adaptations

Fahrenheit 451 was adapted as a film, Universal, 1966; *The Illustrated Man* was adapted as a film, Warner Bros./Seven Arts, 1969; *The Martian Chronicles* was adapted as a television movie, NBC-TV, 1979; *The Electric Grandmother* was adapted as a television movie (based on *I Sing the Body Electric*), NBC-TV, 1982.

Bradbury's works have also been adapted for other media, including radio dramas, videocassettes, recordings, and filmstrips.

■ Sidelights

"The most beautiful sound in my life, dearly recollected, was the sound of a folded newspaper kiting through the summer air and landing on my front porch. . . . The door burst open. A boy, myself, leapt out, eyes blazing, mouth gasping for breath, hands seizing at the paper to grapple it wide so that the hungry soul of one of Waukegan, Illinois' finest small intellects could feed. . . ."

"That was how I lived," Ray Bradbury remembers in his 1969 introduction to *The Collected Works of Buck Rogers in the 25th Century,* "in a fever, a faint delirium, in semi-hysteria. I was born and bred fanatic. What I loved, I truly loved." "In fact," he concludes, "I still live pretty much that way." Bradbury continues to communicate his passion for imagination and creativity, as well as his major themes of alienation and fear, through his writing. He utilizes a variety of media ranging from nonfiction to poetry, from television and films to short stories and novels. "I have found again and again that the finest minds, the finest colleges, the nicest people, do not know the first thing about Creativity, large C or small," he explains in his introduction to *Buck Rogers*. "In fact I have watched supposedly intelligent men hurl themselves with cruel vigor into attacking and destroying the simple root systems of creativity . . . the outcrop of imagination we call romance."

Greatest Gift Was Falling in Love

Bradbury's family was a literate one. Leonard Spaulding Bradbury, his father, was English by ancestry, although the family had been in the New World since at least the seventeenth century: he counted among his progenitors a woman tried for witchcraft in Salem, Massachusetts. "He came from a family of newspaper editors and printers,"

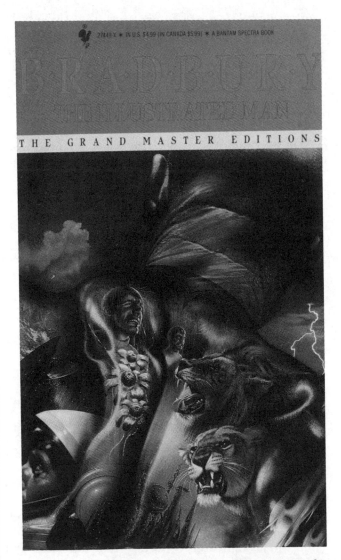

A man is haunted by the often-terrifying stories the tattoos on his body tell in this 1951 collection.

Bradbury explains to William F. Nolan in a biographical sketch accompanying the 1973 Doubleday edition of *The Martian Chronicles*. "My grandfather and great-grandfather formed Bradbury & Sons, and published two northern Illinois newspapers at the turn of the century, so you might say that publishing and writing are in my blood." His mother, Esther Marie Moberg, was the daughter of Scandinavian immigrants. Bradbury himself was born on August 22, 1920, "a Sunday afternoon . . . while my father and brother were attending a baseball game on the other side of town," he tells Nolan.

"I have what might be called almost total recall back to the hour of my birth," Bradbury states in Nolan's *The Ray Bradbury Companion*. "I remember suckling, circumcision, and nightmares-about-being-born experienced in my crib in the first weeks of my life. I know, I know, such things are not possible. Most people don't remember. Psychologists say that babies are born undeveloped, and that only after some few days and weeks are they capable of seeing, hearing, knowing. But, I saw, I heard, I knew." These memories may have helped spur Bradbury's early and profound fear of the dark—a fear that he later drew on in *Switch on the Night* and many of his "dark fantasy" stories. "Some of my first memories," he explains in Sam Moskowitz's *Seekers of Tomorrow*, "concern going upstairs at night and finding an unpleasant beast waiting at the next to the last step. Screaming, I'd run back down to mother. Then, together, we'd climb the stairs. Invariably, the monster would be gone. Mother never saw it. Sometimes I was irritated at her lack of imagination." Such unpleasant experiences did have their benefits, however. "I imagine I should be grateful for my fear of the dark," he concludes. "You have to know fear and apprehension in some form before you can write about it thoroughly, and God knows my first ten years were full of the usual paraphernalia of ghosts and skeletons and dead men tumbling down the twisting interior of my mind. What a morbid little brat I must have been to have around."

Bradbury grew up in the small Illinois town of Waukegan, north of Chicago near the shore of Lake Michigan, where his father was an electrical lineman for the Waukegan Bureau of Power and Light. He draws on his family history and his small-town American upbringing in almost all of his fiction. Waukegan serves as a model for Green

Town, Illinois, the setting of *Dandelion Wine*. It is cut on a north-south axis by a long ditch like the ravine featured in the novel. Moreover, it was reputed to be haunted by a figure who lurked late at night near a bridge over the gully, a character similar to The Lonely One featured in *Dandelion Wine*. "The preoccupation with libraries most evident in *Something Wicked This Way Comes*," writes Gary K. Wolfe in the *Dictionary of Literary Biography*, ". . . is certainly related to the ten-year-old Bradbury's spending each Monday evening with his brother at the Waukegan Public Library. His fascination with circuses and carnivals may be related to the traveling shows of his youth, and in particular to a day in 1931 when he appeared on stage as an audience volunteer with Blackstone the Magician."

The films and books young Bradbury saw and read also helped to fire his romantic literary imagination. "A number of people changed my life forever in various ways," Bradbury writes in his introduction to Irwin Porges' biography *Edgar Rice Burroughs: The Man Who Created Tarzan*. "Lon Chaney put me up on the side of Notre Dame and swung me from a chandelier over the opera crowd in Paris. Edgar Allen Poe mortared me into a brick vault with some Amontillado. Kong chased me up one side and down the other of the Empire State." Other influences included the early science fantasy comic strip *Buck Rogers in the 25th Century*, the *Amazing Stories* science fiction magazine, L. Frank Baum's fantasy series about the magical Land of Oz, the "Tom Swift" science adventure series about a young inventor, and the works of Poe, Jules Verne, and H. G. Wells. "In all of the years of all the laughing, the snorting, the doubtful, the derisive people, only a few made sense to me . . . truly inspired me, filled me with love, and allowed my intuition to come out to play forever in the fields of space," Bradbury states in his introduction to *The Collected Works of Buck Rogers in the 25th Century*. "Boys need to take courage wherever they can find it. . . . We live by example."

Going Mad with Mr. Burroughs

It was Edgar Rice Burroughs's "Tarzan" and "Martian" novels, however, that influenced Bradbury the most—not because of Burroughs's grasp of scientific principles, but because of his huge, awesomely romantic imagination. "Mr. Burroughs convinced me that I could talk with the animals, even if they didn't answer back, and that late nights when I was asleep my soul slipped from my body and frolicked across town . . . ," Bradbury continues in his introduction to the Porges biography. The writer tells *Contemporary Authors New Revision Series* interviewer Jean Ross that "The very first thing I did, when I was twelve, was to write a sequel to an Edgar Rice Burroughs novel because I couldn't afford to buy it. Burroughs was a very sly character. He wrote one of his Martian novels and left his heroine trapped in the Sun Prison, and you had to buy the next book to find out how she got out. I had no money, so I wrote the sequel and got her out." Bradbury turned to this practice on other occasions as well. "It was a long way to my next birthday and Christmas," Bradbury explains in David Morgan's study *Ray Bradbury*, "so that's why I sat down with my friend, Bill Arno, and why we got out a roll of butcher paper and wrote and illustrated a sequel to *The Gods of Mars*." Burroughs' fantasies became a significant influence on the young Bradbury. "Some part of [my] soul," he declares in the Porges biography introduction, "always stayed in the ravine running through the center of Waukegan . . . up in a tree, swinging on a vine, combating shadow-apes." But Burroughs' greatest gift, he concludes, "was teaching me to look at Mars and ask to be taken home."

Bradbury's tastes in reading and his active imagination helped him survive some of the realities of his family's life. "Twice during his childhood, in 1926–1927 and again in 1932–1933," Wolfe writes, "Bradbury lived with his family in Arizona, where his father hoped to find work after being laid off during the Depression. . . . But both moves were abortive, and in both cases the family returned to Waukegan." In 1934, however, Leonard Bradbury uprooted his family once again—this time permanently. "Because he thought he'd have better luck getting a job on the West Coast," Bradbury tells *Detroit Free Press* contributor Sandra Shevey, "my father . . . moved us from Waukegan, Ill., to Los Angeles. He'd walk for miles every day looking for work, and the only two times I ever remember seeing him cry were when my sister died and when he couldn't find a job." The family's financial situation remained bleak. "We were so poor," he continues, "that we were on relief the day I graduated from the Los Angeles High School. My parents couldn't even afford to buy me a graduation suit, so I wore the suit an uncle of mine had been killed in. He'd been shot by a holdup man, and the bullet hole went through the front and out the back of the suit. We didn't have enough money to have the bullet hole repaired." Undaunted, Bradbury found ways to enjoy Los Angeles that did not require money. He worked at station KGAR as a gofer and wound up performing bit parts in radio dramas. He learned to sneak into Los Angeles theaters without paying to see the latest MGM films. Accompanied by a friend, he served as the first live audience for one of George Burns and Gracie Allen's radio shows. He showed up for auditions for his high school talent show and found himself serving as announcer, director, sound effects man, and scriptwriter. "It should seem obvious by now," he states in Nolan's *The Ray Bradbury Companion,* "that I was always out of breath, always going somewhere, always wanting something, and there weren't enough days or hours for me to fill with my loves." Science fiction, he notes, "was one among half a dozen such grand affairs I had with life. And I wrote it amongst 4,000 students at Los Angeles High School who neither knew nor cared whether or not one damned rocket was ever built or pointed toward the Moon, Mars, or the Universe."

Bradbury's enthusiasm as a reader of science fiction helped him break into the genre as a writer. According to Nils Hardin in the *Dictionary of Literary Biography,* Bradbury became active in science fiction fandom in his seventeenth year and soon began writing and illustrating for the Los Angeles Science Fantasy Society's *Imagination!* His first published short story appeared in the fanzine early in 1938. Bradbury's zeal soon outran *Imagination!*'s publication schedule, however, and "in June 1939 he began his own mimeographed fanzine, *Futuria Fantasia,* Hardin explains. "He published, edited, and contributed fiction, columns, and verse to the four issues he published, the last one being distributed in September 1940. All four issues were typed mimeographed sheets, printed in green ink. Each issue had a cover by the later well-known fantasy artist, Hannes Bok. Bradbury's own contributions to the fanzine issues appeared under his own name, anonymously, and under various pseudonyms." In 1941, drawing on his experience in the fanzines, Bradbury made his first professional sale—"Pendulum," a story co-written with his friend Henry Hasse—to *Super Science Stories.* "My share of the check came to $13.75 . . .

and it seemed like a million to me! . . . I was a *writer!,*" he exclaims in the biographical sketch accompanying *The Martian Chronicles.* "When 1941 ended I had written fifty-two new stories in fifty-two weeks, and had sold three of them."

Many of Bradbury's earliest stories appeared in *Weird Tales,* which specialized in fantasy and horror fiction rather than the science fiction emphasis of magazines like *Amazing Stories* and *Super Science Stories.* He also was able to sell stories to mainstream periodicals such as *American Mercury* and *Mademoiselle.* Stories such as "The Small Assassin," about a baby who kills its parents, and "The Lake," in which a young man visits the shore of a lake where his childhood sweetheart drowned ten years before only to discover her body, appealed to a different audience than that of most of the major science fiction pulps. Bradbury's poetic style and his concentration on the emotion of fear proved to be a good match for the *Weird Tales* readers, and the stories themselves helped Bradbury come to terms with his childhood fears. "In the horror tales," declares Anita T. Sullivan in *English Journal,* "he was completely serious and trying his best to achieve a shock effect upon his readers. In the best of these, he probably succeeded because he also achieved, in the writing process, a shock effect upon himself. He was trying to exorcise something in himself as he wrote. Thus his horror tales were not written to enable his readers to escape, but rather to cause them to suffer so that they might be cleansed."

"The Lake" was first purchased by August Derleth, a Wisconsin-based publisher whose press, Arkham House, reprinted the dark fantasy of H. P. Lovecraft in book form. Derleth recognized that Bradbury was a talented writer. After accepting "The Lake" for inclusion in a 1945 anthology, *Who Knocks?,* he challenged Bradbury to collect enough of his stories to create a volume of his own. As a result, *Dark Carnival* appeared under the Arkham House imprint in 1947. In that same year Bradbury married Marguerite McClure, an English teacher who also "worked in a downtown bookstore," Bradbury states in Nolan's biographical sketch. "Each afternoon she'd watch this shaggy fellow come in, carrying a briefcase. He'd nose around, pick up several books, discard them, then leave. When a number of volumes were reported missing, Maggie was convinced she'd found the thief—which was *me!* That's how we met. Luckily, the missing books were found, and I ended up stealing Maggie."

The two of them decided to wed, despite a certain amount of uncertainty about their financial situation. "The day we married, in late September," he continues in an article for the periodical *Making Films in New York,* "I had ten dollars in the bank. I offered it to the minister who handed it back, saying, 'You're a writer, aren't you?' I nodded. 'Then you'll need this more than I will,' he said. Dear man."

The Red Fields of Mars

Like *Dark Carnival,* Bradbury's first novel, *The Martian Chronicles,* came about through the suggestion of a publisher. Bradbury had already written a number of stories dealing with the colonization of Mars: "The Million-Year Picnic," for instance, was published in *Planet Stories* in 1946. But "The book market for fantastic literature was more receptive to novels than to short-story collections. When Walter Bradbury, a Doubleday editor, suggested in 1949 that Bradbury put together a book with at least a semblance of narrative continuity, the author's response was almost immediate," reports Wolfe. "I went to my room at the YMCA," Bradbury relates in an article written for the *New York Times,* "brooded, and suddenly realized that all the Martian stories fell into an atmosphere, a pattern, a place, a time. By midnight that night I had done an outline of a novel."

The Martian Chronicles is a generally optimistic work about the first Terran settlers on Mars and the difficulties they encounter there. The telepathic native Martians sense the impending arrival of the humans. Some react with a romantic sense of wonder; others become fearful and kill the aliens, destroying the first expedition to the planet. A second expedition to the planet meets a similar fate, destroyed by Martians who regard them merely as hallucinations. The third expedition is lured into a trap: upon arriving on Mars, they discover their own families and childhoods, reconstructed from their own memories. "Seduced by this telepathic hallucination," Wolfe explains, "they too are destroyed, unable until it is too late to overcome the powerful pull of their own past lives. To survive in the new environment, one must be willing to forgo the past entirely."

The narrative, however, indicates that the continuing expeditions have taken their toll on the native Martians as well. The fourth expedition discovers that most of the natives have succumbed to Terran diseases. The focus of the stories then turns to the settlers. Some arrive looking for opportunities to exploit the environment; others come seeking an escape from oppression, censorship, and the threat of nuclear war. When the threatened war actually breaks out, however, most of the settlers choose to return home, leaving only a few individuals and families. At the end of the volume, in "The Million-Year Picnic," a family that has travelled to Mars to escape the nuclear war begins to reject the remnants of their own past and to adapt to their new environment. They be-

The effects of Man's colonization of Mars is the focus of this series of tales.

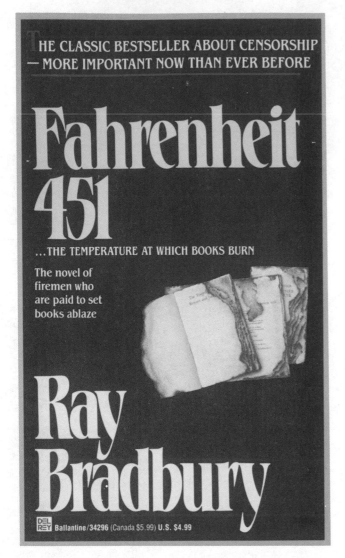

THE CLASSIC BESTSELLER ABOUT CENSORSHIP — MORE IMPORTANT NOW THAN EVER BEFORE

Fahrenheit 451

...THE TEMPERATURE AT WHICH BOOKS BURN

The novel of firemen who are paid to set books ablaze

Ray Bradbury

DEL REY Ballantine/34296 (Canada $5.99) U.S. $4.99

In this 1953 work, the author presents a society where books and reading have been declared illegal.

gin to think of themselves as Martians rather than transplanted Terrans.

The Martian Chronicles, according to some reviewers, is less about the fanciful topic of interplanetary colonization and more about life, death, and culture in mid-twentieth century America. Racism is the underlying theme of "Way in the Middle of the Air," while in "The Off-Season," the exploiters of Mars realize the futility of their actions when their markets on Earth collapse as a result of a nuclear holocaust. The only way to survive both as individuals and as a species, as Bradbury demonstrates in "The Million-Year Picnic," is to accept the new environment and adapt to it, to reject the technological trappings of the Terran past and look toward a truly Martian future. "This

new paradise," declares George Edgar Slusser in the *Dictionary of Literary Biography,* "is a doubly barren planet: life is still firmly rooted in death. Again, the new world is one of timidity and fearful restriction. Yet there is . . . hope." He describes *The Martian Chronicles* as "a magic and ephemeral moment of balance between individual and social concerns, between fallen nature and man's ability to abide." Slusser concludes that, "to Bradbury, science is the forbidden fruit, destroyer of Eden, and continuing mark of man's fall."

Hellfire and Damnation

Bradbury pursues related topics in his novel *Fahrenheit 451.* "I didn't know it, but I was literally writing a dime novel," Bradbury reveals in his afterword to the 1982 Ballantine edition of the book. "In the spring of 1950 it cost me nine dollars and eighty cents in dimes to write and finish the first draft of *The Fire Man* which later became *Fahrenheit 451.* In all the years from 1941 to that time, I had done most of my typing in the family garages," he continues, but his growing family proved to be a distraction, and Bradbury moved the center of his operations to the typing room in the college library at UCLA—where the available typewriters were rented out at a price of ten cents every half hour. "Between investing dimes and going insane when the typewriter jammed . . . and whipping pages in and out of the device, I wandered upstairs. There I strolled, lost in love, down the corridors, and through the stacks, touching books, pulling volumes out, turning pages, thrusting volumes back, drowning in all the good stuffs that are the essence of libraries. What a place, don't you agree, to write a novel about burning books in the future!"

Fahrenheit 451 is also about repression and escape in the future, and it evokes the same sense of fear that Bradbury practiced in *Dark Carnival.* It was based in part on a short story, "Dark Phoenix," that Bradbury had begun in the late 1940s. It takes place on Earth in a society that has rejected freedom of thought and condones book-burning as a means of ensuring conformity. The protagonist, Guy Montag, is one of the official book-burners. However, a young woman he meets raises doubts in his mind about himself and his society and he begins to read books himself. Eventually he escapes his oppressive society and goes to live with a band of bibliophiles in the wilderness. The book-lovers in the novel fight back against the book-burners by each choosing one book and memorizing it, preserving it from society's traditional means of destruction.

Like *The Martian Chronicles* and *Dark Carnival, Fahrenheit 451* is less about technology than it is about people. Montag alienates himself from the society he originally swore to protect after he begins to read books. "From then on he is isolated," declares Slusser: "deeds prove pointless, all attempts at communication . . . futile. Society's course leads fatally to holocaust. The hero can only escape to a nature still fallen, where the new fire of human companionship remains a feeble spot in the dark forest." Even the technological devices that Bradbury introduces—such as the Mechanical Hound, which hunts down social deviants by tracing changes in their body chemistry—evoke less fear, according to Donald Watt in *Ray Bradbury,* than "the specter of that witless mass of humanity in the background who feed on manhunts televised live and a gamey version of highway hit-and-run.

"Themes of alienation and fear appear in many of Bradbury's short stories as well. "The Foghorn," included in Bradbury's 1953 short story collection *The Golden Apples of the Sun,* is a representative example. The story concerns a lonely monster that mistakes the foghorn of a ship for a mating call and became the basis for the 1953 Warner Brothers film, *The Beast from 20,000 Fathoms.* Many of the stories in *The Illustrated Man*—which are generated by the tattoos on the man's back—address the same topics and concerns. Some, such as "The Veldt" and "The City," echo the fantasy and horror that dominated *Dark Carnival.* One—"The Exiles"—has clear connections with both *The Martian Chronicles* and *Fahrenheit 451:* it depicts the ghosts of great fantasists surviving on Mars, only to be finally destroyed when their books are burned on Earth.

Something Wicked This Way Comes also deals with fear. It tells the story of two midwestern boys, Will Halloway and Jim Nightshade, who visit Cooger and Dark's Pandemonium Shadow Show, a carnival that has set up shop in a local meadow. They are overcome by the evil forces that manage the carnival, but are rescued by Will's father, Charles Halloway. "As in much of Bradbury's earlier fiction," Wolfe writes, "the car-

nival represents not only present evil, but also the vulnerability of the human form and the seductive dangers of the past." Halloway emerges triumphant, though, despite the fact that, as Wolfe notes, his weapon is "nothing more than the power of laughter. The carnival is vanquished, but in the closing scene Halloway explains that it will return, that it ultimately resides in each individual, and that the struggle never really ends." *Switch on the Night* provides a more reassuring view of darkness. It looks at Bradbury's childhood fear of the dark in terms familiar to a child: rather than switching off the light in the room, the child switches on the night and its sounds become faiar and comforting rather than terrifying.

280325 ✻ IN U.S. $5.50 (IN CANADA $6.99) ✻ A BANTAM SPECTRA BOOK

B·R·A·D·B·U·R·Y
SOMETHING WICKED THIS WAY COMES
THE GRAND MASTER EDITIONS

Two Midwestern boys discover their dark side when evil—in the guise of a mysterious carnival—creeps into a small town.

Young Douglas Spaulding finds out a lot about himself and his world during the momentous summer depicted in this 1957 novel.

Green Town, U.S.A.

Despite "the fact that it cannot be called science fiction," writes A. James Stupple in the essay collection *Voices for the Future,* "*Dandelion Wine* closely resembles *The Martian Chronicles* and much of Bradbury's other writing in that it is essentially concerned with the same issue—the dilemma created by the dual attractions of the past and the future, of stasis and change." "Essentially a series of sketches based on Bradbury's childhood in Waukegan," Wolfe explains, "*Dandelion Wine* is distinguished primarily for its evocative style; its only real theme is that, through a series of experiences in a single summer, young Douglas Spaulding . . . comes to realize that he is alive." The youth is at a crossroad in his personal

growth. "At twelve," declares Stupple, "Douglas Spaulding finds himself on the rim of adolescence. On one side of him lies the secure, uncomplicated world of childhood, while on the other is the fascinating yet frightening world of 'growing up.'" In *Dandelion Wine,* he continues, "Bradbury seems to be reiterating what he has said in *The Martian Chronicles*—that the past, or stasis, or both, is enticing but deadly, and that Douglas, like the colonists, must forsake the past and give himself up to change and progress."

Critics recognized *Dandelion Wine* as a lyrical, almost surrealistic, celebration of youth in small-town America in the early decades of the twentieth century. "All the lives chronicled," reports Slusser, "seem to be encapsulated by the existence of Douglas, bottled like dandelion wine for his private consumption. His final act is to stand in a cupola high above the town and, moving his arms like an orchestra leader, direct the world to sleep." The book is widely recognized as one of Bradbury's most enduring works. "More than any other single book, perhaps," Wolfe contends, "*Dandelion Wine* consolidated Bradbury's reputation as a poet of small-town nostalgia and provided the clearest perspective to date on the essential sources of his overall vision."

"What you have . . . in this book then is a gathering of dandelions from all those years," Bradbury explains in his introduction to the 1975 edition of *Dandelion Wine.* "I was gathering images all my life, storing them away, and forgetting them. Somehow I had to send myself back, with words as catalysts, to open the memories out and see what they had to offer. He describes this process to interviewer Jean Ross: "You begin with the simple association of the feeling of grass the first night of summer when you run barefoot. What do you find in the grass? Old bits of the fourth of July left over from the year before, little pieces of junk or firecrackers that didn't go off or a piece of a rocket stick. . . . Then you remember the ferns, which were like green fountains sprinkling up around the porch," Bradbury continues. "And then all of your relatives seated on the porch, which ones were there and how they were dressed and who did what. And you wanted to listen to the mysterious talk of these wise people who knew everything, so . . . you crept around behind all the rocking chairs and the swing and put your head down on the porch floor and listened to your grandfather's voice thunder-

The author ventured into television with his popular anthology series, *The Ray Bradbury Theatre.*

ing down through the rocking chair into the floor-boards and into your ear, and you've got a xylo-phone there being played by the voices."

Bradbury draws on a somewhat later period in his life for the setting of his murder mystery *Death Is a Lonely Business*. The novel recalls his young adult years in Venice, California, and depicts the detective Elmo Crumley's attempts to solve a series of deaths in the aging beachside community. Crumley, however, shares the spotlight with an anonymous writer who publishes short fiction in pulp magazines of the era such as *Weird Tales* and *Amazing Stories*. Like *Dandelion Wine*, *Death Is a Lonely Business* both evokes and illuminates Bradbury's own life in the early 1950s. Paul Barber declares in the *Los Angeles Times Book Review* that "even if you were never there in the '50s, you are likely to feel that you remember Venice to have been just the way [Bradbury] describes it."

Bradbury's most recent novel, *A Graveyard for Lunatics*, concerns the same unnamed writer featured in *Death is a Lonely Business*. This narrator, while anonymous, is strongly reminiscent of Bradbury himself. The novel itself "combines elements of the detective story, the Hollywood novel, and the monster fable in a manner that is intermittently effective, nearly unique and frequently charming," writes Tom Nolan in *The New York Times Book Review*. As is the case with so much of Bradbury's fiction, the book seeks to describe a world that is simultaneously nostalgic and magical.

Despite his reiterated theme that the past cannot be allowed to destroy the future, Bradbury also stresses the need to maintain contact with one's own sources of inspiration and respect one's childhood's affections as valuable. "As long as we're reading," he tells Ross, "that's the important thing; we can just take off and fly. Then, along the way, you move from Edgar Rice Burroughs to Jules Verne and H. G. Wells and finally to Shakespeare and George Bernard Shaw; they're all great loves to me. The important thing is not to tell people to give up on their loves, but to accept all of them. I can get just as much a bang out of looking at my old 'Prince Valiant' Sunday strips, which I began to

collect when I was seventeen, as I do from reading Alexander Pope."

Bradbury himself continues to inspire others. In words from his introduction to the Porges biography—which he applied to Edgar Rice Burroughs but which might also apply to Bradbury himself—"We have commuted because of [him]. Because of him we have printed the Moon. Because of him and men like him, one day in the next five centuries, we will commute forever, we will go away . . . . And never come back. And so live forever."

■ Works Cited

Barber, Paul, review of *Death Is a Lonely Business*, *Los Angeles Times Book Review*, November 17, 1985, p. 1.

Bradbury, Ray, "At What Temperature Do Books Burn?," *New York Times*, September 13, 1966.

Bradbury, "Buck Rogers in Apollo Year 1," *The Collected Works of Buck Rogers in the 25th Century*, edited by Robert C. Dille, Chelsea House, 1969, pp. xi-xiv.

Bradbury, "Tarzan, John Carter, Mr. Burroughs, and the Long Mad Summer of 1930," *Edgar Rice Burroughs: The Man Who Created Tarzan*, Brigham Young University Press, 1975, pp. 17-21.

Bradbury, *Dandelion Wine: A Novel*, Knopf, 1975.

Bradbury, "Afterword," *Fahrenheit 451*, Ballantine, 1982.

Bradbury, interview with Jean Ross, *Contemporary Authors New Revision Series*, Volume 30, Gale, 1990, pp. 37-43.

Hardin, Nils, "Science-Fiction Fanzines: The Time Binders," *Dictionary of Literary Biography*, Volume 8: *Twentieth Century American Science Fiction Writers*, Gale, 1981, pp. 280-94.

Morgan, David, *Ray Bradbury*, Twayne, 1986.

Moskowitz, Sam, *Seekers of Tomorrow: Masters of Modern Science Fiction*, World Publishing, 1966.

Nolan, Tom, review of *A Graveyard for Lunatics*, "Strange, Even for Hollywood," *New York Times Book Review*, September 2, 1990.

Nolan, William F., "Ray Bradbury: A Biographical Sketch," *The Martian Chronicles*, Doubleday, 1973.

Nolan, William F., *The Ray Bradbury Companion*, Gale, 1975.

"Ray Bradbury: I Was Always Rich, but Too Dumb to Know It," *Making Films in New York,* October 1975.

Shevey, Sandra, "For Ray Bradbury, Earth Is Just the Starting Point," *Detroit Free Press,* October 5, 1975.

Slusser, George Edgar, "Ray Bradbury," *Dictionary of Literary Biography,* Volume 2: *American Novelists since World War II,* Gale, 1978, pp. 60-65.

Stupple, A. James, "The Past, the Future, and Ray Bradbury," *Voices for the Future: Essays on Major Science Fiction Writers,* Volume 1, edited by Thomas D. Clareson, Bowling Green University Press, 1976, pp. 175-84.

Sullivan, Anita R., "Ray Bradbury and Fantasy," *English Journal,* December, 1972, pp. 1309-14.

Watt, Donald, "Burning Bright: 'Fahrenheit 451' as Symbolic Dystopia," *Ray Bradbury,* edited by Martin H. Greenberg and Joseph D. Olander, Taplinger, 1980, pp. 195-213.

Wolfe, Gary K., "Ray Bradbury," *Dictionary of Literary Biography,* Volume 8: *Twentieth Century American Science Fiction Writers,* Gale, 1981, pp. 61-76.

■ For More Information See

BOOKS

Authors in the News, Gale, Volume 1, 1976, Volume 2, 1976.

Bleiler, E. D., editor, *Science Fiction Writers: Critical Studies of the Major Authors from the Early Nineteenth Century to the Present Day,* Scribner, 1982.

Bleiler, E. F., editor, *Supernatural Fiction Writers: Fantasy and Horror,* Volume 2, Scribner, 1985.

Breit, Harvey, *The Writer Observed,* World Publishing, 1956.

Concise Dictionary of American Literary Biography: Broadening Views, 1968–1988, Gale, 1989.

Contemporary Literary Criticism, Gale, Volume 1, 1973, Volume 3, 1975, Volume 10, 1979, Volume 15, 1980, Volume 42, 1987.

Gunn, James, editor, *The New Encyclopedia of Science Fiction,* Viking, 1988.

Johnson, Wayne L., *Ray Bradbury,* Ungar, 1980.

Kirk, Russell, *Enemies of the Permanent Things: Observations of Abnormality in Literature and Politics,* Arlington House, 1969.

Knight, Damon, *In Search of Wonder: Critical Essays on Science Fiction,* 2nd edition, Advent, 1967.

Platt, Charles, *Dream Makers: Science Fiction and Fantasy Writers at Work,* Ungar, 1987.

Slusser, George Edgar, *The Bradbury Chronicles,* Borgo, 1977.

Touponce, William F. *Ray Bradbury and the Poetics of Reverie: Fantasy, Science Fiction and the Reader,* UMI Research Press, 1984.

Wollheim, Donald, *The Universe Makers,* Harper, 1971.

World Literature Criticism, Gale, 1992.

PERIODICALS

Extrapolation, Fall 1984.

Future, October 1978.

Los Angeles Times, April 27, 1975.

Midwestern Miscellany, Volume 8, 1980.

National Review, April 4, 1967.

Newsday, November 2, 1975.

New York Times, April 24, 1983; January 17, 1987.

New York Times Book Review, August 8, 1951; December 28, 1969; October 29, 1972; October 26, 1980.

Omni, February 1987; January 1989.

Reader's Digest, September 1986.

Time, March 24, 1975; October 13, 1980; October 28, 1985; August 6, 1990.

Washington Post, July 7, 1989.

Writer's Digest, December 1974; February 1976.

—*Sketch by Kenneth R. Shepherd*

Brock Cole

■ Personal

Born May 29, 1938, in Charlotte, MI; married; wife's name, Susan (a classical studies professor); children: two sons. *Education:* Kenyon College, B.A; University of Minnesota, Ph.D.

■ Addresses

Home—158 Lombard Ave., Oak Park, IL 60302.

■ Career

University of Minnesota, instructor in English composition; University of Wisconsin, instructor in philosophy until 1975; writer and illustrator, 1975—.

■ Awards, Honors

Juvenile Award, Friends of American Writers, 1980, for *The King at the Door;* California Young Reader Medal, California Reading Association, 1985, and Young Reader's Choice Award, Pacific Northwest Library Association, both for *The Indian in the Cupboard,* which was also named a *New York Times* outstanding book, 1981; Smarties "Grand Prix," for children's books, Book Trust, 1985; Parent's Choice Award, 1986, for *The Giant's Toe;* Carl Sandburg Award, Friends of Chicago Public Library, 1988, for *The Goats,* which was also named a *New York Times* notable book, an American Library Association (ALA) best book for young adults, and an ALA notable book, all 1987.

■ Writings

YOUNG ADULT

The Goats (young adult novel), Farrar, Straus, 1987.
Celine (young adult novel), Farrar, Straus, 1989.

SELF-ILLUSTRATED

The King at the Door, Doubleday, 1979.
No More Baths, Doubleday, 1980.
Nothing but a Pig, Doubleday, 1981.
The Winter Wren, Farrar, Straus, 1984.
The Giant's Toe, Farrar, Straus, 1986.
Alpha and the Dirty Baby, Farrar, Straus, 1991.

OTHER

(Illustrator) Lynne Reid Banks, *The Indian in the Cupboard,* Avon, 1980.
(Illustrator) Jill Paton Walsh, *Gaffer Samson's Luck,* Farrar, Straus, 1984.

■ Sidelights

Stripped naked and abandoned on a wilderness island, the protagonists of *The Goats* overcome their castaway status and learn a valuable lesson about the human condition. Brock Cole's first juvenile novel, *The Goats,* was a remarkable success, earning both critical praise and popular acclaim. While Cole had showed writing and artistic talent as the creator of several picture books for children, many people were taken with the excellence of *The Goats.* Patty Campbell, writing in *Wilson Library Bulletin,* comments that Cole's "style is deceptively simple and straightforward, completely free of sentimentality. The boy and the girl are funny and touching and quite real, but without the false smart-aleck sophistication that is the trademark of many young adult novelists." She concludes that *The Goats* is "a remarkable book to enjoy first and ponder later, and one that deserves to become a YA classic."

Cole grew up in the small town of Charlotte, Michigan, and small town life influenced him greatly. In *Junior Literary Guild,* he recalled that Charlotte was "a place where a six year old could wander into the feed mill or the auto body shop and watch men work without being chased out." His family moved to different places in the Midwest several times during his childhood, and he ended up graduating from high school in Royal Oak, Michigan. After graduation he attended Kenyon College in Ohio. He briefly considered writing as a career, but instead decided that he wanted to be a teacher. He taught English at the University of Minnesota, where he was also studying for a graduate degree. After completing his Ph.D., Cole began teaching philosophy at the University of Wisconsin.

Teaches Himself Illustration

In 1975, Cole's wife Susan got a job at the University of Illinois, and the family moved to the Chicago area with their two sons. By that time, Cole realized that teaching wasn't really his interest. He was mainly interested in writing books for children. Realizing that the books would need to be illustrated, Cole also decided to learn how to illustrate. He had no previous art training, and he didn't take classes to learn. Instead, he studied the work of other illustrators whom he admired. It seemed like a monumental task for the author to undertake, but he had a very simple, yet effective, plan of action. "I looked at illustrators I liked and tried to draw like they did," Cole told Christine McDonnell in an interview in *Horn Book* magazine. In particular, Cole studied the work of Maurice Sendak, Ernest Shepard, Margot Zemach and Edward Ardizzone. This technique worked well for Cole and his first picture book, *The King at the Door* was published in 1979, just a few years after he decided to write and illustrate full-time.

The King at the Door is a moral fable set in a time long ago. It is the story of a king who, while dressed in beggar's rags, asks at an inn for food and drink. While the innkeeper looks at the poorly dressed man and offers only pitiful scraps, the young chore-boy, Little Baggit is able to look deeper than the clothing to see the real identity of the king. The boy shares his own humble dinner with the king, and is later richly rewarded when the royal coach arrives for him. "Cole proves that familiar plots can be fashioned into new, refreshing and mighty diverting tales by a gifted craftsman," a *Publisher's Weekly* critic wrote. *Kirkus Reviews* commented that the book was "crisply told, energetically pictured, and unmistakably amusing." In 1980 Cole won a Juvenile Award from the Friends of American writers for the book.

No More Baths features a rebellious young girl named Jessie McWhistle. After a particularly dirty day, her parents have the audacity to try to bathe her in the middle of the day. She decides to leave

In this allegorical 1984 story a brother and sister attempt to wake the spring, but the angry winter turns the girl into a wren.

home so she will never have to take baths again. Jessie studies the cleaning methods of cats, pigs, and chickens and tries to groom herself in the same ways. But she finds that rolling in the sand, licking her hands and trying to smooth her hair, and wallowing in a mud hole don't seem to work for her, so reluctantly she returns home to surrender to the suds. Even though Jessie ends up feeling a lot cleaner, she never loses her rebellious attitude. "The author-artist tells a fresh, funny story with a clear text," McDonnell related in a review in *Horn Book.*

Moving onto another social satire with *Nothing but a Pig,* Cole once again scored a hit. This tale focuses on a pig who is a social climber. He despises his friend and owner because he is just a poor farmer. The pig feels he has hit it big when his social aspirations are realized—he is sold to a wealthy banker. Dressed in fancy clothes, the pig is appalled to find out that the banker only wishes to make him into bacon. His farmer friend returns to save him, and the pig learns a big lesson about friendship. A few critics thought the tale was too fantastical, but Karla Kuskin, writing in the *New York Times Book Review,* praised the illustration highly, indicating that the village where the story is set is "filled with color and clutter and always on the verge of coming apart at the picturesque seams."

The Winter Wren, published in 1984, is an allegorical tale of Simon and his sister Meg who take a journey to wake Spring at Winter's farm. But cold Winter has overheard their plan, and he drenches the children with an ice storm which turns Meg into a wren. Simon then goes to battle Winter. His sister's suggestions aid him in the undertaking. While Winter is sowing sleet, Simon sprinkles the land with meal and a few plants spring to life. While Winter is pruning the buds on the trees, Simon throws an apple down and a tree immediately grows. Simon reaches the house, asks for a "princess in green and gold," and is led to his sister, who has returned to her own form, and they gaze out over fields, now turned to green and gold. Barbara Elleman praised the artistry of the book in *Booklist,* commenting that "strikingly composed double-page spreads flow gracefully across the pages." A few critics found the text confusing, but Elleman wrote that "others will use the ambiguity as a springboard to discuss the tale's transformation and renewal theme."

Cole's award-winning 1987 novel involves two young teenagers who become victims of a cruel prank and are left on an island without food or clothing.

Beanstalk Journeys

Cole showed a quirkier sense of humor with the 1986 book, *The Giant's Toe.* In a variation on the "Jack and the Beanstalk" stories, this tale follows an elderly, dull-witted giant who cuts off his toe by mistake while hoeing cabbages. The toe transforms into an elf-like creature who eludes the giant's attempts at capturing him. When the toe creature gobbles down the giant's pie, the giant, in retribution, tries to put the toe in a pie. But the toe quickly substitutes a hen into the pie, and the giant eats it instead. Only later does he realize that he has eaten the hen who lays golden eggs. The giant, in a rage, once again goes after the toe, who next finds a way to get rid of the giant's magic harp. When Jack finally turns up, there are no treasures left to steal. Giant and toe end up living a happy and undisturbed life. Luann Toth, writing in the *School Library Jour-*

nal, called *The Giant's Toe* "Cole's best effort to date."

A Fallen World

Most of Cole's books have been parables. Cole's first young adult novel, published in 1987, was a parable of another kind. In this book, two thirteen-year-olds—a boy and a girl—are stripped and marooned on Goat Island by their fellow campers. The cruel ritual at Camp Tall Pine is to find two socially backward campers to be "Goats," and leave them overnight to spark their interest in the opposite sex. The prank backfires because Howie and Laura decide to escape when they see someone returning to the island. It turns out to be the counselors, attempting to save them. But the two teens decide ride to the mainland on a floating log and barely make it to land alive. They break into a boarded-up cottage where they sleep and borrow clothes for their journey.

"It's an old story," Cole told McDonnell, reminiscent of Adam and Eve in the Garden of Eden. "The twist is that the kids are searching for Paradise, rather than being driven from it." Realizing that they have been cruelly treated by their campers, the children decide to strike out on their own, battling their way through what Cole has called "a fallen world." They steal clothing and money from people on the beach, yet somehow keep a sense of morality because they realize they have to pay it back. "Without clothing or housing or food, the preteen-age couple feel compelled to lie and steal and trespass over and over again, but there is a rightness and authenticity to that, and they make a rigorous accounting of 'things they would have to come back and pay for' and 'things they had borrowed without asking,'" Ron Hansen wrote in the *York Times Book Review.* They skillfully find their way around in a world that has completely rejected them. In the end, the pranksters have their way, because the boy and the girl do come closer, but in a caring, affectionate way rather than sexually.

In contrast to the competence of the lost children, the adults in the story appear crass, irresponsible, and incompetent. "I decided not to sweeten it up," Cole commented to McDowell. "It's a fair view, not a complete view. It's fragmentary, but it's an honest view." "Critics of the book," wrote Anita Silvey in *Horn Book,* "are concerned with the ab-

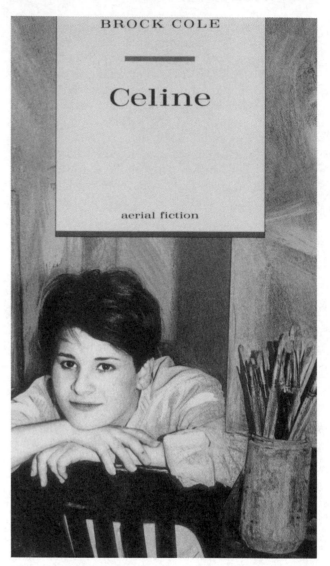

Left to her own devices, a sixteen year old grows up in an unconventional manner in this humorous 1989 young adult novel.

sence of positive adult characters . . . and the change in the young protagonists from innocents to thieves." Cole believes that children have a natural sense of morality. "I have much more faith in children's ability and judgment than a lot of people. They turn away if they find something too scary or too burdensome. I would like to think they can put the book down," he told McDonnell.

While Cole was writing *The Goats,* he had a sense of urgency about finishing it. "I write for the characters in the book, on their behalf. I feel a responsibility to tell their story," he told McDonnell. "I was so engrossed while working on it, that I kept worrying, 'What if I get killed before I get it done?' I couldn't get it out of my head." While driving to visit a friend, he became so distracted by the dialogue unfolding in his head that he was afraid he would have an accident and the book would go unfinished. Silvey comments that *The Goats* "reaffirms my belief that children's literature is alive and thriving." She explains that the novel appeals to so many people because "we know what it means to feel severe alienation from life and one's peers." She concludes that "the publication of a novel like *The Goats* signifies that we are still creating children's books that affirm the human spirit and the ability of the individual to rise above adversity."

Cole's 1989 novel, *Celine,* is a funny tale about a teenager who practically has to grow up by herself. The sixteen-year-old artist is living in a loft in Chicago with her twenty-two-year-old stepmother, Catherine. Celine's mother happens to live on a beautiful yacht off of the island of Antigua.

Cole illustrated Lynne Reid Banks's well-received 1980 work.

Her father has gone off on a lecture tour of Europe, leaving the teen and her barely-adult stepmother with in the hope that they will grow closer together. He leaves with an admonition that his daughter to "show a little maturity." "Really," Celine remarks, "it's hard not to be offended. If I was any more mature, I'd have Alzheimer's disease."

Celine virtually takes possession of her neighbor Jake Barker, whose parents are going through a divorce. Jake's mother claims that she loves spending time with him, but Celine ends up being his foster mother most of the time. At the same time, she is attempting to finish high school a year early, partly because she feels like a misfit there. Celine finds herself having a crush on Jake's father, Mr. Barker, while she tries to deal with the cute but stupid Dermot, who has a crush on her. She rushes home from school with an idea for a painting that is so compelling, she is afraid she'll die before she finishes it, only to be coaxed into polishing Catherine's toenails instead.

"Start to finish, this book is a delight," wrote Lynn Freed in *The New York Times Book Review.* "It is funny, witty and poignant. . . . At the end of the novel, the reader emerges curious to know what becomes of Celine as an adult. What becomes of such sharp vision, such wry insight, such wise innocence?" Diane Roback, writing in *Publisher's Weekly,* thinks that one of the strengths of the novel is Celine's "wry comments on everything from modern art to divorce." Karen Berlin observes in *Voice of Youth Advocates* that "events and people just seem to swirl about Celine, filtering through her artist's eyes into the meaningful patterns of an adolescent's life." An *Entertainment Weekly* critic observed "since (Celine's) mind shoots off in daring flights of speculation at the slightest provocation, we're in for a wild, funny ride."

Brock Cole explained his approach to writing children's books in his interview with McDonell: "Don't falsify. Be honest. Be responsible to the characters you're writing about." Furthermore, he commented that "It's not right to create a book with messages or to look for messages in books. Books with messages are confidence tricks. This is fiction. To persuade people by means of fiction seems dishonest." He concludes that writers "want your books to be influential, so they enlarge a person's experience. A book gives you a set of hypotheses that you can test out against your own experiences."

■ Works Cited

Berlin, Karen, review of *Celine*, *Voice of Youth Advocates*, February, 1990, p. 341.

Campbell, Patty, review of *The Goats*, *Wilson Library Bulletin*, January 1988, p. 75.

Review of *Celine*, *Entertainment Weekly*, May 4, 1990, p. 114.

Cole, Brock, autobiographical sketch in *Junior Literary Guild*, September, 1979.

Elleman, Barbara, review of *The Winter Wren*, *Booklist*, vol. 81, No. 5, November 1, 1984, p. 366.

Freed, Lynn, review of *Celine*, *New York Times Book Review*, April 15, 1990, p. 23.

Hansen, Ron, "Discovering the Opposite Sex," *New York Times Book Review*, November 8, 1987, p. 31.

Review of *The King at the Door*, *Kirkus Reviews*, September 15, 1979, p. 1063.

Review of *The King at the Door*, *Publishers Weekly*, October 29, 1979, p. 82.

Kuskin, Karla, "The Art of Picture Books," *New York Times Book Review*, November 15, 1981, pp. 57, 60.

McDonnell, Christine, "New Voices, New Visions: Brock Cole," *Horn Book*, September/October, 1989, pp. 602-05.

McDonnell, Christine, review of *No More Baths*, *Horn Book*, August, 1980, pp. 393-94.

Roback, Diane, review of *Celine*, *Publishers Weekly*, October 27, 1989, p. 70.

Silvey, Anita, review of *The Goats*, *Horn Book*, January/February, 1988, p. 23.

Toth, Luann, review of *The Giant's Toe*, *School Library Journal*, October, 1986, p. 158.

■ For More Information See

BOOKS

Children's Literature Review, Volume 18, Gale, 1989, pp. 81-85.

Sixth Book of Junior Authors, H.W. Wilson, 1989, pp. 62-63.

PERIODICALS

Bulletin of the Center for Children's Books, December, 1979; October, 1984; July/August, 1986; October, 1987.

Kirkus Reviews, September 1, 1984, p. J-59.

School Library Journal, May, 1980, p. 52.

—Sketch by Nancy E. Rampson

Roald Dahl

■ Personal

Given name is pronounced "Roo-aal"; born September 13, 1916, in Llandaff, Glamorgan, Wales; died November 23, 1990, in Oxford, England; son of Harald (a shipbroker, painter, and horticulturist) and Sofie Magdalene (Hesselberg) Dahl; married Patricia Neal (an actress), July 2, 1953 (divorced, 1983); married Felicity Ann Crosland (a fashion coordinator), 1983; children: (first marriage) Olivia (deceased), Tessa, Theo, Ophelia, Lucy. *Education:* Llandaff Cathedral School; St. Peter's Preparatory School; Repton School, Derbyshire, 1932. *Hobbies and other interests:* Fine wine, collecting avant-garde paintings, collecting antiques, breeding and raising greyhounds, orchid breeding, gardening.

■ Addresses

Agent—Watkins Loomis Agency, 150 East 35th Street, New York, NY 10016.

■ Career

Writer. Shell Oil Co., London, England, member of eastern staff, 1933–37; Shell Oil Co., Dar-es-Sa-laam, Tanzania, 1937–39. Host of series of half-hour television dramas, *Way Out,* during the early 1960s. *Military service:* British Army, temporary officer, 1939; Royal Air Force, Nairobi and Habbanya, flight training, 1939–40, Western Desert, fighter squadron, 1940, Greece and Syria, hospitalization, 1941, Washington, DC, assistant air attache, 1942–43, North America, British Security Coordination (achieved the rank of wing commander), 1943–45.

■ Awards, Honors

Edgar Allan Poe Awards, Mystery Writers of America, 1954, 1959, and 1980; New England Round Table of Children's Librarians Award, 1972, and Surrey School Award, 1973, both for *Charlie and the Chocolate Factory;* Surrey School Award, 1974, and Nene Award, 1978, both for *Charlie and the Great Glass Elevator;* Surrey School Award, 1978, and California Young Reader Medal, 1979, both for *Danny: The Champion of the World;* Federation of Children's Book Groups Award, 1982, for *The BFG;* Massachusetts Children's Award, 1982, for *James and the Giant Peach;* Outstanding Books Award, *New York Times,* 1983, Whitbread Award, 1983, and West Australian Award, 1986, all for *The Witches;* World Fantasy Convention Lifetime Achievement Award, and Federation of Children's Book Groups Award, both 1983; Kurt Maschler Award Runner-up, 1985, for *The Giraffe and the Pelly and Me; Boston Globe/Horn Book* Nonfiction Honor Citation, 1985, for *Boy: Tales of Childhood;* International Board on Books for Young People

Awards, 1986, for Norwegian and German translations of *The BFG*; Smarties Award, 1990, for *Esio Trot*.

■ Writings

CHILDREN'S BOOKS

The Gremlins, illustrated by Walt Disney Productions, Random House, 1943.

James and the Giant Peach: A Children's Story, illustrated by Nancy Ekholm Burkert, Knopf, 1961, illustrated by Michel Simeon, Allen & Unwin, 1967, Cornerstone Books, 1991.

Charlie and the Chocolate Factory, illustrated by Joseph Schindelman, Knopf, 1964, illustrated by Faith Jaques, Allen & Unwin, 1967, Cornerstone Books, 1989.

The Magic Finger, illustrated by William Péne du Bois, Harper and Row, 1966, illustrated by Tony Ross, Puffin, 1966, illustrated by Pat Marriot, Puffin, 1974.

Fantastic Mr. Fox, illustrated by Donald Chaffin, Knopf, 1970.

Charlie and the Great Glass Elevator: The Further Adventures of Charlie Bucket and Willy Wonka, Chocolate-Maker Extraordinary, illustrated by Schindelman, Knopf, 1972, illustrated by Jaques, Allen & Unwin, 1973.

Danny: The Champion of the World, illustrated by Jill Bennett, Knopf, 1975.

The Enormous Crocodile, illustrated by Quentin Blake, Knopf, 1976, Puffin, 1993.

The Complete Adventures of Charlie and Mr. Willy Wonka (contains *Charlie and the Chocolate Factory* and *Charlie and the Great Glass Elevator*), illustrated by Jaques, Allen & Unwin, 1978.

The Twits, illustrated by Blake, J. Cape, 1981, Knopf, 1982.

George's Marvelous Medicine, illustrated by Blake, J. Cape, 1981, Knopf, 1982.

Roald Dahl's Revolting Rhymes, illustrated by Blake, J. Cape, 1982, Knopf, 1983, Puffin, 1995.

The BFG, illustrated by Blake, Farrar, Straus, 1982, Viking Penguin, 1985.

Dirty Beasts (verse), illustrated by Rosemary Fawcett, Farrar, Straus, 1983, Puffin, 1986.

The Witches, illustrated by Blake, Farrar, Straus, 1983, Puffin, 1985.

Boy: Tales of Childhood (autobiography), Farrar, Straus, 1984.

The Giraffe and the Pelly and Me, illustrated by Blake, J. Cape, 1985, Puffin, 1994.

Matilda, illustrated by Blake, Viking Kestrel, 1988, Knopf, 1988, Puffin, 1990.

Roald Dahl: Charlie and the Chocolate Factory, Charlie and the Great Glass Elevator, The BFG (boxed set), Viking, 1989.

Rhyme Stew (comic verse), illustrated by Blake, Viking Kestrel, 1989, Viking, 1990.

Esio Trot, illustrated by Blake, Viking, 1990, Puffin, 1992.

The Dahl Diary, 1992, illustrated by Blake, Puffin, 1991.

The Vicar of Nibbleswicke, illustrated by Blake, Viking, 1992.

The Minpins, illustrated by Patrick Benson, Puffin, 1994.

My Year, illustrated by Blake, Viking, 1994.

Roald Dahl's Revolting Recipes, illustrated by Blake, Viking, 1994.

ADULT BOOKS

Sometime Never: A Fable for Supermen (novel), Scribner, 1948.

My Uncle Oswald (novel), M. Joseph, 1979, Knopf, 1980.

Going Solo (autobiography), Farrar, Straus, 1986.

SHORT STORY COLLECTIONS

Over to You: Ten Stories of Flyers and Flying, Reynal, 1946.

Someone Like You, Knopf, 1953.

Kiss, Kiss, Knopf, 1953.

Selected Stories of Roald Dahl, Modern Library, 1968.

Twenty-Nine Kisses from Roald Dahl (contains *Someone Like You* and *Kiss, Kiss*), M. Joseph, 1969.

Switch Bitch, Knopf, 1974.

The Wonderful World of Henry Sugar and Six More, J. Cape, 1977.

The Best of Roald Dahl (includes selections from *Over to You, Someone Like You, Kiss, Kiss,* and *Switch Bitch*), introduction by James Cameron, Random House, 1978.

Roald Dahl's Tales of the Unexpected, Vintage, 1979.

"Taste" and Other Tales, Longman, 1979.

A Roald Dahl Selection: Nine Short Stories, edited and introduced by Roy Blatchford, photographs by Catherine Shakespeare Lane, Longman, 1980.

More Tales of the Unexpected, Penguin, 1980, published in England as *More Roald Dahl's Tales of the Unexpected,* M. Joseph, 1980, and as *Further Tales of the Unexpected,* Chivers, 1981.

Roald Dahl's Book of Ghost Stories, Farrar, Straus, 1983.

Two Fables ("Princess and the Poacher" and "Princess Mammalia"), illustrated by Graham Dean, Viking, 1986, Farrar, Straus, 1987.

The Roald Dahl Omnibus, Hippocrene Books, 1987.

A Second Roald Dahl Selection: Eight Short Stories, edited by Helene Fawcett, Longman, 1987.

Ah, Sweet Mystery of Life, illustrated by John Lawrence, J. Cape, 1988, Knopf, 1989, Penguin, 1990.

The Collected Short Stories of Roald Dahl (an omnibus volume containing *Kiss, Kiss, Over to You, Switch Bitch, Someone Like You,* and *Eight Further Tales of the Unexpected*), Penguin, 1991.

The Collected Short Stories of Roald Dahl, Penguin, 1992.

SCREENPLAYS

"Lamb to the Slaughter" (teleplay), *Alfred Hitchcock Presents,* Columbia Broadcasting System (CBS), 1958.

(With Jack Bloom) *You Only Live Twice,* United Artists (UA), 1967.

(With Ken Hughes) *Chitty Chitty Bang Bang,* UA, 1968.

The Night Digger (based on *Nest in a Falling Tree* by Joy Crowley), Metro-Goldwyn-Mayer, 1970.

Willy Wonka and the Chocolate Factory (adaptation of *Charlie and the Chocolate Factory*), Paramount, 1971.

Also author of screenplays *Oh Death, Where Is Thy Sting-a-Ling-a-Ling,* United Artists; *The Lightening Bug,* 1971; and *The Road Builder.*

RECORDINGS

Bedtime Stories to Children's Books (interview), Center for Cassette Studies, 1973.

Charlie and the Chocolate Factory, Caedmon, 1975.

James and the Giant Peach, Caedmon, 1977.

Fantastic Mr. Fox, Caedmon, 1978.

Roald Dahl Reads His "The Enormous Crocodile" and "The Magic Finger," Caedmon, 1980.

OTHER

The Honeys (play), produced on Broadway, 1955.

Contributor of short fiction to *Penguin Modern Stories 12,* 1972. Contributor to anthologies and periodicals, including *Atlantic, Collier's, Esquire, Harper's, New Yorker, Playboy, Saturday Evening Post,* and *Town and Country.* Various works have been translated into foreign languages, including Norwegian and German.

■ Adaptations

"Beware of the Dog" (short story) was adapted for the film *36 Hours,* Metro-Goldwyn-Mayer, 1964; *Charlie and the Chocolate Factory* was adapted as *Roald Dahl's Charlie and the Chocolate Factory: A Play* by Richard R. George, with an introduction by Dahl, Knopf, 1976; an excerpt from the film *Willy Wonka and the Chocolate Factory* was distributed as the film *Delicious Inventions* and the filmstrips *Willy Wonka and the Chocolate Factory—Storytime* and *Willy Wonka and the Chocolate Factory—Learning Kit,* all Films, Inc., 1976; *The Great Switcheroo* was recorded by Patricia Neal, Caedmon, 1977; *Tales of the Unexpected* was broadcast by WNEW-TV, 1979; *James and the Giant Peach* was adapted as *Roald Dahl's James and the Giant Peach: A Play* by George, with an introduction by Dahl, Penguin, 1982; *Charlie and the Great Glass Elevator* was adapted as the play *Charlie and the Great Glass Elevator: Roald Dahl's Fantasy Adventure for Children* by George, Dramatic Publishing Company, 1984; *The Witches* was filmed by Lorimar, 1990; *The BFG* was adapted as the play *The BFG (big friendly giant) by Roald Dahl* by David Wood, S. French, 1991.

■ Sidelights

Roald Dahl was flying over the African desert for the Royal Air Force during World War II when he was forced to make an emergency landing. He wrote in his first short story, "A Piece of Cake," "I remember the dipping of the nose of the aircraft and I remember looking down the nose of the machine at the ground and seeing a little clump of camel-thorn growing there all by itself. . . . Then there was a small gap of not-remembering." When Dahl regained consciousness, he thought that something was burning. "I rolled about a bit in the sand, then crawled away from the fire on all fours and lay down." It was then that Dahl began to feel pain. "Things were beginning to hurt. My face hurt most. There was something wrong with my face. Something had happened to it. Slowly I put a hand to feel it. It was sticky. My nose didn't seem to be there."

While it would take Dahl six months to recover and he would live with the recurrent pain of his injuries for the rest of his life, Dahl's crash land-ing set him on a course that led him to his ca-reer as a writer. It was not long before Dahl earned the title "our Supreme Master of Wicked-ness" from the *New Republic's* J. D. O'Hara for his adult fiction. "Dahl's trademark was his mer-cilessness," wrote Frederic Raphael in *Times Liter-ary Supplement.*

Despite his early success as a writer for adults, Dahl is perhaps best known for a book he wrote for children, *Charlie and the Chocolate Factory.* What Dahl "does in *Charlie* and in his other children's stories is to home unerringly in on the very nub of childish delight, with brazen and glorious dis-regard for what is likely to furrow the adult brow," commented Gerald Haigh in *Times Educa-tional Supplement.* The publication and popularity of *Charlie and the Chocolate Factory* evoked criti-cism from experts in children's literature who thought that the violence, insensitivity, or sup-posed racism in the text was offensive or inap-propriate for children. "It is difficult to avoid the feeling that Dahl . . . enjoys writing about vio-lence, while at the same time condemning it," remarked David Rees in *Children's Literature in Education,* adding: "Dahl . . . parades his own ir-ritations—television addiction . . . overindulgence in sweets, gum-chewing, shooting foxes, beards, ugly faces, fat bodies, cranky old people, spoiled children—and presents them as moral objections."

Throughout his life, Dahl maintained that he was writing to suit the tastes of children, who, he ar-gued, appreciate a sense of humor that adults cannot understand. He insisted that his primary goal was to amuse children and to make them laugh. "If I offend some grown-ups in the pro-cess," he told Mark I. West in *Trust Your Children: Voices against Censorship in Children's Books,* "so be it. It's a price I'm willing to pay." If critics dis-agreed about the suitability of some of Dahl's books for children, most agreed that Dahl was a talented writer. According to Michael Wood of *New Society,* "Dahl is at his best when he reveals the horrible thinness of much of our respectabil-ity; at his worst and most tiresome when he nudges us towards the contemplation of mere naughtiness . . . what is striking about Dahl's work, both for children and adults, is its carefully pitched appeal to its different audiences. . . . He has tact, timing, a clean, economic style, an abun-dance of ingenuity . . . above all he knows how to manipulate his readers."

From British Boardings to Battle

Dahl was just four years old when his sister Astri died of an appendicitis and his father succumbed to pneumonia. His mother, Sofie, was left to care for the family with an estate of a quarter of a million pounds. She took the family on trips to visit their Norwegian grandparents, doted on Dahl, and fulfilled her husband's wish to educate Dahl in the best English schools, even when she had to sell her jewelry to do so. Dahl's experi-ences at these schools contributed much to the success of his later work in children's literature.

One childhood incident is particularly memorable. Dahl made a habit of stopping at the sweet shop with friends on the way home from the Llandaff Cathedral school. There, the mean-spirited Mrs. Pratchett complained and nagged as she waited on them. When Dahl and his friends slipped a dead mouse into a candy jar to teach her a les-son, she reacted with surprise, spilling candy and smattering glass all over the store. Mrs. Pratchett, however, had her turn to get even. When the boys entered the store the next day, Headmaster Coombes from school beat them while Mrs. Pratchett hooted and cheered.

The severity of the beating Dahl received prompted his mother to remove him from Llandaff Cathe-dral School. Dahl described his time at St. Peters, his new boarding school, in the story "Lucky Break," in *The Wonderful World of Henry Sugar and Six More.* "Those were the days of horrors, of fierce discipline . . . the fear of the dreaded cane hung over us like the fear of death all the time." He continued, "The welts were always very long, stretching right across both buttocks, blue-black with brilliant scarlet edges, and when you ran your fingers over them ever so gently afterward, you could feel the corrugations. . . . The impor-tant thing was never to flinch upward or straighten up when you were hit. If you did that, you got an extra one."

In 1929, Dahl moved on to Repton, a distin-guished preparatory school in Derbyshire; he re-called in "Lucky Break" that the "beatings at Repton were more fierce and more frequent than anything I had yet experienced." Standing six feet, six inches tall, Dahl played football and served as the captain of the squash and handball teams, but did not excel in school. One teacher, comment-ing on the fourteen-year-old boy's English com-

During his stay at Repton—a distinguished preparatory school—Dahl was known more for his excellence in sports than his scholarship.

position work, wrote, as Dahl related in "Lucky Break," "I have never met a boy who so persistently writes the exact opposite of what he means. He seems incapable of marshaling his thoughts on paper." One year later, a comment on another English composition read: "A persistent muddler. Vocabulary negligible, sentences mal-constructed. He reminds me of a camel."

Although Dahl's mother offered to send him to Oxford when he turned eighteen, the young man decided to work for the Shell Oil Company instead. Dahl was in Dar-es-Salaam, Tanzania, working for the company when World War II erupted. To enlist in the Royal Air Force, he drove alone through one thousand miles of jungle to Nairobi, Kenya. After training in Nairobi and Habbaniya, Iraq, Dahl was sent to fly a bi-wing Gladiator with a fighter squadron in Libya. It was there that he was given misleading directions on a mission, and his plane was shot by Italian machine-gun fire. Dahl was too low to bail out of the plane, and so he made the emergency landing that would change his life.

Fortunately, Dahl was rescued by another pilot and transported to a hospital in Alexandria. His skull was fractured and plastic surgery was necessary to repair the damage to his nose. After six months, in 1941, he had recuperated to the point that he could fly a Hurricane airplane with his squadron in Greece against the Germans. Dahl shot four planes down, and his own plane was one of the four out of the thirty Hurricanes in that campaign to survive. Then, as Dahl's old injuries began to cause dangerous blackouts when he flew, he returned to England. At a club one night, he met the Undersecretary of State for Air, Harold Balfour, and Balfour gave Dahl his next post as an Assistant Air Attache in Washington, D.C.

Becomes Writer with "A Piece of Cake"

One day, as Dahl sat in his Washington office, C. S. Forester stopped by. "He asked if he could interview me," recalled Dahl in an article by Willa Petschek for the *New York Times Biographical Service*. "America wasn't in the war then, and I suppose I was one of the few men in Washington who had 'seen action.' Forester said he wanted to write up my most exciting war experience" for a *Saturday Evening Post* article. Forester took Dahl to lunch for the interview, and as Forester could not eat and take notes at the same time, Dahl offered to write some notes later for Forester. Those notes became the story, "A Piece of Cake."

As he told Petschek, the way his writing career began was a "fluke." "Without being asked to, I doubt if I'd ever have thought of beginning to write." The *Saturday Evening Post* paid Dahl one thousand dollars to publish "A Piece of Cake"; he lost this money playing poker with Senator Harry S. Truman (who would later become the President of the United States), but developed his talent as a writer. Dahl began to write stories for *Collier's, Harper's, Ladies' Home Journal,* and other large magazines. "A Piece of Cake" was later published, along with eleven other stories originally printed in the *Saturday Evening Post,* in *Over to You: Ten Stories of Fliers and Flying*. In a review of this collection, Nona Balakian of the *New York Times Book Review* praised Dahl's "singular brand of talent," and noted that Dahl could "communicate a feeling, a sensation, a state of mind that has often nothing to do with us earthbound creatures."

In Dahl's first book for children, he did not stray far from the fighter pilot stories he had created for adults. *The Gremlins* (1943) reveals the existence of the little men, Gremlins, as Dahl named them, who caused war planes to crash. After the Gremlins are discovered, they are convinced to work for the pilots instead of against them. *The Gremlins* was a popular success. Mrs. Roosevelt, the First Lady, read the book to her children and invited Dahl to dinner at the White House; and Walt Disney was so taken with the story that he planned to transform it into a motion picture. May Lamberton Becker, writing in the *New York Herald Tribune Weekly Book Review*, advised her readers to preserve *The Gremlins* "as a firsthand source book on the origin of a genuine addition to folklore. That is, preserve it if the children in the family don't read it to bits. . . ." Despite the success of *The Gremlins*, Dahl did not write another book for children for seventeen years.

Although initially wary of the giant who snatches her in the middle of the night, Sophie eventually joins forces with her large captor to defeat some rather nasty ogres.

In 1945, Dahl moved to Buckinghamshire, England. There he bred and raised greyhounds, enjoyed fine wines, collected paintings and antiques, and meticulously crafted new stories and a novel. The stories were published in various magazines, including the *New Yorker*, and the novel, *Sometime Never: A Fable for Supermen*, appeared in 1948. In 1952, Dahl met Patricia Neal (the famed beauty who starred in *The Fountainhead* with Gary Cooper) at a dinner party hosted by playwright Lillian Hellman. Although Dahl had to persuade Neal to date him, they soon became a fashionable couple and were married in July of 1953. After a small wedding and reception, they honeymooned in Italy, Switzerland, and France. The couple then moved into an apartment on the West Side of New York, where Dahl continued to write stories and Neal pursued her acting career off-Broadway.

Some critics assert that Dahl wrote some of his best stories during this time of his life. *Someone Like You* (1953), which includes eighteen stories (some of which were previously published in the *New Yorker, Harper's, Collier's*, and other magazines), established Dahl's reputation as a master of the macabre. One of the most famous of these stories, "Lamb to the Slaughter," describes how a woman kills her policeman husband with a frozen leg of lamb and then feeds the cooked and garnished weapon to detectives investigating the death. Another well-known piece, "The Great Automatic Grammatisator," asserts the existence of a computer which writes short stories and novels and gradually puts great writers out of work. "Taste," in the words of James Kelly of the *New York Times Book Review*, "captures the high drama and gourmet flavor of a dinner party" and demonstrates what happens when a wine expert cheats to win a bet. Kelly compared Dahl to authors like Saki, O. Henry, Guy de Maupassant, and W. Somerset, Maugham, and praised Dahl's use of "honed dialogue," his "masterful hand with nuance," and his "ability to keep the reader off balance through sheer astonishment." In the opinion of Kelly, "Mr. Dahl could be a cult without half trying, and he deserves the warm welcome he'll get."

Dahl's success with *Someone Like You* and the prestigious Edgar Allen Poe Award he won from the Mystery Writers of America allowed him to experiment during the mid-1950s. He began his first attempts at writing plays with encouragement from producer Cheryl Crawford. *The Honeys,* a three-act comedy, opened on Broadway on April

28, 1955, and ran for thirty-six performances. Dahl also found himself under pressure from producers to allow them to adapt his stories for television. Finally, Alfred Hitchcock, the acclaimed director of suspense thrillers, persuaded Dahl to give him the rights to produce "Lamb to the Slaughter" and directed the work himself.

Kiss, Kiss, another short story collection for adults, was well received upon its publication in 1959. This collection includes stories about a poacher who drugs pheasants ("The Champion of the World"), a bee-keeper who fuels his baby daughter's aberrant growth with royal jelly ("Royal Jelly"), and another about a cat which seems to possess the spirit of the composer Franz Liszt ("Edward the Conqueror"). Reviewing *Kiss, Kiss,* Malcolm Bradbury of the *New York Times Book Review* praised Dahl as "a true craftsman" and commented that "his punch-lines have so much punch that I was reeling for several days. . . . [Dahl] does all the things that people say may not be done."

Theo Dahl Survives Terrible Accident

As Dahl and Neal's children, Olivia, Tessa, and Theo, were born in 1954, 1957, and 1960, respectively, Dahl began the pleasant practice of telling the children bedtime stories every evening. This practice allowed the author to develop his understanding of the kind of stories children enjoyed. Dahl explained this in an article for *The Writer.* According to him, children love suspense, action, magic, "new inventions," "secret information," and "seeing the villain meet a grisly death." Children "hate descriptive passages and flowery prose," and "can spot a clumsy sentence."

Dahl was busy writing *James and the Giant Peach* in New York on December 5, 1960, when the first of several traumatic events to plague the Dahl-Neal family occurred. Neal was out shopping while the children's nurse, Susan, set out to pick up Olivia from nursery school. Young Tessa walked beside her, and Theo, just four months old, rode in the pram. After seeing the light change at the corner of Eighty-Second and Madison, Susan pushed the pram out into the street. At that moment, a taxi cab burst into the pram and the carriage flew forty feet into the side of a bus. Neal, who heard the sirens of emergency vehicles as they rushed to aid her son, did not find out about the accident until she returned home and answered the ringing telephone.

Although Theo miraculously survived the accident, he suffered multiple head injuries which left him with hydrocephalus. The shunt that drained excess fluid from the child's brain had to be constantly monitored. For years, Dahl and Neal watched for the signs of a blocked shunt: "groggy" eyes. Dahl explained what would happen when they spotted the sign in a 1965 *Ladies' Home Journal* article: "Then comes the drive to the hospital, the walk through the snow (it was always snowing) to the hospital entrance, the swift elevator ride to the neuro-surgical floor, and suddenly there you are again, standing in the pale yellow corridor with the child in your arms, handing him over, consigning him, trusting him to the ruthless but precise alchemy of the neurosurgeons: the subdural taps, the lumbar punctures, the manometers, the myelograms, and finally, inevitably, comes the operation itself." Theo was subjected to eight operations during the three years the shunt was in place. Dahl's frustration with the unreliable, uncomfortable shunt led him to collaborate with his friends Stanley Wade, an inventor, and Kenneth Till, an English neurosurgeon. Since the Dahl-Wade Valve was introduced and produced by a non-profit organization in 1963, its use around the world has saved countless lives.

Controversial Charlie

In the meantime, Dahl and his family began to make important decisions about how to deal with the consequences of Theo's accident. In 1961, Dahl decided to host the half-hour television drama series *Way Out* to help pay for Theo's medical expenses. Also, Neal resolved to end the practice of spending summers in England at their "Gipsy House" in Great Missenden and winters in the United States. She and Dahl thought that England would provide a safe, stable environment for the children and they took up permanent residence in their Great Missenden home.

Finally, in 1961, *James and the Giant Peach* was published. According to Rees, this is Dahl's "most original novel." The story begins when an enormous peach crushes James's nasty aunts and he climbs into the peach through a worm hole. With the spider, ladybug, centipede, and silkworm that inhabit the peach, James is flown by a flock of seagulls over the sea from England to New York's

Central Park. Although Alice Dalgliesh of *Saturday Review* believed that some children may appreciate the "exciting" aspects of this "rambunctious fantasy," she worried that other children may be bothered by the fact that James's aunts are suddenly killed in the beginning of the story. According to a *Times Literary Supplement* critic, the verse is "splendid" and the work is "vivid, robust, entertaining, and funny." Over thirty years after it was published, *James and the Giant Peach* was still a children's favorite and had sold more than 350,000 hardcover copies.

Despite Dahl's and Neal's expectations, England did not provide a safe haven for the their family. In November, 1962, Olivia suddenly contracted measles encephalitis and died within one day. To add to the grief they felt over losing their first child, Dahl and Neal coped with the idea that Olivia wouldn't have died if the family had stayed in New York, where measles inoculations were available. And soon after Olivia's death, the couple noticed that Theo was a bit feverish and groggy and that his appetite had decreased. They thought his condition was improving, and faulted the shunt with causing such symptoms; after consulting with his doctors, the shunt was removed. For fifteen days, they waited in suspense until they could be sure that Theo was free from the need for the shunt. The joy they felt about Theo's recovery was reinforced by the birth of another girl, Ophelia, and Neal's Academy Award for her role in *Hud* (1963) opposite Paul Newman.

Dahl dedicated *Charlie and the Chocolate Factory* (1964) to Theo. In this work, an impoverished boy, Charlie Beckett, longs to win entrance into the mysterious chocolate factory owned by Willy Wonka. Unlike many rich children, he can barely afford to buy a few Wonka candies. Yet, amazingly, he finds a candy bar with the winning golden wrapper and is included on a tour of the wondrous chocolate factory with his grandfather.

The other children on the tour exhibit severe character flaws: Augustus Gloop is voracious and greedy for chocolate; Veruca Salt is spoiled and throws fits until she has her own way; Little Mike Teavee cannot stop watching television; and Violet Beauregarde will not stop chewing gum. One by one, these nasty children suffer gruesome punishments and are subjected to the morality chants of the factory's Oompa Loompa workers. Charlie's character, however, is as golden as the prize-winning candy-bar wrapper. Willy Wonka surprises him by announcing that he will become Wonka's heir and Willy, Charlie, and Charlie's family fly away in a magic elevator.

A reviewer for the *Times Literary Supplement* wrote that the work was highly enjoyable, inventive, and original, and John Gillespie and Diana Lembo noted the book's "infectious fun and outlandish episodes" in *Introducing Books: A Guide for the Middle Grades.* Aileen Pippett remarked in the *New York Times Book Review* that Willy Wonka "is a Dickensian delight, and his factory, with its laughing, singing, tiny Oompa-Loompa workers, is sheer joy." J. S. Jenkins of *Children's Book News* commented, "Children laugh and gasp at his splendid fantasies—the waterfalls of chocolate, the everlasting gobstoppers, the chewing gum machines." *Charlie and the Chocolate Factory* eventually sold over one million hardcover copies in the United States and was later made into a movie from a screenplay written by Dahl. As Rees noted, the book was voted the number one best children's book in a *Sunday Times* survey.

Despite its popular success, however, *Charlie and the Chocolate Factory* incited a controversy about what types of books are appropriate for children and about censorship. The controversy was fueled by Eleanor Cameron's criticism in *Horn Book* that the book displayed "tastelessness," "overtones of sadism," a "phony presentation of poverty," and even moral "hypocrisy." Various reviewers presented their own critiques of the book. In "A New Look at Old Favorites: *Charlie and the Chocolate Factory*," published in *The Black American in Books for Children: Readings in Racism,* Lois Kalb Bouchard described the "racism" which came out in "time-dishonored stereotypes" and argued that the Black Oompa Loompas were presented as "dehumanized," "dependent," and "exploited." A reviewer for the *Times Literary Supplement* lamented Charlie's "passive," accepting character and the association of "good" with such attributes. Myra Pollack Sadker and David Miller Sadker, in *Now Upon a Time: A Contemporary View of Children's Literature,* criticized the way Charlie and Willy ignored the wishes of Charlie's grandparents and pushed them into the elevator against their own will at the end of the story. "The message with which we close the book is that the needs and desires and opinions of old people are totally irrelevant and inconsequential."

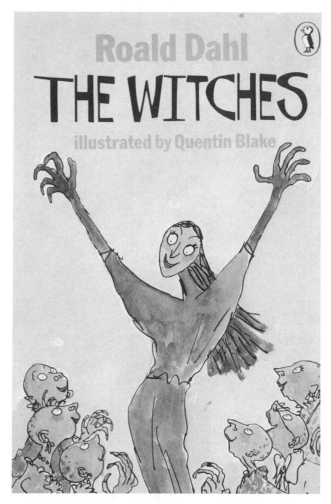

Roald Dahl
THE WITCHES
illustrated by Quentin Blake

A young boy uncovers a plot by some rather nasty witches in this 1983 work.

Dahl was affronted by some of Eleanor Cameron's comments in her 1972 *Horn Book* article. As he asserted in *Horn Book* in 1973, "it would not have been difficult for her [Cameron] to check her facts . . . . We have had some massive misfortunes and some terrific struggles, and we have emerged from these, I think, quite creditably. I deeply resent, therefore, the subtle insinuations that Mrs. Cameron makes about my character." Dahl also responded to Cameron's question of whether or not the book was harmful to young readers. Noting that the book was dedicated to Theo, he asserted, "We fought a long battle to get him where he is today, and we all adore him. . . . The thought that I would write a book for him that might actually do him harm is too ghastly to contemplate." "Mrs. Cameron" would stop Dahl's children from reading *Charlie and the Chocolate Factory* "only over" his "dead body." While

Dahl later told Petschek that "some librarians order 40 copies of my books, but there's a certain bunch of American lady librarians who flay me for what they consider the violence in my children's stories" and that these women had "no sense of humor," the 1973 edition of *Charlie and the Chocolate Factory* was revised so that, as Ellen Chamberlain of *Horn Book* noted, the Oompa Loompas bore "no resemblance" to any racial group.

Another Crisis and More Children's Books

The year after the publication of *Charlie and the Chocolate Factory,* another blow struck the Dahl-Neal family. On February 17, 1965, when Neal was pregnant with the couple's fifth child, Lucy, she suffered three strokes. They began as Neal was bathing her daughter; she experienced a searing pain in her head. As she later told Andrea Chambers of *People,* Neal thought, "I have children to care for. I can not die," as she slipped into a coma. Given the quick work of surgeons and Neal's will, she survived the strokes but was paralyzed on her right side. Although with Dahl's help, insistence, and years of therapy, Neal regained various functions, she walked with a cane, was blind in her right eye, and would experience memory lapses for the rest of her life.

While Dahl assisted Neal's recovery, he felt it was best to continue earning a living for the family. He adapted *You Only Live Twice,* a James Bond book, for a film in 1966 and wrote the screenplay for *Chitty Chitty Bang Bang* in 1967. Children's books were also written as Dahl kept up a steady pace, writing for four hours every day in a tiny hut in his apple orchard. As he once commented in *Something about the Author:* "Normally, I am completely oblivious to the surroundings. When I am up here I see only the paper I am writing on, and my mind is far away with Willy Wonka or James or Mr. Fox or Danny or whatever else I am trying to cook up. The room itself is of no consequence. It is out of focus, a place for dreaming and floating and whistling in the wind, as soft and silent and murky as a womb."

The Magic Finger, published in 1966, begins when an eight-year-old girl casts a spell on a duck hunting family with a "magic finger." The family members sprout wings and are forced to live in a tree while ducks take over their house. By the book's end, however, the father of the family de-

Angelica Huston played the Grand High Witch in the 1990 film adaptation of *The Witches.*

stroys their guns. According to Zena Sutherland of *Bulletin of the Center for Children's Books,* "this is an unusual and effective fanciful story." Constantine Georgiou, in his book *Children and Their Literature,* appreciated the "delightful vein of humor" in the book. And Dalgliesh of the *Saturday Review* exclaimed, "Great merriment here if this is allowed to crash the gates of the Establishment!"

Charlie and the Great Glass Elevator (1972) begins where *Charlie and the Chocolate Factory* left off. In this book, Wonka's glass elevator takes Charlie, his parents, and grandparents on a strange adventure. They orbit the earth, find themselves attacked by creatures, and even save some astronauts. This book received mixed reviews. A critic for *Publishers Weekly* asserted that *Charlie and the Great Glass Elevator* is "all good fun and suspense," while a *Kirkus Reviews* contributor described the book as "perfectly silly and pointlessly tasteless." In her *Bulletin of the Center for Children's Books* review Sutherland wrote that the sequel possessed "ex-

aggeration and action and little else" and was "a comedown" after *Charlie and the Chocolate Factory.* According to Julia Whedon of the *New York Times Book Review, Charlie and the Great Glass Elevator* "becomes just a string of random jokes and adventures held together by . . . glibness."

During the late 1970s, Dahl focused his attention on business affairs and gained attention for *My Uncle Oswald,* the explicit adult novel which is based on Dahl's famous short story, "Switch Bitch" (1974). Dahl sold the paperback rights to six of his books for children for $1,150,000 in 1977, and in 1979, he sold twenty-four stories for adults which became the syndicated television series, *Roald Dahl's Tales of the Unexpected,* hosted by Dahl himself. In 1983, years after Dahl began a relationship with Neal's friend Felicity Ann Crosland, Dahl and Neal divorced; Dahl married Crosland, a fashion coordinator, that same year. Despite the growing discomfort caused by Dahl's spinal problems and metal hips, he continued to write and also to collaborate with illustrator Quentin Blake.

Published in 1983, *The Witches* begins when a young boy's parents are killed in a car accident and his elderly, cigar-smoking grandmother begins to take care of him. While the boy and his grandmother vacation at a hotel, he realizes that a convention of the RSPCC (The Royal Society for the Prevention of Cruelty to Children) is really a convention of witches. After he sees the Grand High Witch reveal her true, ugly, face, the boy is turned into a mouse. Despite this transformation, the brave and clever child-mouse manages to foil the witches' plans with the help of his loving Grandmamma, who understands the needs of the boy-as-mouse as well as the weaknesses of the witches. Erica Jong of the *New York Times Book Review* wrote that this "curious" yet "honest" story "deals with matters of crucial importance to children: smallness, the existence of evil in the world, mourning, separation, death." While Edward Blishen, writing in the *Times Educational Supplement,* expressed concern about the "distrust" of the world the story may evoke, he concluded that *The Witches* is "mesmerizingly readable." Rees, however, wrote that "*The Witches* is sexist and gratuitously frightening." *The Witches* formed the basis for the movie of the same title directed by Nicolas Roeg and staring Anjelica Huston as Miss Ernst, the Grand High Witch of All the World.

In *Boy* (1984), Dahl recalls for younger readers the stories of his childhood that he could not forget. The differences between his life at school and at home, vacations in Norway, the beating at Llandaff after he and his friends put the mouse in Mrs. Pratchett's candy jar, an adenoids operation during which Dahl received no anesthetic, and his decision to go to Africa are all discussed. The stories are accompanied by report cards, drawings, letters to his mother, and photographs. According to Hazel Rochman of the *New York Times Book Review,* these stories are "as frightening and funny" as Dahl's fiction and possess "the intense drama and simplicity of the fairy tale, and its unequivocal extremes of good and evil." Blishen decided in the *Times Literary Supplement* that "one sees in these memories the origin of much of his [Dahl's] fiction, in which the cruel reap a harvest of cruelty." And Rees commented that "*Boy* is very readable, a nice mixture of anecdote and incident, laughter and excitement."

Although *Going Solo* was written when Dahl was seventy, it is, according to Alan Ross of *Times Literary Supplement,* "a young man's book." *Going Solo* begins where *Boy* leaves off, at Dahl's journey to Africa in 1938. By the time Dahl reaches the year 1941 in his memories, he has recalled his experiences in Tanganyika, his training with the R.A.F., his first flight missions, his crash in the desert, his hospitalization, and finally, his return to England. Old letters to his mother, pages from his pilot's log, and photographs enliven the text. *Going Solo* "is made up of powerful, startling scenes, spun by a master storyteller . . . a thoroughly enjoyable account," wrote a reviewer for *People* magazine.

According to Linda Taylor of *Times Literary Supplement,* Dahl "created a safe moral universe in which children are given the inventive powers to bounce back and revenge themselves humorously against their oppressors" in his 1988 children's book *Matilda.* Matilda is a brilliant young child who has managed to teach herself to read despite her obnoxious, neglectful, ignorant, and even criminal parents, Mr. and Mrs. Wormwood. She has also learned how to seek revenge, whether by tricking her father into wearing a hat lined with super-glue or replacing her father's hair tonic with her mother's hair bleach. Matilda develops strange powers when she is not allowed to use her talents in school. She uses these to help Miss Honey, the only adult who recognizes Matilda's gifts, and to confound Miss Turnbull, the "fierce tyrannical" headmistress with a "bull-neck" who throws girls by their pigtails. Vicki Weissman of the *New York Times Book Review* asserted that the book "will surely go straight to children's hearts." Writing in the *Wilson Library Bulletin,* Frances Bradburn concluded that "middle readers will thrill to see a clever five-year-old win out over mean, uncaring parents and a truly vile teacher."

One of Dahl's later works, *Esio Trot,* published in 1990, dwells on the situation created when Mr. Hoppy, a shy retiree, falls in love with Mrs. Silver, a widow who lavishes all her attention on a small tortoise. Mr. Hoppy attempts to find his way to Mrs. Silver's heart by pretending to invoke a Bedouin charm beginning with the words "Esio trot" (tortoise spelled backwards) to make the small tortoise grow larger. He manages this feat by purchasing over one hundred tortoises resembling Alfie but of different sizes, and replacing the tortoise sunning on Mrs. Silver's balcony each week with a specially devised tortoise clamp. When Alfie seems to grow too large to fit in his little house, Mr. Hoppy manages to shrink him

Dahl recalled numerous adventures from his childhood in this 1984 autobiography.

to just the right size. According to George Szirtes of the *Times Literary Supplement,* Dahl's purpose in this work is to celebrate human ingenuousness, the triumph of obsessions and the larger glories of appetite." "*Esio Trot* reveals Roald Dahl at his sunniest and best," commented Brian Alderson of the *Times.*

Another sunny and magical tale, *The Minpins* (1994) was published after Dahl's death and tells the story of a small boy who wanders into the forest despite warnings to stay away. The Minpins are the little tree-dwellers who save Billy from the great monster of the forest and inspire him to battle it. In her review of the tale, *Booklist's* Hazel Rochman maintained that *The Minpins* is "vintage Dahl for reading aloud." Denis Woychuk of the *New York Times Book Review* concluded that the

"story is as brilliant and as unexpected as a dream, filled with soaring excitement and happy resolutions."

Dahl died in a hospital in Oxford, England, on November 23, 1990. Writing after Dahl's death in the *New York Times Book Review,* Ann Hulbert offered this view of the author's contribution to children's literature: "The truth is that Dahl was a tamer phenomenon in children's literature than he ever wanted to acknowledge. To be sure, he was eager to offend taste, and did it with a zest that kids appreciate." Yet, continued Hulbert, "Dahl's abiding theme is nostalgic and idealistic. . . . The heart of almost every book is a paean to the possibility of perfect love and true sympathy between a very small person and a very big person of a special, 'sparky' kind."

■ Works Cited

Alderson, Brian, review of *Esio Trot, Times,* April 21, 1990.

Balakian, Nona, "Gremlins—and Mr. Dahl," *New York Times Book Review,* February 10, 1946, p. 6.

Becker, May Lamberton, review of *The Gremlins, New York Herald Tribune Weekly Book Review,* July 18, 1943, p. 8.

Blishen, Edward, "Bewitched," *Times Educational Supplement,* January 13, 1984, p. 38.

Blishen, "The Unsuspecting Author," *Times Literary Supplement,* November 30, 1984, p. 1376.

Bouchard, Lois Kalb, "A New Look at Old Favorites: *Charlie and the Chocolate Factory,*" in *The Black American in Books for Children: Readings in Racism,* edited by Donnarae MacCann and Gloria Woodard, Scarecrow, 1972, pp. 112-15.

Bradburn, Frances, review of *Matilda, Wilson Library Bulletin,* February, 1989, p. 84.

Bradbury, Malcolm, "Always a Dog beneath the Skin," *New York Times Book Review,* February 7, 1960, p. 5.

Cameron, Eleanor, review of *Charlie and the Chocolate Factory, Horn Book,* October, 1972, p. 440.

Cameron, "McLuhan, Youth, and Literature," *Horn Book,* October, 1972, published as "At Critical Cross-Purposes: McLuhan, Youth, and Literature," in *Crosscurrents of Criticism: Horn Book Essays, 1968–1977,* edited by Paul Heins, Horn Book, 1977, pp. 98-120.

Chamberlain, Ellen, review of *Charlie and the Chocolate Factory, Horn Book,* 1973, p. 227.

Chambers, Andrea, "Patricia Neal Looks Back at a Glorious and Grueling Life," *People,* May 9, 1988, pp. 118-22.

Review of *Charlie and the Chocolate Factory, Times Literary Supplement,* December 14, 1967, p. 1225; June 15, 1973, p. 683.

Review of *Charlie and the Great Glass Elevator, Kirkus Reviews,* July 15, 1972, p. 802.

Review of *Charlie and the Great Glass Elevator, Publishers Weekly,* September 4, 1972, p. 51.

Dahl, Roald, "A Piece of Cake," in *Over to You: Ten Stories of Flyers and Flying,* Reynal, 1946.

Dahl, "My Wife, Patricia Neal," *Ladies' Home Journal,* September, 1965.

Dahl, "At Critical Cross-Purposes: *Charlie and the Chocolate Factory,* A Reply," *Horn Book,* February, 1973, published in *Crosscurrents of Criticism: Horn Book Essays, 1968–1977,* edited by Paul Heins, Horn Book, 1977, pp. 121-22.

Dahl, "Writing Children's Books," *The Writer,* August, 1976, pp. 18-19.

Dahl, "Lucky Break," in *The Wonderful World of Henry Sugar and Six More,* J. Cape, 1977.

Dahl, comments in *Something about the Author,* Volume 26, Gale, 1982.

Dalgliesh, Alice, review of *James and the Giant Peach, Saturday Review,* February 17, 1962, p. 32.

Dalgliesh, "That Pointing Finger," *Saturday Review,* September 17, 1966, pp. 40-41.

Georgiou, Constantine, *Children and Their Literature,* Prentice-Hall, 1969, p. 294.

Gillespie, John, and Diana Lembo, review of *Charlie and the Chocolate Factory,* in *Introducing Books: A Guide for the Middle Grades,* Bowker, 1970, p. 62.

Review of *Going Solo, People,* November 3, 1986.

Haigh, Gerald, "For Non Squiffletrotters Only," *Times Educational Supplement,* November 19, 1982, p. 35.

Hulbert, Ann, review of *Roald Dahl,* by Jeremy Treglown, *New York Times Book Review,* May 1, 1994, pp. 1, 26, 28.

Review of *James and the Giant Peach, Times Literary Supplement,* December 14, 1967, p. 1225.

Jenkins, J. S., review of *Charlie and the Chocolate Factory, Children's Book News,* March-April, 1968.

Jong, Erica, review of *The Witches, New York Times Book Review,* November 13, 1983, p. 45.

Kelly, James, "With Waves of Tension," *New York Times Book Review,* November 8, 1953, p. 5.

O'Hara, J. D., article in *New Republic,* October 19, 1974, p. 23.

Petschek, Willa, "Roald Dahl at Home," *New York Times Biographical Service,* December, 1977, pp. 1615-16.

Pippett, Aileen, review of *Charlie and the Chocolate Factory, New York Times Book Review,* October 25, 1964, p. 36.

Raphael, Frederic, "Stories from the Source of Heartlessness," *Times Literary Supplement,* October 4, 1991, p. 28.

Rees, David, "Dahl's Chickens: Roald Dahl," in *Children's Literature in Education,* Agathon Press, 1988, pp. 143-55.

Rochman, Hazel, review of *Boy, New York Times Book Review,* January 20, 1985, p. 27.

Rochman, review of *The Minpins, Booklist,* October 15, 1991, p. 447.

Ross, Alan, review of *Going Solo, Times Literary Supplement,* September 12, 1986, p. 996.

Sadker, Myra Pollack, and David Miller Sadker, *Now Upon a Time: A Contemporary View of Children's Literature,* Harper, 1977.

Sutherland, Zena, review of *The Magic Finger, Bulletin of the Center for Children's Books,* April, 1965, p. 40.

Sutherland, review of *Charlie and the Great Glass Elevator, Bulletin of the Center for Children's Books,* September, 1973, p. 5.

Szirtes, George, review of *Esio Trot, Times Literary Supplement,* May 11-17, 1990, p. 509.

Taylor, Linda, "Annihilating the Blighters," *Times Literary Supplement,* May 6, 1988, p. 513.

Weissman, Vicki, review of *Matilda, New York Times Book Review,* January 15, 1989.

West, Mark T., interview with Dahl in *Trust Your Children: Voices against Censorship in Children's Books,* Neal-Schuman, 1988, pp. 71-76.

Whedon, Julia, review of *Charlie and the Great Glass Elevator, New York Times Book Review,* September 17, 1973, p. 142.

Wood, Michael, "The Confidence Man," *New Society,* December 20-27, 1979, pp. xiv-xvi.

Woychuk, Denis, review of *The Minpins, New York Times Book Review,* October 27, 1991, p. 27.

■ For More Information See

BOOKS

Children's Literature Review, Volume 1, Gale, 1976.

Contemporary Literary Criticism, Gale, Volume 1, 1973, Volume 6, 1976, Volume 18, 1981, Volume 79, 1994.

Farrell, Barry, *Pat and Roald,* Random House, 1969.

Powling, Chris, *Roald Dahl*, Hamish Hamilton, 1983.
Treglown, Jeremy, *Roald Dahl: A Biography*, Farrar, Straus, 1994.
Warren, Alan, *Roald Dahl*, Starmont, 1988.
West, Mark I., *Roald Dahl*, Twayne, 1992.

PERIODICALS

Atlantic, December, 1962.
Booklist, January 15, 1976, p. 683.
Christian Science Monitor, November 16, 1961.
Kirkus Reviews, May 1, 1984, p. 29.
Library Journal, March 1, 1980, p. 635.
New Statesman, October 29, 1960; March 5, 1971; November 4, 1977.
New York Times Book Review, September 23, 1984, p. 47.
School Library Journal, May, 1992, p. 112.
Washington Post Book World, November 13, 1977; April 20, 1980; May 8, 1983; January 13, 1985.

—Sketch by R. Garcia-Johnson

Genaro González

■ Personal

Born December 28, 1949, in McAllen, TX; son of Leonel González (a migrant farmworker) and Dolores Portales Guerra (a migrant farmworker); married Elena Maria Bastida; children: Carlos Gabriel, Claudia Daniela, Mariella Elena. *Education:* Attended Pan American University, 1968–70; Pomona College, B.A., 1973; graduate study at University of California at Riverside, 1973–74; University of California at Santa Cruz, M.S., 1979, Ph.D., 1982.

■ Addresses

Office—Psychology Department, University of Texas at Pan American, Edinburg, TX 78539.

■ Career

Writer and educator. Pan American University, Edinburg, TX, psychology instructor, 1979–82; University of the Americas, Puebla, Mexico, associate professor of psychology, 1983–85; Texas Governor's School, U.T., Austin, TX, instructor, 1986; Wichita State University, Wichita, KS, assistant professor of

minority studies, 1986–88; University of Texas at Pan American, Edinburgh, TX, associate professor in psychology, 1988—. *Member:* National Hispanic Council of Aging, 1987—; Southwestern Social Science Association, 1988—.

■ Awards, Honors

Seminars Abroad (American University, Cairo, Egypt) Fulbright Fellowship, 1988; Critic's Choice Selection, *Los Angeles Times Review of Books,* 1988, and American Book Award nomination, both for *Rainbow's End;* Creative Writing Fellowship, National Endowment for the Arts, 1990; Summer Seminar (University of Virginia), National Endowment for the Humanities, 1990; Dubic-Paisano Fellowship, Texas Institute of Letters, University of Texas at Austin, 1990.

■ Writings

BOOKS

Rainbow's End (novel), Arte Publico Press, 1988.
Only Sons (short story collection), Arte Publico Press, 1991.

SHORT STORIES

"Un hijo del sol," in *The Chicano: From Caricature to Self-Portrait,* edited by Edward Simmen, New American Library, 1971.
"Soil from the Homeland," in *Nuestro,* July, 1978.

"A Simple Question of $200 a Month," in *Riversedge,* fall, 1980.

"The Heart of the Beast," in *Riversedge,* fall, 1980.

"Too Much His Father's Son," in *Denver Quarterly: Journal of Modern Culture,* fall, 1981.

"A Bad Back," in *Quilt 1,* edited by Ishmael Reed and Al Young, Quilt, 1981.

"Real Life," in *Riversedge,* 1982.

"Home of the Brave," in *A Texas Christmas,* Volume 2, edited by John Edward Weems, Presswork, 1986.

OTHER

"Too Much His Father's Son" and "Boys' Night Out" were published by North of the Border in 1990. Scholarly articles include: "Psychological Strengths in the Hispanic Elderly," *Hispanic Elderly,* 1989; and "Hispanics in the Last Two Decades, Latinos in the Next Two," *La Causa Latina,* 1990.

■ Sidelights

"A large wall mirror faces him. He tries to look at the mirror with detached inspection, but his gaze immediately locks him into the mirror," Genaro González writes in his short story "Un hijo del sol." "Adán stared. . . . Two pairs of eyes—those of himself and of his reflection—mesmerized each other and met at some distance between the mirror and Adán. He felt himself as being some place outside his body. Where am I? he thought. Space. Spaced out. Estoy afuera. Yo soy . . . Adán nadA. . . ."

Just as his character Adán struggles to find himself and understand his heritage in "Un hijo del sol," González grapples with "the existential angst felt by many young Chicanos," according to Manuel M. Martín-Rodríguez in the *Dictionary of Literary Biography.* Besides entertaining readers, however, González's fictional explorations of Chicano "angst" have contributed to the definition of Chicano identity. Scholars of Chicano literature, such as Charles Tatum in *The Identification and Analysis of Chicano Literature* and Ramón Saldívar in *Chicano Narrative,* count González among the most influential writers in the development of Chicano literature. In fact, authors like González, who write "mainly from personal experience . . . create a group consciousness, a Chicano consciousness," according to Tatum.

González was born in McAllen, Texas, to migrant farmworkers of Texan and Mexican descent. When his parents divorced, he went with his mother, Dolores, to live with her family. That situation, which was often uncomfortable, continued until he was nine, when Dolores remarried. Life with his new family was also difficult for González. Due to financial difficulties, he had to work packing produce alongside his mother. Nevertheless, when his mother was diagnosed with tuberculosis and sent to a state hospital, the young boy refused to return to his father.

González did not let his family problems or the fact that he had to work stop him from excelling in school. His dedication and talent in high school earned him an honors scholarship to Pan American University. At Pan American, González distinguished himself academically and voiced his opinions through political activism as well as his writing. González's first short story, "Un hijo del sol" (A Son of the Sun), was published in an anthology of Chicano works in 1971, during his sophomore year.

First Story Enjoys Strong Critical Reception

In "Un hijo del sol," which consists of five sections, Adán (the Spanish equivalent of "Adam") is tormented by the knowledge that he doesn't really know himself or understand his heritage. In the passage quoted above, for example, Adán describes how he feels *afuera* (outside) himself and decides that he is empty, or *nada* (nothing). When Adán realizes that his quest for understanding cannot be meaningful unless he travels to Mexico, the home of his recent and ancient ancestors, he begins to make progress.

Finally, in the last section of "Un hijo del sol," a fight breaks out among Chicanos and Anglos in a bar. Adán joins the Chicanos in the struggle and makes a choice that brings him the self-definition he has been searching for: "Adán suspends the knife in final decision, weighing the victim versus the act. . . . An obsidian blade traces a quick arc of instinct—somewhere in time an angry comet flares, a sleeping mountain erupts, an Aztec sun explodes in birth." The killing is "narrated in highly symbolic terms that suggest the reconciliation of Adán's roots, his inner life, and his new participation in social action," according to Martín-Rodríguez. "Adán's discovery of his identity conveys to the reader a message of hope. It reveals itself as a starting point for a new life that transcends the isolation of the individuals into a collective struggle."

"Un hijo del sol" and the message it carries brought the young writer immediate critical attention. Though some critics decried what they saw as a "socially unproductive" message in the work, González nevertheless won a spot in the history of the development of Chicano literature. Juan Rodríguez, writing in *The Identification and Analysis of Chicano Literature*, calls the story "the best of all until now," and claims that it "is the only one in all Chicano literature which offers a search for and an encounter of identity in positive and viable terms."

While González seemed to be a hit with literary critics, his political activities were not appreciated by college officials. Upon learning that his affiliation to Chicano organizations was being investigated by Pan American University, González left the school and Texas and transferred to Pompano College in California. At Pompano, González became an active member of La Raza Unida and contributed his efforts to the campaign to elect Ramsey Muñiz governor of Texas. In 1973, however, he became discouraged with La Raza Unida and left the party.

González began graduate studies at the University of California at Riverside and then earned an M.S. and Ph.D. from the University of California at Santa Cruz. He began work as a professor of social psychology at Pan American University in 1979. During graduate school and his years at Pan American, González continued to write. Most of the short stories González produced during this time "revolved around isolation versus integration," Martín-Rodríguez states in *Dictionary of Literary Biography*. "Soil from the Homeland" (1978), "A Simple Question of $200 a Month" (1980), and "A Bad Back" (1981) were later integrated into *Rainbow's End.*

"The Heart of the Beast" (1980) tells the story of a boy who suffers from ill health. Taunted by children and even his grandfather for his sickliness, Arturo is reluctant to disclose any new information about his health. The situation deteriorates to the point that, although he believes he has been bitten by a rabid dog, Arturo cannot bring himself to tell his family. His emotional isolation, however, bears fruit when he begins to

Gonzalez spent part of his youth in McAllen, Texas, where his parents worked on a number of farms.

appreciate himself. In "Too Much His Father's Son" (1981), a boy must deal with the confusion and pain generated by his parents' frequent arguments and his own difficult relationship with his father. In this work, "González's psychological characterization is at its best," according to Martín-Rodríguez. "Real Life" (1982) features orphaned Ernesto, who has been raised by his aunt and uncle and must help them make a difficult choice. His aunt is dying, and his uncle calls upon him to help decide whether to let her die naturally or support her artificially.

Rainbow's End Elicits Praise

By 1982, when Pan American declined to offer him tenure and he left the university, González devoted most of his time to writing. He was finally ready to begin a project he had put off—writing a novel intended for publication by Grove Press. He wrote a long first draft and then left the United States for Mexico. González continued to write and taught at the Universidad de las Américas in Puebla from 1983 to 1985. Arte Publico decided to publish a revised and shortened draft of González's novel as *Rainbow's End,*

After a dangerous Rio Grande crossing, Don Heraclio Cavazos discovers a life of both pleasure and pain in the United States.

and he returned to the United States. González began to teach at Texas Governor's School at the University of Texas at Austin in 1986, and then became an assistant professor of minority studies at Wichita State University.

It was during this time that his story "Home of the Brave" was first published in an anthology. In this short story, a Vietnam veteran becomes frustrated with the war and confronts his family with his decision to desert the army. While his family objects to the plan, an uncle who survived the Korean war advises the young man to flee to Mexico. According to Martín-Rodríguez, this story "depicts army life as a false hope for eventual social integration."

Two triumphs mark the year 1988 for González: he was hired as an associate professor in psychol-

ogy at the University of Texas at Pan American, and *Rainbow's End* was published. *Rainbow's End* begins in the 1930s, as Don Heraclio Cavazos stands at the threshold of his future life in the United States. He is just about to cross the Rio Grande for the first time by swimming through the swollen water when he thinks he sees a bridge joining Mexico and the United States. While the bridge Cavazos imagines is really a rainbow, no pot of gold lies on the U.S. side of the river. Cavazos soon finds that he must earn his living with tedious, back-breaking labor: years after his arrival in the United States he and his family are still cheated by the "gringo" farm owners for whom they toil. Martín-Rodríguez asserts that "the pot at the end of the rainbow, although never mentioned explicitly, provides the basis for the pervasive irony of the work. González's novel is, in this way, connected to the satirical tradition of Chicano literature that demythologizes the popular belief of quick riches in the United States."

Once González establishes the symbolism of the rainbow, his novel flows along, telling the story of three generations with flashbacks. The reader learns how, as a young man, Cavazos lives in Doña Zoila's rooming house with migrant workers nicknamed Tomcat, Rooster, Elephant, Greased Pig, Frog Prince, Love Bandit, and El Bruto. He leaves the rooming house to marry Chaca, and they have two children together. When Chaca dies, Cavazos raises them with the help of Chaca's family. During Cavazos's last years, he stubbornly refutes the superficial reality imposed upon him by reminding those around him of disagreeable facts and events. For example, he greets neighbors by remarking, "They shot Kennedy." And when he stands before an official to receive U.S. citizenship, to the question "Who discovered America?" Cavazos replies, "Los indios" (the Indians). Cavazos refuses to respond to the injustice that pervades his life with anything less than pride and dignity.

While Cavazos is not happy with the lifestyles his children and grandchildren choose as they are assimilated into American society, he cannot persuade them to live as he has taught them. Cavazos' son earns his money illicitly, and other members of his family are involved in the drug trade. His daughter and her husband embrace popular culture. One of Cavazos' grandsons, a Vietnam veteran, cannot recover from the psychological trauma of war. Hope remains in the fact that one of Cavazos' grandsons journeys to Mexico and begins to understand himself and his grandfather, and optimism is manifested when Cavazos' sister-in-law Fela (a sorceress who has never married) decides to give her knowledge to an eager young apprentice so that it does not die with her.

Critics have appreciated various scenes in *Rainbow's End*. Tom Miller of the *Los Angeles Times Book Review,* for example, calls the scene in which a girl excites the barrio with the news that she has seen the devil (who has to dance on a hoof and a rooster foot instead of human feet) at the Saturday night dance "wonderfully comic." Miller also described a scene in which Cavazos goes to the mall to shop for a new hat as "poignant and comical." Stuart Klawans of the *Nation* praises a scene from *Rainbow's End* that "happens almost entirely in Don Heraclio's mind." In the scene, Cavazos is working in the tomato field when his nose begins to bleed. Just as he leans his head back to stop the bleeding, he gets a glimpse of his wife and his oldest friend, whose deaths he has been mourning. It is all Cavazos can do to keep from lowering his head and confirming what he has seen. A storm brings him back to reality with a rush of color, and he realizes that the figures he saw were not those of the departed: "suddenly sporadic patches of the world caught color all around. A pair of dungy objects in a nearby field combusted into twin calico cows with huge rust freckles, grazing without a care on the good, green earth. Even the fire ants under his feet seemed to ignite in redness." Klawans claims that when "González writes at this level, the creatures of his imagination combust into their own living, full-color reality."

Rainbow's End has elicited some enthusiastic reviews from critics. Miller writes that González's "bilingual puns enrich" *Rainbow's End,* and that the work "captures the *ambiente* of the life of a borderland household as well as any book I've ever read." Klawans said that the novel would make a good movie, but claimed that what "can't be transferred to film is González's writing, which at its best deals in epiphanies." *Rainbow's End* was a *Los Angeles Times Book Review Critic's Choice* selection, and was nominated for the American Book Award. González also received several awards that indicate his talent as a writer. These include a prestigious Fulbright Fellowship and a coveted Creative Writing Fellowship from the National Endowment for the Arts.

The tales in this collection take place in a Texas border town where racism, sexism and injustice are part of everyday life.

Publishes Short Story Collection

Like *Rainbow's End,* the stories in the collection *Only Sons* (1991) are set in a Texas border town. Readers of González's first novel and this collection will recognize similar themes and even characters. For example, in both works a tension between Chicanos of different generations is prominent. The problem of justice, observes Jim Christie of *Hispanic,* also appears in both books. In one story, a judge must deal with the son of a campaign contributor who is accused of raping his family's maid. González's character tries to justify his actions: "'She's also a wetback,' said the son. 'Twice! From some country I never even heard of.' He looked at her and smiled, satisfied that his revenge had thwarted his case. Don Benito covered his eyes as the last glimmer of justice seemed to dim from the world."

In another story, an old man whose hand was mangled during his work as a farmhand tries to find the Anglo employer who paid him to keep quiet about the accident. When Vincente finds him in a trailer park, he slowly removes the glove from his hand to the horror of his former employer. By contrast, Elena, the woman Vincente had asked to accompany him because of her educated dislike of Anglos, cannot find the courage to confront them. In the opinion of Christie, González "loves to play with anxiety and ambiguity; *Only Sons* seems to have been an exercise in refining and adapting those emotions over and over again in many different settings."

González, who is the father of three children, continues to write fiction and conduct research in cross-cultural psychology at Pan American University. Scholars, critics, and fans alike look forward to the voices that will emerge in his future work. In the words of Martín-Rodríguez, González's "mature style holds great promise for his future literary contributions to Chicano letters."

■ Works Cited

Christie, Jim, review of *Only Sons, Hispanic,* May, 1992, p. 56.

González, Genaro, "Un hijo del sol," in *The Chicano: From Caricature to Self–Portrait,* edited by Edward Simmen, New American Library, 1971, pp. 308–17.

González, *Rainbow's End,* Arte Publico Press, 1988.

González, *Only Sons,* Arte Publico Press, 1991.

Klawans, Stuart, review of *Rainbow's End, Nation,* November 14, 1988, p. 502.

Martín-Rodríguez, Manuel M., "Genaro González," *Dictionary of Literary Biography,* Volume 122, Gale, 1991, pp. 115–18.

Miller, Tom, "It's Doggy–Dog along the Rio Grande," *Los Angeles Times Book Review,* March 13, 1988, p. 8.

Rodríguez, Juan (translated by R. Garcia-Johnson), "La búsqueda de identidad y sus motivos en la literatura chicana," *The Identification and Analysis of Chicano Literature,* edited by Francisco Jiménez, Bilingual Press, 1979, pp. 170–78.

Saldívar, Ramón, *Chicano Narrative: The Dialectics of Difference,* University of Wisconsin Press, 1990.

Tatum, Charles M., "Contemporary Chicano Prose Fiction: Its Ties to Mexican Literature," *The Identification and Analysis of Chicano Literature,* edited by Francisco Jiménez, Bilingual Press, 1979, pp. 47–57.

■ For More Information See

PERIODICALS

Children's Book Watch, Volume 12, November, 1991, p. 9.

Multi-Cultural Review, Volume 1, January, 1992, p. 46.

Palabra (Spanish-language), fall, 1979, pp. 3–16.

—*Sketch by R. Garcia–Johnson*

Patricia Hermes

■ Personal

Born Patricia Mary Martin, February 21, 1936, in Brooklyn, NY; daughter of Frederick Joseph (a bank vice-president) and Jessie (Gould) Martin; married Matthew E. Hermes (a research and development director for a chemical company), August 24, 1957 (divorced, 1984); children: Paul, Mark, Timothy, Matthew, Jr., Jennifer. *Education:* St. John's University, Jamaica, NY, B.A., 1957. *Politics:* Democrat. *Religion:* Roman Catholic.

■ Addresses

Home and office—1414 Melville Ave., Fairfield, CT 06430. *Agent*—Dorothy Markinko (juvenile books) and Julie Fallowfield (adult books), McIntosh & Otis, Inc., 310 Madison Ave., New York, NY 10017.

■ Career

Writer. Rollingcrest Junior High School, Takoma Park, MD, teacher of English and social studies, 1957–1958; Delcastle Technical High School, Delcastle, DE, teacher of home-bound children, 1972–1973; Norfolk Public School System, Norfolk, VA, writer in residence, beginning 1981; Sacred Heart University, Fairfield, CT, teacher of English and writing, 1986–87. *Member:* Authors Guild, Authors League of America, Society of Children's Book Writers and Illustrators.

■ Awards, Honors

A Solitary Secret was named Best Book for Young Adults for 1985, American Library Association; several Children's Choice awards.

■ Writings

YOUNG ADULT NOVELS

Friends Are Like That, Harcourt, 1984.
A Solitary Secret, Harcourt, 1985.
Be Still My Heart, Putnam, 1989, Archway, 1992.
My Girl (novel based on a screenplay by Laurice Elehwany), Pocket Books, 1991.
My Girl 2 (novel based on a screenplay by Janet Kovalcik, with characters created by Laurice Elehwany), Pocket Books, 1994.

OTHER

A Time to Listen: Preventing Youth Suicide (nonfiction), Harcourt, 1987.

CHILDREN'S BOOKS

What If They Knew, Harcourt, 1980, Dell, 1989.

Nobody's Fault?, Harcourt, 1981, Dell, 1983.

You Shouldn't Have to Say Good-bye, Harcourt, 1982, Scholastic, 1989.

Who Will Take Care of Me?, Harcourt, 1983.

Kevin Corbett Eats Flies, illustrated by Carol Newsom, Harcourt, 1986, Minstrel, 1987.

A Place for Jeremy (sequel to *What if They Knew*), Harcourt, 1987.

Heads, I Win (sequel to *Kevin Corbett Eats Flies*), Harcourt, 1988, Minstrel, 1989.

I Hate Being Gifted, Putnam, 1990, Minstrel, 1992.

Take Care of My Girl, Little, Brown, 1992.

Mama, Let's Dance, Little, Brown, 1991, Scholastic, 1993.

Someone to Count On, Little, Brown, 1993.

Nothing but Trouble, Trouble, Trouble, Scholastic, 1994.

"COUSINS' CLUB" SERIES

I'll Pulverize You, William, Minstrel, 1994.

Everything Stinks, Minstrel, 1995.

Thirteen Things Not to Tell a Parent, Minstrel 1995.

Contributor to periodicals, including *Woman's Day, Life and Health, Connecticut, American Baby,* and *Mother's Day.*

■ Sidelights

"An author is a spy," Patricia Hermes admitted in an interview with Sarah Verney for *Authors and Artists for Young Adults (AAYA).* "I watch children, how they act with each other and with their teachers. I listen to their conversations. I write down things I see and hear that are interesting. And yes, sometimes I do use these things in my books." For Hermes, finding the opportunity to spy on children isn't as easy as it used to be. As the mother of five, watching children interact with each other and with adults used to be an integral part of daily life. Her own children are grown now, though, so Hermes finds the best way to gather material is through frequent visits to elementary schools. She goes to the schools to discuss writing, but these visits also allow her to gather bits and pieces of information that become the telling details that are sprinkled throughout her work. And these little things are important in writing because, as Hermes expressed in *The Sixth Book of Junior Authors,* "no writer is worth the paper the books are written on if she or he is not in tune with the details of the lives of children."

Sometimes the things Hermes observes can spark her imagination and lead to something larger than those telling details. "Once," Hermes told *AAYA,* "I was visiting an elementary school and a tiny girl, about six years old, ran past, chasing a little boy and yelling, 'I'll pulverize you, William.' At the time I thought, what a great piece of dialogue that would make. Right off the bat, those four words tell you so much about this child—she's intelligent, she's spunky, and she's really mad at William. Later, I realized that those four words would also make a great title." Eventually that little girl grew into Meghann, the feisty heroine of *I'll Pulverize You, William,* the first book in Hermes's "Cousins' Club" series.

A Painful Childhood

For the overall thrust of her stories, Hermes generally relies on personal experiences and memories. Hermes has what one friend has termed "a dangerous memory," because she remembers almost everything. By her own account in *The Sixth Book of Junior Authors,* "the joy, the sadness, the vulnerability, the sense of powerlessness" of childhood are still very clear in her mind. "I think that each of us has a little kid who lives inside us, and mine is ten or eleven years old," she explained to Verney. Perhaps this explains why many of Hermes's characters are fifth- or sixth-graders, and why her stories seem fairly realistic. Hermes remembers well what it was like to be a child—and passes those memories along through her characters.

Hermes's own childhood was sometimes lonely and painful. The third of four children, she described herself in the *AAYA* interview as having been "very much a middle child," and said that "like everyone, I wanted to feel special, but always felt sort of lost in the family." Most difficult, however, was the fact that she had rheumatic fever, and was often ill. This disease—and later, epilepsy—made her feel weird and different from other children, and frequent hospital stays added to her feelings of isolation. Hermes points out that the year she was ten happened to be particularly traumatic, partly due to having surgery for a burst appendix and partly because her family moved from a small community to a much bigger one. "I was a smart kid in my first school," she told Verney, "but they were way ahead of us in the new school, and I wasn't so smart anymore." To make matters worse, her new class had 57 children in it, which made it particularly difficult to get any attention or recognition.

Ironically, though, Hermes's illnesses and sense of isolation also led her to discover one of the greatest joys of her childhood: a love of books. "In a book," she stated in *The Sixth Book of Junior Authors,* "I was never lonely, never sad. Open a book, and I was surrounded by a world of people, imaginary ones, true, but imaginary ones who were sometimes more real to me than the ones with whom I lived." The author's love of books continued into adulthood, but for many years Hermes did not seriously consider becoming a writer. Upon graduating from college, she married and immediately took a job teaching junior high school. She left that position when her first child was born, and during the next nine years she had five more children, one of whom died in infancy. For the next several years, Hermes mainly devoted herself to raising her children, although she did return to teaching for short periods of time in the early 1970s and again in the early 1980s.

From Full-Time Mother to Novelist

Even though she did not consider getting her work published during this time, Hermes did write for herself and for her children. Then, in the late 1970s, she began to seriously consider trying to get published, and submitted an essay to the *New York Times* editorial page. The *Times* published the piece, in which Hermes described the experience of returning to an important place from her childhood with one of her own children. As luck would have it, a children's book editor read the essay and liked it, and called to ask Hermes if she had ever considered writing a novel for children. Hermes hadn't—at least not seriously—but enthusiastically rose to the challenge. The result was *What If They Knew,* Hermes's first published novel.

With *What If They Knew,* Hermes began her own tradition of mixing her memories of childhood with what she calls "lies"—fiction. "Children sometimes ask me if the things that happen in my stories really happened to me," Hermes explained to Verney—a testament, it would seem, to her convincing first-person voice. "I tell them authors tell lies. We take one little thing that's true,

In this sequel to Hermes's first book, *What If They Knew?,* Jeremy stays with her grandparents in her old neighborhood while she tries to adjust to the idea of a new adoptive sibling.

and tell lots of lies about it. I write fiction. But everything I write has a little bit of truth in it."

The "little bit of truth" in *What If They Knew* can be found in the main character's feelings about having epilepsy, which are drawn directly from Hermes's own life. Jeremy is a ten-year-old girl who is apprehensive about attending a new school, because she is afraid she might have a seizure and be labeled as weird by her new friends. In spite of the serious subject at its core, however, the novel also details the lighter side of childhood. *What If They Knew* was a success, and in 1981 was selected as a Children's Choice book by a joint committee of the International Reading Association and the Children's Book Council. The book's sequel, *A Place for Jeremy,* was published in 1987, and was also named a Children's Choice book.

A Reputation for "Doing Death"

Many of the novels that followed *What If They Knew* deal with even more serious and painful subjects. Among these are *You Shouldn't Have to Say Good-bye* and *Mama, Let's Dance,* two of the author's most critically acclaimed works. *You Shouldn't Have to Say Good-bye* is the story of a thirteen-year-old girl who must come to terms with her mother's terminal illness. *Mama, Let's Dance* concerns three children who attempt to cover up their mother's abandonment by carrying on as if she had never left. Both books deal with death and grief, as do several of Hermes's other novels, including *Nobody's Fault* and *Who Will Take of Me?* In fact, as Hermes once said jokingly, she has earned a reputation in the children's publishing industry as an author who "does death." That doesn't mean that her books are somber or morbid, but simply that she isn't afraid to take a close look at grief through a child's eyes.

In doing so, Hermes infuses her characters with emotions she has experienced first-hand. "Children will often ask if my mother died when I was thirteen, or if my brother or sister died. The answer is no—but I did lose a child in infancy, and in writing about a character's feelings about death, I know I go back to that. When Mary Belle is grieving for her sister Callie in *Mama Let's Dance,* her feelings are definitely drawn from my own," the author explained in her *AAYA* interview. Hermes's infant daughter died of Sudden Infant Death Syndrome (SIDS). Like all SIDS victims, the baby was apparently healthy until she suddenly died in her sleep. "One day I was calling everyone to invite them to the christening, and the next I was calling them back to tell them to come to the funeral instead. It was terrible," Hermes recalled.

However Hermes achieves her characterizations, they generally seem to ring true with critics as well as with readers. *Kevin Corbett Eats Flies* "has both humor and warmth as well as solid characterizations," according to *Booklist* reviewer Ilene Cooper, and Vicki Hardesty of *VOYA* called *You Shouldn't Have to Say Goodbye* "an excellent portrayal of a teenager adjusting to the terminal illness of a parent." Similarly, Donna S. Rodda,

In order to prove to her parents that she is responsible enough to hold a babysitting job, Alex tries to stay out of trouble for two whole weeks—with mixed results.

writing in *School Library Journal,* praised *Friends Are Like That* for its "real and believable" characterizations, and *Booklist* reviewer Karen Stang Hanley called *Who Will Take Care of Me?* "an affecting story that is especially moving in its portrayal of the complex, tender relationship between two brothers."

In creating realistic characters and portraying their feelings about things like death, child abandonment, and life in foster care, Hermes attempts to reach out to young people who, for one reason or another, may be having a difficult time. "As adults," she noted in an interview for *Contemporary Authors (CA),* "we often try to deceive ourselves that childhood is a safe, pleasant place to be. It isn't—at least not much of the time. For me, it is important to say this to young people, to let them know they are not alone and that others share their feelings, their dreams and fears and hopes. It is important for them to know that things aren't so great in other children's lives either, because I have long believed that anything is bearable when we know that we are not alone." In addition, whether she is dealing with the really tough problems, like grieving, or more common ones, like the desire to be popular, Hermes likes to give her readers hope that things will get better. "Hope is the most important thing I can hold out to them," she told *CA*.

Children seem to be getting the message, but some parents don't always understand why Hermes finds it important to speak to these issues. "People sometimes say to me, 'I won't let my child read *that*'" Hermes told Verney. "But I think children know everything there is to know about emotions by the time they are three or four. As parents we sometimes want to protect our children from anything that is painful, but what we're really trying to do is protect ourselves, and in doing so, we harm them. When you're dealing with these things in a book—if it gets too scary or too painful—you can close it, or go talk to someone about it. I think its ironic," she added, "that no one tries very hard to protect children from TV."

Hermes' ability to create realistic characters and write about grief may have led, in part, to her being asked to write the novelization of the movie *My Girl,* in which a child dies. Turning the screenplay into a novel was an enjoyable experience because the author had such a good script to work from. Although the plot was established, Hermes had a relatively free hand with the character's "voice" and what is known as "backfilling"—developing the character's thoughts, feelings, and memories—so Hermes was able to put her own stamp on the story. The author was essentially happy with the finished product, and was pleased to have the opportunity to write the sequel, *My Girl 2.*

The Lighter Side of Childhood

While Hermes may be known for taking on tough subjects, even her most serious books are infused with a healthy dose of humor. As she once commented, "I also write about the fun, and nonsense and glee of childhood." Throughout the author's writing career, Hermes' five children have helped provide some of the material for these lighter

moments. Her children "teach me the language of childhood that I have long forgotten. They teach me the tricks that children can play on the adult world," she noted.

Hermes's children are all grown now, but that hasn't stopped her from continuing to explore childhood's more humorous moments. In fact, if there is a trend in her latest novels, it seems to be a tendency to lighten up. Her characters still have their painful moments, but in books like those in the "Cousins' Club" series, the overall tone is decidedly less serious. For example, in *I'll Pulverize You, William,* Meghann's biggest problem is finding the escaped baby boa constrictor that she's supposed to be taking care of (the boa is trapped in the house, so Meghann doesn't have to look far). However, Hermes explained to *AAYA* that any change in subject matter was not really a conscious decision: "As an author," she noted,

SELECTED FOR A CHILDREN'S CHOICE AWARD IN 1986

This humorous Children's Choice selection for younger readers features the author's trademark humor in telling of the friendship between a boy who performs strange stunts for attention and a tough-talking foster child.

"if you're at all lucky, you are well-rounded. It just feels like it's time to do this now."

It is also time for branching out into previously unexplored genres. Hermes began work on her first historical novel, *On Winter's Wind,* which is set in the 1850s, and on a picture book, *When Snow Lay Soft on the Mountain.* In addition to these books and the "Cousins' Club" series, she also began work on a novel entitled *Love Me Love Me Not.* All of these books add up to a big increase in productivity for Hermes, who for many years published just one novel a year. The increase in her output, she said, is largely due to the fact that she no longer has children at home. Her house, which was once a gathering place for all the neighborhood children, is mostly quiet, except when her grandchildren come to visit.

The quiet gives Hermes the opportunity to work on her novels and, when her busy schedule permits, answer some of the many fan letters she receives. She loves getting letters from her readers, she said, although she's not as crazy about those that are done as part of a class assignment. Still, the unprompted letters help keep her connected with her readers and allow her glimpses—sometimes funny, sometimes sad—into their lives. "Some of the letters about *You Shouldn't Have to Say Good-bye* were just heartbreaking," she explained to Verney, citing one from a girl who had received the book from her mother, who was dying of cancer. "I corresponded with her for years, until she went away to college."

Other letters provide a chuckle, Hermes told *AAYA,* like the one from the boy who wrote: "My name is _____. My mother says I'm cute. If you would like me to be a character in one of your books, write back." Hermes doesn't plan to take him up on his generous offer at the moment. But that little boy might want to read her future books carefully, because he sounds like just the kind of exuberant child who could spark Hermes's imagination—and maybe inspire a new character.

■ *Works Cited*

Cooper, Ilene, review of *Kevin Corbett Eats Flies, Booklist,* August 1986, p. 1688.

Contemporary Authors, New Revision Series, volume 22, Gale, p. 188.

Hanley, Karen Stang, review of *Who Will Take Care of Me?, Booklist,* September 15, 1983, p. 171.

Hardesty, Vicki, review of *You Shouldn't Have to Say Goodbye, Voice of Youth Advocates (VOYA),* October 1993, p. 203.

Hermes, Patricia, autobiographical note in *The Sixth Book of Junior Authors,* edited by Sally Holmes Holtze, H. W. Wilson, 1989, pp. 124-26.

Hermes, Patricia, interview with Sarah Verney for *Authors and Artists for Young Adults,* conducted 1994.

Hermes, Patricia, *My Girl,* Pocket Books, 1991.

Rodda, Donna S., review of *Friends Are Like That, School Library Journal,* May 1984, p. 80.

—Sketch by Sarah Verney

Zora Neale Hurston

■ Personal

Born January 7, 1891 (Hurston claimed various birth years, primarily 1903 but ranging from 1898 to 1910; scholars have established 1891 as the correct year), in Eatonville, FL; died January 28, 1960, in Fort Pierce, FL; buried in the Garden of the Heavenly Rest, Fort Pierce, FL; daughter of John (a minister and carpenter) and Lucy Ann (a schoolteacher and seamstress; maiden name, Potts) Hurston; married Herbert Sheen, May 19, 1927 (divorced, July 7, 1931); married Albert Price III, June 27, 1939 (divorced November 9, 1943). *Education:* Attended Howard University, 1923–24; Barnard College, B.A., 1928; graduate study at Columbia University.

■ Career

Writer and folklorist. Collected folklore in the South, 1927–31; assistant to writer Fannie Hurst, late 1920s; Bethune-Cookman College, Daytona, FL, instructor of drama, 1933–34; collected folklore in Jamaica, Haiti, and Bermuda, 1937–38; collected folklore in Florida for the Works Progress Administration, 1938–39; Paramount Studios, Hollywood,

CA, staff writer, 1941; collected folklore in Honduras, 1946–48; worked as a maid in Florida, 1950; freelance writer, 1950–56; librarian at Patrick Air Force Base, FL, 1956–57; writer for the *Fort Pierce Chronicle* and part-time teacher at Lincoln Park Academy, Fort Pierce, FL, 1958–59. Also worked as a librarian at the Library of Congress, Washington, DC, and as professor of drama at North Carolina College for Negroes (now North Carolina Central University), Durham. c. 1950s. *Member:* American Folklore Society, American Anthropological Society, American Ethnological Society, Zeta Phi Beta.

■ Awards, Honors

Guggenheim fellowships, 1936, 1938; Litt.D., Morgan College, 1939; Anisfield-Wolf Award (race relations), 1943, for *Dust Tracks on a Road.*

■ Writings

FICTION

Jonah's Gourd Vine (novel), introduction by Fannie Hurst, Lippincott, 1934, published with a introduction by Larry Neal, 1971, published with an new foreword by Rita Dove, Harper, 1990.

Their Eyes Were Watching God (novel), Lippincott, 1937, published with a foreword by Ruby Dee and an introduction by Sherley Anne Williams, University of Illinois Press, 1991.

Moses, Man of the Mountain (novel), Lippincott, 1939, published as *The Man of the Mountain*, Dent, 1941.

Seraph on the Suwanee (novel), Scribner, 1948, published with a foreword by Hazel V. Carby, Harper, 1991.

Spunk: The Selected Stories of Zora Neale Hurston, Turtle Island Foundation, 1985.

The Gilded Six-Bits (story), Redpath Press, 1986.

The Complete Stories, HarperCollins, 1992.

Contributor of stories to periodicals, including *Challenge, Opportunity, Saturday Evening Post, Spokesman,* and *Stylus,* and to anthologies.

PLAYS

Color Struck!: A Play in Four Scenes, published in *Fire!!: A Quarterly Devoted to the Younger Negro Artists,* November, 1926, pp. 7–15.

The First One: A Play (one-act), in *Ebony and Topaz,* edited by Charles S. Johnson, National Urban League, 1927.

(With Clinton Fletcher and Tim Moore) *Fast and Furious* (musical), published in *Best Plays of 1931–32,* edited by Burns Mantle and Garrison Sherwood, 1931.

(With Langston Hughes) *Mule Bone: A Comedy of Negro Life in Three Acts,* 1931, published in *Drama Critique,* spring, 1964, updated version edited by George H. Bass and Henry Louis Gates, Jr. (produced at Ethel Barrymore Theatre, New York), Harper, 1991.

(With Dorothy Waring) *Stephen Kelen-d'Oxylion Presents Polk County: A Comedy of Negro Life on a Sawmill Camp With Authentic Negro Music* (three-act play), [New York], ca. 1944.

OTHER

Mules and Men (folklore), introduction by Franz Boas, Lippincott, 1935, published with a new foreword by Arnold Rampersad as *Mules and Men: A Treasury of Black American Folklore,* Harper, 1989.

Tell My Horse (nonfiction), Lippincott, 1938, published as *Voodoo Gods: An Inquiry into Native Myths and Magic in Jamaica and Haiti,* Dent, 1939, published with an introduction by Ishmael Reed as *Tell My Horse: Voodoo and Life in Haiti and Jamaica,* Harper, 1989.

Dust Tracks on a Road (autobiography), Lippincott, 1942, 2nd edition published as *Dust Tracks on a Road: An Autobiography,* edited with an introduction by Robert E. Hemenway, University of Illi-nois Press, 1984, published with a foreword by Maya Angelou, Harper, 1991.

I Love Myself When I Am Laughing . . . And Then Again When I Am Looking Mean and Impressive: A Zora Neale Hurston Reader, edited by Alice Walker, Feminist Press, 1979.

The Sanctified Church, Turtle Island Foundation, 1981.

Three Classic Works by Zora Neale Hurston: Their Eyes Were Watching God, Dust Tracks on a Road, Mules and Men, HarperCollins, 1991.

Complete Works, two volumes, Library of America, 1995.

Author of weekly column "Hoodoo and Black Magic," *Fort Pierce Chronicle,* 1958–1959. Contributor of poetry to *Howard University Record* and *Stylus;* contributor of essays, reviews, and nonfiction to *American Legion Magazine, American Mercury, Essence, Fort Pierce Chronicle, Forum, Interview, Journal of American Folklore, Journal of Negro History, Messenger, New York Herald Tribune Books, Pittsburgh Courier, Saturday Evening Post, Saturday Review, Utne Reader, Washington Tribune,* and *World Tomorrow.*

■ Adaptations

Spunk: Three Tales was adapted as a play by George C. Wolfe, with music by Chic Street Man, produced at the Public Theatre, New York, 1990, and published by Dramatists Play Service, 1992. *Their Eyes Were Watching God* was produced as a sound recording, 1991. Producer Quincy Jones has purchased rights to one of Hurston's novels.

■ Work in Progress

At the time of her death, Hurston left an unfinished three-hundred-page novel manuscript, *The Life of Herod the Great.*

■ Sidelights

"Zora was funny, irreverent (she was the first to call the Harlem Renaissance literati the 'niggerati'), good-looking and sexy," wrote Alice Walker. Having been one of the most prolific African-American women writers of her time, Zora Neale Hurston was a renowned member of the Harlem Renaissance in the 1920s, a preeminent folklorist, and author of four novels, three nonfiction works, and numerous short stories, essays, and plays. In 1942 she reached the peak of her career with a

Saturday Review cover story about her autobiography *Dust Tracks on a Road;* by 1950 she was working as a maid in Miami; and in 1960 she died in obscurity and was buried in an unmarked pauper's grave in Fort Pierce, Florida.

Robert E. Hemenway's *Zora Neale Hurston: A Literary Biography* described this enigmatic writer as "flamboyant and yet vulnerable, self-centered and yet kind, a Republican conservative and yet an early black nationalist." Such contradictory characteristics enraged her black male contemporaries, who criticized her lack of social consciousness. Langston Hughes noted her dependence on white patronage for financial support, commenting that she was "simply paid just to sit around and represent the Negro race." Some criticized her for advancing her career by portraying herself and other blacks as childlike primitives and for sacrificing her integrity in ignoring racism. While blacks criticized her refusal to acknowledge resentment of white oppression, predominantly white reviewers generally liked her lively stories of black culture at a time when whites were fascinated to know what blacks were "really like." Recent scholars have recognized her importance as a writer, particularly on the basis of her masterpiece, the novel *Their Eyes Were Watching God.*

Born in Eatonville, Florida, just north of Orlando, Hurston set most of her fiction in this first incorporated black township in the United States. The puzzle of her life begins with confusion about her birth date, since no record of her birth exists. She wrote in *Dust Tracks on a Road* that she "heard tell" she was born on January 7, 1903, one of eight children. Although Hurston used various birth dates (ranging from 1898 to 1910) on public documents, scholar Cheryl Wall used Eatonville census records to establish that Hurston was nine in 1900. Hurston's parents—Lucy Ann Potts, a country schoolteacher, and John Hurston, a carpenter and Baptist minister—met and married in Alabama before moving to Eatonville three years before Hurston's birth. After her mother died, her father quickly remarried and sent Zora, along with a sister and brother, to a Jacksonville school where she felt different and unwanted. As she recounted in her autobiography, when her father stopped paying room and board—and even suggested the school adopt her—she returned to Eatonville to a miserable life of "ragged dirty clothes and hit-and-miss meals." Three siblings and Zora were passed around to their mother's friends "like a bad

Hurston (right) poses with Langston Hughes and Jessie Fauset by the Booker T. Washington statue at Tuskegee Institute in 1927.

penny." She continued in *Dust Tracks* to describe how she left home, working for eighteen months as a wardrobe girl with a Gilbert and Sullivan repertory company that traveled around the South. She read a great deal to educate herself and in 1917 enrolled in a Baltimore high school, Morgan Academy (now Morgan State University) while working as a live-in maid.

Hurston entered Howard University, supporting herself as a barbershop manicurist and as a maid for prominent black families. At Howard she met Herbert Sheen, also a student, and they married in 1927 in St. Augustine, Florida. They lived together only eight months, however, and divorced amicably in 1931. Sheen later claimed that the demands of her career doomed the marriage. In a 1953 letter to him, Hurston recalled the idealistic youthful dreams they once shared but regretted nothing because she had lived life to the fullest. Her second marriage ended on less friendly terms. She married Albert Price III, a Works

Progress Administration playground worker fifteen years her junior, in 1939 in Fernandina, Florida, and divorced him in 1943. Sheen contended that he feared for his life because Hurston had threatened to "fix him" with voodoo if he "would not perform her wishes," according to Hemenway's biography.

Hurston's literary career began at Howard with her first short story, "John Redding Goes to Sea," published in the university's literary magazine. Depicting a young man unable to achieve his ambitions because his mother and wife prevent him from following his traveling instinct, this story came to the attention of Charles Johnson, editor of *Opportunity: A Journal of Negro Life,* the leading periodical of the Harlem Renaissance. He published her "Drenched in Light," a story of another

ZORA NEALE HURSTON

AUTHOR OF THEIR EYES WERE WATCHING GOD

A NOVEL

JONAH'S GOURD VINE

"A bold and beautiful book, many a page priceless and unforgettable."—Carl Sandburg

This 1934 novel incorporates biblical elements and folklore into its story of a minister and his wife—characters modeled loosely after Hurston's own parents.

dreamer—a lively girl of eleven whose energies are stifled by her strict Grandmother Potts. Encouraged by Johnson, Hurston moved to New York City in 1925 with "$1.50, no job, no friends, and a lot of hope."

When Hurston won second prize in an *Opportunity*-sponsored contest in 1925 for her short story "Spunk," she quickly furthered her literary career amid the influential people she met at the awards banquet. One of the judges, writer Fannie Hurst, hired Hurston as a live-in secretary because she was so impressed with Hurston's charm, rich Southern dialect, and laughter. Hemenway recorded that Hurston became Hurst's chauffeur when Hurst found her secretarial skills sadly lacking: her shorthand was nearly illegible, "her typing hit or miss, mostly the latter; her filing, a game of find-the-thimble." She secured a scholarship to Barnard College through another white benefactor, Annie Nathan Meyer (founder of Barnard, a novelist, and philanthropist who supported Harlem Renaissance artists). So, in the fall of 1925 Hurston became Barnard's first black student. In 1926 she won second place in an *Opportunity* contest with "Muttsy," a story about a worldly gambler's relationship with an innocent young girl. Then she published "Sweat," about another black couple, in *Fire!!,* a magazine founded by Wallace Thurman, Langston Hughes, and Hurston. For the *Messenger* she wrote three installments of "Eatonville Anthology"—fourteen brief sketches about a backwoods farmer, a great liar, a cheating husband, a beggar woman, and other characters. The series, blending folklore and fiction, marks the beginning of her career as folklorist.

Having studied under the renowned anthropologist Franz Boas, Hurston received a $1400 fellowship to work with him as a graduate student at Columbia University after she graduated as an English major in 1928. Her publications by this time included short stories, poetry, plays, and an article, "Cudjo's Own Story of the Last African Slaver," which describes the sole survivor of the last slave ship to America in 1859, as well as descendants of the last shipped slaves, living in Plateau, Alabama. But Hemenway revealed that in 1972 a scholar proved Hurston had plagiarized many passages from Emma Langdon Roche's *Historic Sketches of the Old South* (1914).

Be that as it may, Hurston pursued her interest in folklore during the next few years. Unable to enter Columbia University's Ph.D. program, she continued to study folklore with the aid of fellowships and a $200 a month subsidy from another New York patron, Mrs. Rufus Osgood Mason. Her first novel, *Jonah's Gourd Vine,* incorporates black folklore into a story about characters modeled after her parents. From the tall-tale sessions (telling "lies") she heard from her travels among sharecroppers and migrant workers in Alabama, Louisiana, and Florida, she compiled *Mules and Men* (1935). Basing the collection on her academic studies and anthropological field work, Hurston included tales, descriptions of voodoo practices, work songs, legends, and rhymes. Thus, the work reflected the social and philosophical messages of black American society and served as a framework for all of her subsequent writing. For example, she blended black folklore and storytelling in "Hoodoo in America," published in the respected *Journal of American Folklore,* and *Tell My Horse,* her study of Caribbean voodoo practices.

From Harlem Renaissance Writer to Obscurity

Hurston's devotion to anthropology, however, disappointed friends who encouraged her to focus on her fiction. Others considered her opportunistic. According to Hemenway, Wallace Thurman modeled his character Sweetie May Carr in *Infants of the Spring* (1932) on Hurston. He depicted this character as indifferent to writing serious literature, unwilling to create fiction out of the stories "she told so well." Carr rationalizes, "I have to eat. I also wish to finish my education. Being a Negro writer these days is a racket and I'm going to make the most of it while it lasts. . . . I don't know a tinker's damn about art. . . . And the only way I can live easily until I have the requisite training is to pose as a writer of potential ability." Thurman wrote that Carr (like Hurston in the early 1930s) was "more noted for her ribald wit and personal effervescence than for any actual literary work." Furthermore, his fictional character was based on Hurston's relationship with white patrons: "She was a great favorite among those whites who went in for Negro prodigies. Mainly because she lived up to their conception of what a typical Negro should be. . . . Her repertoire of tales was earthy, vulgar and funny. Her darkies always smiled through their tears, sang spirituals on the slightest provocation, and performed buck dances. . . . Sweetie May was a master of Southern dialect, and an able raconteur . . . [who] knew her white folks." Langston

Hughes, in his autobiography *The Big Sea* (1940) similarly remembered that Hurston "was full of sidesplitting anecdotes, humorous tales, and tragicomic stories." He called Hurston "a perfect 'darkie' in the nice meaning whites give the term—that is a naive, childlike, sweet, humorous, and highly colored Negro. But Miss Hurston was clever too—a student who didn't let college give her a broad 'a' and who had great scorn for all pretensions, academic or otherwise."

Hurston never reached the pinnacle of literary success, despite some recognition of her novels, folklore, and autobiography. As Hemenway recounted, in the 1940s she worked for four months at Paramount Studios but failed to have her novels turned into movies. She lectured on the black college circuit and worked on her autobiography and her fourth novel. However, in 1948 her professional and private world collapsed when she was arrested on a morals charge in New York City. Although she was cleared of this false charge of sodomizing a ten-year-old, she felt betrayed by her own race when a national black newspaper, the *Baltimore Afro-American,* gave the story sensationalized, inaccurate front-page coverage. She lamented to her friend, critic Carl Van Vechten, "All that I have ever tried to do has proved useless. All that I have believed in has failed me. I have resolved to die. . . . No acquittal will persuade some people I am innocent. I feel hurled down a filthy privy hole."

Attempting to restore her professional reputation, Hurston published various nonfiction articles in national magazines. She taught drama at North Carolina College for Negroes in Durham for a brief time. Her last published story, "The Conscience of the Court," came out in the *Saturday Evening Post* while she was working as a maid for a white family in Miami in 1950. Hurston knew what would sell to white, middle-class America—her protagonist Laura Lee Kimble's humility, dependence, and loyalty toward her white employer. As Hemenway noted, this story (which she allowed to be heavily edited because she badly needed the nine hundred dollars payment) further perpetuated stereotypical images about blacks. To cover her desperate need of money, she explained to a newspaper reporter that she worked as a maid just for the experience so she could begin a magazine for domestics; she even told her employer that she had bank accounts overseas where her books had been published but refused to be unpatriotic and spend the money abroad. Soon after this feature article was picked up by the national wire services, she wrote her agent that she was "cold in hand" (penniless), confessing "God! What I have been through. . . . Just inching along like a stepped-on worm."

She spent her last decade working at different jobs around Florida—Belle Glade, Eau Gallie, Merritt Island, and finally Fort Pierce, where, following a stroke, she entered the St. Lucie County Welfare Home in October 1959 and died on January 28, 1960, of heart disease. Hemenway revealed that her middle name was misspelled as Neil on her death certificate, and her funeral was delayed a week while friends and family raised the four hundred dollars for expenses. She was buried in an unmarked grave in Fort Pierce's segregated cemetery, Garden of the Heavenly Rest.

A Hurston Revival

There has been tremendous interest in Hurston in recent years. Books and essays by scholars, as well as new editions of her works, have established a favorable reappraisal. Among the famous writers who have added forewords and introductions to her reissued works just since 1990 are Maya Angelou, Ishmael Reed, Ruby Dee, and Rita Dove. Much has been written about Hurston's personal life and professional career, as demonstrated by the sums of critical opinion about her short stories, novels, and folklore anthologies. Her literary executor, Arna Bontemps, prophesied in 1972 that Hurston "still awaits the thoroughgoing critical analysis that will properly place her in the pattern of American fiction." In Bontemps's edited work, The Harlem Renaissance Remembered, Hemenway established Hurston's importance to the Harlem Renaissance in providing the largely urban literary participants of the Renaissance (Langston Hughes, Arna Bontemps, Wallace Thurman, Countee Cullen, and Jean Toomer) with the "richness in the racial heritage" of the rural South; he argued that she "added new dimensions to the interest in exotic primitivism" to the movement. Becoming an academic anthropologist, Hemenway explained, was "alien to her exuberant sense of self, her admittedly artistic and sometimes erratic temperament." Hurston thus created Eatonville as a model of black folklore and racial experience not distorted into racial stereotypes.

Her early short stories "showed a command of folklore and idiom excelled by no earlier Negro novelist," asserted Sterling Brown in his 1969 study of African-American fiction and drama, "Negro Poetry and Drama" and "The Negro in American Fiction." Robert Bone, in his Down Home: A History of Afro-American Short Fiction from Its Beginnings to the End of the Harlem Renaissance, saw a central "thrust toward freedom" in Hurston's early stories ("John Redding Goes to Sea," "Drenched in Light," and "Magnolia Flower"), which conflicted with the impulse "to celebrate the singularity of Eatonville." Other stories of the 1920s, such as "Spunk" and "Sweat," continued this local-color theme, portraying the people, folkways, and idiom of this specific landscape of the Florida lake country. Bone found in her 1933 story, "The Gilded Six-Bits," the central core of Hurston's values; writing in the depths of the Depression, "she attacks the acquisitive society" and her "mature style emerges whose metaphors, drawn from folk speech, function as a celebration of agrarian ideals." Having "discovered her subject and mastered her idiom," concluded Bone, Hurston could turn to novels, where her greatest achievement as a writer lies.

Hurston's debut novel, Jonah's Gourd Vine, blends folklore with biblical themes in depicting John Pearson, minister and town leader, and his wife Lucy Potts—characters loosely based on the author's parents. In the book's introduction, Fannie Hurst praised the realistic characterization: "Rising above the complicated machinery of color differentiations, they bring the reader to fresh realization that races, regardless of pigmentation, behave like human beings." New York Herald Tribune Books contributor Josephine Pinckney commended the "deftly-drawn personalities, childlike, shrewd, violent, gay" and remarked that whites are "portrayed but little and then without bitterness" for Hurston "is not to be deflected by controversy from her preoccupation with her characters." Sterling Brown found the portrayal of "handsome, stalwart John Buddy from plowboy to moderator of the Baptists of Florida" less developed than the "authentic scenes of timber camps, railroad gangs with the 'hammer-muscling men, the liars, fighters, bluffers and lovers.'" Applauding Hurston's "rich, expressive" language, with its "rolling and dignified rhythms," New York Times Book Review contributor Margaret Wallace called Jonah's Gourd Vine "the most vital and original novel about the American Negro that has yet been written by a member of the Negro race."

Mules and Men also appealed to the white community, this time presenting a collection of folktales ("lies"), voodoo practices, and beliefs. Hurston's mentor Franz Boas, writing in the book's foreword, saw its value to cultural history as "the peculiar amalgamation of African and European tradition which is so important for understanding historically the character of American Negro life." He praised her ability "to penetrate through that affected demeanor by which the Negro excludes the White observer effectively from participating in his true inner life." Yet black critic Sterling Brown disagreed, charging in his essay "Southern Realism" that Hurston ignored racial oppression and exploitation. While Brown admitted Hurston's "zestful" approach to her material, the first substantial collection of folktales by a black scholar, made it "a delight to read," he regretted that Hurston omitted the misery and exploitation blacks suffered—"The picture is too pastoral, with only a bit of grumbling about hard work, or a few slave anecdotes that turn the tables on old marster." A contemporary British reviewer for the *Times Literary Supplement* saw this compilation of stories as reflecting the American imagination—"with its whimsicality, its American love of exaggeration, and its under-dog's admiration of victorious cunning constantly pitted against the dominance of the white man." Indeed, in the scholarly *Journal of American Folklore,* John Roberts pointed to the imaginative, exaggerated quality of this work, giving credence to accusations that Hurston made "her folklore studies too literary and her literary works too folkloristic." He recommended caution in approaching *Mules and Men* because Hurston does not mention recording equipment or even pencil and pad to insure authentic transcription. Roberts suspected that Hurston took liberties with folklore texts as well as dialogue, making the work problematic for the professional folklorist, yet "worthwhile and extremely useful" in capturing black speech rhythms and cultural lifestyles.

An American Classic

Their Eyes Were Watching God is Hurston's best work, a classic in African-American and feminist literature for its portrayal of a black woman's quest for fulfillment and freedom from exploitation. Janie struggles to find an equal, rewarding relationship with a man, despite her grandmother's warnings that "de nigger woman is de mule uh de world" and that love is "de very

"Simply the most exciting book on black folklore and culture I have ever read."
—Roger D. Abrahams

Based on stories Hurston compiled during her travels through the American south, this 1935 collection includes folktales, work songs, and rhymes.

prong all us black woman gits hung on." Told in flashback to her friend Pheoby Watson, the narrative is a story within a story. After two loveless marriages, Janie's romantic vision of finding a man who loves her as an equal becomes a reality—at 37, Janie finds love with vibrant, loving Vergible "Tea Cake" Woods, twelve years her junior.

At the time of its publication, critical opinion varied. James Robert Saunders noted in a 1988 *Hollins Critic* article that the novel "was not fully appreciated during the 1930s when women were to a large extent still controlled by chauvinistic attitudes." Thus, contemporary reviewers paid more attention to the novelty of the black lifestyle and speech rather than Janie's story as a woman seeking an identity. Otis Ferguson, for instance, although he found the novel to be "free of Uncle

ZORA NEALE HURSTON

Their Eyes Were Watching God

This 1937 novel, detailing the life and loves of a middle-aged black woman, has become a landmark in African-American feminist literature.

Toms," lamented in the *New Republic* the sloppy dialect which sets "a mood of Eddie Cantor in blackface." Novelist Richard Wright accused Hurston of manipulating white stereotypes of blacks to pander to white readers and attacked her for lacking racial consciousness. In his *New Masses* review, Wright faulted Hurston for perpetuating the minstrel tradition that makes the "white folks" laugh; furthermore, he questioned whether Hurston even had the desire to move toward serious fiction because she addressed her novel not "to the Negro, but to a white audience whose chauvinistic tastes she knows how to satisfy." Other criticism involved technical aspects. George Stevens considered the flashback too confusing and the hurricane story too hurriedly told, but praised the dialogue: "No one has ever reported the speech of Negroes with a more accurate ear for its raciness, its rich invention, and its music."

Critic Lucy Tompkins likewise found the dialect "easy to follow" and stated that the love story of Janie and Tea Cake is "a little epic all by itself." Even Sterling Brown, who criticized *Mules and Men* for ignoring racism, praised this novel, especially in its dramatizing whites' bigotry after a hurricane in refusing to bury white and black victims together. Brown explained in his *Nation* review, "To detect the race of the long-unburied corpses, the conscripted grave-diggers must examine the hair. The whites get pine coffins; the Negroes get quick-lime."

Contemporary critics have demonstrated that Hurston does indeed affirm black culture and the strength of the black community. Many scholars in the 1970s focused on the novel's self-identity theme. Writing in *Modern Fiction Studies*, S. Jay Walker put the novel in the context of the liberation movements for blacks and for women, concluding that Hurston's neglected masterpiece is "virtually unique in the annals of black fiction" because it "deals far more extensively with sexism, the struggle of a woman to be regarded as a person in a male-dominated society, than racism, the struggle of blacks to be regarded as persons in a white-dominated society." Addison Gayle, Jr. saw the work as "a novel of intense power," with characters as "outsiders in America because they were the inheritors of a culture different from that of others." Gayle concluded in *The Way of the New World: The Black Novel in America* that Janie represents the beginning of "the new paradigm" of liberated women because after returning to the town where she began her search for freedom "she remains an outsider and yet is not able to continue her rebellion beyond the immediate present." Writing in the foreword to the 1978 edition of the novel, Sherley Anne Williams agreed that the character of Janie lacks a certain forcefulness—a "questing quality that characterized Zora's own life"; to wit, "Where Janie yearns, Zora was probably driven; where Janie submits, Zora would undoubtedly have rebelled." Williams also praised Hurston's "fidelity to diction, metaphor, and syntax." But not all critics concurred with this assessment. Roger Sale, critiquing the work in *Hudson Review,* called the language the novel's main problem, illustrating the sudden shift from black English to a formal literary narrative voice with the following passage: just after Grandma advises Janie, "Youse young yet. No tellin' whut mout happen befo' you die," the narrator states, "Nanny sent Janie along with a stern mien, but she dwindled all the rest of the day as she worked."

In the 1980s many critics debated whether or not Janie is a fully realized character. As Jennifer Jordan noted in *Tulsa Studies in Women's Literature,* Hurston wrote *Their Eyes Were Watching God* as an attempt to "embalm all the tenderness of [her] passion" for A. W. P., a 23-year-old West Indian whom she gave up because he did not approve of her career. Jordan argued that this novel fails, however, to meet the often conflicting criteria of black feminism: "individual transformation, feminine bonding, and racial communalism." On the other hand, Gay Wilentz, discussing the book in *Faith of a (Woman) Writer,* considered Janie to be one of the few characters in early black American fiction "to emerge whole." The critic found it ironic that the title of this story about one woman refers to "their," suggesting the contradiction of looking to God for answers yet having to watch out for cruel false gods, particularly those of the white world. Maria Tai Wolff's reader-response analysis showed how the narrative is a woman's story as well as "the presentation of a model of reading, of understanding an oral or written text." Wolff asserted in *Black American Literature Forum* that the theme is "the transformation of the outside world into a personal vision," and that the lyric images of the blossoming pear tree and spreading pollen of spring represent Janie's inner world. Cheryl A. Wall similarly argued that Hurston's language proves her to be in full command of her narrative talents, especially her skill with recurring metaphors of the pear tree and the horizon that unify the narrative. In her essay "Zora Neale Hurston: Changing Her Own Words," Wall stated: "The first symbolizes organic union with another, the second, the individual experiences one must acquire to achieve selfhood." Many other critics acknowledged these metaphors as well as Hurston's symbolic use of objects to present Janie's quest for freedom: she flings her apron, the mark of servility to first husband Logan Killicks, in a bush as she leaves with Jody, and she burns all her headrags in a similar symbolic gesture of emancipation from second husband Jody Starks. When she finds happiness with Tea Cake, she realizes her quest for self. As many feminist critics pointed out, Janie has achieved self-fulfillment at the novel's conclusion: "Here was peace. She pulled in her horizon like a great fish-net. Pulled it from around the waist of the world and draped it over her shoulders. So much

of life in its meshes! She called in her soul to come and see."

Back to Folklore Material

Tell My Horse impressed her contemporary Carl Carmer with its "vitality and imagination" in interpreting the folklore of Jamaica and Haiti with vivid details such as hunting the wild hog, marriage customs, and the "Night Song After Death." The *New York Herald Tribune Books* reviewer remarked that being black, Hurston could make her readers understand "the deep current of racial poetry that runs beneath the rituals"; thus, Carmer considered this the "authentic work of an honest, painstaking scholar." Yet Darwin T. Turner criticized its lack of legitimacy from an academic standpoint. He acknowledged Hurston's skills in gathering and reporting material and noted her intriguing descriptions of witch doctors and Zombies (the living dead). However, Turner, writing in his *In a Minor Chord: Three Afro-American Writers and Their Search for Identity,* considered *Tell My Horse* a "travelogue" rather than a serious study and concluded that Hurston "became neither an impeccable raconteur nor a scholar" because she remained "superficial and shallow in her artistic and social judgments."

Hurston's third novel, 1939's *Moses, Man of the Mountain,* was praised by Carmer for its "distinction inflections and sharply defined rhythms." *Christian Century* critic Philip Slomovitz called her portrait of Moses as voodoo man a "brilliant study of the problem of emancipation." Percy Hutchison in the *New York Times Book Review* was also impressed with Hurston's Moses, "just about the greatest magician ever in the world," and called the novel "an exceptionally fine piece of work far off the beaten tracks of literature." Nearly 50 years later, *New York Times Book Review* contributor Henry Louis Gates, Jr. lauded Blyden Jackson's new edition for its great insights about Hurston's sources. In addition to the popular play *Green Pastures,* which depicted a black Jehovah and heaven, and Freud's two controversial essays on Moses's Egyptian origins (published a year before Hurston's *Moses*), Gates suggested Hurston's primary source was Frances E. W. Harper, a black woman whose allegorical "Moses: A Story of the Nile" (1869) also stressed Moses's identity as conjurer and utilized multiple voices. Gates thus found it fitting that just as a black female literary ancestor (Harper) inspired Hurston, Hurston in turn shaped this generation's black women writers, including Alice Walker, Toni Morrison, Toni Cade Bambara, Gloria Naylor, and Jamaica Kincaid.

Dust Tracks on a Road, Hurston's story of her life, received mixed reactions from critics. Arna Bontemps's 1942 *New York Herald Tribune Books* appraisal was that she "deals very simply with the more serious aspects of Negro life in America—she ignores them." On the other hand, *New York Times Book Review* contributor Beatrice Sherman admired Hurston's treating problems of blacks as just "those of any other race," and applauded "her fighting spirit" in her struggle to achieve the education that led to her "considerable reputation as anthropologist and writer." Readers did not have the book as Hurston wrote

ZORA NEALE HURSTON

AUTHOR OF *THEIR EYES WERE WATCHING GOD*

AN AUTOBIOGRAPHY

DUST TRACKS ON A ROAD

"Warm, witty, imaginative, and down-to-earth by turns, this is a rich and winning book by one of our few genuine, Grade A folk writers."
—*The New Yorker*

Although Hurston's 1942 autobiography provided her thoughts on political and racial issues, it deliberately obscures some personal details and reveals little about the author's development as an artist.

it until 1984, however, when editor Robert Hemenway restored three chapters on topics such as racial chauvinism, imperialism, and economic exploitation—controversial topics that had been either heavily revised or deleted from the book when first published in 1942. Gates acknowledged that even her most devoted readers have had problems with her politics, especially her disapproval of the U.S. Supreme Court decision banning racial segregation in public schools. To explain the controversial aspect of her politics, this new edition of her autobiography more fully details her distrust of "race consciousness" and her criticism of neocolonialism: "One hand in somebody else's pocket and one on your gun, and you are highly civilized. Your heart is where it belongs—in your pocketbook. . . . Democracy, like religion, never was designed to make our profits less." Gates admired the way Hurston used the linguistic rituals of both the black and white speech communities, finding this "double voice unreconciled—a verbal analogue of her double experiences as a woman in a male-dominated world and as a black person in a non-black world" was Hurston's great achievement. On the other hand, Hemenway, in his introduction to this 1984 edition, said *Dust Tracks on a Road* "fails as autobiography because it is a text deliberately less than its author's talents, a text diminished by her refusal to provide a second or third dimension to the flat images of her adult image." He cited as examples her devoting only eight pages to her writing career, one paragraph on her role in the Harlem Renaissance, and her deliberate ambiguity about many events of her personal and professional life. Thus, the mystery of this "enigmatic" woman remains despite the revised autobiography.

Seraph on the Suwanee, which followed Hurston's autobiography by six years, is thematically similar to *Their Eyes Were Watching God* but is not as successful in telling the story of a woman's search for self-esteem and her attempt to return the love of her husband. The plot follows the marriage of Arvay Henson, daughter of Florida "Crackers," and James Kenneth Meserve, son of plantation owners, over a twenty-year span. Critical commentary over the years reflects the change in emphasis from the fascination with rural white and black lifestyles to the concern with feminist themes. In a 1948 *New York Herald Tribune Weekly Book Review* article, Worth Tuttle Hedden praised the local color of Hurston's west Florida turpentine camp setting, peopled by characters such as "Titty-

Nipple" and "Cup-Cake," and found it "incredible" that a writer "not born to the breed" could so well depict the mores and language of the Florida Cracker. But some black critics attacked the author's use of white characters; for example, Darwin T. Turner wrote that Hurston's final novel "reveals her conscious adjustment to the tastes of a new generation of readers," using "sex and sensation" and "the deep and bitter emotions of a sick world." More recently, Cheryl A. Wall posited that Hurston's experiment in depicting upwardly mobile whites was "disappointing" because in Arvay's search for self-identity, she accepts her subordinate role as wife. Arvay's "whole duty as a wife was to just love him good, be nice and kind around the house and have children for him. She could do that and be more than happy and satisfied, but it looked too simple." Wall concluded that "the problem is Hurston's inability to grant her protagonist the resources that would permit her to claim autonomy." Most reviewers, then, seemed to agree with Wall that this novel "represents an artistic decline" from Hurston's best work, whose creative power was drawn directly from black folk culture.

Hurston's Literary Influence

Hurston has finally received the recognition that eluded her for many decades. Her biographer Hemenway suggested that she "chose to write of the positive effects of black experience because she did not believe that white injustice had created a pathology in black behavior." Aimed at a popular white middle-class audience, her books "did not receive the attention they deserved," Hemenway concluded. Despite Hurston's successful Harlem Renaissance days of the 1920s and 1930s, she died in obscurity in 1960, but today she is considered a key figure in black literature. Rosemary L. Bray, writing about Harper's reissue of four Hurston books in the *New York Times Book Review*, remarked that it "took a renaissance of a different sort to give works by Hurston a new life"—the civil rights and women's movements and a new generation that appreciates Hurston's "lyrical grace" and "affirming vision." Modern readers have a more accurate picture of Hurston's mind with these new editions, a perspective which might have softened the criticism of her harshest critics. Gates noted that today's black women writers "have grounded their fictions in the works of Zora Neale Hurston," acknowledging her narrative strategies as an influence in creating their own voices. Gates saw Hurston's lasting contribution to be her original way of "so splendidly" creating "black and female perspectives," pointing to Alice Walker's 1983 Pulitzer Prize-winning novel *The Color Purple*, whose diction and character development extend "potentials Hurston registered" in *Their Eyes Were Watching God*.

Hurston was the main inspiration to Walker's own life and career—despite being so "outrageous" and full of "contradictions and complexity." Walker's *Ms.* essay about her pilgrimage in 1973 to seek an understanding of Hurston's life helped revive her critical reputation. Gates called Walker's essay a "moving account of her search for and discovery of her own literary lineage"; he credited Walker especially with revitalizing Hurston's reputation after several decades of neglect. Shortly after Hemenway's biography, Walker edited *I Love Myself When I Am Laughing . . . And Then Again When I Am Looking Mean and Impressive: A Zora Neale Hurston Reader*, making her all-but-forgotten work accessible for today's readers. In her dedication essay (titled "On Refusing to Be Humbled by Second Place in a Contest You Did Not Design: A Tradition by Now"), Walker recounted the time Hurston dramatically entered a room full of people after having won second prize in a 1925 contest for her play *Color Struck!*, which portrays blacks' bigotry in favoring light-skinned over dark-skinned blacks. She "flung her scarf dramatically over her shoulder, and yelled 'COLOR..R.R STRUCK..K.K!' at the top of her voice." Walker admitted that "it isn't easy to like a person who is not humbled by second place," yet found Hurston admirable for her work and for herself—for "the humor and courage with which she encountered a life she infrequently designed."

When Walker visited Hurston's birthplace and then her unmarked grave in 1973, she had a monument inscribed with Hurston's name, a quote from one of Jean Toomer's poems—"A genius of the South," "novelist, folklorist, anthropologist," and the dates 1901–1960. Walker confessed that she could afford only a plain stone—"ordinary, not at all like Zora." Walker thus paid tribute to the woman who inspired not only her but also countless others. "That Hurston held her own, literally, against the flood of whiteness and maleness that diluted so much other black art of the period in which she worked," Walker concluded, "is a testimony to her genius and her faith."

Upon her death in 1960, Hurston was buried in an unmarked grave in a segregated cemetery until novelist Alice Walker had this headstone erected in 1973.

■ Works Cited

Boas, Franz, foreword to *Mules and Men* by Zora Neale Hurston, Kegan, Paul, Trench, Trubner & Co., 1936, p. 5.

Bone, Robert, *Down Home: A History of Afro-American Short Fiction From Its Beginnings to the End of the Harlem Renaissance,* Putnam, 1975, pp. 122–150.

Bontemps, Arna, "From Eatonville, Fla. to Harlem," *New York Herald Tribune Books,* November 22, 1942, p. 3.

Bray, Rosemary L., "Now Our Eyes Are Watching Her," *New York Times Book Review,* February 25, 1990, p. 11.

Brown, Sterling A., "'Luck Is a Fortune,'" *Nation,* October 16, 1937, pp. 409–10.

Brown, Sterling, "Southern Realism," in his *"Negro Poetry and Drama" and "The Negro in American Fiction,"* Atheneum, 1969, pp. 151–68.

Carmer, Carl, "In Haiti and Jamaica," *New York Herald Tribune Books,* October 23, 1938, p. 2.

Carmer, Carl, "Biblical Story in Negro Rhythm," *New York Herald Tribune Books,* November 26, 1939, p. 5.

Ferguson, Otis, "You Can't Hear Their Voices," *New Republic,* October 13, 1937, p. 276.

Gates, Henry Louis, Jr., "'A Negro Way of Saying,'" *New York Times Book Review,* April 21, 1985, pp. 1, 43, 45.

Gayle, Addison, Jr., "The Outsider," *The Way of the New World: The Black Novel in America,* Anchor Press/Doubleday, 1975, pp. 129–52.

Hedden, Worth Tuttle, "Turpentine and Moonshine," *New York Herald Tribune Weekly Book Review,* October 10, 1948, p. 2.

Hemenway, Robert E., "Zora Neale Hurston and the Eatonville Anthropology," in *The Harlem Renaissance Remembered,* edited by Langston Hughes and Arna Bontemps, Dodd, Mead, 1972, pp. 190–214.

Hemenway, Robert E., *Zora Neale Hurston: A Literary Biography,* University of Illinois Press, 1977.

Hemenway, Robert E., introduction to *Dust Tracks on a Road: An Autobiography* by Zora Neale Hurston, 2nd edition, University of Illinois Press, 1984, pp. ix–xxxix.

Hughes, Langston, *The Big Sea,* Knopf, 1940.

Hurst, Fannie, introduction to *Jonah's Gourd Vine* by Zora Neale Hurston, Lippincott, 1934, pp. 7–8.

Hurston, Zora Neale, *Dust Tracks on a Road: An Autobiography,* 2nd edition, University of Illinois Press, 1984.

Hutchison, Percy, "Led His People Free," *New York Times Book Review,* November 19, 1939, p. 21.

Jordan, Jennifer, "Feminist Fantasies: Zora Neale Hurston's 'Their Eyes Were Watching God,'" *Tulsa Studies in Women's Literature,* spring, 1988, pp. 105–17.

Review of *Mules and Men, Times Literary Supplement,* March 7, 1936, p. 200.

Pinckney, Josephine, "A Pungent, Poetic Novel about Negroes," *New York Herald Tribune Books,* May 6, 1934, p. 7.

Roberts, John, review of *Mules and Men* and *Their Eyes Were Watching God, Journal of American Folklore,* October-December, 1980, pp. 463–66.

Sale, Roger, "Zora," *Hudson Review,* spring, 1979, pp. 151–54.

Saunders, James Robert, "Womanizing as the Key to Understanding Zora Neale Hurston's 'Their Eyes Were Watching God' and Alice Walker's 'The Color Purple,'" *Hollins Critic,* October, 1988, pp. 1–11.

Sherman, Beatrice, "Zora Hurston's Story," *New York Times Book Review,* November 29, 1942, p. 44.

Slomovitz, Philip, "The Negro's Moses," *Christian Century,* December 6, 1939, p. 1504.

Stevens, George, "Negroes by Themselves," *Saturday Review of Literature,* September 18, 1937, p. 3.

Tompkins, Lucy, "In the Florida Glades," *New York Times Book Review,* September 26, 1937, p. 29.

Turner, Darwin T., "Zora Neale Hurston: The Wandering Minstrel," *In a Minor Chord: Three Afro-American Writers and Their Search for Identity,* Southern Illinois University Press, 1971, pp. 89–120.

Walker, Alice, "In Search of Zora Neale Hurston," *Ms.,* March, 1975, pp. 74–79, 85–89.

Walker, Alice, "On Refusing to Be Humbled by Second Place in a Contest You Did Not Design: A Tradition by Now," *I Love Myself When I Am Laughing . . . And Then Again When I Am Looking Mean and Impressive* by Zora Neale Hurston, edited by Walker, The Feminist Press, 1979, pp. 1–5.

Walker, S. Jay, "Zora Neale Hurston's 'Their Eyes Were Watching God': Black Novel of Sexism," *Modern Fiction Studies,* winter, 1974–75, pp. 519–27.

Wall, Cheryl A., "Zora Neale Hurston: Changing Her Own Words," *American Novelists Revisited: Essays in Feminist Criticism,* edited by Fritz Fleischmann, 1982, pp. 371–93.

Wallace, Margaret, "Real Negro People," *New York Times Book Review,* May 6, 1934, pp. 6–7.

Wilentz, Gay, "Defeating the False God: Janie's Self-Determination in Zora Neale Hurston's 'Their Eyes Were Watching God,'" *Faith of a (Woman) Writer,* edited by Alice Kessler-Harris and William McBrien, Greenwood Press, 1988, pp. 285–91.

Williams, Sherley Anne, foreword to *Their Eyes Were Watching God: A Novel* by Zora Neale Hurston, University of Illinois Press, 1978, pp. v–xv.

Wolff, Maria Tai, "Listening and Living: Reading and Experience in 'Their Eyes Were Watching God,'" *Black American Literature Forum,* spring, 1982, pp. 29–33.

Wright, Richard, "Between Laughter and Tears," *New Masses,* October 5, 1937, pp. 22, 25.

■ For More Information See

BOOKS

Awkward, Michael, "The Inaudible Voice of It All': Silence, Voice, and Action in *Their Eyes Were Watching God,*" *Studies in Black American Literature: Black Feminist Criticism and Critical Theory,* edited by Joe Weixlmann and Houston A. Baker, Jr., Penkevill, 1988, pp. 57–109.

Bethel, Lorraine, "'This Infinity of Conscious Pain': Zora Neale Hurston and the Black Female Literary Tradition," in *All the Women Are White, All the Blacks Are Men, But Some of Us Are Brave: Black Women's Studies,* edited by Gloria T. Hull, Patricia Bell Scott, and Barbara Smith, Feminist Press, 1982, pp. 176–88.

Bloom, Harold, editor, *Zora Neale Hurston: Modern Critical Views,* Chelsea House, 1986, p. 192.

Contemporary Literary Criticism, Gale, Volume 7, 1977, pp. 170–172, Volume 30, 1984, pp. 207–229, Volume 61, 1990, pp. 235–276.

Cooke, Michael G., "Solitude: The Beginnings of Self-Realization in Zora Neale Hurston, Richard Wright, and Ralph Ellison," *Afro-American Literature in the Twentieth Century: The Achievement of Intimacy,* Yale University Press, 1984, pp. 71–109.

Davis, Arthur P., *From the Dark Tower: Afro-American Writers, 1900–1960,* Howard University Press, 1974.

Glassman, Steve, and Kathryn Lee Seidel, editors, *Zora in Florida,* University Presses of Florida, 1991.

Howard, Lillie P., *Zora Neale Hurston,* Twayne, 1980.

Howard, Lillie P., "Zora Neale Hurston," *Dictionary of Literary Biography* Volume 51: *Afro-American Writers from the Harlem Renaissance to 1940,* edited by Trudier Harris, Gale, 1987, pp. 133–145.

Lyons, Mary E., *Sorrow's Kitchen: The Life and Folklore of Zora Neale Hurston,* Scribner, 1990.

Meese, Elizabeth A., "Orality and Textuality in Zora Neale Hurston's 'Their Eyes Were Watching God,'" in *Crossing the Double Cross: The Practice of Feminist Criticism,* University of North Carolina Press, 1986, pp. 39–53.

Nathiri, N. Y., editor, *Zora! Zora Neale Hurston: A Woman and Her Community,* Sentinel Books, 1991.

Zaidman, Laura M., "Zora Neale Hurston," in *Dictionary of Literary Biography,* Volume 86: *American Short-Story Writers, 1910–1945, First Series,* edited by Bobby Ellen Kimbel, Gale, 1989, pp. 159–171.

PERIODICALS

African American Review, spring, 1992, p. 147; winter, 1992, p. 605, 610; summer, 1993, p. 167.

American Literature, May, 1986, pp. 181–202.

Black American Literature Forum, fall, 1983, pp. 109–15; winter, 1985, pp. 152–57; spring-summer, 1987, pp. 185–97.

Black Review, Number 2, 1972, pp. 11–24.

Black World, August, 1972, pp. 68–75; August, 1974, pp. 6–7, 20–30.

Booklist, July, 1985, p. 1514.

Callaloo, summer, 1988, pp. 627–35.

Christian Century, November 16, 1988, p. 1035.

Chronicle of Higher Education, June 5, 1991, p. B4.

CLA Journal, December, 1987, pp. 189–200.

Detroit Free Press, February 20, 1995, pp. 1E, 6E.

English Journal, November, 1989, p. 70.

Library Chronicle of the University of Texas, Number 35, 1986, pp. 20–43.

Library Journal, July, 1985, p. 76; November 1, 1991, p. 85.

Modern Maturity, February-March, 1989, p. 56.

Negro American Literary Forum, summer, 1972, pp. 52–3, 60.

New Statesman & Society, July 19, 1991, p. 28.

Newsweek, February 13, 1995, p. 81.

New York Herald Tribune Books, September 26, 1937, p. 2.

New York Times Book Review, November 10, 1935, p. 4.

North American Review, March, 1936, pp. 181–83.

Papers on Language and Literature, fall, 1976, pp. 422–37.

Publishers Weekly, April 19, 1991, p. 34.

Southern Literary Journal, fall, 1982, pp. 45–54; spring, 1985, pp. 54–66.

Studies in American Fiction, autumn, 1988, pp. 169–80.

Women's Studies, 1986, pp. 163–169.

OBITUARIES

Newsweek, February 15, 1960.

New York Times, February 5, 1960, p. 27.

Publishers Weekly, February 15, 1960.

Time, February 15, 1960.

Wilson Library Bulletin, April, 1960.*

—Sketch by Laura M. Zaidman

Barbara Kingsolver

■ Personal

Born April 8, 1955, in Annapolis, MD; daughter of Wendell R. (a physician) and Virginia (a homemaker; maiden name, Henry) Kingsolver; married Joseph Hoffmann (a chemist), April 15, 1985 (divorced, 1993); children: Camille. *Education:* DePauw University, B.A. (magna cum laude), 1977; University of Arizona, M.S., 1981, and additional graduate study. *Politics:* "Human rights activist." *Religion:* Pantheist. *Avocational interests:* Music, hiking, gardening, parenthood.

■ Addresses

Home—P.O. Box 5275, Tucson, AZ 85703. *Agent*—Frances Goldin, 305 East 11th St., New York, NY 10003.

■ Career

Worked a number of jobs, including X-ray technician, typesetter, researcher, and translator; University of Arizona, Tucson, research assistant in department of physiology, 1977–79, technical writer in office of arid lands studies, 1981–85; free-lance journalist, 1985–87; full-time writer, 1987—. *Member:* International Women's Writing Guild, Amnesty International, PEN West, Committee for Human Rights in Latin America, Phi Beta Kappa.

■ Awards, Honors

Feature-writing award, Arizona Press Club, 1986; American Library Association awards, 1988, for *The Bean Trees,* and 1990, for *Homeland;* citation of accomplishment from United Nations National Council of Women, 1989; PEN fiction prize and Edward Abbey Ecofiction Award, both 1991, for *Animal Dreams.*

■ Writings

The Bean Trees (novel), HarperCollins, 1988.
Homeland: And Other Stories (includes "Homeland," "Islands on the Moon," "Quality Time," "Covered Bridges," "Rose-Johnny," and "Why I Am a Danger to the Public"), HarperCollins, 1989.
Holding the Line: Women in the Great Arizona Mine Strike of 1983 (nonfiction), ILR Press, 1989.
Animal Dreams (novel), HarperCollins, 1990.
Pigs in Heaven (novel), HarperCollins, 1993.
Another America: Otra America (poetry), translations by Rebeca Cartes, Seal Press, 1994.

Work represented in anthologies, including *Rebirth of Power,* edited by P. Portwood, M. Gorcey, and P. Sanders, Mother Courage Press, 1987; *Florilegia, an Anthology of Art and Literature by Women,* edited by M. Donnelly, Calyx Books, 1987; and *New*

Stories from the South: The Year's Best, 1988, edited by S. Ravenel, Algonquin Books. Contributor of fiction, nonfiction, and poetry to numerous periodicals, including *Calyx, Cosmopolitan, Heresies, Mademoiselle, McCall's, New Mexico Humanities Review, Redbook, Sojourner, Tucson Weekly, Virginia Quarterly Review, Progressive,* and *Smithsonian.* Reviewer for the *New York Times Book Review. The Bean Trees* has been published in more than sixty-five countries around the world.

■ Adaptations

The Bean Trees has been optioned for film production.

■ Sidelights

The daughter of a country doctor, Barbara Kingsolver grew up in Nicholas County in rural

Kingsolver wrote this novel while plagued with insomnia during a difficult pregnancy.

Kentucky. It was a place with such limited opportunities that one would not expect it to nurture the future writer of such acclaimed novels as *The Bean Trees, Animal Dreams,* and *Pigs in Heaven.* "The options were limited," Kingsolver said in a *People* article by Michael Neill and Michael Haederle "—grow up to be a farmer or a farmer's wife. . . . I didn't date and I didn't have boyfriends." In such a setting, there was only one thing for a bright young woman to do: get out. Yet, years later, Kingsolver has never disconnected herself from her roots. Her writing resonates with the world of the rural South and its people, as well as the lives of those who make their homes near her current home of Arizona. Surrounded as she has always been by people with scant financial resources, yet who possess a powerful sense of community, Kingsolver is sometimes surprised by critics who, as Lisa See put it in a *Publishers Weekly* interview, "contend that Kingsolver's characters live on the margins of society. 'That's a shock to me,' [the author] bristles. 'I write about people who are living in the dead center of life. The people who are actually living on the margins of society are those you see on *Lifestyles of the Rich and Famous.*'"

Inspired early in life by such authors as Flannery O'Connor, Eudora Welty, and Carson McCullers, Kingsolver had long fostered an urge to create literature. She wrote short stories and poems in high school and kept a daily journal, but her parents taught their daughter to be more practical than to dream of success as a writer. Kingsolver was a product of her background and her era; she told Michael Freitag in the *New York Times Book Review,* "I never had any illusions about being able to do what I pleased and not worry about where the rent would come from." Instead of studying English literature, therefore, she majored in biology after receiving a scholarship to Depauw University, followed by graduate study at the University of Arizona. At university, she supplemented her regular studies with a creative writing course—taken at Depauw—and a growing interest in the socialist writings of Karl Marx and Friedrich Engels, along with the feminist works of Betty Friedan and Gloria Steinem. Their books blended well with her graduate studies in ecology and evolutionary biology. Her concern for balance in the environment and society grew, and she became involved in some of the student protests against the Vietnam War.

It was while at Arizona that Kingsolver had "a crisis of faith," she told Neill and Haederle, "and realized I didn't want to be an academic." Nevertheless, she continued her studies and, after receiving her master's degree from Arizona, found work at the university as a research assistant. Here she got the chance to try her hand at science writing. "I think that's the first time it really occurred to me that it was something I could do for a living," she told *Contemporary Authors* interviewer Jean W. Ross. "From there I eased into free-lance journalism and then wrote my first novel." Before that first novel, however, Kingsolver honed her writing skills by briefly studying under writer Francine Prose and becoming a contributing journalist to the *Progressive, Smithsonian,* and other similar publications. Eventually, she also submitted short stories, some of which were published in *Redbook* and *Mademoiselle.*

In 1983, her journalism work led Kingsolver to a dramatic story of a copper mine strike in Clifton, Arizona. Focusing her attention on how the women of the town had been affected by the eighteen-month-long strike and had managed to hold their community and families together despite unbearable hardships, Kingsolver was motivated to write a book on the story of their plight. By 1984 she had completed half the book, but her agent couldn't find a publisher for it, so the project was dropped. Returning to her regular work as a journalist, Kingsolver put aside her ambition to write a book for a while. In 1985, she married Joseph Hoffman, a chemist at the University of Arizona, and the couple had a daughter, Camille, one year later. Her pregnancy was somewhat troubled, causing Kingsolver to suffer from insomnia. To occupy her time on those sleepless nights, she set to work on a new project: a novel called *The Bean Trees.*

First Book Has Autobiographical Roots

The author discussed the origins of her first book with Ross: "For almost as long as I had lived in Tucson, I had been thinking about this imaginary place called Roosevelt Park," she recalled, "which was an amalgamation of several actual neighborhood parks and neighborhoods where I had lived. I imagined that all the people who lived around Roosevelt Park were women and children, just because of circumstances; that's what happens in marginally poor neighborhoods a lot of times. So I was thinking about characters and setting and

things that might happen, but it just simmered for five or six years." "Then I wrote a short story," Kingsolver continued, "which I thought was completely unrelated to the Roosevelt Park novel, and I showed it to a friend, who said, 'I really love this, but it's not a short story, it's the first chapter of a novel.' At first I said, Oh no, that's impossible. And then I looked at it again and realized that it probably was the beginning of my novel."

Kingsolver readily admits that her first novel contains strongly autobiographical elements. The author confessed to See, "People always say that a first novel sounds so much like the author. . . . I think that's certainly true of *The Bean Trees.*" *The Bean Trees* is about a woman—Taylor Greer—who flees her rural Kentucky homeland for greater opportunities out west. On her way, however, she is sidetracked by a startling development. After her Volkswagen breaks down in the middle of a Oklahoma Cherokee reservation, which she is visiting because she is part Cherokee, Taylor is startled to discover an abandoned child in the front seat of her car. Despite not being prepared for such a heavy responsibility, Taylor takes the child, a three-year-old Cherokee girl whose abuse at the hands of her elders has left her mute, to her heart, and the two of them continue the drive together. They get as far as Tucson, where the Volkswagen finally expires for good, and Taylor decides the desert city is as good a place as any for her and "Turtle" to settle down.

In Tucson, Taylor finds work with a woman named Mattie, who owns the Jesus Is Lord Used Tire Co., and she finds a room to rent from a woman named Lou Ann Ruiz, who, like Taylor, is from Kentucky. The casting is further complicated with the addition of two refugees named Estevan and Esperanza, who have been hiding out in Mattie's safe house for political refugees. Once Kingsolver has brought all of these characters into play, the rest of the novel is mostly concerned with the issues of how to best help Turtle and how to get Estevan and Esperanza safely to Guatemala.

The Bean Trees received a warm critical reception, as well as a 1988 American Library Association award. *New York Times Book Review* critic Jack Butler discussed the merits of Kingsolver's first attempt in his review of what he called a "Southern novel taken west." He was particularly impressed with the author's ability to create not only an individually "vivid and realistic scene," but also a succession of scenes that work together as a harmonious whole. It "is extremely rare to find the two gifts in one writer," Butler claimed, later adding that "Kingsolver doesn't waste a single overtone. . . . *The Bean Trees* is as richly connected as a fine poem, but reads like realism." Butler did have one problem with the novel, in that he felt that in the latter part of the story Kingsolver sacrifices convincing characterization in favor of bringing her plot to a happy conclusion. "Perhaps the problem is one of overmanipulation," the critic surmised. "At the same time the characters faded on me, I started to see the images and the plot coming. And the story began to feel a bit like an upbeat novel for teen-agers—because, although it considers true and terrible realities, only certain resolutions are permitted."

Most of the reviews for *The Bean Trees*, however, were positive. Many critics praised Kingsolver's use of characterization and her ear for language. Karen Fitzgerald, for one, remarked in *Ms.*: "From the very first page, Kingsolver's characters tug at the heart and soul. It is the growing strengths of their relationships . . . that gives the novel its energy and appeal." Reviewing *The Bean Trees* in the *Women's Review of Books*, Margaret Randall declared that the novel possesses "a marvelous ear, a fast-moving humor and the powerful undercurrent of human struggle."

Political, Social Concerns Are Central

The Bean Trees reveals the author's concern for a variety of issues, including child abuse, divorce, and political injustice. As she told Ross, "I only feel it's worth writing a book if I have something important to say." She realizes, as she pointed out in another part of her interview, the dangers of imbuing a story with a "message." "I have to work hard to refrain from diatribe," she admitted to Ross, "because I feel very strongly about human rights and human justice." Her political convictions are tempered by another common thread that runs through much of Kingsolver's fiction: the importance of a sense of community. "If there's one homeground that I always come back to in my writing, regardless of the social concern or the plot or the particular device, it's community," she stated to Ross. "That's something I grew up in."

Community is the central theme to Kingsolver's collection, *Homeland: And Other Stories*. "All the stories are about people who are finding a home," the author told Ross. In the title story, an elderly Cherokee woman returns to her birthplace in Tennessee to find that it has been turned into a cheap tourist trap. After a discouraging visit with her family, she leaves only to die far away from the land of her ancestors. Other stories in the collection are set variously in California, Arizona, Kentucky, and the Caribbean, and the narrators are either women or young girls growing to adulthood; her female characters are often single mothers (a prophetic touch, since Kingsolver became a single mother herself after her 1993 divorce). As Russell Banks describes Kingsolver's characters in the *New York Times Book Review*, they are people "just getting by economically and trying, against all odds, to make moral sense of their lives. This is what ennobles them, makes them more than mere case histories. For all of Ms. Kingsolver's characters it is not enough to endure poverty, abandonment, the dissolution of community and tribe: they also struggle to make sense of what happened to them and pass that sense on to their children, lovers, husbands and in some cases even their parents."

In the last story in the collection, "Why I Am a Danger to the Public," Kingsolver uses her writing skills to dramatize the issues of the Clifton copper mine strike she had covered years earlier. In this fictional version of the strike, a crane operator named Vicki Morales resists the authorities and is thrown into prison. "That story was a collection of things that didn't happen but could have, and I sort of wish had," Kingsolver told Ross. She later added, "I collected all those what-ifs and turned them into this short story that was fictional but very much grounded in the truth of that strike."

Although Kingsolver sticks to the facts in *Holding the Line: Women in the Great Arizona Mine Strike in 1983*, which was finally published six years after she first began work on the project, her approach to her subject is similar to her techniques as a fiction writer. The nonfictional account is organized into scenes, and the women speak not as if they are being interviewed but more like characters uttering dialogue in a story. Not all reviewers appreciated Kingsolver's devices, however. *Library Journal* contributor Frieda Shoenberg Rozen, for example, felt that though the book was a useful account, "additional industry and strike background would have made the account more effective." On the other hand, a *Publishers Weekly* critic called the book a "powerful tribute to [the strikers'] resolve and passion for economic justice."

With her second novel, *Animal Dreams,* Kingsolver continued to address the topics that most concerned her, while making a conscious effort to avoid repeating what she had done in *The Bean Trees.* "I have the disturbing idea that I'm writing the same book again and again," she confessed to *New York Times Book Review* contributor Joseph A. Cincotti. To break away from that possibility, she made certain not to bring back Taylor Greer in a story that would be a sequel to her first novel. Kingsolver also told See how the "voice of Taylor . . . was very strong, and she wanted to tell all of my stories. I've had to lock her away."

This collection of stories, concerned with the theme of people finding a home, won the 1990 American Library Association award.

Kingsolver the Eco-Feminist

By the time *Animal Dreams* was published, Kingsolver was being classified by some critics as belonging to a new class of writers—including authors like Louise Erdrich and Alice Walker—who write "eco-feminist" fiction. This subgenre of fiction, explains Paul Gray in a *Time* article, involves women characters who, "relying on intuition and one another, mobilize to save the planet, or their immediate neighborhoods, from the ravages—war, pollution, racism, etc.—wrought by white males. This reformation of human nature usually entails the adoption of older, often native American, ways." *Animal Dreams* tackles not just one of these issues, but many of them all at once. See lists these issues in her interview with Kingsolver in *Publishers Weekly* as "Native Americans, U.S. involvement in Nicaragua, environmental issues, parental relationships, [and] women's taking charge of their own lives." Teenage pregnancy, racism, and class ostracism can also be added to this list.

Kingsolver told See about her difficulty with tying all these themes together: "About two-thirds of the way through I realized I wasn't *just* a fool; I had jumped out of a plane and the parachute wouldn't open. I wanted to go back to bed, but Harper had already designed the book jacket." Despite her feelings of frustration, Kingsolver succeeded in completing the novel, which concerns Codi Noline's return to her hometown of Grace, Arizona, after a fourteen-year absence. Codi is troubled by a lack of self-confidence that has its origins in the miscarriage of her baby when she was fifteen and which bore bitter fruit when she failed to complete medical school. Discouraged, she returns to the town where her ailing father, Doc Homer, still lives, while her sister Hallie goes to Nicaragua to lend aid to its beleaguered citizens. Grace is no haven from the outside world, however, and Codi discovers that serious environmental problems, brought about by the local mining company, plague the town. To further complicate matters, she runs into her old high school sweetheart, Loyd Peregrina, and their romance is rekindled.

Writing in the *New York Times Book Review,* Jane Smiley expressed her concern that Kingsolver tries to cover too much ground in a single book, calling the attempt only "partly successful." Smiley also complained that "Codi comes across too of-

NEW YORK TIMES BESTSELLER
BARBARA KINGSOLVER
PIGS IN HEAVEN

A NOVEL BY THE AUTHOR OF *THE BEAN TREES* AND *ANIMAL DREAMS*
"A novel full of miracles." —Newsweek

In this sequel to *The Bean Trees,* Kingsolver contemplates the rights of adoptive parents versus biological ones in a story about a Native-American girl being raised away from her people.

ten as a whiner," and that by focusing on Codi's personal despair, Kingsolver "frequently undermines the suspense and the weight of her book." Other critics, however, have asserted that *Animal Dreams* is a testimony to Kingsolver's growth as a writer of importance. "Kingsolver's maturation as a writer has been astonishingly rapid," declared one *Publishers Weekly* reviewer, adding that *Animal Dreams* is a "well-nigh perfect novel, masterfully written, brimming with insight, humor and compassion." The critic concluded, "This richly satisfying novel should firmly establish Kingsolver among the pantheon of talented writers."

When Kingsolver left her native Kentucky in 1977, she got rid of her southern accent as quickly as she could for fear of being labelled as an ignorant hillbilly. By the late 1980s, however, she had

rediscovered the richness of her native dialect and its worth in her writing as it was captured through Taylor Greer's use of dialect and southern colloquialisms. Kingsolver discovered that she not only didn't have to abandon her accent, she didn't have to forsake her character Taylor forever. With *Pigs in Heaven,* the author continues the story of Taylor and Turtle. In this sequel, Turtle and her adoptive mother are asked to appear on the "Oprah Winfrey Show" after Turtle helps to save the life of a man who almost drowns near Hoover Dam. Trouble brews when a lawyer for the Cherokee tribe sees the broadcast and vows to have Taylor's adoption of Turtle annulled so that the child can be returned to her people.

"I conceived of the idea for *Pigs in Heaven* as I watched native American children being adopted by outsiders," Kingsolver explained to *New York Times Book Review* contributor Lynn Karpen. Sensing that this important issue had been ignored in *The Bean Trees,* the author said she "had the option and the *obligation*" to write about it. As with her other novels, *Pigs in Heaven* touches on several important topics, including the problems of single-parent families, the dangers of television, and the tragedy of eating disorders. But the central complications in this novel are, as Antonya Nelson describes them in the *Los Angeles Times Book Review,* "the rights of adoptive parents as opposed to biological ones, and the rights of jurisprudence in tribal matters." And again there is the theme of the importance of community. As R. Z. Sheppard pointed out in his *Time* review, "Home, family and tribe are central to" the novel.

While critics found much to praise about *Pigs in Heaven*—*New York Times Book Review* contributor Karen Karbo called it a "resounding achievement"—some felt the resolution of the story's central conflict too pat. Taylor decides to become a part of the Cherokee community, satisfying both sides: Taylor is allowed to keep Turtle, and Turtle is able to remain with her Cherokee tribe. Nelson claimed that "the genuine controversy of community versus individual rights is trivialized" by this conclusion. The critic also complained that, as the story's title indicates, the world and characters portrayed in *Pigs in Heaven* are "idealized," thus making it a place that the author "can't make us believe in." Karbo, on the other hand, took a contrary view when she wrote that Kingsolver "manages to maintain her political views without sacrificing the complexity of her characters' predicaments." Karbo later concluded: "Possessed of an extravagantly gifted narrative voice, [the author] blends a fierce and abiding moral vision with benevolent, concise humor. Her medicine is meant for the head, the heart and the soul—and it goes down dangerously, blissfully, easily."

Kingsolver has always written with the aim that her stories would have a kind of medicinal value for her readers and that her books could somehow change their lives, if only a little. "I've always had this absolute belief in my ability to change things," she told Neill and Haederle, adding that "I do what I do because that's the only moral option to me." But for her books to affect as many people as possible, her writing has to be accessible. "I have a serious commitment to accessibility," she told Ross. "I don't believe that art is only for the highly educated. . . . I want to write books that anybody can read. I also want my books to be artful and as well crafted as I can make them: I don't want to offend educated people. I want to challenge people who like literature, to give them something for their trouble, without closing any doors to people who are less educated." In this way, Kingsolver has maintained her ties to her humble origins, while still finding fulfillment as the creative, talented person she has become.

■ Works Cited

Review of *Animal Dreams, Publishers Weekly*, June 22, 1990, p. 45.

Banks, Russell, "Distant as a Cherokee Childhood," *New York Times Book Review*, June 11, 1989, p. 16.

Butler, Jack, "She Hung the Moon and Plugged in All the Stars," *New York Times Book Review*, April 10, 1988, p. 15.

Cincotti, Joseph A., "Intimate Revelations," *New York Times Book Review*, September 2, 1990, p. 2.

Fitzgerald, Karen, review of *The Bean Trees, Ms.*, April, 1988, p. 28.

Freitag, Michael, "Writing to Pay the Rent," *New York Times Book Review*, April 10, 1988, p. 15.

Gray, Paul, "Call of the Eco-Feminist," *Time*, September 24, 1990, p. 87.

Review of *Holding the Line, Publishers Weekly*, October 13, 1989, p. 47.

Karbo, Karen, "And Baby Makes Two," *New York Times Book Review*, June 27, 1993, p. 9.

Karpen, Lynn, "The Role of Poverty," *New York Times Book Review*, June 27, 1993, p. 9.

Kingsolver, Barbara, in an interview with Jean W. Ross, *Contemporary Authors*, Volume 134, Gale, 1992, pp. 284-90.

Neill, Michael, and Michael Haederle, "La Pasionaria," *People*, October 11, 1993, pp. 109-10.

Nelson, Antonya, "Heaven in Oklahoma," *Los Angeles Times Book Review*, July 4, 1993, pp. 2, 8.

Randall, Margaret, review of *The Bean Trees, Women's Review of Books*, May, 1988.

Rozen, Frieda Shoenberg, review of *Holding the Line, Library Journal*, November 1, 1989, p. 104.

See, Lisa, "PW Interviews: Barbara Kingsolver," *Publishers Weekly*, August 31, 1990, pp. 46-47.

Sheppard, R. Z., "Little Big Girl," *Time*, August 30, 1993, p. 65.

Smiley, Jane, "In One Small Town, the Weight of the World," *New York Times Book Review*, September 2, 1990, p. 2.

■ For More Information See

PERIODICALS

Booklist, March 1, 1988, p. 1095.

Library Journal, May 15, 1989, p. 90; June 15, 1993, p. 97.

Los Angeles Times Book Review, March 12, 1988, p. 14.

Times Literary Supplement, July 13, 1990, p. 956.

—Sketch by Janet L. Hile

Tanith Lee

■ Personal

Born September 19, 1947; daughter of Bernard and Hylda (Moore) Lee. *Education:* Attended Catford Grammar School, London, England; studied art at college level. *Hobbies and other interests:* Past civilizations (Egyptian, Roman, Incan); psychic powers (their development, use, and misuse); music.

■ Addresses

Agent—c/o Macmillan London Ltd., 4 Little Essex Street, London WC2R 3LF, England.

■ Career

Writer. Former librarian.

■ Awards, Honors

August Derleth Award, 1980; World Fantasy Convention Award, 1983.

■ Writings

NOVELS

The Birthgrave, DAW, 1975, Futura, 1977.
Don't Bite the Sun, DAW, 1976.
The Storm Lord, DAW, 1976, Futura, 1977.
Drinking Sapphire Wine, DAW, 1977, published with *Don't Bite the Sun,* Hamlyn, 1979.
Volkhavaar, DAW, 1977, Hamlyn, 1981.
Vazkor, Son of Vaskor, DAW, 1978, published as *Shadowfire,* Futura, 1979.
Night's Master (part of series), DAW, 1978, Hamlyn, 1981.
Death's Master (part of *Tales From the Flat Earth* series), DAW, 1979, Hamlyn, 1982.
Electric Forest, DAW, 1979.
Kill the Dead, DAW, 1980.
Day by Night, DAW, 1980.
Delusion's Master (part of *Tales From the Flat Earth* series), DAW, 1981.
Sabella; or, The Blood Stone, DAW, 1982, Unwin, 1987.
The Silver Metal Lover, DAW, 1982, Unwin, 1986.
Sung in Shadow, DAW, 1983.
Anackire, DAW, 1983, Futura, 1985.
Days of Grass, DAW, 1985.
Dark Castle, White Horse, DAW, 1986.
Delirium's Mistress (part of *Tales From the Flat Earth* series), DAW 1986.
The White Serpent, DAW, 1988.
A Heroine of the World, DAW, 1989.
The Blood of Roses, Century, 1990.
Lycanthia, Legend, 1990.
Heart Beast, Dell, 1992.
Personal Darkness, Dell, 1993.

SHORT STORY COLLECTIONS

The Betrothed, Slughorn, 1968.
Cyrion, DAW, 1982.
Red as Blood; or, Tales from the Sisters Grimmer, DAW, 1983.
The Beautiful Biting Machine, Cheap Street, 1984.
Tamastara; or, The Indian Nights, DAW, 1984.
The Gorgon and Other Beastly Tales, DAW, 1985.
Dreams of Dark and Light, Arkham House, 1986.
Night Sorceries, DAW, 1987.
Women as Demons, Women's Press, 1989.
Forests of the Night, Unwin, 1990.
The Book of the Damned (book one of *The Secret Books of Paradys*), Unwin, 1988, Overlook, 1990.
The Book of the Beast (book two of *The Secret Books of Paradys*), Unwin, 1988, Overlook, 1991.
The Book of the Dead (book three of *The Secret Books of Paradys*), Overlook, 1991.
The Book of the Mad (book four of *The Secret Books of Paradys*), Overlook, 1993.

CHILDREN'S BOOKS

The Dragon Hoard, Macmillan (London), 1971, Farrar Straus, 1971.
Princess Hynchatti and Some Other Surprises, Macmillan (London), 1972, Farrar Straus, 1973.
Animal Castle, Macmillan (London), 1972, Farrar Straus, 1972.
Companions on the Road, Macmillan (London), 1975.
The Winter Players, Macmillan (London), 1975.
Companions on the Road, and The Winter Players, St. Martin's Press, 1977.
East of Midnight, Macmillan (London), 1977, St. Martin's Press, 1977.
The Castle of the Dark, Macmillan (London), 1978.
Shon the Taken, Macmillan (London), 1979.
Prince on a White Horse, Macmillan (London), 1982.
Madame Two Swords, Donald M. Grant, 1988.
Black Unicorn, Macmillan (London), 1991, Atheneum, 1991.

RADIO PLAYS

Bitter Gate, BBC Radio, 1977.
Red Wine, BBC Radio, 1977.
Death is King, 1979.
The Silver Sky, 1980.

OTHER

Sarcophagus, 1980, and *Sand,* 1981 (television plays for *Blake's Seven* series.
Unsilent Night, NESFA Press, 1981.

■ Sidelights

"I wrote my first story at the age of nine (an embarrassingly trite thing to do)," notes Tanith Lee in *Something about the Author.* But as she indicates in an interview with *Contemporary Authors,* "I began to write, and continue to write, out of the sheer compulsion to fantasize. I can claim no noble motives, no aspirations . . . I just want to write, can't stop, don't want to stop, and hope I never shall."

Lee, the prolific and highly original creator of works of fiction that combine science fiction, humor, a dark imagination, and the power of the erotic, was born in London, England. She attended school in London as well, where she began to develop her tastes in art and literature. In discussing factors that have molded her work, Lee says in *Contemporary Authors* that "I think I can say that I've been influenced by everything I've read and liked. But I'm influenced by symphonies and concertos, too, by paintings and by films. And sometimes by people. A character. A sentence."

While Lee has authored dozens of novels and short stories generally categorized as fantasy or science fiction, she also has written numerous works for young audiences as well as plays for radio and television. Her work consistently explores themes relating to the individual's ability to control fate, the search for identity, and the nature of morality. Critics note that Lee's stories typically feature a vividly imagined fictional world peopled by unique characters. Using language that is both highly expressive yet deeply disciplined, she spins journeys of thought and imagination that have captured the hearts and minds of devoted readers worldwide.

Science Fiction and Fantasy

Lee's chief works of adult fiction begin with *The Birthgrave* (1975), her first adult novel. Several characters which appear in later books by Lee were first featured in this novel. *The Birthgrave* concerns a goddess who, unable to recall her past, must come to terms with the moral and personal implications of her lack of identity. The tale is an episodic series of adventures in which the god–dess confronts her own moral ignorance, as well as societal conflicts between men and women, and between technology and science. The novel fea–

This first volume of the author's "Secret Books of Paradys," *The Book of the Damned,* introduces readers to the lost city of Paradys, a macabre world forgotten by time where the secrets of the dead fail to remain buried in crypts and cemeteries.

(and world) is so original that she provides a glossary explaining the meaning of words used by her characters. Indeed, this invented vocabulary, called "Jang slang" in the book, is filled with words that describe the heroine's character and the nature of the society she creates.

The primary theme explored in these stories concerns human society and its failures, a common topic for Lee. The struggles of the main characters in the novels provide a context for the examination of society as a whole. Paul G. Maguire, writing in *Science Fiction Review* about *Don't Bite The Sun,* described it as follows: "The heroine is a product of her world, it reflects her, and we see it through her perceptions, with special impact. The desert blossoming scene and its aftermath culminating in a tender and bittersweet, although pathetic, attempt at affection; and her failure to grasp real love, are truly moving. The novel has deep insights. A pleasure to find a real science fiction novel which succeeds in making its ideas seem fresh."

Scheherezade Rides Again

Lee has also produced a number of tales that are somewhat reminiscent of *The Thousand and One Nights.* She uses these stories to examine the moral content of myths and legends. Known as the *Tales from the Flat Earth* series, these books include *Night's Master* (1978), *Death's Master* (1979), *Delusion's Master* (1981) and *Delirium's Mistress* (1986). All share a common time and place, an imaginary period when the earth is thought to be flat, and all share the use of elements of sword and sorcery fiction to relate the interaction of demons and human beings. As was the case with *The Thousand and One Nights,* these books utilize episodic plots and a structure of interrelated short stories. Lee also employs a prose tone that is reminiscent of the structure of many old myths and fairy tales. Like the main characters in Lee's other novels, the demons in these stories have the ability to influence the direction of world events with their behavior. Thus the stories take on a highly moral focus, and make it possible for Lee to expose the ambiguities in the relationship between behavior and morality, especially as they relate to sexual relationships.

tures larger–than–life protagonists, but resolves itself in human terms, a more traditional form of science fiction. Joan Gordon, discussing the novel in *Fantasy Review,* called it "a powerful book" exemplifying "Lee's interest in myth" as well as "her characteristic reshaping of mythic elements."

In later novels such as *Vaskor, Son of Vaskor* (1978) and *Quest for the White Witch* (1978), the central characters remain powerful and mythic figures. The style of her writing during this period became increasingly fantastic in tone. In *Don't Bite the Sun* (1976) and *Drinking Sapphire Wine* (1977), Lee chronicles a young woman's search for love and meaning in a hedonistic and technologically advanced society. When the protagonist kills a man in a duel, she finds herself exiled and forced to set up a new society. Here Lee's prose style

Peter Stampfel, in a review published in the *Village Voice Literary Supplement,* dubbed Tanith Lee the "Princess Royal of Heroic Fantasy and God-

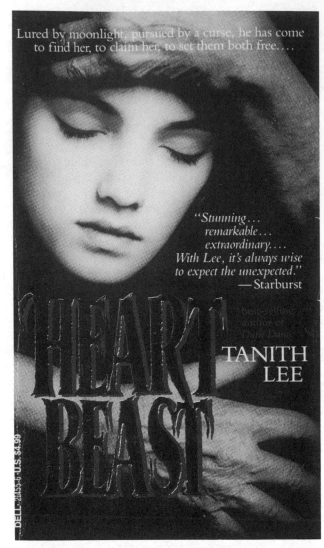

Lured by moonlight, pursued by a curse, he has come to find her, to claim her, to set them both free....

"*Stunning... remarkable... extraordinary.... With Lee, it's always wise to expect the unexpected.*" —Starburst

HEART BEAST

TANITH LEE

Lee's ability to combine dark fantasy with romance and eroticism is in evidence in *Heart Beast*, a tale of love gone awry.

dess–Empress of the Hot Read" before proceeding to discuss the Flat Earth Series. Wrote Stampfel: "Lee's series is inspired by *The Arabian Nights* and the fairy tales of Oscar Wilde, as well as all the myths that have ever strode and stormed through the mind and soul of mankind." Michael E. Stamm, reviewing *Death's Master* for *Fantasy Review*, found the prose to be "very rich, reminiscent of Clark Ashton Smith's." Michael R. Collings, discussing *Death's Master* in *The Scope of the Fantastic—Theory, Technique, Major Authors: Selected Essays from the First International Conference on the Fantastic in Literature and Film*, celebrated Lee's superb use of "archaic, exotic and elevated" language to create "the emotional effect in the reader of suddenly being immersed in an unfamiliar world."

"Tanith Lee has published at least two dozen books in her career," Stamm wrote in a subsequent *Fantasy Review* article, "11 since *Delusion's Master* appeared. But the quality of her work is not lessened by its quantity. The prose in *Delirium's Mistress* is as luxuriant as ever, imparting some of the qualities of a fever dream; it is not read easily (though her style in other books can be very different). These books should be read gradually, but they should be read, and they will be enjoyed."

Maturing Vision

In the 1980s and 1990s the prolific Lee continued publishing science fiction and fantasy novels at a rapid pace. She notes in an interview with *Contemporary Authors* that she produces this large volume of work despite an "undisciplined and erratic" approach to writing. "One day I will commence work at four in the afternoon and persevere until four the next morning. Sometimes I start at four in the morning, and go on until physical stamina gives out. Sometimes I get stuck on some knotty problem, and worry about said problem for days, pen poised, eyes glazed. Frequently I race through 150 pages in a month, and then stick for three months over one page. It's a wonder to me I get anything done."

As with her novels of the 1970s, Lee's more recent work is marked by its originality and use of traditional myth reshaped for modern themes and sensibilities. Michael Swanwick, in a *Washington Post Book World* article about Lee's work, described her style as follows: "Tanith Lee writes fantasy for adults. It is darkly, lushly romantic stuff, with silvery veins of eroticism and sinister beauty . . . Her prose practically shimmers on the page."

Lee's first novel of the 1980s, *Day by Night* (1980), is a story within a story. The plot revolves around a writer's highly entertaining fables that become (unbeknownst to her) reality on the other side of her planet. *Publisher's Weekly* termed *Day by Night* one of Lee's "longest and most ambitious" novels "with a complicated plot involving mirror existences on the bright side and dark side of a planet that does not rotate." Catherine Monnin, writing for *Voice of Youth Advocates*, thought the novel was "well written and suspenseful . . . a better than average SF tale" that successfully employs the story–within–a–story form.

Other works by Lee during this period reflect an exploration of a variety of storylines. *Sabella: or, The Blood Stone* (1980) is, as described by Roland Green in *Booklist*, a "short novel of a young female vampire's search for a way to live in a human world. The author's gifts for characterization and realistic detail are particularly noteworthy." *The Silver Metal Lover* (1982) relates the futuristic story of a love affair between a woman and a robot. Roger C. Schlobin commented in *Science Fiction and Fantasy Book Review* that the novel "is marked by her always striking prose and her ability to endow her characters with persuasive humanity." The protagonist, Jane, whose physical appearance has been pre–determined scientifically, is "the perfect consumer of the future," according to Schlobin. When Jane falls in love with a robot called S.I.L.V.E.R. (Silver Ionized Locomotive Verisimulated Electronic Robot) the story takes off and becomes, in Schlobin's words, "a chronicle of a poignant love that is highly engaging and powerful." Roland Green, reviewing the novel for *Booklist*, agreed. He found *The Silver Metal Lover* a perfect vessel for "Lee's diverse talents at their best—her eye for detail, her deft hand with decadence and corruption, her brisk pacing."

Sung in Shadow (1983) is set in "an alternate Renaissance Italy," according to Jeff Clark of the *Library Journal*. Lee utilizes this medieval setting, complete with warring families, to artfully rework a Romeo and Juliet tale of rebellious love, adding a few supernatural twists for good measure. According to Clark, "Lee is indeed retelling *Romeo and Juliet*, but she has elaborated it novelistically, filling out secondary people and relationships." Roland Green, reviewing the novel in *Booklist*, found Lee's prose up to her "usual high standard . . . Lee does not appear to be slacking off from her three– books–a–year pace, nor (if this book is any indication) is her genius diminishing."

Lee's rich imagination was next displayed in *Days of Grass* (1985), a tale about a young girl on the verge of womanhood who confronts aliens who have taken over the earth and forced the human race to live in underground cities. Though Gregory Frost, reviewing the book for *The Washington Post Book World*, found it "a flawed book, and a despairing novel," he also could not help but note that it is also "one that sinks deeply into the substance of myth."

In *A Heroine of the World* (1990), a noblewoman named Ara who has been taken captive by invaders learns that it is her destiny to be the focus of great events. Ara subsequently launches herself upon a fantastic journey of self–discovery that utilizes all of Lee's notable gifts for rich and exotic storytelling. According to a review in *Publisher's Weekly*, "The novel's events unfold at a breakneck pace: rape, murder, marriage, widowhood, inheritance of riches, and imperial romance. . . . Lee's heated prose is both striking and convincing as the first–person narrative of her idealistic, intelligent young heroine." Roland Green's review of the story in *Booklist* was complimentary as well: "Ara's adventures make for another splendid, large scale Tanith Lee story, the latest from one of contemporary fantasy's undoubted masters."

Turning Worlds Upside Down and Inside Out

As Tanith Lee's body of work has grown, certain trademarks in her highly stylized writing have emerged. Reviewers point to the extraordinary sensory awareness in the details she conjures in so many of her stories: the feel of exotic fabrics, the taste of strange fruits, the scent of haunting perfumes, and the amazing colors of a variety of barbaric and sophisticated peoples. Her original use of language, character, and place draws readers in with a sense of the familiar, then delights with sudden changes and departures from the expected. Lee often creates real characters using stock villains and heroes from the fantasy/fairy tale genre as well. In mixing these styles together, she has created sympathetic wolves and wicked Cinderellas that defy reader expectations.

In Lee's short story collection *Red as Blood: Or Tales From the Sisters Grimmer* (1983), she turns the familiar tales of the Brothers Grimm upside down. Or, as Susan L. Nickerson describes it in *The Library Journal*, "She turns some familiar fairy tales inside–out, investing them with an unearthly aura." Roland Green, writing about *Red as Blood* in *Booklist*, applauded Lee for having "conceived something unique and executed it superlatively well, displaying gifts as both a fantasy writer and a folklorist." *Publisher's Weekly* observed that "Lee's entrancing and vivid style make what may seem a minor exercise into a collection of essentially new stories with some of the resonances of folklore." Lee has published several other collections of short stories in various other genres as well, including *Cyrion* (1982), *Tamastara; or, The Indian Nights* (1984), *Night Sorceries* (1987), and a series of books known collectively as *The Secret Books of Paradys.*

Cyrion (1982) is a collection of stories of the sword and sorcery genre. These stories feature the exploits of a compelling, gorgeous, masculine protagonist named Cyrion. Susan L. Nickerson, reviewing the collection for *The Library Journal,* noted that "Lee has created another exquisite male character. Her continuing success with rich fantasy is remarkable."

Lee's gift for describing radically different worlds is on display in a couple other short story collections, too. *Night Sorceries* concerns events, told in a series of interconnected stories, surrounding a love affair between two gods: Azhram, the daughter of the Lord of Darkness, and Chuz, the Prince of Madness. When these two lovers inhabit the depths of a great forest it becomes enchanted, and the magic unleashed affects all who inhabit the forest and the surrounding country. Another collection, *Tamastara: or, the Indian Nights,* contains seven tales that conjure up mythic and historic India, and incorporates themes of reincarnation and self discovery. The style of the writing is firmly rooted in the tradition of folklore, but the tales are set in the twentieth century.

The trilogy of lost Paradys books (*The Book of the Damned, The Book of the Beast,* and *The Book of the Dead*) are all set in the lost city of Paradys, a land forgotten by time and history. Here Lee mines the traditions of the macabre, horror, and dark fantasy. Jackie Cassada, reviewing *The Book of the Dead* for the *Library Journal,* notes that Lee "infuses her stories with a restless, evocative sultriness." *Publisher's Weekly* commented that the stories are infused with "the ambience of fin de siecle France," terming these "gothic tales" of "the tortured lives once led by those buried in the crypts and cemeteries of the mythical (or forgotten) city of Paradys."

Books for Children and Young Adults

While a noted practitioner of adult fantasy, Lee is also a prolific and popular writer of children's and young adult stories. Indeed, her publishing career began in 1971 with the publication of her first book for children, *The Dragon Hoard.* Since

Lee often takes popular myths, legends, and fairy tales and transforms them into her own, as in this novel about a group of immortal, sophisticated vampires.

that time Lee has continued to pepper her publishing career with a steady stream of stories for children and young adults.

In *Animal Castle* (1972), a prince who presides over a land that has no animals ventures on a journey to collect animals to come and live in a castle he has built especially for them. When the prince returns the animals he has brought with him are pampered to such a great degree that they become spoiled and unpleasant, an amusing turn of events that is illustrated with entertaining, action packed drawings. In the end the prince banishes the animals once more and the animals, realizing how good they had it, promise to behave if allowed to stay.

In *Companions on the Road* (1975), a book for young adults, Lee portrays a classic struggle between good and evil. This tale features Havor, a disenchanted soldier who resigns his commission in the King's army following the destruction of a city called Avillis. But upon resigning he engages in an act of theft that, though it was meant to help the poor family of a dead boy, unwittingly releases mystical and evil powers. Graham Hammond, writing in the *Times Literary Supplement*, found the book "imaginative and impressive . . . with something of the deceptive simplicity and compelling mystery of an old folk tale. Tanith Lee has refined a language of pared down precision to convey Havor's desolation and evoke a chilling sense of menace."

East of Midnight (1977) is a "trading places" type of story, in which a transference of minds takes place between a lowly page and a queen's consort (the latter who has been sentenced to death) on a planet where women rule. Peter Hunt, writing in the *Times Literary Supplement*, applauded Lee's imagination: "Whereas the interchange of minds is rather circumstantial for magic, the world of women–kings who ride lions and dispose of their weak male consorts every five years flashes with ideas. It also touches deeper themes of love, sex, and honour, and reaches a moving climax."

Other books for children written by Lee include *Princess Hynchatti and Some Other Surprises* (1972), *The Castle of the Dark* (1978), *Prince on a White Horse* (1982), *Madame Two Swords* (1988), and *Black Unicorn* (1991). Lee says in *Something about the Author* that while these book's are labeled children's books, "I intend my books for anyone who will enjoy them. Frankly," she adds, "I write for me, I can't help it. My books are expressions of my private inner world. I love the idea that other people may read and perhaps relish them, but that, if it happens, is a delightful by product."

■ Works Cited

Cassada, Jackie, review of *The Book of the Dead*, *Library Journal*, February 15, 1992, p. 200.

Caywood, Carolyn, review of *Tamastara: or, the Indian Nights*, *Voice of Youth Advocates*, October 1984, p. 206.

Clark, Jeff, review of *Sung in Shadow*, *Library Journal*, May 15, 1983, p. 1019.

Collings, Michael R., *The Scope of the Fantastic—Theory, Technique, Major Authors: Selected Essays from the First International Conference on the Fantastic in Literature and Film*, edited by Robert A. Collins and Howard D. Pearce, Greenwood Press, 1985, p. 173.

Frost, Gregory, review of *Days of Grass*, *Washington Post Book World*, December 22, 1985, p. 8.

Gordon, Joan, review of *The Birthgrave*, *Fantasy Review*, April 1986, p. 25.

Green, Roland, *Booklist*, July 1, 1980, p. 1596.

Green, review of *A Heroine of the World*, *Booklist*, August 1989, p. 1949.

Green, review of *Red as Blood*, *Booklist*, February 1, 1983, p. 715.

Green, review of *The Silver Metal Lover*, *Booklist*, June 1, 1982, p. 1299.

Green, review of *Sung in Shadow*, *Booklist*, August 1983, p. 1448.

Hammond, Graham, review of *Companions on the Road*, *Times Literary Supplement*, April 2, 1976, p. 383.

Hunt, Peter, review of *East of Midnight*, *Times Literary Supplement*, October 21, 1977, p. 1246.

Maquire, Paul G., review of *Don't Bite the Sun*, *Science Fiction Review*, August 1976, p. 34.

Monnin, Catherine, review of *Day by Night*, *Voice of Youth Advocates*, April 1981, p. 40.

Nickerson, Susan L., review of *Cyrion*, *Library Journal*, September 15, 1982, p. 1772.

Nickerson, review of *Red as Blood*, *Library Journal*, January 15, 1983, p. 147.

Review of *The Book of the Dead*, *Publisher's Weekly*, January 1, 1992, p. 50.

Review of *Day by Night*, *Publisher's Weekly*, September 26, 1980, p. 119.

Review of *A Heroine of the World*, *Publisher's Weekly*, July 21, 1989, p. 55.

Review of *Red as Blood*, *Publisher's Weekly*, November 26, 1982, p. 57.

Schlobin, Roger C., review of *The Silver Metal Lover, Science Fiction & Fantasy Book Review*, April 1982, p. 17.

Stamm, Michael E., review of *Death's Master*, *Fantasy Review*, April 1985, p. 25.

Stamm, review of *Delirium's Mistress*, *Fantasy Review*, July August 1986, p. 30.

Stampfel, Peter, *Village Voice Literary Supplement*, October 1981, p. 6.

Swanwick, Michael, *Washington Post Book World*, July 27, 1986, p. 4.

■ For More Information See

PERIODICALS

Booklist, June 1, 1973, p. 948; April 15, 1985, p. 1162; March 15, 1988, p. 1223.
Junior Bookshelf, February 1976, p. 48; April 1978, p. 105; February 1979, p. 54.
Library Journal, April 15, 1984, p. 826; August 1989, p. 167.

Publishers Weekly, October 23, 1972, p. 45.
Science Fiction Review, May 1977, p. 16; May 1979, p. 49; August 1981, p. 11; May 1983, p. 19.
Times Literary Supplement, July 14, 1972, p. 808.
Voice of Youth Advocates, April 1983, p. 45; August/September 1987, p. 131.

—Sketch by Mindi Dickstein

Lurlene McDaniel

■ Personal

Born Lurlene Nora Gallagher, April 5, 1944, in Philadelphia, PA; daughter of James (a chief petty officer in the U.S. Navy) and Bebe (a homemaker; maiden name, Donaldson) Gallagher; married Joe McDaniel, March 12, 1966 (divorced, 1987); children: Sean Clifford, Erik James. *Education:* University of South Florida, B.A., 1965. *Politics:* Republican. *Religion:* Conservative Presbyterian.

■ Addresses

Home—Chattanooga, TN. *Agent*—Meg Ruley/Jane Rotrosen, 318 East 51st St., New York, NY 10022.

■ Career

Novelist and freelance writer, including radio and television scripts, and promotional and advertising copy. Frequent speaker and lecturer at writers' conferences. *Member:* Romance Writers of America, East Tennessee Romance Writers of America.

■ Awards, Honors

Six Months to Live was placed in a literary time capsule in the Library of Congress, November, 1990; RITA Award, 1991; *Somewhere between Life and Death, Too Young to Die,* and *Goodbye Doesn't Mean Forever* were selected as Children's Choice books by the International Reader's Association.

■ Writings

YOUNG ADULT NOVELS

What's It Like to Be a Star?, Willowisp Press/School Book Fairs, 1982.

I'm a Cover Girl Now, Willowisp Press/School Book Fairs, 1982.

Will I Ever Dance Again?, Willowisp Press/School Book Fairs, 1982.

Head over Heels, Willowisp Press/School Book Fairs, 1983.

If I Should Die before I Wake, Willowisp Press/School Book Fairs, 1983.

Sometimes Love Just Isn't Enough, Willowisp Press/School Book Fairs, 1984.

Three's a Crowd, Willowisp Press/School Book Fairs, 1984.

Six Months to Live, Willowisp Press/School Book Fairs, 1985.

The Secret Life of Steffie Martin, Willowisp Press/School Book Fairs, 1985.

Why Did She Have to Die?, Willowisp Press/School Book Fairs, 1986.

I Want to Live, Willowisp Press/School Book Fairs, 1987.

More Than Just a Smart Girl, Willowisp Press/School Book Fairs, 1987.

Mother, Please Don't Die, Willowisp Press/School Book Fairs, 1988.

My Secret Boyfriend, Willowisp Press/School Book Fairs, 1988.

Too Young to Die, Bantam, 1989.

Goodbye Doesn't Mean Forever, Bantam, 1989.

So Much to Live For, Willowisp Press/School Book Fairs, 1991.

Somewhere between Life and Death, Bantam, 1991.

Time to Let Go, Bantam, 1991.

Now I Lay Me Down to Sleep, Bantam, 1991.

When Happily Ever after Ends, Bantam, 1992.

Baby Alicia Is Dying, Bantam, 1993.

No Time to Cry, Willowisp Press/School Book Fairs, 1993.

Don't Die, My Love, Bantam, 1995.

I'll Be Seeing You, Bantam, in press.

Saving Jessica, Bantam, in press.

"ONE LAST WISH" YOUNG ADULT SERIES

A Time to Die, Bantam, 1992.

Mourning Song, Bantam, 1992.

Mother, Help Me Live, Bantam, 1992.

Someone Dies, Someone Lives, Bantam, 1992.

Sixteen and Dying, Bantam, 1992.

Let Him Live, Bantam, 1992.

The Legacy: Making Wishes Come True, Bantam, 1993.

Please Don't Die, Bantam, 1993.

She Died Too Young, Bantam, 1994.

All the Days of Her Life, Bantam, 1994.

A Season for Goodbye, Bantam, 1995.

JUVENILE NOVELS

A Horse for Mandy, Willowisp Press/School Book Fairs, 1981.

The Pony Nobody Wanted, Willowisp Press/School Book Fairs, 1982.

The Battle of Zorn, Willowisp Press/School Book Fairs, 1983.

Peanut Butter for Supper Again, Willowisp Press/School Book Fairs, 1985.

OTHER

Fiction editor for the children's magazine *Guideposts for Kids*. McDaniel's books have been translated into German, Norwegian, and Dutch.

While McDaniel's books—particularly those in the "One Last Wish" series—deal with the devastating impact of illness on teens, the stories also often present the healing benefits of a hopeful attitude.

■ Sidelights

Talking to Lurlene McDaniel about her work is similar to reading a book of inspirational sayings; her conversation is sprinkled with such phrases as "life works out if you give it a chance," and "all things work to the good of those who love God." She is unflaggingly upbeat and cheerful—traits that seem surprising in the author of dozens of novels that portray teenagers faced with terminal illnesses and their own mortality. More often than not, some form of the word "death" finds its way into the titles of McDaniel's novels, as it does in the following: *A Time to Die, Sixteen and Dying,* and *She Died Too Young.*

As the titles suggest, McDaniel's specialty is dealing with some of life's most difficult blows. In *Somewhere between Life and Death,* Erin's younger sister is severely injured in a car accident. When the doctors declare her brain dead, Erin and her family must decide whether or not to turn off life-support systems and donate her organs to be transplanted. In *Please Don't Die,* heart transplant recipient Katie O'Roark spends the summer at "Jenny House," a retreat for critically ill adolescents. She befriends three girls: Chelsea, a candidate for a heart transplant; Amanda, a victim of leukemia; and Lacey, a diabetic. Not everyone makes it through the summer. Desi, the protagonist of *Baby Alicia Is Dying,* is a teenage volunteer at a home for babies with AIDS. She becomes very attached to a baby who seems healthy but then suddenly succumbs to the disease.

It's not exactly the stuff of young adult romances, or even the horror novels that currently fill the shelves in teen sections of bookstores. Nevertheless, McDaniel has carved out a niche in the young adult publishing world—one that some people never dreamed existed. "Adults are often prejudiced against my books," McDaniel says in her interview with Sarah Verney for *Authors and Artists for Young Adults (AAYA).* "They don't understand why kids would want to read them." The problem, McDaniel speculates, may be that the adults haven't read the books themselves. "They look at the titles and erroneously assume that the books are morbid. They aren't," McDaniel attests.

Illness, death and dying may be at the core of McDaniel's novels, but the stories themselves are really about life, and getting beyond the grieving process. While some people have referred to her books as "ten-hankie novels," McDaniel prefers to think of them as "bibliotherapy"—a means of working out one's grief in a book. To do that, her readers need to get a glimpse of the big picture—"the totality of life, not just the individual moments," as McDaniel told Verney.

Most importantly, though, McDaniel's readers also need to feel hope. "I end all my stories on a note of hope," she points out in her *AAYA* interview. Hope is the one thing McDaniel most wants to give her readers, whether they are kids like her characters, facing extraordinary challenges, or ordinary teens with ordinary problems. McDaniel recognizes that many teens face difficulties that those of her own generation never even imagined. "We worried about someone cutting in line," she explains in her interview with Verney. "They worry about getting shot." When terrible things do happen in their lives, teens may have nowhere to turn.

"No one is talking to teenagers about the grieving process," asserts McDaniel in an interview with Mark Curnutte for the Raleigh (NC) *News & Observer.* So she does, by offering them a look into the lives of characters who have been through the process and emerged on the other side. As she attests, positive messages abound in her books, as they do in the following passage from *Somewhere between Life and Death:* "The flowers, the butterflies, the greening of the grass, told her that life was cyclic, season after season. It came, it went. It came again. . . . Erin gazed at Amy's coffin . . . and knew with certainty that Amy wasn't in it. Maybe her body would be buried, but the person of Amy, her spirit, would not. For Amy was with Erin still and would live in her heart for all the days of her life." And a similar theme of hope and peace is found in the following excerpt from *All the Days of Her Life:* "As she turned to go inside, she saw a shooting star arc through the darkness. . . . Was it an answer sent to her from a world beyond the rainbows? Lacey found renewed hope within her heart. She'd been given a second chance for all the days of her life. Beginning now, she'd make the most of it."

A Christian Perspective

The hope reaching out to young adults in McDaniel's novels springs from the author's own personal well, which is fed by her faith. She is a devout Christian, and is certain her books reflect the inspiration she receives from her religion. But while McDaniel strives to maintain "a biblical perspective" and "a sense of eternal purpose" in her novels, she makes a point of not being dogmatic. "I don't push a Christian agenda on my readers," McDaniel maintains in her *AAYA* interview, pointing out that they come from a variety of religious backgrounds. "I don't preach to them—if someone wants a sermon, they can go to church."

One obvious way McDaniel's Christian perspective comes through is in her treatment of death. "I never send a character to the grave without the hope of eternal life," she explains to Verney.

And although her doomed characters suffer plenty, in the end they generally make their peace with God. As Melissa, a high school junior dying of leukemia writes to her best friend in *Goodbye Doesn't Mean Forever,* "I'm not mad at God anymore. . . . I've had some heart-to-heart talks with Him and I've come to believe that He loves me enough to want me with Him in heaven. And that once I'm in heaven, I'll never have to die again." In coming to terms with her own death, Melissa also seems confident that she is going on to an afterlife. She finishes her letter with, "I'll be watching you. And when you least expect it, you'll hear me call you in the wind. I promise."

Author of *Six Months to Live*

Lurlene McDaniel

Too Young to Die

Books like *Too Young to Die* explore the effect of severe illness on entire families, a subject the author is familiar with from her own experiences as the mother of a diabetic.

McDaniel's faith, in addition to inspiring her young protagonists, has helped her through the tough times in her own life. The most difficult of these resulted from her older son's diabetes. Sean, who is now an athletic, healthy (though still diabetic) adult, was only three when diagnosed with the disease. At the time, he was losing weight and was constantly fatigued—all classic signs of diabetes; McDaniel consulted a doctor, but he failed to recognize Sean's illness. "I was getting him undressed that night," McDaniel remembers in her *AAYA* interview, "and I could count every rib on his little body. It was as if there was a voice in my head—I just knew he wasn't going to make it through the night." McDaniel, who was then in the early stages of her second pregnancy, took her son to an emergency room, and the doctors there immediately recognized his condition. Still, it took a tremendous medical effort for Sean to stabilize, and he came perilously close to dying in McDaniel's arms.

When Sean's crisis was over, McDaniel turned to the business of learning everything she could about diabetes management, a process that includes monitoring blood sugar levels and being extremely careful about diet and exercise. She quickly saw how chronic illness takes over one's life, and how it affects the dynamics of a family. Nevertheless, she feels her own experiences with Sean's illness support two of the hopeful messages she tries to convey in her novels: "Good can come from bad," and "life works out if you give it a chance." "What possible good could come of my beautiful little red-haired boy having diabetes?" she asks in her interview with Verney, then answers her own question: "If it weren't for Sean's illness, I don't know that I would ever have written my first novel. Would I go back and give up writing if it meant Sean wouldn't have diabetes? Absolutely. But you don't get to pick what happens to you. You do get to pick how you respond to it, however."

One way McDaniel responded to Sean's illness was to choose to work at home as a freelance writer, so that she would be available to care for him. She had previously worked as a promotion copywriter for television stations in Florida and Michigan, and so was able to write advertising and promotional copy at home for a number of different sources. Among the things McDaniel wrote were commercials for local companies, public service announcements, and promotional materials for real estate agencies.

Discovering a Talent for Fiction

The beginning of McDaniel's career as a novelist can be traced back to when Sean was ten or eleven and was asked to model in a poster for the Diabetes Research Institute. As McDaniel waited for Sean, she happened to strike up a conversation with a woman there whose father had founded a company, School Book Fairs, that sold remainders of already published books to schools. The company was just starting to branch out into publishing their own titles, and the woman suggested that McDaniel write one. "I think they were just looking for someone who could meet a deadline, and I was used to that," McDaniel relates to Verney.

McDaniel wrote several children's books, including picture books, for School Book Fairs before publishing *Will I Ever Dance Again?* This book, which is the story of how diabetes changes the life of a teenage ballet student, did very well for Willowisp, School Book Fairs' imprint. Asked to do more titles that featured teenage characters overcoming physical adversity, McDaniel followed up with *If I Should Die before I Wake,* and later, *Six Months to Live,* which eventually sold more than half a million copies and was placed in a literary capsule at the Library of Congress.

McDaniel had found her voice and her subject matter, but it wasn't until she ended her relationship with Willowisp that she really hit her stride as a writer. She and her husband of twenty-one years divorced in 1987, and McDaniel suddenly needed to earn more money. She felt she had stayed at home too long to go back out into the work force, so instead she concentrated on making her career as a novelist more lucrative. She found a literary agent and within weeks had a contract with Bantam Books. In addition to increasing her financial security, the move to Bantam gave McDaniel an opportunity to work with an editor in a way she hadn't previously experienced. Her books for Willowisp were edited and then sent to press without McDaniel participating in the process. Looking back, she says she realizes that, due to lack of constructive feedback, she wrote "a lot of bad books" before signing on with Bantam. She now works more closely with her editor and feels that the editorial give-and-take

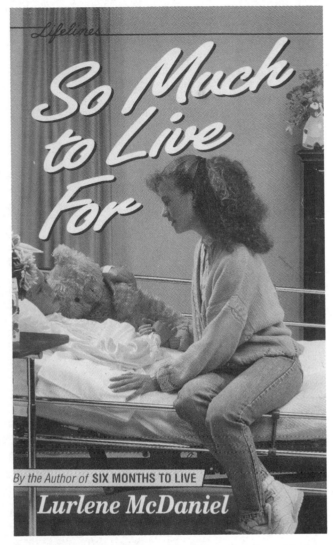

Although Dawn has won her own battle with leukemia, the death of a fellow cancer patient she befriended leaves her with many questions in *So Much to Live For.*

has helped her to grow artistically. Nevertheless, McDaniel is grateful to her two editors at Willowisp for their instrumental role in establishing her as an author, and they remain friends to this day.

In spite of her feeling that some of her earlier books were not as well-crafted as they might have been, McDaniel comments that "I did have an ability to tap into the reader's emotions," and credits that ability with much of her success. "Fiction is about feelings," she says, "and empathy is the name of the game." Without that empathy, McDaniel might never be able to get her message of hope across. Luckily, empathy comes easily to

In this sequel to *Somewhere between Life and Death,* Erin continues to mourn the sister she lost in a car accident even as she tries to get on with her own life.

McDaniel, perhaps because—even though she has not experienced the diseases that her characters endure—serious illness has often touched her life. In addition to Sean's diabetes, her father-in-law had multiple sclerosis, a progressive nerve disease, and her mother-in-law died of liver cancer while still relatively young. "I felt like I was always standing at a hospital bedside," McDaniel remembers in her Verney interview.

From this vantage point, she had the opportunity to observe both the emotional effects of illness and the high-tech world of medicine. "I was always fascinated by things medical," McDaniel explains in her *AAYA* interview. "Maybe I'm really a frus-

trated doctor." This fascination led to another hallmark of McDaniel's novels, perhaps the flip side to her inspirational themes: realistically stark portrayals of illness and medical procedures. This is another aspect of her books that parents sometimes don't understand, but judging by the comments in her fan mail, McDaniel's readers are as interested in the details as she is. (One girl, a premed student, wrote that she had become so interested in medicine while reading McDaniel's novels that she intended to become a pediatric oncologist.)

In order to keep the medical information as up-to-date and accurate as possible, McDaniel sometimes employs the services of a librarian, who faxes her information from medical journals, and interviews scores of medical experts. She also works with cancer societies, hospice organizations, the Tennessee Organ Donor Services, and an AIDS agency in Atlanta. All of this research, coupled with McDaniel's graphic descriptions, leads to passages that should put to rest anyone's fears that McDaniel somehow romanticizes illness or dying. "I have a responsibility to my readers to be accurate," McDaniel relates in her interview with Curnutte. "I call a spade a spade. If somebody vomits, they vomit." Her dedication to realism results in passages like the following, which appears in *She Died Too Young:* "Jillian was on the bed, lead wires from monitors snaking to her chest. Two tubes protruded from her groin area, from the femoral arteries, and led to the ECMO machine. One tube carried her oxygen-poor blood into the machine, where it was oxygenated by a special membrane, and the other tube carried the blood into her body to her oxygen-starved system. The machine was eerily quiet."

Personal Illness Brings New Insight

Ironically, McDaniel recently got her first glimpse of what it feels like to be on the receiving end of all the medical care she describes in her novels. In August of 1993 the author was diagnosed with breast cancer. Although the diagnosis was frightening, McDaniel considers herself lucky: the disease was caught early enough that she was able to have a lumpectomy (removal of just the cancerous lump, not the entire breast) plus radiation treatment, and she is considered to have made a full recovery. Still, the act itself of facing the cancer gave her a slightly different outlook. And McDaniel believes this comes through in one of her recent novels, *Don't Die, My Love,* in which a high school football star fights Hodgkin's disease, a form of cancer that affects the lymphatic system.

Perhaps her readers will notice the difference in McDaniel's outlook, but perhaps not; in the past the author had no difficulty convincing her audience that she knows precisely how her characters feel. It is this realistic portrayal of teen crisis that is praised by McDaniel's critics. In a review of *Now I Lay Me Down to Sleep,* a *Booklist* contributor asserts that "McDaniel deals honestly and directly with the emotional and physical challenges of her characters." And Barbara Flottmeier, writing in *Voice of Youth Advocates,* points out in a review of *Somewhere between Life and Death* and *Time to Let Go:* "The issues of healing after a loved one dies, sustaining or ending life support systems, and organ donation are handled with care and thoughtfulness."

On the other hand, those who disparage McDaniel's work describe her novels as being too contrived and predictable. "The plot is trite and overly sentimental, with obvious twists and a predictable ending," says Tina Smith Entwistle in a review of *Mourning Song* for *School Library Journal. Somewhere between Life and Death* and it's sequel, *Time to Let Go,* are similarly criticized by a *Publishers Weekly* contributor: "These forgettable, lightweight novels have no place among the many wonderful books that offer young readers an authentic vision of what it means to love and lose."

McDaniel is characteristically upbeat about any negative reviews. "I'm a mass market writer, a commercial writer," she explains to Verney. "I'll never win a Newbery Award." And as long as she continues receiving letters at the rate of 200 to 300 a month from her readers, McDaniel will feel confident she's touching their hearts. For girls

like Elizabeth, who writes, "In August of 1993, I had a double lung transplant. . . . Your books are so touching and realistic, and I am so thankful for them," McDaniel will continue spreading her message of hope.

■ Works Cited

Curnutte, Mark, "Teen Tear-Jerkers," *News & Observer* (Raleigh, NC), April 10, 1992, pp. 1D, 6D.

Entwistle, Tina Smith, review of *Mourning Song, School Library Journal,* June, 1993, pp. 130, 132.

Flottmeier, Barbara, review of *Somewhere between Life and Death* and *Time to Let Go, Voice of Youth Advocates,* April, 1991, pp. 32-33.

McDaniel, Lurlene, *Goodbye Doesn't Mean Forever,* Bantam, 1989.

McDaniel, *Somewhere between Life and Death,* Bantam, 1991.

McDaniel, *She Died Too Young,* Bantam, 1994.

McDaniel, *All the Days of Her Life,* Bantam, 1994.

McDaniel, in an interview with Sarah Verney for *Authors and Artists for Young Adults,* 1995.

Review of *Now I Lay Me Down to Sleep, Booklist,* June 15, 1991, p. 1977.

Review of *Somewhere between Life and Death* and *Time to Let Go, Publishers Weekly,* November 23, 1990, p. 66.

■ For More Information See

PERIODICALS

Booklist, March 15, 1991, p. 1506.

Publishers Weekly, June 9, 1989, pp. 70-71; April 6, 1992, pp. 23-24; June 7, 1993, p. 71.

School Library Journal, August, 1989, pp. 152-54; July, 1993, pp. 101-2.

Voice of Youth Advocates, June, 1991, p. 98; August, 1992, p. 169; December, 1992, pp. 283-84; August, 1993, p. 154.

—*Sketch by Sarah Verney*

Larry McMurtry

■ Personal

Born Larry Jeff McMurtry, June 3, 1936, in Wichita Falls, TX; son of William Jefferson (a rancher) and Hazel Ruth (McIver) McMurtry; married Josephine Ballard, July 15, 1959 (divorced, 1966); children: James Lawrence (a musician). *Education:* North Texas State College (now University), B.A., 1958; Rice University, M.A., 1960; additional study at Stanford University, 1960.

■ Addresses

Office—Booked Up Book Store, 1209 31st Street N.W., Washington, DC 20007. *Agent*—Irving Paul Lazar, The Irving Paul Lazar Agency, 120 El Camino, Beverly Hills, CA 90212.

■ Career

Writer, 1961—. Texas Christian University, Fort Worth, TX, instructor, 1961–62; Rice University, Houston, TX, lecturer in English and creative writing, 1963–69; Booked Up Book Store, Washington, DC, co-owner, 1970—. Visiting professor at George Mason College, 1970, and at American University,

1970–71. Has worked as a rare book scout and dealer for book stores in Texas and California. *Member:* PEN American Center (president, 1989), Texas Institute of Letters.

■ Awards, Honors

Wallace Stegner fellowship, 1960; Jesse H. Jones Award, Texas Institute of Letters, 1962, for *Horseman, Pass By;* Guggenheim fellowship, 1964; Academy of Motion Picture Arts and Sciences Award (Oscar), best screenplay based on material from another medium, 1972, for *The Last Picture Show;* Barbara McCombs/Lon Tinkle Award for continuing excellence in Texas letters, Texas Institute of Letters, 1986; Pulitzer Prize for fiction, Spur Award, Western Writers of America, and Texas Literary Award, Southwestern Booksellers Association, all 1986, all for *Lonesome Dove.*

■ Writings

NOVELS

Horseman, Pass By, Harper, 1961, published as *Hud,* Popular Library, 1961.
Leaving Cheyenne, Harper, 1963.
The Last Picture Show, Dial, 1966.
Moving On, Simon & Schuster, 1970.
All My Friends Are Going to Be Strangers, Simon & Schuster, 1972.
Terms of Endearment, Simon & Schuster, 1975.
Somebody's Darling, Simon & Schuster, 1978.

Cadillac Jack, Simon & Schuster, 1982.

The Desert Rose, Simon & Schuster, 1983.

Lonesome Dove, Simon & Schuster, 1985.

Texasville (sequel to *The Last Picture Show*), Simon & Schuster, 1987.

Anything for Billy, Simon & Schuster, 1988.

Some Can Whistle (sequel to *All My Friends Are Going to Be Strangers*), Simon & Schuster, 1989.

Buffalo Girls, Simon & Schuster, 1990.

The Evening Star (sequel to *Terms of Endearment*), Simon & Schuster, 1992.

Streets of Laredo (sequel to *Lonesome Dove*), Simon & Schuster, 1993.

(With Diana Ossana) *Pretty Boy Floyd,* Simon & Schuster, 1994.

Three Complete Novels: Lonesome Dove, The Last Picture Show, Leaving Cheyenne, Random House, 1994.

ESSAYS

In a Narrow Grave: Essays on Texas, Encino Press, 1968, Simon & Schuster, 1989.

It's Always We Rambled: An Essay on Rodeo, Hallman, 1974.

Film Flam: Essays on Hollywood, Simon & Schuster, 1987.

SCREENPLAYS

(With Peter Bogdanovich) *The Last Picture Show* (based on McMurtry's novel of same title), Columbia, 1970.

Texasville (based on McMurtry's novel of same title), Columbia, 1990.

Montana (cable television movie), Turner Network Television (TNT), 1990.

Falling from Grace, Columbia, 1992.

(With Cybill Shepherd) *Memphis* (cable television movie; based on novel by Shelby Foote), Turner Home Entertainment, 1992.

(And executive producer) *Streets of Laredo* (television miniseries; based on McMurtry's novel of same title), CBS, 1995.

OTHER

Also author of the forewords for *Journey through Texas: or, A Saddle-Trip on the Southwestern Frontier,* by Frederick L. Olmsted, University of Texas Press, 1978; *Panhandle Cowboy,* by John R. Erickson, University of Nebraska Press, 1980; and *Growing Up Western,* edited by Clarus Backes, Knopf, 1990. Contributor of introductions to books, including *Canyon Visions: Photographs and Pastels of the Texas Plains,* by Dan Flores, Texas Tech University Press,

1989; and *Liberty Denied: The Current Rise of Censorship in America,* by Donna A. Demac, Rutgers University Press, 1990. Also contributor to *Texas in Transition,* Lyndon Baines Johnson School of Public Affairs, 1986; and *Rodeo,* by Louise L. Serpa, Aperture Foundation, 1994. Contributor of numerous articles, essays, and book reviews to magazines and newspapers, including *Atlantic, Gentleman's Quarterly, New York Times, Saturday Review,* and *Washington Post.* Contributing editor of *American Film,* 1975—.

■ Adaptations

Hud (based on McMurtry's novel *Horseman, Pass By;* starring Paul Newman, Patricia Neal, and Melvyn Douglas; directed by Martin Ritt), Paramount, 1962.

Lovin' Molly (based on McMurtry's novel *Leaving Cheyenne;* starring Blythe Danner), Columbia, 1974.

Terms of Endearment (starring Shirley MacLaine, Jack Nicholson, and Debra Winger; directed by James L. Brooks), Paramount, 1983.

Lonesome Dove (television miniseries; starring Robert Duvall, Tommy Lee Jones, and Anjelica Huston; directed by Simon Windsor), Columbia Broadcasting System (CBS), 1989.

Return to Lonesome Dove (television miniseries; based on characters from *Lonesome Dove*), CBS, 1993.

Buffalo Girls (television miniseries; starring Anjelica Huston, Melanie Griffith, Gabriel Byrne, Sam Elliott, and Reba McEntire), CBS, 1995.

■ Sidelights

"I remember laboring, around 1971, on a screen offering for John Wayne, James Stewart, and Henry Fonda, a bittersweet, end-of-the-West Western, in which no scalps were taken and no victories were won," Larry McMurtry recalled in *New Republic.* "The three actors were horrified, genuinely and touchingly horrified. Over? The Old West? They couldn't quite articulate it, but what they were struggling to say, I think, in response to the disturbing script that eventually became *Lonesome Dove,* was that the only point of the movies, and thus, more or less, of their lives, was that the Old West need never be over. You might as well say that America could be over, a notion so high-concept as to be, at the time, unthinkable, or at least unproduceable."

In the years since this unsuccessful effort, however, McMurtry's acclaimed novels and their popular screen adaptations have exposed a large audience to his views about the mythology surrounding the American West. A native of rural Texas, McMurtry drew inspiration from his own experiences as well as those of his ancestors: "All through my youth I listened to stories about an earlier, a purer, a more golden and more legendary Texas than I had been born to see," he told Walter Clemons in *Newsweek*. Much of McMurtry's fiction reflects his home state's struggle to reconcile its frontier past with its urbanized future. "Being a writer and a Texan is an amusing fate, one that gets funnier as one's sense of humor darkens," the author continued in *In a Narrow Grave: Essays on Texas*. "The transition that is taking place is very difficult, and the situations it creates are very intense. Living here consciously uses a great deal of one's blood; it involves one at once in a birth, a death, and a bitter love affair."

Besides being known as a Texas writer, however, McMurtry has been hard to categorize. According to Malcolm Jones in *Newsweek*, McMurtry has "consistently confounded his readers' expectations," because "over the course of his career, in a plain style that's ice-water clear but on a scale that rivals Faulkner's, he has spun Old West legends, contemporary domestic dramas, tragedy, comedy and satire." McMurtry's early novels, such as *Horseman, Pass By* and *The Last Picture Show*, deal with the boredom and frustration teenagers face while growing up on rural ranches or in small towns in Texas. His works from the 1970s, like *Terms of Endearment*, present contemporary problems facing adults in urban centers such as Houston, Washington, D.C., and Hollywood. His novels from the 1980s return to rural Texas, but take place nearly 100 years in the past. His best-known work, *Lonesome Dove*, tells the gripping, realistic story of a turn-of-the-century cattle drive from Texas to Montana. Winner of the 1986 Pulitzer Prize for fiction and an immediate bestseller, *Lonesome Dove* also became one of the most successful television miniseries of all time.

Throughout his career, McMurtry has earned critical praise for "his characters, his readability, his original narrative voice, his mixture of humor and bleakness, and always, when he writes about Texas, his sense of place," according to Sarah English in the *Dictionary of Literary Biography*.

While the popular success of his novels may cause some reviewers to regard him less seriously, still others rank McMurtry among the best American fiction writers. "As much as I hate to say it about somebody who can sell 200,000 copies of just about any novel he writes, I think Larry McMurtry may be a great writer. He's doing something with the American West that is very much like what William Faulkner did with the Mississippi . . . weaving a complete history," Jack Butler stated in the *New York Times Book Review*. "None of this would matter if he were not a poet, a resonant scene-setter and a master of voice, but he is; and since the West figures so strongly in our vision of what it means to be American, Mr. McMurtry's labor is, I think, essential literature."

Growing Up in the West

McMurtry was born June 3, 1936, in Wichita Falls, Texas—a sparsely populated, rural community in the north central part of the state. Both his father and grandfather were cattle ranchers, although even before McMurtry was born his father recognized that this way of life was quickly becoming a thing of the past. "Always I wondered, as a boy, at my father's tragic sense. What did he see that was so sad? We didn't have much, but we had as much as our neighbors. We even had better horses. What did he see? What he saw was that the frontier was over. . . . The time had come to awaken from the great dream of the West," McMurtry explained in the *New Republic*. "Even ninety years ago, when my father was born, anyone smart could see that cattle weren't going to last. In the fast twentieth century, it wouldn't do just to let steers graze around on the grass until they got fat enough for suburbanites to eat; such a method was too slow, too inefficient, too capital-intensive. Ranching and cowboying and all that my father and thousands like him lived would soon end—and now it has. But not the yearning for it."

McMurtry was more interested in reading than ranching during his childhood, but the family stories he heard as a boy nevertheless helped shape his life. In fact, in the *Los Angeles Times* he called writing "the ultimate analogue to my herding tradition. I herd words, I herd them into sentences and then I herd them into paragraphs and then I herd these paragraphs into books." McMurtry was an honor student at his high school in Archer City, Texas, but in general he did not find small-town

LARRY McMURTRY

THE PULITZER-PRIZE
WINNING AUTHOR OF
LONESOME DOVE

HORSEMAN, PASS BY

"Excellent...a tough, nostalgic narrative of a young man growing up in Texas."
—*THE NEW YORK TIMES*

The stark loneliness of cowboy life is portrayed in this 1961 novel about a teenager growing up in a small town in Texas.

life very stimulating. Instead, he claimed that his real education began when he entered college: "I grew up in a bookless town, in a bookless part of the state—when I stepped into a university library, at age eighteen, the whole of the world's literature lay before me unread, a country as vast, as promising, and, so far as I knew, as trackless as the West must have seemed to the first white men who looked upon it," McMurtry wrote in *In a Narrow Grave*.

McMurtry began his studies at North Texas State University in 1955, which he found to be "a very lively, interesting school, partly because at that time they had hired a number of really good teachers," he recalled in an interview with Si Dunn for the *Dallas News*. Since the university housed a prominent jazz school, McMurtry also noted that "they brought in all sorts of musicians

and road bands and things like that, that you wouldn't have at most state teachers colleges. So it was very stimulating in the years that I was there." During his college years, McMurtry published some of his first stories in the campus literary magazine, *Aresta*. After earning his bachelor of arts degree in English in 1958, McMurtry went on to receive his master's degree from Rice University in Houston in 1960.

In 1961, at the age of 25, McMurtry published his first novel, *Horseman, Pass By*. The story takes place on a rural ranch and in a small town much like the area where the author grew up. Lonnie Bannon, the teenaged narrator, describes what happens when deadly hoof-and-mouth disease strikes his grandfather's herd of cattle. Lonnie also struggles to define his personal relationships with his proud and stubborn grandfather Homer, his arrogant and irresponsible uncle Hud, and their caring housekeeper Halmea. Although the book did not sell particularly well at the time, it did earn positive reviews among critics of Western literature. In a letter to McMurtry's agent quoted in *Contemporary Authors*, for example, critic John Howard Griffin stated, "This is probably the starkest, most truthful, most terrible and yet beautiful treatment of [ranching country] I've seen. It will offend many, who prefer the glamour treatment—but it is a true portrait of the loneliness and pervading melancholy of cowboying; and of its compensations in nature, in human relationships." Like several of McMurtry's later novels, *Horseman, Pass By* was made into a successful feature film. The movie version, released as *Hud* in 1962, starred Paul Newman and won three Academy Awards.

McMurtry's second novel, *Leaving Cheyenne*, was published in 1963 to positive reviews, though fewer than 1,000 copies were sold at that time. It tells the life story of Molly Taylor, who becomes the main love interest of friends Gideon, a rancher, and Johnny, a cowboy. Molly eventually marries another man, but has a son with each of the friends. Writing in the *New York Times Book Review*, Walter Clemons called *Leaving Cheyenne* a "funny, wonderful, and heartbreaking book," and "a rarity among second novels in its exhilarating ease, assurance, and openness of feeling." McMurtry, however, stated in *New York* in 1974 that he considered his first two novels to be immature works: "It is perhaps worth pointing out that both [*Leaving Cheyenne*] and my first novel were written in the same year—my twenty-third. I revised around on both books for a while, but essentially both incorporate, at best, a 22-year-old's vision. . . . I don't want that vision back, nor am I overjoyed to see the literary results of it applauded." *Leaving Cheyenne* was made into a movie called *Lovin' Molly* in 1974, with Blythe Danner in the title role.

The Last Picture Show, McMurtry's third novel about small-town life in rural Texas, was published in 1966. It describes the struggles of a group of teenagers to reach adulthood in the fictional town of Thalia. "A sorrier place would be

LARRY McMURTRY

Pulitzer Prize-Winning Author of *Lonesome Dove*

POCKET BOOKS FICTION 75380●0 $5.99 U.S. $6.99 CAN.

Leaving Cheyenne

"A rarity...funny, wonderful, heartbreaking, exhilarating." —*The New York Times Book Review*

Written when McMurtry was twenty-three years old, this 1963 novel tells of a woman who is loved by two friends, has sons by each of them, but eventually marries someone else.

hard to find," Thomas Lask explained in the *New York Times.* "It is desiccated and shabby physically, mean and small-minded spiritually. McMurtry is an expert in anatomizing its suffocating and dead-end character." Sex becomes an outlet for frustration and boredom for the people of Thalia, which stirred up some controversy at the time of the novel's publication. In an article for *Western American Literature,* however, Charles D. Peavy defended McMurtry's graphic portrayal of teenage sexuality, stating: "Some of McMurtry's sexual scenes are highly symbolic, all are important thematically, and none should be taken as sensationalism . . . neither Updike nor Salinger has been successful as McMurtry in describing the gnawing ache that accompanies adolescent sexuality."

In 1972, McMurtry admitted in the *Colonial Times* that the fictional portrait of his hometown in *The Last Picture Show* was "too bitter." Archer City "had not been cruel to me, only honestly indifferent, and my handling of many of the characters in the book represented a failure of generosity for which I blame no one but myself." When an opportunity arose to work on the script for the movie version of *The Last Picture Show,* McMurtry collaborated with director Peter Bogdanovich and created a more sympathetic portrait. The movie, starring Jeff Bridges, Timothy Bottoms, and Cybill Shepherd, was filmed in black and white in Archer City. It won three Academy Awards in 1972, including one for best screenplay.

During the period when he was writing his early novels, McMurtry pursued additional graduate studies at Stanford University on a Stegner fellowship, and then returned to Rice, where he taught creative writing from 1963 to 1969. Throughout the 1960s, as he continued to build his literary reputation, McMurtry also revealed his self-deprecating sense of humor. For instance, he was often spotted wearing a black sweatshirt that said "Minor Regional Novelist" on the front. Much to his publishers' relief, however, he lost the shirt in a laundromat around 1970.

Moving away from Texas

In 1970, at age 33, McMurtry left his home state. He gave up his teaching position and moved to Washington, D.C., to open a rare book store, called Booked Up, in the city's exclusive Georgetown district. He explained that he enjoyed combining the social activity of selling books with the solitary activity of writing them. The change of scenery soon became apparent in his fiction, as he stopped writing about rural Texas and instead embarked upon what some critics referred to as his "urban trilogy": *Moving On, All My Friends Are Going to Be Strangers,* and *Terms of Endearment.* The main characters in all three books are adults who live in urban Houston. In *Moving On,* which was less favorably reviewed than his earlier novels, McMurtry compares the relationships of several couples over time as they travel around the West somewhat aimlessly. In *All My Friends Are Going to Be Strangers,* he introduces frustrated novelist Danny Deck and chronicles his relationships with several women.

Terms of Endearment became the most popular segment of the trilogy. The main characters include Aurora Greenway, an elegant but cantankerous widow who is pursued by many humble suitors, and her daughter Emma Horton, a simple woman struggling in an unhappy marriage. Although much of the story is somewhat comical, in the end Emma dies of cancer. While critics praised McMurtry's writing throughout, some found the ending a bit jarring. According to Robert Towers in the *New York Times Book Review,* "The final scenes between the dying Emma and her stricken boys are the most affecting in the book, but the ending—a real tear-jerker—dangles from the rest of the novel like a broken tail." *Terms of Endearment* was also made into a feature film, which was directed by James L. Brooks and starred Shirley MacLaine, Debra Winger, and Jack Nicholson. The movie won five Academy Awards, including one for best picture of 1983.

According to McMurtry, *Terms of Endearment* marked a turning point in his fiction, when he began moving away from Texas as his main setting. Although the characters in the novel live in Houston, they provide an outsiders' view since none of them are originally from Texas. "I lived in Texas quite a while, and for my own creative purposes I had kind of exhausted it," McMurtry told Dunn. "Texas is not an inexhaustible region." In the *Atlantic,* he explained that he had covered the major issues affecting Texans in his earlier novels: "The move off the land is now virtually completed, and that was the great subject that Texas offered writers of my generation. The one basic subject it offers us now is loneliness, and one can only ring the changes on that so many times."

Beginning in 1978—eight years after he had moved away from his home state—McMurtry published three consecutive novels that were set elsewhere, *Somebody's Darling, Cadillac Jack,* and *The Desert Rose.* The first book is set in Hollywood, a place McMurtry became familiar with during the filming of his novels. It tells the story of Jill Peel, a young director who is suddenly very much in demand, and her struggle to balance a longtime friendship with her newfound fame. A *Publishers Weekly* reviewer praised McMurtry's realistic and complex portrait of Jill, calling *Somebody's Darling* "an endearing, exasperating, sometimes funny, sometimes sad account of a woman who never quite gets it all together." *Cadillac Jack,* told in first person by travelling antiques dealer Jack McGriff, provides a satirical view of the elite social circles of Washington, D.C.

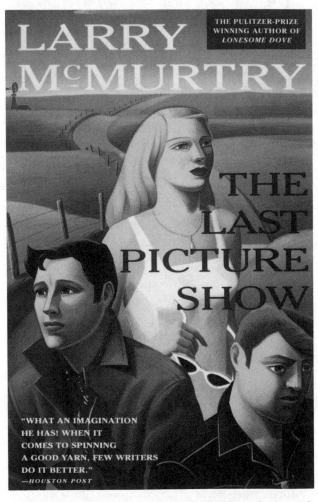

The author's third novel, written in 1966, deals with the boredom and frustration several teenagers face while growing up in a small town in Texas.

In *The Desert Rose,* McMurtry again takes the female point of view effectively. The novel follows a character named Harmony during a week when she loses her job as a Las Vegas showgirl, gets swindled by her boyfriend, and argues with her teenaged daughter, Pepper, who wants to drop out of school to become a dancer. Despite these trials, however, Harmony remains optimistic. "Women are always the most admirable characters in my novels," the author told Patrick Bennett in *Talking with Texas Writers: Twelve Interviews.* "I feel I write about them well, but that's not necessarily to say that I understand them." McMurtry originally intended the story to be a screenplay about the dying craft of Las Vegas showgirls, but he enjoyed writing in Harmony's voice so much that he soon realized it would become a novel. In fact, he completed the book in just three weeks, during a break from his work on the book that would change his status forever: *Lonesome Dove.*

Reinventing the Western

Lonesome Dove, an 800-page epic published in 1985, was a phenomenal success by any standard. It sold 300,000 copies in hardcover and 1.2 million in paperback, it was awarded the Pulitzer Prize, and it launched one of the most successful television miniseries of all time. It also had a predictable effect on McMurtry's life, as Jones reported in *Newsweek:* "McMurtry went from Minor Regional Novelist to Famous American Author in one shot. He was deluged with fan mail, and curiosity seekers made it impossible for him to visit his own bookstores." At one point, the author even learned that several men across the country had been impersonating him in order to seduce women or cheat people out of money.

The book marked yet another new direction in McMurtry's work: chronicling Texas history. McMurtry explained in the *New York Times Book Review* that the novel "grew out of my sense of having heard my uncles talk about the extraordinary days when the range was open. In my boyhood I could talk to men who touched this experience and knew it, even if they only saw the tag end of it. I wanted to see if I could make that real, make it work fictionally." *Lonesome Dove* tells the story of two former Texas Rangers who, having helped settle the West, decide to drive a herd of cattle to Montana in search of the last unsettled country. Woodrow Call is a planner, silent and tense, while his partner Gus McCrae is the oppo-

site, talking constantly but often insightfully. They both seem to recognize, somewhat sadly, that the romantic era of cattle drives, outlaws, and Indian wars is all but over.

At the same time his characters mourn the loss of the frontier, however, McMurtry consistently presents a realistic picture of the hardships they must endure in this way of life. On their journey, the heroes encounter violent thunderstorms, dangerous quicksand, a cloud of locusts, a nest of angry water moccasins, and a blizzard. "You can easily believe that this is how it really was to be there, to live, to suffer and rejoice, then and there," George Garrett wrote in the *Chicago Tribune Book World.* "And thus, the reader is most subtly led to see where the literary conventions of the Western came from, how they came to be in the first place, and which are true and which are false."

CBS spent over $16 million to produce *Lonesome Dove* as a television miniseries in 1989. The network hired top actors—many of whom rarely consented to appear on TV—shot on location in remote areas of Texas and New Mexico for three months, and even checked against photographs in archives to be sure the costumes were historically accurate. The miniseries starred Tommy Lee Jones as Call and Robert Duvall as McCrae, as well as Ricky Schroeder as Call's unacknowledged son Newt and Angelica Huston as McCrae's mistress Clara. "In terms of epic sweep, depth of characterization, superlative acting and unflinching fidelity to its source, this eight-hour adaptation proves what television can achieve when it forgets that it's only television," Harry F. Waters stated in *Newsweek.* "Scriptwriter William Wittliff, a fellow Texan and old friend of the author, was savvy enough to lift most of the talk straight from the novel. The result is the rarest of video phenomena—a mini-series that engages the ear as well as the eye." The success of *Lonesome Dove,* which came at a time when Westerns were not considered commercially viable, paved the way for the return of the genre to television.

McMurtry went on to complete two other historical novels that contrasted the reality of the Old West with popular myths—*Anything for Billy,* published in 1988, and *Buffalo Girls,* published in 1990. In these books, McMurtry made a conscious effort to expose the myths surrounding cowboys: "If you actually read the biography of any of the

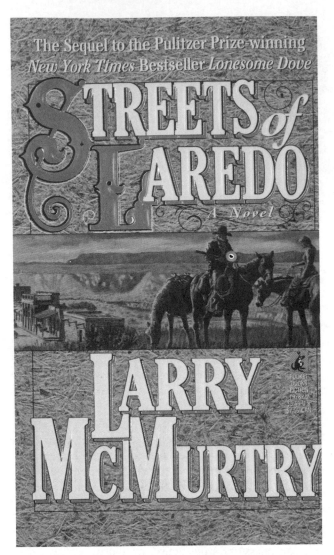

The Sequel to the Pulitzer Prize-winning
New York Times Bestseller *Lonesome Dove*
STREETS of LAREDO
A Novel
LARRY McMURTRY

While McMurtry recovered quickly from quadruple heart bypass surgery, it took writing this 1993 sequel to *Lonesome Dove* to help him recover from a lack of inspiration.

famous gunfighters," he explained in *Contemporary Authors*, "they led very drab, mostly very repetitive, not very exciting lives. But people cherish a certain vision, because it fulfills psychological needs. People need to believe that cowboys are simple, strong and free, and not twisted, fascistic and dumb, as many cowboys I've known have been." *Anything for Billy* tells the story of legendary outlaw Billy the Kid, although in the book he is anything but heroic. Instead, McMurtry's character is homely, nearsighted, stupid, and mean. But since Eastern pulp fiction writer Ben Sippy narrates the story, Billy's exploits seem larger than life.

Buffalo Girls features many famous characters from the Old West, including Calamity Jane, Wild Bill Hickok, Buffalo Bill Cody, and Sitting Bull. But McMurtry shows them many years after their prime, as they join together to act out their past deeds in a travelling Wild West Show. "Almost everyone in *Buffalo Girls* knows himself and his world to be on the verge of extinction," Susan Fromberg Schaeffer noted in the *New York Times Book Review*. "They begin to understand that they have outlived their time. The question then becomes whether they can find a new way to live, or at least a new meaning that will justify their lives. That most of them fail to do so should be no surprise, because the Wild West . . . is the childhood of our country and, like all childhoods, it must pass." *Buffalo Girls* was filmed as a television miniseries by CBS for release in 1995, starring Anjelica Huston, Melanie Griffith, and Sam Elliott.

Revisiting Favorite Characters

During the late 1980s and early 1990s, McMurtry kept extremely busy. He opened new Booked Up branches in Dallas, Houston, and California, bought a ranch in his hometown in Texas, and continued writing Hollywood screenplays. As he explained in the *Dictionary of Literary Biography*, his many interests involved a lot of travel: "I have a little track that I follow about once a month. I start in Washington and go to Texas, Arizona, and California in easy stages. I check on my stores and see family and friends." In 1989, he gave up some of his privacy to become president of the American chapter of PEN, a prestigious international writers' organization. At the same time, McMurtry published sequels to four of his popular novels. Partly due to this decision, and partly due to the successful film versions of his earlier work, he began to receive some criticism for being too commercial. However, two of his sequels earned positive reviews, and all four served the author's—and his readers'—desire to revisit favorite characters.

Texasville, the 1987 sequel to *The Last Picture Show*, came about because of McMurtry's work on the movie version of his 1966 novel about small-town life. "I discovered the real reason why writers are ill-advised to script their own books . . . in scrutinizing his old text time after time, the writer will suddenly glimpse the book he ought to have written," McMurtry admitted in *Film Flam: Essays on*

Hollywood. "In the case of *The Last Picture Show,* the better book I discovered had to do with the older couples in the story. While Peter [Bog-danovich] was working out his fascination with youth, I was beginning to develop mine with middle age." *Texasville* joins the residents of Thalia thirty years later, as they prepare for the town's centennial celebration. Most of the characters still feel stifled and unhappy, and the town is declining rapidly after experiencing a brief period of prosperity during the oil boom. In the *Times Literary Supplement,* critic John Clute remarked upon "the gleaming ferocity McMurtry has at his command, the extravagance of wit and comic invention that makes every page of *Texasville* bristle with such hilarious and unstoppable despair."

Some Can Whistle, the 1989 sequel to *All My Friends Are Going to Be Strangers,* rejoins novelist Danny Deck after he has become extremely wealthy from the success of a television sitcom based on his work. Fame and fortune are not enough to make him happy, however, as he fails to connect emotionally with his long-lost daughter. The novel was less well-received than McMurtry's previous books, with Paul Gray of *Time* calling it an "uncharacteristically spotty performance." *The Evening Star,* the 1992 sequel to *Terms of Endearment,* picks up the story of Aurora Greenway several years after her daughter's death, as she struggles with the problems of her three adult grandchildren. This book was also not particularly well-received, with a *Time* reviewer calling it "big, flabby, and aimless."

At first, McMurtry had no intention of writing a sequel to *Lonesome Dove.* In fact, he agreed to let CBS develop its own sequel to the successful miniseries, *Return to Lonesome Dove,* in 1993 without his input. He changed his mind, however, after undergoing quadruple heart bypass surgery. "I went about the physical recovery very quickly," McMurtry explained to Malcolm Jones in *Newsweek,* "and went about my life doing the things I had done—running bookshops, writing screenplays, writing fiction, traveling, lecturing, etc. And it just sort of gradually emptied out of content, until it was like a ghost doing these things, not me at all, until there was nothing but an outline." During this difficult period, McMurtry claimed that *Streets of Laredo* suddenly came to him, as if it had been "faxed to me by my former self." The novel takes place fifteen years after the original, and finds Woodrow Call chasing an evil young

Sam Bottoms stars as Billy, the deaf-mute boy in the 1970 Oscar-winning film *The Last Picture Show.*

Mexican train robber. While some reviewers were inevitably disappointed with the sequel, Jones called it "a splendid addition to the literary portrait of his native Texas and the West that McMurtry's been creating for three decades. It's also one of his most affectingly melancholy books. Its heroes are frail, and their ideals are often compromised." Despite the fact that the network had already launched its own sequel—which killed off some characters who were still alive in McMurtry's version—CBS also filmed *Streets of Laredo* as a miniseries for release in 1995, starring James Garner, Sissy Spacek, and Sam Shepard.

Explaining the Writing Process

In addition to publishing numerous popular and well-received novels, McMurtry has written and spoken extensively on the craft of writing. "I consider it a process of discovery, writing a novel," the author explained to Bennett. "But I always start with an ending. My novels begin with a scene that forms itself in my consciousness, which I recognize as a culminating scene . . . and the writing of the novel is a process in which I discover how these people got themselves to this scene." "First, I do a long draft in which I discover the book I am developing. I let characters come out and take me wherever they want to take me," McMurtry elaborated in his interview with Dunn. "In the second draft, I remove redundancies and tighten. And the third draft I consider a polishing draft. I attend to style. So I participate in the emotions of a book three times. It's like a husband and wife having the same fight over and over again." In the preface to *Cadillac Jack*, he concluded: "Once I finish a book, it vanishes from my mental picture as rapidly as the road runner in the cartoon. I don't expect to see it or think about it again for a decade or so, if ever."

Despite his own success, McMurtry expressed reservations about the state of the publishing industry and its effect on young writers. "Publishers have become indifferent toward discovering and developing young literary talent," he told Dunn. "The lust for the blockbuster is getting out of hand. . . . Writing novels has become a process of getting the right manuscripts into the hands of the right people at the right time." "I really don't envy young writers at all," McMurtry continued. "I know several young writers who have written five or six novels lately without getting any of them published. It was easy to publish a novel in the late Fifties and early Sixties; a publisher would publish a young writer out of a belief in his talent, knowing that the first book or two wouldn't make any money. Now is a very difficult time for a young writer to develop." Nevertheless, McMurtry professed his confidence in the intellectual abilities of future generations, claiming in *Contemporary Authors* that they "may keep something of the frontier spirit even though the frontier is lost. What they may keep is a sense of daring and independence, transferred from the life of action to the life of the mind."

■ Works Cited

Atlantic, March, 1975.

Bennett, Patrick, "Larry McMurtry: Thalia, Houston, and Hollywood," *Talking with Texas Writers: Twelve Interviews*, Texas A & M University Press, 1980.

Butler, Jack, review of *Buffalo Girls*, New York Times Book Review, October 7, 1990, p. 3.

Clemons, Walter, "The Last Word: An Overlooked Novel," *New York Times Book Review*, August 15, 1971, p. 39.

Clemons, "Saga of a Cattle Drive," *Newsweek*, June 3, 1985, p. 74.

Clute, John, "Ghosts at the Feast," *Times Literary Supplement*, September 18, 1987, p. 978.

Colonial Times, December 21-January 12, 1972.

Contemporary Authors, New Revision Series, Volume 43, Gale, 1990, p. 306.

Dunn, Si, "Larry McMurtry Moves On," *Dallas News*, January 18, 1976.

English, Sarah, "Larry McMurtry," *Dictionary of Literary Biography Yearbook*, Gale, 1987, p. 265.

Garrett, George, review of *Lonesome Dove, Chicago Tribune Book World*, June 9, 1985.

Gray, Paul, "Movie-Cute," *Time*, October 16, 1989, p. 89.

Griffin, John Howard, quoted in *Contemporary Authors, New Revision Series*, Volume 43, Gale, 1990, p. 306.

"Jokey but Not Funny," *Time*, May 25, 1992, p. 73.

Jones, Malcolm, "The Ghost Writer at Home on the Range: Larry McMurtry Revisits the Old West for a Bleak and Brilliant Sequel to *Lonesome Dove*," *Newsweek*, August 2, 1993, p. 52.

Lask, Thomas, "Dead End," *New York Times*, December 3, 1966, p. 37.

Los Angeles Times, September 28, 1990, p. F1.

McMurtry, Larry, preface to *Cadillac Jack*, Simon & Schuster, 1982.

McMurtry, *Film Flam: Essays on Hollywood*, Simon & Schuster, 1987.

McMurtry, "How the West Was Won or Lost: The Revisionists' Failure of Imagination," *New Republic*, October 22, 1990, p. 32.

McMurtry, *In a Narrow Grave: Essays on Texas*, Encino Press, 1968.

New York, April 29, 1974.

Peavy, Charles D., "Coming of Age in Texas: The Novels of Larry McMurtry," *Western American Literature*, Fall, 1969, p. 171.

Schaeffer, Susan Fromberg, "Lonesome Jane," *New York Times Book Review*, October 7, 1990, p. 3.

Sheppard, R. Z., "It's a Long, Long Tale Awinding," *Time*, June 10, 1985, p. 79.

Review of *Somebody's Darling, Publishers Weekly*, September 18, 1978, p. 162.

Towers, Robert, "An Oddly Misshapen Novel by a Highly Accomplished Novelist," *New York Times Book Review*, October 19, 1975, p. 4.

Waters, Harry F., "How the West Was Once: *Lonesome Dove* Shakes the Dust off a Trail-Weary TV Genre," *Newsweek,* February 6, 1989.

■ For More Information See

BOOKS

Contemporary Literary Criticism, Volume 44, Gale, 1987.
Peavy, Charles D., *Larry McMurtry,* Twayne, 1977.

—Sketch by Laurie Collier Hillstrom

Arthur Miller

■ Personal

Born October 17, 1915, in New York, NY; son of Isidore (a manufacturer) and Augusta (Barnett) Miller; married Mary Grace Slattery, 1940 (divorced, 1956); married Marilyn Monroe (an actress), June, 1956 (divorced, 1961); married Ingeborg Morath (a photojournalist), 1962; children: (first marriage) Jane Ellen, Robert Arthur; (third marriage) Rebecca Augusta, Daniel. *Education:* University of Michigan, A.B., 1938. *Hobbies and other interests:* Carpentry, farming.

■ Addresses

Agent—International Creative Management, 304 East 65th St., Apt. 5A, New York, NY 10021–6783.

■ Career

Writer, 1938—. Associate of Federal Theater Project, 1938; author of radio plays, 1939–1944; dramatist and essayist, 1944—. Also worked in an automobile parts warehouse, the Brooklyn Navy Yard, and a box factory. Resident lecturer, University of Michigan, 1973–74.

■ Awards, Honors

Avery Hopwood Awards from the University of Michigan, 1936, for *Honors at Dawn,* and 1937, for *No Villain: They Too Arise;* Bureau of New Plays Prize from Theatre Guild of New York, 1938; Theatre Guild National Prize, 1944, for *The Man Who Had All the Luck;* Drama Critics Circle Awards, 1947, for *All My Sons,* 1949, for *Death of a Salesman,* and 1953, for *The Crucible;* Donaldson Awards, 1947, for *All My Sons,* 1949, for *Death of a Salesman,* and 1953, for *The Crucible;* Pulitzer Prize for drama, 1949, for *Death of a Salesman;* National Association of Independent Schools Award, 1954; L.H.D. from the University of Michigan, 1956, and Carnegie–Mellon University, 1970; Obie Award from *Village Voice,* 1958, for *The Crucible;* American Academy of Arts and Letters gold medal, 1959; Anglo–American Award, 1966; Emmy Award, National Academy of Television Arts and Sciences, 1967, for *Death of a Salesman;* Brandeis University creative arts award, 1969; George Foster Peabody Award, 1981, for *Playing for Time;* John F. Kennedy Award for Lifetime Achievement, 1984; Algur Meadow award, Southern Methodist University, 1991.

■ Writings

PLAYS

Honors at Dawn, first produced in Ann Arbor, MI, 1936.

No Villain: They Too Arise, first produced in Ann Arbor, 1937.

The Man Who Had All the Luck, produced on Broadway at Forest Theatre, November 23, 1944.

All My Sons (produced on Broadway at Coronet Theatre, January 29, 1947; also see below), Reynal, 1947.

Death of a Salesman (produced on Broadway at Morosco Theatre, February 10, 1949; also see below), Viking, 1949, published as *Death of a Salesman: Text and Criticism,* edited by Gerald Weales, Penguin, 1977.

(Adaptor) Henrik Ibsen, *An Enemy of the People* (produced on Broadway at Broadhurst Theatre, December 28, 1950), Viking, 1951.

The Crucible (produced on Broadway at Martin Beck Theatre, January 22, 1953), Viking, 1953, published as *The Crucible: Text and Criticism,* edited by Weales, Viking, 1977.

A View from the Bridge, [and] *A Memory of Two Mondays* (produced together on Broadway at Coronet Theatre, September 29, 1955; also see below), Viking, 1955, published separately, Dramatists Play Service, 1956, revised version of *A View from the Bridge* (produced Off–Broadway at Sheridan Square Playhouse, January 28, 1965; also see below), Cresset, 1956.

After the Fall (produced on Broadway at American National Theatre and Academy, January 23, 1964), Viking, 1964.

Incident at Vichy (produced on Broadway at American National Theatre and Academy, December 3, 1964), Viking, 1965.

The Price (produced on Broadway at Morosco Theatre, February 7, 1968; also see below), Viking, 1968.

The Creation of the World and Other Business (produced on Broadway at Shubert Theatre, November 30, 1972), Viking, 1972.

Up from Paradise, with music by Stanley Silverman (musical version of *The Creation of the World and Other Business;* first produced in Ann Arbor at Trueblood Theatre, directed and narrated by Miller, April, 1974; produced Off–Broadway at Jewish Repertory Theater, October 25, 1983), Viking, 1978.

The Archbishop's Ceiling (produced in Washington, DC, at Eisenhower Theatre, Kennedy Center for the Performing Arts, April 30, 1977), Dramatists Play Service, 1976.

The American Clock (first produced in Charleston, SC, at Dock Street Theatre, 1980; produced on Broadway at Harold Clurman Theatre, 1980), Viking, 1980.

Elegy for a Lady [and] *Some Kind of Love Story* (one–acts; produced together under the title *Two–Way Mirror* in New Haven, CT, at Long Wharf Theatre, 1983), published separately by Dramatists Play Service, 1984.

Playing for Time (stage adaptation of screenplay; produced in England at Netherbow Art Centre, August, 1986; also see below), Dramatic Publishing, 1985.

Danger: Memory! Two Plays: "I Can't Remember Anything" and "Clara" (one–acts; produced on Broadway at Mitzi E. Newhouse Theatre, Lincoln Center for the Performing Arts, February 8, 1987), Grove, 1987.

(Also author of introduction) *The Archbishop's Ceiling* [and] *The American Clock,* Grove, 1989, second play published as *The American Clock: A Vaudeville,* Dramatists Play Service, 1992.

The Last Yankee, Dramatists Play Service, 1991, published with an essay about theatre language, Penguin, 1994.

The Ride Down Mt. Morgan, Penguin, 1991.

Broken Glass, Penguin, 1994.

SCREENPLAYS

(With others) *The Story of G.I. Joe,* produced by United Artists, 1945.

The Witches of Salem, produced by Kingsley–International, 1958.

The Misfits (produced by United Artists, 1961; also see below), published as *The Misfits: An Original Screenplay Directed by John Huston,* edited by George P. Garrett, Irvington, 1982.

The Price (based on play of same title), produced by United Artists, 1969.

The Hook, produced by MCA, 1975.

Fame (also see below), produced by National Broadcasting Company (NBC–TV), 1978.

Playing for Time, produced by Columbia Broadcasting System (CBS–TV), 1980.

(Also author of preface) *Everybody Wins,* Grove, 1990.

FICTION

Focus (novel), Reynal, 1945, reprinted with introduction by the author, Arbor House, 1984.

The Misfits (novella; also see below), Viking, 1961.

Jane's Blanket (juvenile), Collier, 1963.

I Don't Need You Anymore (stories), Viking, 1967.

"The Misfits" and Other Stories, Scribner, 1987.

NONFICTION

Situation Normal (reportage on the army), Reynal, 1944.

In Russia, with photographs by wife, Ingeborg Morath, Viking, 1969.

In the Country, with photographs by Morath, Viking, 1977.

The Theatre Essays of Arthur Miller, edited by Robert A. Martin, Viking, 1978.

Chinese Encounters, with photographs by Morath, Viking, 1979.

Salesman in Beijing, with photographs by Morath, Viking, 1984.

Timebends: A Life (autobiography), Grove, 1987.

Homely Girl: A Life, with etchings by Louise Bourgeois, Peter Blum Edition, 1992.

(With Steve Centola) *Arthur Miller in Conversation* (interviews), Northouse & Northouse, 1993.

OMNIBUS VOLUMES

(Also author of introduction) *Arthur Miller's Collected Plays* (contains *All My Sons, Death of a Salesman, The Crucible, A Memory of Two Mondays,* and *A View from the Bridge*), Viking, 1957.

The Portable Arthur Miller (includes *Death of a Salesman, The Crucible, Incident at Vichy, The Price, The Misfits, Fame,* and *In Russia*), edited by Harold Clurman, Viking, 1971.

(Also author of introduction) *Collected Plays, Volume II,* Viking, 1980.

OTHER

Contributor of plays to collections, including *Cross–Section 1944,* Fischer, 1944; *Radio's Best Plays,* Greenberg, 1947; *One-Act: Eleven Short Plays of the Modern Theatre,* Grove, 1961; and *Six Great Modern Plays,* Dell, 1964. Contributor of essays, commentary, and short stories to periodicals, including *Collier's, New York Times, Theatre Arts, Holiday, Nation, Esquire,* and *Atlantic.* The University of Michigan at Ann Arbor, the University of Texas at Austin, and the New York Public Library have collections of Miller's papers.

■ Adaptations

All My Sons was filmed as a movie by Universal in 1948 and as a television special by the Corporation for Public Broadcasting in 1987; *Death of a Salesman* was filmed as a movie by Columbia in 1951 and as a television special by CBS–TV in 1985; *The Crucible* was filmed in France by Kingsley–International in 1958; *A View from the Bridge* was filmed by Continental in 1962; *After the Fall* was filmed as a television special by NBC–TV in 1969.

■ Sidelights

After his first Broadway play failed, Arthur Miller vowed never to write another play. But within a few years, Miller was hailed as one of the world's most important playwrights, following successful Broadway productions of *All My Sons* in 1947 and *Death of a Salesman* in 1949. Since that time, Miller has solidified his reputation as one of the finest American playwrights of the post–World War II era with the plays *The Crucible, A View from the Bridge, The Price,* and several others. Miller's plays capture the often tragic failure of the individual to come to terms with the complex social forces around him. Though his situations are quintessentially American, exploring the tensions within Puritan New England, a salesman's family in Brooklyn, and an Italian–American community, for example, the issues his plays confront are universal. Miller's plays have been produced around the world and remain popular decades after their first productions.

For a time, Miller's real life actions drew as much attention as those actions he set in motion on the stage. Miller became an international celebrity in 1956 when he married the film star and sex symbol Marilyn Monroe. Though the marriage kept Miller from devoting much energy to his play writing, he did write a screenplay for the movie *The Misfits,* with a woman's role written especially for Monroe. Miller's notoriety was strengthened in 1957, when he was called before a Congressional Committee on Un–American Activities and asked to name people who had attended a 1947 meeting of Communist writers which he had attended. Miller's refusal to name names earned him the charge of contempt of Congress and newspaper headlines, and echoed the themes of his earlier play, *The Crucible.* By the 1960s, however, Miller felt out of touch with American culture, though he continued to play the role of public intellectual, speaking at antiwar protests, attending the 1968 Democratic Party convention in Chicago, and becoming the president of PEN International, a human rights organization. Though his plays are still produced in the United States, they are more popular with Europeans, who seem more comfortable with Miller's calls for moral commitment and community solidarity in the face of the bewildering odds presented by modern society.

The Call of Idealism

Miller's paternal grandparents had left Germany for America before the turn of the century, leaving Miller's father, Isidore, behind with relatives. When the family at last earned the money for his ticket, Miller remembers in his autobiography, *Timebends,* Isidore "was put on a train for the port of Hamburg [Germany] with a tag around his neck asking that he be delivered, if the stranger would be so kind, to a certain ship sailing for New York on a certain date." Amazingly, Isidore found his family and after several months of schooling was put to work operating a sewing machine in the family business. When he was thirty–two, Isidore met and married Augusta Barnett, a teacher, and the couple had their second son, Arthur Miller, on October 17, 1915.

Following family tradition, Isidore opened his own company, the Miltex Coat and Suit Company, shortly after the end of World War I, and employed many members of his large family. Miller's first memories are of the pride he felt in being shown around the clothing shops, sensing his importance as "the owner's son" in the eyes of the workers. Miller describes himself as a "funny looking" kid in *Timebends,* "with ears that stuck out and forced me to endure my [uncle] Moe's inevitable salutation when he came to visit, 'Pull in your ears, we're coming to a tunnel.'" Miller biked to school in then–fashionable Harlem and, to his mother's dismay, displayed far more interest in athletics than in school. When the Millers moved to Brooklyn in 1928, following a downturn in the family's business, the proximity to the amusement park of Coney Island, football, and neighborhood fun seemed far more compelling than school. Miller described the mood of his friends in a 1955 article for *Holiday* magazine: "Because the idea all of us subscribed to was to get out onto the football field with the least possible scholastic interference, I can fairly say we were none of us encumbered by anything resembling a thought."

On a sunny day in the summer of 1932, Miller stood watching some boys play a game of handball against the wall of a local drugstore and worrying about the troubles his family had coping with the economic downturn of the 1930s. "On this particular day there were no accidents," Miller recalled in *Timebends,* "and sunlight shone over the street as I straddled my bike watching the game while an older boy . . . stood beside me explaining that although it might not be evident to the naked eye, there were really two classes of people in society, the workers and the employers." So began Miller's introduction to socialism, an ideology that appealed to many Americans in an era when the dream of success promised by capitalism had turned into a nightmare. "For me," wrote Miller, "as for millions of young people then and since, the concept of a classless society had a disarming sweetness that called forth the generosity of youth. The *true* condition of man, it seemed, was the complete opposite of the competitive system I had assumed was normal, with all its mutual hatreds and conniving."

Disappointed with his father's inability to cope with economic failure and uncertain about his own ability to make a living, Miller found an ideal in Marxism. It was a romance that could only happen to an adolescent, he thought later. "Adolescence is a kind of aching that only time can cure, a molten state without settled form, but when at the same time the order of society has also melted and old authority has shown its incompetence and hollowness, the way to maturity is radicalism," he wrote in *Timebends.* Miller's romance with Marxism did not last, though critics have found in his plays, especially *Death of a Salesman,* a critique of capitalism that charges that the pursuit of wealth is deadening to people's souls. What remained, however, was a powerful belief that society could provide for the fulfillment of the individual, instead of creating anxiety and despair.

Coming of Age in the Great Depression

Miller's poor academic record came back to haunt him in the early 1930s, when he was refused admission to both Cornell University and the University of Michigan. Failing to get into college, he had to deal with the problem that faced most Americans: earning a living in the deepest economic depression the country had ever seen. For Miller the task was made harder because he was Jewish and so many of the want ads specified that they wanted "Gentiles," "Protestants," or "Catholics." Finding an ad without such a restriction, Miller applied for a stockboy job at the Chadick–Delamater auto parts warehouse. He got the job after a friend's father intervened, but nothing

Arthur Kennedy, Karl Malden, Beth Merril, Ed Begley, and Lois Wheeler starred in the 1947 adaptation of *All My Sons*, which tells the story of a family torn apart by lies and greed.

could shield him from the anti–Semitic attitudes of his Irish boss and coworkers. This was not the first time Miller faced bigotry, though it was one of the most blatant, and the experience in the warehouse found its way into the play *A Memory of Two Mondays*. But a job was a job, and Miller saved thirteen of the fifteen dollars he earned each week, saving to pay his way through the University of Michigan, which he had finally convinced to accept him on a provisional basis.

The University of Michigan in Ann Arbor, with its intellectual atmosphere, its impressive buildings, and its lush campus, was a long way from the bustle and despair of Brooklyn, and Miller fell in love with his new surroundings. Working several jobs, Miller still found time to write and soon changed his major from journalism to English, where he was encouraged by Professor Kenneth

Rowe. Tempted by a university prize, Miller decided to take one spring break to write a play, something he knew almost nothing about. Having seen just a few plays, he had to ask a housemate how long an act in a play lasted. Writing furiously, he penned an autobiographical drama about an industrial conflict and the relationship between a father and his two sons. In the spring of 1936 this play, *Honors at Dawn*, earned the Avery Hopwood Award and a $250 cash prize. Miller was thrilled, though he later wrote in *Timebends:* "Hardly had I cashed the Hopwood check when I started the habit, which I have never lost, of worrying whether I had anything left to write."

With another Hopwood Award for *No Villain: They Too Arise*, a Bureau of New Plays Prize from the Theatre Guild of New York, and a college degree,

Miller soon found writing jobs in New York City. He worked briefly for the Federal Theater Project, then wrote a series of radio dramas, which provided good practice in writing dialogue and constructing scenes, though Miller soon tired of the formulaic plots and the simple morals that he was required to write. "I despise radio," Miller later told *New York Times* interviewer John K. Hutchens. "Every emotion in a radio script has to have a tag. It's like playing a scene in a dark closet." Miller sought to write more serious plays in his free time, but was dissatisfied with the results until he began a play called *The Man Who Had All the Luck,* which tells the story of a garage mechanic for whom everything always turns out right without his even trying, while his striving brother meets with continual misfortune. The play made it to Broadway, where it failed miserably and closed after just four performances. "Standing at the back of the house during the single performance I could bear to watch, I could blame nobody," remembered Miller. "All I knew was that the whole thing was a well–meant botch, like music played on the wrong instruments in a false scale. I would never write another play, that was sure."

"I Would Never Write Another Play"

For two years Miller avoided plays, writing a nonfiction work called *Situation Normal,* which examined the lives and attitudes of ordinary soldiers going to battle in World War II, and a novel called *Focus,* which explored the irrationality of anti–Semitism. *Situation Normal* was well–received, earning Miller praise for his descriptive abilities and his reporting, and *Focus* sold more than 90,000 copies after its 1945 publication. The novel, writes Benjamin Nelson in *Arthur Miller: Portrait of a Playwright,* "tells the story of the macabre disorientation of a New York personnel executive" whose new eyeglasses make his look stereotypically Jewish. "This embarrassing new look rapidly leads to a series of situations in which he is increasingly persecuted and victimized by a world wherein he had considered himself secure."

By 1946, however, Miller was hard at work on another play, one suggested to him by an offhand remark made by the mother of his wife, Mary Grace Slattery, who he had met in college. "Mary's mother . . . had unknowingly triggered that play when she gossiped about a young girl somewhere in central Ohio who had turned her father in to

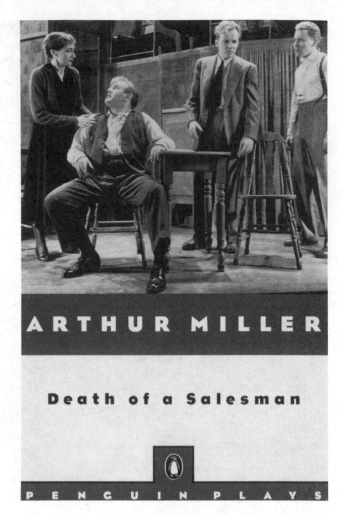

Recipient of the Pulitzer Prize for drama, this 1949 play criticizes the pursuit of wealth.

the FBI for having manufactured faulty aircraft parts during the war," Miller recalled in *Timebends.* Miller shifted the story, which became *All My Sons,* to tell of an aging businessman who sold defective merchandise to the army and then lied when he learned that the merchandise caused war planes to crash in battle, only to discover that one of his two sons died in one of the plane crashes. In *Arthur Miller: A Collection of Critical Essays,* Gerald Weales notes that the businessman, Joe Keller, is "an image of American success, who is destroyed when he is forced to see that image in another context—through the eyes of his idealist son." The irony in Joe Keller's tragedy is that, while pursuing economic success to support his family, he kills one son and alienates the other, who confronts the father, exclaiming "I never saw you as a man. I saw you as my father." The play is unabashedly moral, but Miller suggested in the introduction to *Arthur Miller's Collected Plays* that "It is an assertion not so much of a morality in terms of right and wrong, but of a moral world's being such because men cannot walk away from certain of their deeds."

Though some initial reviews complained about the play's moral didacticism, audiences were impressed with the powerful emotional drama that Miller had created. Nelson wrote: "*All My Sons* is a drama in the service of a message. Fortunately the message is dramatic and substantial, and the play is rooted in enough human conflict and complexity so that it never deteriorates into an illustrated editorial." *All My Sons* began its long run on Broadway on January 29, 1947, earning Miller his first New York Drama Critics Circle Award and enough money on royalties to finally consider himself a success. Miller moved his family to a new house in Brooklyn Heights and purchased a farm in rural Connecticut.

Success did not always sit well with Miller. People recognized him on the street, but their gaze made him feel "unnervingly artificial." He had drawn his characters from the working class but now he no longer had to work. (Trying to stay in touch with working people, he took a job assembling beer box dividers for minimum wage but was quickly bored into quitting.) He felt guilt at succeeding, but was aware that "guilt is a protective device to conceal one's happiness at surpassing others," he wrote in *Timebends,* and he continued: "I had been scratching on the glass from the outside for thirty-one years, until now I was scratching on it from the inside, trying to keep contact with the ordinary life from which my work had grown." Awash in uncertainty about his work, his marriage, and his identity, Miller prowled the waterfront of New York City, travelled to Italy, and wondered whether he would write again.

"I Am Not a Dime a Dozen!"

In April of 1948, Miller drove to his Connecticut farm and began construction of a ten–by–twelve foot writing shack while two lines of dialogue floated in his head, waiting to be transformed into a play. Finishing his building, he began to write. "I wrote all day until dark, and then I had dinner and went back and wrote until some hour in the darkness between midnight and four. . . . By the next morning I had done the first half, the first act or two. When I lay down to sleep I real-ized I had been weeping—my eyes still burned and my throat was sore from talking it all out and shouting and laughing," he remembered in *Timebends*. The play he was writing told the story of Willy Loman, an aging salesman, and of the dreams he had for his sons, Biff and Happy. It would be titled *Death of a Salesman.*

Death of a Salesman opened on Broadway at the Morosco Theater on February 10, 1949. The play centers on the emotional deterioration of Willy Loman as he grapples with the loss of his job and the failure of his two grown sons to achieve wealth and with it, presumably, happiness. Willy had championed a success ethic based on the cult of popularity, good looks, and a winning personality, yet sees that this ethic has left his sons unable to survive in the world. In a last desperate attempt to help his sons, Willy kills himself so that his boys can use the insurance money. Though the play is about a man's despair, Willy Loman asserts a vision of the individual that is ultimately hopeful. In his climactic scene, he thunders: "I am not a dime a dozen! I am Willy Loman." Nelson wrote: "Even as the audience slowly left the theater, still deeply jolted by the emotional experience they had just undergone, the critics of the eight major New York newspapers were formulating their unanimous and unreservedly enthusiastic responses. The performance of *Death of a Salesman* . . . was the first of 742 that would run deep into November of 1950. With his third produced play, Arthur Miller became a force to be reckoned with in the American theater."

Death of a Salesman has drawn critical praise ever since its introduction, as each audience finds anew something to appreciate in the play. American critics have lauded the play for revealing the peculiar neuroses at the core of the American psyche. Foreign audiences have responded to the play as well, for it has been produced successfully throughout Europe and, as Miller records in *Salesman in Beijing,* in communist China. The successful revival of *Death of A Salesman* in 1984, with Dustin Hoffman playing the role of Willy, is a testament to the play's lasting impact. "The very different tone and mood of the revival," commented Helterman, "marks the true test of a classic—a performance that can change to fit the tenor of the times and still not lose its dramatic power or grip on the audience."

Mary Warren, caught up in the paranoia, accuses Proctor of witchcraft in this 1953 performance of *The Crucible*.

Communists and Witches

Miller had always believed, he insisted in *Timebends,* "that art ought to be of use in changing society," and in the early 1950s much in American society seemed to need changing. Many national leaders, including Senator Joseph McCarthy and a young Congressman named Richard Nixon, perceived a threat of communist domination within the borders of the United States. Public figures from all walks of life, including many of Miller's friends and fellow artists, fell under suspicion of conspiring to overthrow the government. As the "Red Scare" hysteria mounted, scores of people were called before investigating committees to explain why, ten or twenty years before, they had attended meetings of Communist or socialist organizations. They were also asked to name others whom they had seen there. Miller wrote: "I saw the civilities of public life deftly stripped from the body politic like the wings of insects or birds by maniac children, and great and noble citizens branded traitors, without a sign of real disgust from any quarter." Braving the sure condemnation of anti–Communist patriots, Miller chose to tackle the culture of suspicion with a new play.

Many critics viewed *The Crucible,* Miller's 1953 play about the 1692 witchcraft trials that took place in the Puritan town of Salem, Massachusetts, as a direct analogy for the McCarthy hearings on communism. As John Gassner notes in *Twentieth Century Interpretations of "The Crucible,"* Miller's motivation "plainly included taking a public stand against authoritarian inquisitions and mass hysteria. . . . It is one of Miller's distinctions that he was one of the very few writers of the period to speak out unequivocally for reason and justice." But Miller insisted in *Timebends* that the play transcended the moment, for "the political question of whether witches and Communists could be equated was no longer to the point. What was manifestly parallel was the guilt, two centuries apart, of holding illicit, suppressed feelings of alienation and hostility toward standard, daylight society as defined by its most orthodox proponents." In the end, Miller was right, for *The Crucible* survived an initially cold reception to become one of Miller's most produced works.

The Crucible is now praised as an invaluable chronicle of the American past and as a standing protest against repression in the name of order.

Robert Martin wrote in *Modern Drama:* "As one of the most frequently produced plays in the American theater, *The Crucible* has attained a life of its own; one that both interprets and defines the cultural and historical background of American society. Given the general lack of plays in the American theater that have seriously undertaken to explore the meaning of the American past in relation to the present, *The Crucible* stands virtually alone as a dramatically coherent rendition of one of the most terrifying chapters in American history." In *Twentieth Century Interpretations of "The Crucible,"* Phillip G. Hill claimed that the work remains "a powerful indictment of bigotry, narrow–mindedness, hypocrisy, and violation of due process of law, from whatever source these evils spring."

Miller came even closer to the anti–Communist hysteria in the years following the first production of *The Crucible.* First, in 1953, the U.S. State Department refused to renew his passport so that he could accept an award in Belgium. A short while later, insinuations about his Communist sympathies helped get Miller expelled from his participation in an effort to publicize the plight of New York City youth gang members. Then, in 1956, Miller was subpoenaed to appear before the House Un–American Activities Committee, where he was queried about his political beliefs and asked to name others who had attended the meetings he had attended. Miller described the situation in *Timebends:* "Of course it was all a game of power entirely; they had the power and were bound to make me concede that I did not by trying to force me to break an implicit understanding among human beings that you don't use their names to bring trouble on them, or cooperate in deforming the democratic doctrine of the sanctity of peaceful association." Miller was charged with contempt of Congress and was tried and convicted in 1957 (His conviction was overturned on appeal). Nelson wrote: "In a time when men and women were being enticed and coerced into giving up their cores and identities, the author of *The Crucible* remained himself. It was a knowledge and a victory that reached far beyond any court decision."

The Playwright and the Sex Symbol

In 1950, Miller met an aspiring young actress at a Hollywood party. "In this roomful of actresses and wives of substantial men, all striving to dress and behave with an emphatically ladylike reserve," he described the scene in *Timebends*, "Marilyn Monroe seemed almost ludicrously provocative, a strange bird in the aviary, if only because her dress was so blatantly tight, declaring rather than insinuating that she had brought her body along and that it was the best one in the room." In the coming days they spent near each other, Miller felt powerfully attracted to her and wanted to protect her, and he returned to New York and his family badly shaken. In 1956, his marriage to Mary Grace Slattery ended, a victim of the changes success had wrought in Miller. On June 29, just seventeen days after his divorce became final, Miller wed Marilyn Monroe, now Hollywood's biggest celebrity and an international sex symbol, in a civil ceremony in White Plains, New York.

Like all of Monroe's actions, the wedding attracted intense publicity, the glare of which the Millers

Montgomery Clift costarred with Clark Gable in the 1961 film *The Misfits*, a screenplay Miller wrote to provide his wife, Marilyn Monroe, with a challenging role.

were unable to escape. A year after their marriage, a *Look* magazine profile found them happily adjusting to marriage, he calling her "too honest and earthy for anything phoney," she insisting that his work would be "the center of our lives." The happy picture did not last, however, as Monroe had first one, then a second miscarriage and Miller proved unable to concentrate on his own writing. Miller became his wife's unofficial manager, but soon found himself clashing with Monroe's acting coach and unable to help his wife through crippling bouts of self–doubt and depression. Nelson wrote: "Bitterness increased as personalities clashed and personal and professional frustrations churned to a boil. She began to distrust his involvement in her affairs. Their life grew more abrasive with each additional pressure, and remorselessly their marriage eroded."

By the late 1950s Miller had begun to doubt that he could save Monroe from her personal turmoil. Still, he had adapted his short story "The Misfits" into a screenplay of the same name, and had written the part of the lead female character with Monroe in mind, purposefully giving her a complex and serious part to prove to her that she was more than Hollywood's sex goddess. The filming of *The Misfits,* which costarred Clark Gable and Montgomery Clift and was directed by John Huston, was a disaster, as Monroe plunged into a depression that was worsened by her deepening dependence on prescription sleeping pills. As the film came to an end, so did their marriage. "Other marriages have survived the goldfish bowl existence that was their lot," Miller is reported commenting in *Arthur Miller: Portrait of a Playwright.* "But we've just resigned ourselves to the plain fact that ours didn't work, that's all." A little over a year later, Marilyn Monroe lay dead, the victim of a drug overdose.

Invisible in His Own Land

Miller had entered the 1950s triumphantly, the leading name on the American stage, and productions of *The Crucible* and *A View from the Bridge*, Miller's 1955 tragedy about jealousy and murder in an Italian–American community, only solidified his reputation. But by the 1960s changes in the American theater and in the national mood left Miller feeling like an outcast. He commented in *Timebends:* "I seemed unable to take anything for granted anymore, and I kept trying to figure out what others were taking for granted. The country had become foreign to me, and I did not understand why or how I had become this culturally hard–of–hearing fellow." A large part of the change that Miller saw came in the changing fashions of American theater. Critics had proclaimed the end of serious drama, and now sung the praises of the Theatre of the Absurd, which denied the social power of theater and questioned the very existence of meaning and value in human interactions. Moreover, the rising costs of producing a play on Broadway pressured theatre owners to promote only those plays that attracted large audiences and had long runs. The result was an increase in the number of flashy but intellectually light spectaculars and a marked decrease in serious social drama. Miller lamented in *Timebends:* "The tradition that a play of any significance had to address human destiny seemed ludicrously presumptuous, was going the way of values themselves. . . . In the sense that we lack any real awareness of a continuity [with] the past, we are, I think, a country without a theatre culture."

Miller persevered despite the growing sense that his generation had passed. Increasingly, his plays explored man's hopeless alienation from himself and from others. *After the Fall,* first produced in 1964 and his first post–Marilyn Monroe play, was at first roundly criticized for exploiting details of Miller's life with Monroe. Later, critics came to recognize that it marked an important turn in Miller's work. The play consists of a series of recollections from the mind of Quentin, an attorney facing the consequences of his actions for the first time. The play probes "the nature of guilt, the limits of personal responsibility, and the means of expiation for crimes real or imagined," wrote critic Jeffrey Helterman. The blatantly autobiographical elements of parts of the play did not keep some critics from recognizing the play's value. Robert Hogan, writing in *Arthur Miller,* called *After the Fall* "Miller's most intellectually probing play," and Harold Clurman, writing in *Arthur Miller: A Collection of Critical Essays,* saw it as "a signal step in the evolution of Arthur Miller as man and artist."

This British production of *The American Clock* was a big hit in London, but the play was not popular in America.

Miller had both successes and failures following *After the Fall*. *The Price*, a 1969 family drama about two middle–aged brothers who meet in an attic to dispose of their deceased parents' furniture, enjoyed a long run on Broadway and was compared favorably to Miller's earlier work, especially *All My Sons*. But *The American Clock*, Miller's 1980 portrait of the Great Depression, opened to poor reviews and never succeeded on Broadway, despite Miller's efforts to rewrite the play to satisfy the demands of producers and directors. Miller took the original version of the play to London, where it was an immediate hit, confirming Miller's suspicion that he was out of tune with American audiences. Later plays by Miller, including *Danger: Memory!* and *The Archbishop's Ceiling*, had fates similar to that of *The American Clock*. A revival of Miller's work in the mid–1980s redressed some of the neglect that Miller's plays had received on the American stage, though it struck Miller in *Timebends* as ironic: "I seemed to have been 'revived' when in fact I had only been invisible in my own land."

Miller became a highly visible presence on quite another stage when he became president of PEN International, an organization of writers dedicated to protecting human rights and artistic freedom around the world. Miller accepted the presidency of PEN in 1966, when it appeared that the organization was becoming irrelevant, and helped forge ties with writers in the Soviet Bloc at a time when the Cold War was increasing the distance between the Soviet Union and the West. Roger Shattuck, writing in the *New York Times Book Review*, commented that Miller "was the only American famous enough and courageous enough in 1966 to inject new vitality into PEN International." Miller also used his influence to help free dissident writers in Spain and Nigeria, promote artistic freedom in South Africa, Latin American countries, the Soviet Union, and Korea, and block the censorship efforts of school boards in the states of Illinois and Texas. PEN had become, Miller wrote in *Timebends*, "the conscience of the world writing community."

Miller lives with his wife, the photographer Inge Morath, whom he married in 1962 and with whom he wrote several books, on the 400 acre farm he bought following the success of *All My Sons*. In his late seventies, Miller still writes every day and also plants trees, gardens, and indulges his love of carpentry. In 1987 he wrote his autobiography, *Timebends: A Life*, which allowed him to cast forward and back in time to record the formation of his identity alongside his experiences. *Publishers Weekly* wrote: "Tough, compassionate, bristling with intelligence and profound reflections of the dramas of life and stage, this is one of the memorable autobiographies of our time." And in 1994, fifty years after he made his Broadway debut, Miller's play *Broken Glass* opened to favorable reviews: *Time* critic William A. Henry III called it "complex, a little mysterious, full of arresting incident." But the play faced an uncertain future on a Broadway that remains uninterested in serious plays. Whether Broadway can sustain his plays or not, Arthur Miller will remain one of the twentieth century's great artists, a voice of reason and hope in an often confusing world.

■ Works Cited

Corrigan, Robert W., editor, *Arthur Miller: A Collection of Critical Essays*, Prentice–Hall, 1969.

Ferres, John H., editor, *Twentieth Century Interpretations of "The Crucible,"* Prentice–Hall, 1972.

Goldfarb, Alvin, "Arthur Miller," in *American Playwrights Since 1945: A Guide to Scholarship, Criticism, and Performance*, edited by Philip C. Kolin, Greenwood Press, 1989.

Hamilton, Jack, "Marilyn's New Life," *Look*, October 1, 1957, p. 110.

Helterman, Jeffrey, "Arthur Miller," *Dictionary of Literary Biography*, Volume 7: *Twentieth–Century American Dramatists*, Gale, 1981.

Henry, William A., III, "Sylvia Suffers," *Time*, May 9, 1994, p. 76.

Hogan, Robert, *Arthur Miller*, University of Minnesota Press, 1964.

Huftel, Sheila, *Arthur Miller: The Burning Glass*, Citadel, 1965.

Hutchens, John K., "Mr. Miller Has a Change of Luck," *New York Times*, February 23, 1947, Theatre section, p. 3.

Martin, Robert, "Arthur Miller's *The Crucible*: Background and Sources," *Modern Drama*, Vol. 20, 1977, pp. 279–292.

Miller, Arthur, *Arthur Miller's Collected Plays*, Viking, 1957.

Miller, Arthur, *Salesman in Beijing*, Viking, 1984.

Miller, Arthur, *Timebends: A Life*, Grove, 1987.

Nelson, Benjamin, *Arthur Miller: Portrait of a Playwright*, McKay, 1970.

Review of *Timebends: A Life*, *Publishers Weekly*, October 16, 1987, p. 76.

Shattuck, Roger, *New York Times Book Review,* November 8, 1987, p. 1.

Weales, Gerald, *American Drama since World War II,* Harcourt, 1962.

■ For More Information See

BOOKS

Bigsby, C. W. E., *Twentieth–Century American Drama,* Volume 2, *Tennessee Williams, Arthur Miller, Edward Albee,* Cambridge University Press, 1984.

Carson, Neil, *Arthur Miller,* Macmillan, 1982.

Clurman, Harold, *Lies Like Truth,* Macmillan, 1958.

Contemporary Literary Criticism, Gale, Volume 1, 1973, Volume 2, 1974, Volume 6, 1976, Volume 10, 1979, Volume 15, 1980, Volume 26, 1983, Volume 47, 1988.

Corrigan, Robert W., editor, *Arthur Miller: A Collection of Critical Essays,* Prentice–Hall, 1969.

Evans, Richard, *Psychology and Arthur Miller,* Dutton, 1969.

Ferres, John H., *Arthur Miller: A Reference Guide,* G. K. Hall, 1979.

Jensen, George, *Arthur Miller: A Bibliographical Checklist,* Faust, 1976.

Koon, Helene Wickham, editor, *Twentieth–Century Interpretations of Death of a Salesman,* Prentice–Hall, 1983.

Martin, Robert A., editor, *Arthur Miller: New Perspectives,* Prentice–Hall, 1982.

Martine, James J., *Critical Essays on Arthur Miller,* G. K. Hall, 1979.

Moss, Leonard, *Arthur Miller,* revised edition, Twayne, 1980.

Schlueter, June, and James K. Flanagan, *Arthur Miller,* Ungar, 1987.

Spindler, Michael, *American Literature and Social Change: William Dean Howells to Arthur Miller,* Macmillan, 1983.

Welland, Dennis, *Arthur Miller: A Study of His Plays,* Methuen, 1979.

Welland, Dennis, *Arthur Miller: The Playwright,* Methuen, 1983.

Williams, Raymond, *Drama from Ibsen to Brecht,* Chatto and Windus, 1968.

—Sketch by Tom Pendergast

Joyce Carol Oates

■ Personal

Also writes under pseudonym Rosamond Smith; born June 16, 1938, in Locksport, NY; daughter of Frederic James (a tool-and-die designer) and Caroline (Bush) Oates; married Raymond Joseph Smith (an editor and former professor of English), January 23, 1961. *Education:* Syracuse University, B.A., 1960; University of Wisconsin, M.A. 1961.

■ Addresses

Office—Princeton University, Department of English, Princeton, NJ 08544. *Agent*—c/o John Hawkins, 71 West 23rd St., Ste. 1600, New York, NY 10010.

■ Career

Writer and editor. University of Detroit, Detroit, MI, instructor, 1961–65, assistant professor of English, 1965–67; University of Windsor, Windsor, Ontario, member of English department faculty, 1967–78; Princeton University, Princeton, NJ, writer in residence, 1978–81, Roger S. Berlind Distinguished Professor, 1987—. *Member:* American Academy and Institute of Arts and Letters, Modern Language Association, Phi Beta Kappa.

■ Awards, Honors

Mademoiselle college fiction award, 1959, for "In the Old World"; National Endowment for the Arts grants, 1966, 1968; Guggenheim fellowship, 1967; O. Henry Awards, 1967, for "In the Region of Ice," 1973, for "The Dead," and 1983, for "My Warszawa"; Rosenthal Award, National Institute of Arts and Letters, 1968; National Book Award nominations, 1968, for *A Garden of Earthly Delights*, and 1969, for *Expensive People*; National Book Award for fiction, 1970, for *them*; O. Henry Special Awards for Continuing Achievement, 1970 and 1986; Lotos Club Award of Merit, 1975; Pushcart Prize, 1976; *Los Angeles Times* Book Prize for fiction nomination, 1989, for *Bellefleur*; St. Louis Literary Award, 1988; Rea Award for the Short Story, 1990; Alan Swallow Award for fiction, 1990; National Book Critics Circle Award nomination, 1992, for *Black Water*; PEN/Faulkner Award nomination, 1995, for *What I Lived For.*

■ Writings

NOVELS AND NOVELLAS

With Shuddering Fall, Vanguard Press, 1964.
A Garden of Earthly Delights, Vanguard Press, 1967.
Expensive People, Vanguard Press, 1967.
them, Vanguard Press, 1969.
Wonderland, Vanguard Press, 1971.

Do with Me What You Will, Vanguard Press, 1973.
The Assassins: A Book of Hours, Vanguard Press, 1975.
Triumph of the Spider Monkey: The First Person Confession of the Maniac Bobby Gotteson as Told to Joyce Carol Oates (novella; also see below), Black Sparrow Press, 1976.
Childwold, Vanguard Press, 1976.
Son of the Morning, Vanguard Press, 1978.
Unholy Loves, Vanguard Press, 1979.
Cybele, Black Sparrow Press, 1979.
Bellefleur, Dutton, 1980.
Angel of Light, Dutton, 1981.
A Bloodsmoor Romance, Dutton, 1982.
Mysteries of Winterthurn, Dutton, 1984.
Solstice, Dutton, 1985.
Marya: A Life, Dutton, 1986.
You Must Remember This, Dutton, 1987.
American Appetites, Dutton, 1989.
I Lock My Door upon Myself, Ecco Press, 1990.
Because it Is Bitter, and Because It Is My Heart, NAL/Dutton, 1990.
The Rise of Life on Earth, New Directions, 1991.
Black Water: A Novel, NAL/Dutton, 1992.
Foxfire: Confessions of a Girl Gang, NAL/Dutton, 1993.
What I Lived For, NAL/Dutton, 1994.

NOVELS; UNDER PSEUDONYM ROSAMOND SMITH

Lives of the Twins, Simon & Schuster, 1987.
Soul-Mate, NAL/Dutton, 1990.
Nemesis, NAL/Dutton, 1991.
Snake Eyes, NAL/Dutton, 1992.

SHORT STORIES

By the North Gate, Vanguard Press, 1963.
Upon the Sweeping Flood and Other Stories, Vanguard Press, 1966.
The Wheel of Love and Other Stories, Vanguard Press, 1970.
Marriages and Infidelities, Vanguard Press, 1972.
The Goddess and Other Women, Vanguard Press, 1974.
Where Are You Going, Where Have You Been?: Stories of Young America, Fawcett, 1974, published as *Where Are You Going, Where Have You Been?: Selected Early Stories*, Ontario Review Press, 1993.
The Hungry Ghosts: Seven Allusive Comedies, Black Sparrow Press, 1974.
The Poisoned Kiss and Other Stories from the Portuguese, Vanguard Press, 1975.
The Seduction and Other Stories, Black Sparrow Press, 1975.

Crossing the Border: Fifteen Tales, Vanguard Press, 1976.
Night Side: Eighteen Tales, Vanguard Press, 1977.
All the Good People I've Left Behind, Black Sparrow Press, 1978.
The Lamb of Abyssalia, Pomegranate, 1980.
A Sentimental Education: Stories, Dutton, 1980.
Last Days: Stories, Dutton, 1984.
Wild Saturday, and Other Stories, Dent, 1984.
Raven's Wing: Stories, Dutton, 1986.
The Assignation: Stories, Ecco Press, 1988.
Heat, and Other Stories, NAL/Dutton, 1991.
Where Is Here? Stories, Ecco Press, 1992.
Haunted: Tales of the Grotesque, Dutton, 1994.

Several of Oates's stories have also been published singly in limited editions.

NONFICTION

The Edge of Impossibility: Tragic Forms in Literature, Vanguard Press, 1972.
The Hostile Sun: The Poetry of D. H. Lawrence, Black Sparrow Press, 1973.
New Heaven, New Earth: The Visionary Experience in Literature, Vanguard Press, 1974.
Contraries: Essays, Oxford University Press, 1981.
The Profane Art: Essays and Reviews, Dutton, 1983.
On Boxing, Doubleday, 1987.
(Woman) Writer: Occasions & Opportunities, NAL/Dutton, 1988.
Conversations with Joyce Carol Oates, edited by Lee Milazzo, University Press of Mississippi, 1989.

PLAYS

The Sweet Enemy, produced Off-Broadway, 1965.
Sunday Dinner, produced Off-Broadway, 1970.
Ontological Proof of My Existence, produced Off-Off Broadway, 1972, published in *Partisan Review, 37*, 1970.
Miracle Play, Black Sparrow Press, 1974.
Three Plays, Ontario Review Press, 1980.
Daisy, produced Off-Off Broadway, 1980.
Presque Isle, produced in New York, 1984.
Triumph of the Spider Monkey (based on her novella), produced at the Los Angeles Theatre Center, 1985.
I Stand Before You Naked (produced Off-Broadway, 1990), Samuel French, 1991.
Tone Clusters, produced in Louisville, KY, 1990, published in *In Darkest America: Two Plays*, 1991.
The Eclipse, produced in Louisville, 1990, published in *In Darkest America: Two Plays*, 1991.
In Darkest America: Two Plays, Samuel French, 1991.

How Do You Like Your Meat?, produced in New Haven, CT, 1991, published in *Twelve Plays*, 1991.

Twelve Plays, NAL/Dutton, 1991.

Black, produced in Williamstown, MA, 1992, published in *Twelve Plays*, 1991.

The Rehearsal, produced in New York City, 1993.

POETRY

Women in Love and Other Poems, Albondocani Press, 1968.

Anonymous Sins and Other Poems (also see below), Louisiana State University Press, 1969.

Love and Its Derangements: Poems (also see below), Louisiana State University Press, 1970.

Angel Fire (see also below), Louisiana State University Press, 1973.

Love and Its Derangements and Other Poems (includes *Anonymous Sins and Other Poems*, *Love and Its Derangements*, and *Angel Fire*), Fawcett, 1974.

The Fabulous Beasts: Poems, Louisiana State University Press, 1975.

Season of Peril, Black Sparrow Press, 1977.

Women Whose Lives Are Food, Men Whose Lives Are Money: Poems, Louisiana State University Press, 1978.

Celestial Timepiece: Poems, Pressworks, 1980.

Invisible Woman: New and Selected Poems 1970–1982, Ontario Review Press, 1982.

The Time Traveler: Poems, 1983–1989, NAL/Dutton, 1989.

EDITOR OR COMPILER

Scenes from American Life: Contemporary Short Fiction, Random House, 1973.

(With Shannon Ravenel) *Best American Short Stories of 1979*, Houghton, 1979.

Night Walks, Ontario Review Press, 1982.

First Person Singular: Writers on Their Craft, Ontario Review Press, 1983.

(With Boyd Litzinger) *Story: Fictions Past and Present*, Heath, 1985.

(With Daniel Halpern) *Reading the Fights*, H. Holt, 1988.

The Best American Essays 1991, Ticknor & Fields, 1991.

(With Halpern) *The Sophisticated Cat: An Anthology*, NAL/Dutton, 1992.

The Oxford Book of Short Stories, Oxford University Press, 1992.

OTHER

Contributor of fiction, essays, and reviews to numerous periodicals, including *Atlantic*, *Cosmopoli-*tan, *Esquire*, *Harper's*, *Ladies Home Journal*, *Life*, *Ms.*, *Nation*, *New Republic*, *Newsweek*, *New York Review of Books*, *New York Times Book Review*, *Omni*, *Playboy*, *Poetry*, *Seventeen*, *Tikkun*, and *Yale Review*. Coeditor, *Ontario Review*, beginning 1974.

■ Adaptations

Several of Oates's short stories have been adapted for various media, including "In the Region of Ice," made into a 1976 Academy Award-winning short feature; "Daisy," adapted for the stage by Victoria Rue and produced Off-Off Broadway, 1980; "Where Are You Going, Where Have You Been?" was made into the film *Smooth Talk*, Spectrafilm, 1981; and "Norman and the Killer," made into a short film.

■ Sidelights

"My writing is full of the lives I might have led," says Joyce Carol Oates in a *Boston Globe Magazine* interview with Jay Parini, explaining that "a writer imagines what could have happened, not what really happened." That her works are only imagination is fortunate, for Oates's prolific output of novels, short stories, plays, poems, and essays have intimately recounted such events as rape, incest, abuse, mutilation, suicide, and murder. Her characters encounter acts of violence and evil that they are at a loss to understand; while many of her protagonists are young and female, Oates has reproduced the lives of people ranging from impoverished migrant workers and city dwellers to nineteenth-century heirs and heiresses to modern-day suburbanites whose wealth and power mask turbulent inner lives. As Greg Johnson summarizes in *Understanding Joyce Carol Oates*, "All her characters, regardless of background, suffer intensely the conflicts and contradictions at the heart of our culture—a suffering Oates conveys with both scrupulous accuracy and great compassion."

One of three children, Oates grew up on her grandparents' farm in Erie County, New York. Frederic, her father, was a tool-and-die designer and her homemaker mother, Caroline, raised Joyce, her brother Frederic, and sister Lynn Ann. Oates was a prolific storyteller even before she could write; as a preschooler she drew pictures to tell her stories. Oates talked about the role of her grandfather in her earliest writing in a *New York Times Magazine* interview with Lucinda Franks: "He influenced me greatly. . . . I listened to his stories and then I began to pretend to write them; I simulated handwriting before I knew letters. And sometimes I just drew symbols—butterflies, cats, trees." In elementary school, she wrote stories and produced 200-page books, which she designed and bound herself. A serious child, Oates's fascination for books set her apart from the rowdy children at the one-room schoolhouse she attended. Her family nurtured and appreciated her, however; early on, her parents recognized their daughter's extraordinary gifts. "She was always so hard-working, a perfectionist at everything," her mother, Caroline Oates, recalled to Parini.

Oates went from the one-room schoolhouse to attend junior and senior high school in town. She seldom talks about her youth, as evidenced in this exchange recounted by Newsweek interviewer Paul D. Zimmerman: "She dismisses her childhood as 'dull, ordinary, nothing people would be interested in,' not because it was really dull and ordinary but because it was terrible to talk about. 'A great deal frightened me,' she said cryptically, but would not elaborate." She later explained to Franks that as a petite teen, she made an easy target for bullies, particularly on the long bus ride to school: "They were rough and ignorant boys and they quit school usually at 16. . . . It was exhausting. A continual daily scramble for existence." During this time, however, the fifteen-year-old Oates submitted her first manuscript for publication. This 250-page novel, about a drug addict redeemed by the gift of a black stallion, was rejected by a New York publisher who felt it was "too depressing for the market of young readers," according to Dictionary of Literary Biography contributor Michael Joslin.

The rejection did not deter her writing, however. After graduating from high school, she entered Syracuse University, where she studied literature and philosophy; along with her studies, she wrote a novel a semester. In her junior year, she won her first literary prize: a Mademoiselle college fiction award in 1959 for her short story, "In the Old World," which was published in the magazine. Oates graduated Phi Beta Kappa in 1960 and entered the masters' degree program at the University of Wisconsin the following semester. There she met Raymond Joseph Smith, a doctoral candidate, and they were married the following January. Oates remained at the university for the spring semester to complete her studies, while her husband went to Beaumont, Texas, to begin his first teaching post. After receiving her degree in June, she followed her husband to Texas.

Still following a career path to teach literature, she entered Rice University, in Houston, to work on a doctorate. During her studies, she found a collection of the year's best fiction at the library and discovered that one of her stories had been named to its "honor roll." "I hadn't known about it until I picked [the book] up and saw it," Joslin quoted her as saying. "I thought, maybe I could be a writer. . . . I went back on the bus and stopped thinking about a Ph.D." Though she had never stopped writing, publishing her work on a freelance basis, Oates decided to leave school and devote all her time to writing. As she explained to Newsweek's Zimmerman, "Art does the same things dreams do. We have a hunger for dreams and art fulfills that hunger. So much of real life is a disappointment. That's why we have art."

Within a year of leaving school her first book, a collection of stories titled By the North Gate, was published. Since then, a continuous stream of poetry, novels, short stories, plays, and essays has emerged from her pen—an average of almost two books a year. Many of these early works would explore the people and environment of her formative years. From the flat farmland of western New York Oates created the fictional area of Eden County, in which her first novel, 1964's With Shuddering Fall, was set. The story of the relationship between Karen, an eighteen-year-old country girl, and Shar, a race car driver twelve years her senior, is marked with violence. Trying to control his lover, the volatile Shar battles against Karen's passiveness, eventually beating her father severely. Though she loves Shar, Karen eventually seeks revenge, which is fulfilled when the driver is killed in a raceway accident. "This material is not as garish as it sounds because of the clarity, grace, and intelligence of the writing," John Knowles states in the New York Times Book Review, foreshadowing future critical evaluations of Oates's work.

A Motown Muse

After Oates and her husband relocated to the Detroit, Michigan, area in the early 1960s, the author began teaching her craft to others, first at the University of Detroit, then across the river at the University of Windsor in Ontario, Canada. The move not only established her teaching career, it initiated a new phase in her writing, exposing her to an urban, decaying environment in which violence was a common occurrence. She began an informal trilogy, examining the problems caused by various economic circumstances and exploring in particular the difficulties young people encounter in struggling to overcome oppressive situations. As Betty DeRamus notes in the *Detroit Free Press*, the author's time in Detroit "gave her a tradition to write from, the so-called American Gothic tradition of exaggerated horror and gloom and mysterious and violent incidents." Oates herself acknowledged the influence of Detroit in the *Michigan Quarterly Review:* "If we had never come to the city of Detroit I would have been a writer (indeed, I had already written my first two books before coming here, age 23) but Detroit, my 'great' subject, made me the person I am, consequently the writer I am—for better or worse."

The first of this "trilogy," 1967's *A Garden of Earthly Delights,* opens in a migrant labor camp in the 1920s as the heroine, Clara, is born in the back of a broken-down transport truck. To escape a life of poverty and support her illegitimate son, Clara becomes the mistress and eventual wife of a wealthy local farmer, who believes he fathered her child. The marriage results in tragedy, however, as Clara's son accidentally causes the death of his stepbrother while hunting—inducing a miscarriage in Clara—and eventually shoots both his stepfather and himself. While many critics have found this conclusion, and Clara's resulting descent into madness, overly melodramatic, Joslin notes that the novel "demonstrates Oates's ability to create a living world in her fiction, for she depicts brilliantly the different societies through which Clara moves." *A Garden of Earthly Delights* earned the author her first National Book Award nomination.

The second novel of the series, *Expensive People,* is set in the wealthier areas of America and was inspired by one of the more exclusive Detroit suburbs. The son of a successful corporate executive and a minor writer, eighteen-year-old Richard Everett tells his story in the first person before beginning a suicide attempt. The frequent desertions of his immigrant mother, a social climber with pretensions of nobility, lead the self-pitying, semi-psychotic Richard to murder her—or so he claims, since his psychiatrists insist that his memory of the murder is just a hallucination. Joslin calls this work "a sharp reversal from Oates's earlier efforts," as its portrayal of the up-

This 1969 work, a National Book Award winner, depicts thirty years in the life of an impoverished Detroit family.

per class lends itself to more satire and irony. In addition, Richard's first-person narrative allowed Oates the opportunity to use more unconventional fictional techniques, such as when Richard discusses the art of writing by quoting fictional books. While the book garnered Oates a second National Book Award nomination, critical reaction was again mixed, Joslin relates: "Some [reviews] were quite enthusiastic, while others were skeptical of the value of this unusual work."

The final volume of the "trilogy," titled *them* (1969), chronicles the survival of a lower-class family living in Detroit, trapped in cycle of violence and poverty. Spanning the years from 1937 to

1967, the novel traces the lives of Loretta Wendall and her children, Jules and Maureen, beginning with the murder of Loretta's lover as he lies sleeping next to her in bed. Seeking assistance from a policeman acquaintance, Loretta ends up marrying him, only to end up being handed from man to man after his death. Loretta's children become obsessed with money as the way to escape from the horrible reality of their lives; the book-loving Maureen turns to prostitution while Jules, enamored of a rich suburban girl, becomes involved in various petty crimes. The novel culminates with the Detroit riots of 1967, after which Jules moves west for a potential government job, while Maureen seduces a community college teacher and moves to the suburbs. In an "Author's Preface," Oates stated: "This is a work of history in fictional form—that is, in personal perspective, which is the only kind of history that exists. In the years 1962–67 I taught English at the University of Detroit. . . . It was during this period that I met the 'Maureen Wendall' of this narrative." However, Oates continued, "the various sordid and shocking events of slum life, detailed in other naturalistic works, have been understated here, mainly because of my fear that too much reality would be unbearable."

The critical reception of *them* was favorable. *New York Times* critic Robert M. Adams, for instance, comments that "Oates writes a vehement, voluminous, kaleidoscopic novel, more deeply rooted in social observation than current fiction usually tends to be." A *Virginia Quarterly Review* reviewer observes that "of its genre she has produced a superb modern instance, certain to please those who are adherents of the pattern, approach, and style." The book won the 1970 National Book Award, making Oates, at age 31, one of the youngest writers ever to receive that honor. Her reputation as one of most talented writers in the United States was secured, and led to increasing critical attention to her work—both positive and negative. As *Newsweek*'s Walter Clemons comments: "If you met her at a literary party and failed to catch her name, it might be hard to imagine her reading, much less writing, the unflinching fiction that has made Joyce Carol Oates perhaps the most significant novelist to have emerged in the United States in the last decade." But, the critic explains, Oates's "sweeping vision of America as a delusive wonderland of colliding forces, where love as often as hate leads to violence, has established Miss Oates as a major—and controversial—figure in American writing."

Throughout the 1970s, Oates continued to explore the entire scope of American people and experiences, combining social analysis and psychological characterizations with a literate style and sometimes poetic prose. But where her earlier works had focused on the everyday lives of average citizens, many of her next novels moved through worlds of authority, examining what she has often described as "the complex distribution of power in the United States." *Wonderland* (1971), for example, focuses on the modern medical community; *Do with Me What You Will* (1973) is set amongst Detroit's legal circles; *The Assassins* (1975) presents the turbulent, shifting landscape of American politics; *Son of the Morning* (1978) revolves around a charismatic preacher and religious society; and *Unholy Loves* (1979) presents the academic world of university professors. While they survey different spheres of command, however, these novels still contain violent events and victimizations, portraying the pitfalls of power. *Wonderland* begins with the mass murder of protagonist Jesse's family and includes the cannibalization of a cadaver; *The Assassins* revolves around a political murder, with the dead man's brother shooting himself, and his widow being shot and dismembered; and the protagonist of *Son of the Morning* is conceived in a gang rape and becomes the target of a murder attempt by his own disciple.

As Oates was producing these intricate, often lengthy, novels at a rapid rate, criticism began to focus on her work as whole, analyzing common themes and issues in her work. Even as some reviewers fault the excess of violence in works like *Wonderland,* S. K. Overbeck defends her content: "She is no more 'gothic' than today's headlines, no more violent than the nightly bloody canapes served up on the six o'clock news," the critic observes in the *Washington Post Book World.* It is her "crushing immediacy of contemporary atmospheres and details," Overbeck explains, combined with "her unabashed fictional virtuosity, [that] makes the terrifying aspects of American life vivid for her readers." *National Review* contributor Charles Shapiro similarly notes that "in novel after novel, story after story, Oates gives us her own tragic America, a personal vision as perceptive as it is instructive and terrifying. . . . Oates' swollen characters are relevant to and complement the horror and dangers of our American landscape. The truths of our lives are exhibited in the excesses." "For her emphasis on self-seeking ferocity we call Oates 'Gothic,' but she is perhaps better understood as a contemporary heir of the Great Tradition," Sara Sanborn offers in a *Nation* assessment. "Like Austen, Eliot, or James in their various ways, but with a gift for violence, she aligns the moral and the social." Oates's work "has its flaws, like most big efforts," the critic concludes, "but they are scarcely worth discussing next to its achievement."

Concentrated Lives and Gothic Tales

At the same time Oates's novels were receiving attention from critics and readers—*Do with Me What You Will* placed on some regional best seller lists—she was earning even more acclaim for her

A man is charged with murder after his wife sustains fatal injuries during a domestic argument in this 1989 work.

short fiction. "Oates has written strong novels," John Alfred Avant remarks in the *New Republic,* "but she is best in the short story. Her most characteristic stories read like dreams or nightmares, urgently written in order to release the dreamer." "Her short stories present the same violence, perversion, and mental derangement as her novels, and are set in similar locations," Joslin observes. Many critics believe that her short stories show this genre to be the one to which she is most naturally suited, for, as Joslin continues, "her style, technique, and subject matter achieve their strongest effects in this concentrated form, for the extended dialogue, minute detail, and violent action . . . are wonderfully appropriate in short fiction." As Peter Straub similarly explains in the *New Statesman,* in her shorter pieces "she is entirely unafraid to extend her normal manner, so that a number of these stories exhibit a stunning technical courage."

For example, the story "Where Are You Going, Where Have You Been" (first published in 1966, then in a collection of the same title in 1974) has been described as a masterpiece of the short-story form. While on the surface the story is about fifteen-year-old Connie's rejection of a family outing and subsequent deflowering by a mysterious stranger named Friend, many critics have observed deeper levels of meaning. "Although Oates uses the trappings of a realist to craft plausible characters" and behavior, Marie Mitchell Olesen Urbanski writes in *Studies in Short Fiction,* "this must not obscure her design. She presents an allegory which . . . represent[s] *Everyman's* transition from the illusion of free will to the realization of externally determined fate." Other analysts have explored the story's portrayal of humanity's dual nature of good and evil, as well as its examination of adolescent coming of age and ending of innocence.

Some writers "intuitively seem to know that the short story is for a different type of material from the novel: a brief and dazzling plunge into another state of consciousness," Erica Jong remarks in the *New York Times Book Review.* "Joyce Carol Oates is one of these." Oates writes short stories at the same time that she is writing novels, and these works are published singly in a variety of literary magazines such as the *Hudson Review, Paris Review,* and *Atlantic;* they are later published in book form, often in thematically linked collections. 1976's *Crossing the Border,* for instance, contains tales relating to characters who live in Canada near the U.S. border. The collection achieves "an organic coherence beyond that of the individual stories," Greg Johnson writes in *Southwest Review,* "and the writing is always skillful, taut, compelling. If the characters are not always admirable, Oates's compassion for them makes their lives absorbing; if events are occasionally unsettling, even grotesque, they nevertheless express the darker aspects of human consciousness with precision, clarity, and truthfulness—and in such coherent expression resides their great value." And of the 1991 collection *Heat, and Other Stories,* Mary Warner Marien remarks in the *Christian Science Monitor* that it "again impresses one with the ability [Oates] has to palpably envision the circumstances and inner lives of fictional characters."

During the 1980s, Oates began to explore new avenues of storytelling, experimenting with modern retellings of classic tales. For example, in her 1981 novel *Angel of Light,* Oates adapts the classical Greek tragedy of the fall of the house of Atreus, in which a sister urges her brother to avenge their father's murder by killing their mother and her lover. Even though the novel received positive reviews and widespread attention, it has been somewhat overshadowed by the books that came before and after it—*Bellefleur, A Bloodsmoor Romance,* and *Mysteries of Winterthurn*—commonly known as her Gothic series. These family sagas span generations, and feature stock elements of conventional Gothics: ghosts, haunted mansions, and mysterious deaths. Given their historical context, the stories are also tied to noteworthy events. "I set out originally to create an elaborate, baroque, barbarous metaphor for the unfathomable mysteries of the human imagination," Oates was quoted as saying by Johnson, "but soon became involved in very literal events."

Bellefleur (1980) is an ambitious novel dealing with six generations of the Bellefleur family. Instead of a contemporary setting where violence intrudes into everyday life, Oates creates a gothic setting where strange occurrences seem normal. The plot is complex and not easily summarized. The story goes back and forth from generation to generation, while the main focus is on Gideon Bellefleur and his wife, Leah, who seek to restore the Bellefleur empire to its original grandeur. *New York Times* critic John Leonard calls *Bellefleur* "Gothic pulp fiction, cleverly consuming itself," involving a generational saga and a family curse; on an-

Oates chronicles six generations of the Bellefleur family in this gothic novel from 1980.

other level, the work is also "fairy tale and myth, distraught literature. There is a walled garden, a decayed tower, a sinister cat, a swamp monster, a spider as big as a humming bird, a man who turns into a bear, a pond that breathes, [and other such elements]."

Critics have been generally enthusiastic, finding some flaws in an otherwise excellent work. *New York Times Book Review* contributor John Gardner, for instance, writes that "though *Bellefleur* is not [Oates's] best book," citing some slow passages and overly-complex construction, "in my opinion it's a wonderful book all the same." Calling the work her "most ambitious," the critic explains that *Bellefleur* "is a symbolic summation of all this novelist has been doing for 20-some years, a magnificent piece of daring, a tour de force of imagination and intellect" that provides "proof, if any seems needed, that she is one of the great writers of our time." The first novel Oates produced under a new publisher, *Bellefleur* began a new period in Oates's career, one in which she was considered a popular as well as literary writer. As John Calvin Batchelor observes, "this novel is for the beach, sidewalk cafe lunches, airplane rides," the critic comments in the *Village Voice*. "It has some very serious themes, such as time, justice, true religion; but its most serious . . . accomplishment is that it is funny."

The second of the author's "Gothics," 1982's *A Bloodsmoor Romance,* has been referred to as Oates's version of *Little Women.* This saga of a Victorian American family explores the customs and attitudes that restricted women in the nineteenth century, through the lives of the five daughters of John Quincy Zinn. The tomboy Constance deserts her fiance on the day of their marriage; Malvinia runs away with an actor, has an affair with Mark Twain, and ends up as a faculty wife; Octavia's first husband is given to sexual perversity and she kills him; Samantha, who inherits her father's scientific inclinations, elopes with an obscure young man and invents the baby stroller and disposable diapers; and Deirdre, who was abducted in a balloon as the story opens, returns as a famous medium. "The book is a feminist romance with a lot of axes to grind, and it grinds them wittily till their edges are polished to a fine sharpness," Diane Johnson observes in the *New York Times Book Review.* Because of the wealth of information about nineteenth-century life, "even those who find balloon abductions thin should be satisfied by this richness of detail," the critic adds. *A Bloodsmoor Romance* "is the finest novel yet by Joyce Carol Oates, the richest, the most admirably complex, and the most enjoyable," *Los Angeles Times Book Review* writer Alice Adams states, "and I speak as one who has vastly admired her work."

The third in this trilogy, *The Mysteries of Winterthurn* (1984) is set in nineteenth-century upstate New York, again reflecting the geography of the author's own early life. Using nineteenth-century conventions of an ever-present narrator, a slow pace, and ornate language, Oates works within the conventions of the detective story to develop the theme of the invisibility of women. In the book, a young consulting detective named Xavier Kilgarven discusses three of his cases; each involves a crime against women, and each he has failed to solve. Allusions to classic literature appear throughout the work: for example, Kilgarven is modeled after Sherlock Holmes; his cousin

Georgina, a reclusive poet, is patterned after Emily Dickinson and, through her pen name Iphigenia, is connected with Greek myth; the detective's other cousins are like creations of the Brontë sisters. The novel received fewer strongly positive reviews than its predecessors, with reviewers like Patricia Craig of the *New York Times Book Review* stating that "at times it's unclear to the reader whether [Oates is] reproducing a 19th-century detective novel, overturning it, expanding it or sending it up." But Eileen Teper Bender, author of *Joyce Carol Oates, Artist in Residence,* believes that *Winterthurn* and its predecessor *Bloodsmoor* "demonstrate one of Oates's most interesting literary discoveries"—the similarities between detective fiction and romance. Both "affirm the drive for control," according to the critic, while in *Winterthurn* "Oates reveals a Gothic grimace beneath the mask of ratiocination."

Trials of Coming of Age

Two coming of age novels set in the upstate New York of the author's youth—1986's *Marya: A Life* and 1987's *You Must Remember This*—were hailed by several critics as marking a turning point in Oates's fiction, where she reaches a mature stage by successfully combining the best characteristics of her early and later work. Christopher Lehmann-Haupt of the *New York Times,* for instance, calls *Marya: A Life* "a fresh departure for Miss Oates— quieter, more controlled and realistic, and personal to the point of suggesting autobiography." The critic explains: "It is as if she had consolidated whatever she learned from her rather recent experiments—the gothic excesses of 'Bellefleur,' 'A Bloodsmoor Romance,' and 'Mysteries of Winterthurn,' the nearly clinical psychological realism of 'Solstice'—and started over again on a smaller scale."

The novel is a portrait of a journalist and teacher who has overcome a traumatic childhood: she was abused and later abandoned by an alcoholic mother; her father was murdered when she was seven years old; she was sent to live with an uncle's family, where she was sexually abused by a cousin. Mary Gordon, in the *New York Times Book Review,* describes Marya as "a deprived child mysteriously transformed not into a princess but a scholarship girl." As Marya perseveres, she does exceedingly well in high school, winning scholarships to a state college and then to an Ivy League university. For Gordon, the novel's "strength emanates from the brilliance of Miss Oates's descriptions of objects and places," particularly the details of Marya's dirt-poor family and home; in addition, "the landscape of western New York is rendered with damning precision."

Each chapter in the book is almost a short story in itself that presents a slice of Marya's life; each focuses on important people in her life. Dean Flower, writing in the *Hudson Review,* believes that "Marya's central problem" is that "she is defined by others." In particular, notes the critic, are three men, all of whom die and who "succeed—for a time—in providing Marya with a self, 'a life.'" The novel ends as Marya, in her mid-thirties and successful, suddenly seeks out her mother. "The book's ending," according to Gordon, is "a marvelous, elliptical return to her hometown. . . . We last see Marya trying to get a better look at her mother's unfocused face. And this is just right. For the real romance of the novel has nothing to do with men. It is the romance of the daughter abandoned by her witch mother."

Oates's next novel, *You Must Remember This,* is again set in upstate New York of the 1950s. The story is primarily about fifteen-year-old Enid Maria, the youngest child in the Stevick family, and the affair between her and a half-uncle twice her age, the former boxer Felix. The novel opens with Enid's suicide attempt, and also relates a rape, an abortion, several brutal beatings, a severe boxing injury, and two car accidents. This establishes what John Updike, in the *New Yorker,* calls the pattern of Enid's "flirtation with nothingness." These blendings of "her erotic and her self-destructive compulsions" include masturbation, reckless jumping on a trampoline, swimming to exhaustion, shoplifting, contemplating her wallpaper, an attraction to heights, and her affair with Felix. Updike describes the novel as an "allegorical" fairy tale of 1950s options for women, commenting about the three Stevick sisters: "Geraldine marries into a local life of chronic pregnancy and domestic drudgery; Lizzie becomes a singer, an entertainer, and possibly a hooker in New York City; and Enid goes off to college."

By setting such violent acts against the background of post-World War II revelations of Nazi concentration camps, the trial and execution of the Rosenbergs for treason, the McCarthy anti-Communist hunts, and anxieties about the atomic bomb, Oates uses the characters' inner turmoil to reflect "a larger, public sense of dislocation," Michiko Kakutani of the *New York Times* writes. In this fashion *You Must Remember This* "recalls Ms. Oates's highly acclaimed novel *Them,* in which the disorders in her characters' lives converge with the Detroit riots of 1967." But unlike that novel, which "held the author's penchants for the naturalistic and the Gothic in an uneasy balance," the critic continues, "*Remember* welds them together to create a portrait of family life in the 50's that is both recognizable and horrifying, mundane and disturbing." *America* contributor Robert Phillips likewise notes a major development in this work; as her recent novels "seem more personal, more psychologically penetrating, than her earlier, more violent novels," so in this work the author "applies her penetration and technique to produce her best novel."

Another feature of the novel that earned praise from several critics was the power of Oates' descriptions of boxing bouts. Although Oates primarily writes fiction, the extensive research for *You Must Remember This*'s fight scenes resulted in an essay, and the essay became a book, *On Boxing.* In an interview with Jean W. Ross for *Contemporary Authors (CA),* she talked about the sequence of the work: "First [was] the research for [*You Must Remember This*], much of which I imagined from Felix's point of view. Then an editor at the *New York Times Magazine* asked me to write an essay for them, so I wrote a mosaic-like piece I called 'Notes on Boxing,' which, when finally published—it took me a staggeringly long and dense six months to write hardly more than a dozen pages—excited a fair amount of comment locally; with the result that I was invited to expand the essay into a book, to accompany photographs by the superb photographer John Ranard. While reading about boxing I came to see how many really first-rate articles and pieces had been done on the subject, and got the idea of assembling an anthology, and asked my good friend Dan Halpern to help me with it since Dan knows about boxing, and knows much of the literature. So *Reading the Fights* came into being. . . . And that is the last, or nearly, I will be writing about boxing." *On Boxing* received widespread attention, much of it positive and from sources new to the author's work.

About the same time, Oates developed a mystery novel, 1987's *Lives of the Twins,* that she circulated to publishers under the pseudonym Rosamond

"Eloquent...Penetrating...[A] remarkable book."
—*The New York Times*

JOYCE
CAROL
OATES

ON BOXING

"A welcome addition to boxing literature."
—Budd Schulberg, *Chicago Tribune*

"Never has a woman's touch packed more wallop in the
boxing ring. Joyce Carol Oates hits like a heavyweight."
—Gay Talese

WITH PHOTOGRAPHS BY JOHN RANARD

ZEBRA/0-8217-2370-7 ⹝ (CANADA $4.95) U.S. $3.95

Initially, this 1988 story collection began as an essay about the boxing world written for the *New York Times Magazine*.

Smith. Gratifyingly, it was accepted before anyone knew that it was Oates' work, but the true identity of "Rosamond Smith" was revealed long before the book's actual publication, and it was reviewed—generally positively—as Oates's work. Though she continued to use the pseudonym, producing three additional novels as Rosamond Smith, she told *CA,* "I don't think I'll ever publish secretly again."

Youth, Victims, and Violence

The 1990s brought more stories with young heroines, tales of victims and violence. 1992's *Black Water* is the story of a young woman, Kelly Kelleher, who works for a magazine following

graduation from college; she struggles with her own identity, as she follows her interests in politics. When she meets the politician who was the subject of her college thesis—a man identified only as The Senator—it begins a chain of events that leads to her drowning, in circumstances reminiscent of the infamous real-life tragedy at Chappaquiddick that destroyed the presidential hopes of Senator Edward Kennedy. While the historical inspiration for Oates's fiction was obvious to critics and readers, Oates revealed to Susannah Hunnewell in the *New York Times Book Review* that her intent was to create something "somewhat mythical, the almost archetypal experience of a young woman who trusts an older man and whose trust is violated."

The result is that "*Black Water* is as audacious as anything I know in recent fiction," writes Richard Bausch in the *New York Times Book Review,* "for Ms. Oates dares to treat the sensational in the most ordinary terms," focusing on Kelly's character and thoughts. "The life of the book, its essence and outrage, is the drowning voice of Kelly," according to *Los Angeles Times Book Review* critic Richard Eder. The story is told in two voices, the critic continues: "One is Kelly's, confused, uncertain of who she is, what she wants, what she has done. It is fragmented; it relives the incidents of the day and brief moments of the past. It speaks, pain-shocked, of imaginary rescue in the car's trapped air bubble, and it speaks as the water fills her lungs. The other voice, weaving among narrative, lament and judgment, adopts the musical reiteration and the emotion fortified by distance of the ballad singer." As a consequence, when "the book draws to its conclusion, the refrain 'as the black water filled her lungs, and she died' is repeated with very much the same frequency and engenders much the same feeling of cathartic recognition, that one experiences hearing the choruses of the ancient Greek tragedies," Bausch states. "Indeed, what *Black Water* does is what all the great tragedies do. It portrays an individual fate, born out of the protagonist's character and driven forward by the force of events."

The short, 154-page novel earned widespread praise and was a finalist for National Book Critics Circle Award. A *Publishers Weekly* critic notes that "Oates is at the top of her stunning form" in extracting "a deeper, more terrible meaning" from her familiar theme of a young woman encountering violence. "In its suspense and tragedy, this story is painful to read, and in its allusiveness and brevity frustrating," a reviewer for the *New Yorker* comments. "But its power of evocation is remarkable." As Bausch concluded: "Taut, powerfully imagined and beautifully written, *Black Water* ranks with the best of Joyce Carol Oates's already long list of distinguished achievements. It can be read in a single afternoon, but, like every good book, it continues to haunt us."

This novella, which depicts the final moments and thoughts of a young woman's life, might seem to be the culmination of a literary career which has focused on violence and its victims. Critics have often remarked on the incidence of violence in Oates's work, sometimes criticizing her for it. But, as she explained to Parini, the violence in her work is only reflecting the reality of today's society: "A writer's job, ideally, is to act as the conscience of his race. People frequently misunderstand serious art because it is often violent and unattractive. I wish the world were a prettier place, but I wouldn't be honest as a writer if I ignored the actual conditions around me." Responding more specifically in a *New York Times Book Review* article to the question "Why is your writing so violent?," the author observed: "Since it is commonly understood that serious writers, as distinct from entertainers or propagandists, take for their natural subjects the complexity of the world, its evils as well as its goods, it is always an insulting question; and it is always sexist. The serious writer, after all, bears witness." The author believes her work has been misinterpreted, as she told Hunnewell: "I write about the victims of violence . . . and yet my critics say I'm writing about violence. From my point of view, I've always been writing about its aftermath."

In contrast to the turbulent world she often portrays in her writing, Oates lives peacefully with her husband, Raymond Smith, and several cats in a house nestled into a wooded landscape several miles from Princeton University, where she teaches. Smith runs the Ontario Review Press and is editor of *The Ontario Review,* a small literary magazine he and Oates cofounded in 1974. Mornings are usually reserved for writing, the author told Franks. Working at a desk that sits in front of a large window that looks out on grass and trees, "I usually work from about 8:30 A.M. to 1 P.M.," Oates recounted. Afternoons are open for her teaching duties and related meetings and conferences at the university, while evenings include

more writing. Oates also spends time preparing for talks about and readings from her works, especially in relation to promoting her latest publication.

The process of creating isn't limited to time in front of the typewriter, however. As Oates told Franks: "If you are a writer, you locate yourself behind a wall of silence and no matter what you are doing, driving a car or walking or doing housework, which I love, you can still be writing, because you have that space." The author further explained, as Joslin relates: "It's mainly daydreaming, I sit and look out at the river, I daydream about a kind of populated empty space. There's nothing verbal about it. Then there comes a time when it's all set and I just go write it. With a story it's one evening, if I can type that fast." In contrast to some critics' speculation that her prolific output implies hasty preparation, Oates revealed to Franks that "as I get older, I find I

In this 1993 novel, five high school girls growing up in the fifties form their own gang.

can't write as fast, and I have to rewrite again and again, sometimes as much as 17 times."

Strangely enough, Oates's exceptional literary output has generated controversy about her reputation. Calling rumors of Oates's nomination for the Nobel Prize for Literature "idiotic," for instance, *Washington Post Book World* critic Jonathan Yardley states: "To be sure, were writers to be recognized solely for their productivity, then certainly Oates would get all the prizes; they'd have to invent new ones just for her. . . . Writers, reviewers and readers gaze at her in awe; she is, in the words they occasionally apply reverently to her, a 'writing machine.' It seems not to have occurred to anyone that writing is like anything else: if it is done too hastily and too profusely, it almost inevitably is done badly." As an example, Yardley calls *Solstice* "a hysterical little novel . . . [that has] nothing at all to say." Gordon, however, notes that "we punish Joyce Carol Oates for the crime of her productivity . . . as if she did it just to make us look bad." The critic continues: "If we as readers allow ourselves to see Joyce Carol Oates as an industry or a phenomenon rather than the serious writer she is, we do her and ourselves an injustice. It should not be forgotten that she has rendered better than anyone else the texture of the daily life of a particular kind of American: the lower-middle- or working-class woman whose limited possibilities can quickly move from simple frustration to nightmare."

Despite any critical disputes over the content or volume of her work, there is no doubt that Oates holds a place of distinction in contemporary American literature. "Oates is one of our most audaciously talented writers. Her gift is so large, her fluency in different genres—poems, short stories; novels, essays—so great, that at times she seems to challenge the ability of readers to keep up with her," Jong concludes. "In an age of specialization she is that rarest of generalists, a woman of letters. She gives her gifts with such abundance and generosity that we may pick and choose, preferring this Oates to that, quibbling about which of her many talents we like best." "To view Oates' fiction in retrospect is to be surprised that what seemed to be basically 'realistic' fiction has so many variations, and shows such range of experimentation, such wealth of literary antecedent," Linda W. Wagner similarly states in *Great Lakes Review.* "But whether she writes a comic *Expensive People,* an impressionistic *Childwold,* or that

strangely heightened realism of *them* and the short stories, her interest is less in technical innovation than it is in trying the border between the real and the illusory, in testing the space in which those two seemingly separate entities converge."

It may seem unusual that a writer that attracts such critical and scholarly attention is also a popular favorite, but Oates's books enjoy steady sales and she is a celebrated speaker at colleges and universities. Her stylishly written works may address the larger social themes that draw critical examination, but it is her extraordinary ability to render how terror intrudes on ordinary, everyday life that appeals to a wider audience. As Gardner explains: "Oates is a 'popular' novelist because her stories are suspenseful (and the suspense is never fake: The horror will really come, as well as, sometimes, the triumph), because her sex scenes are steamy and because when she describes a place you think you're there. . . . To real intellectuals Miss Oates's work tends to be appealing, partly because her vision is huge, well-informed and sound, and partly because they too like suspense, brilliant descriptions and sex."

While critics treat each new Oates book as a subject for continuing analysis of her work, they refrain from speculating about what future generations will consider her single greatest accomplishment. As Victoria Glendinning notes in the *New York Times Book Review:* "We cannot know whether it is her whole oeuvre that will seem the sum of her achievement . . . or whether one novel, say, will survive as a classic." Joslin observes: "With each succeeding work Oates demonstrates her growing ability to write highly artistic, yet socially relevant, fiction: her potential is limited only by her energy and her control. Of her energy there is no question; already her output resembles the prodigious collections of the prolific novelists of the nineteenth century. . . . That Oates is today a major American novelist is an established fact, for her powerful imagination presents compelling visions of contemporary society which cannot be ignored." "What matters to Oates is the work itself, not its critical reception or notoriety," Greg Johnson relates. "Despite her occasional remarks hinting at exhaustion, her passionate engagement with her craft continues. . . . Despite the occasional criticism, her reputation continues to grow not only in the United States but worldwide." The critic concludes that while "possibly she has not yet written the book that will be viewed as representing the full range of her talents . . . it is clear that Joyce Carol Oates has already earned her place alongside the major American writers of the twentieth century."

■ Works Cited

Adams, Alice, review of *A Bloodsmoor Romance, Los Angeles Times Book Review,* September 19, 1982, pp. 1, 4.

Adams, Robert M., review of *them, New York Times,* October 1, 1969, p. 45.

Avant, John Alfred, review of *The Hungry Ghosts, New Republic,* August 31, 1974, pp. 30-31.

Batchelor, John Calvin, "Hot News: Funny Oates," *Village Voice,* July 30-August 5, 1980, p. 34.

Bausch, Richard, "Her Thoughts While Drowning," *New York Times Book Review,* May 10, 1992, pp. 1, 29.

Bender, Eileen Teper, *Joyce Carol Oates, Artist in Residence,* Indiana University Press, 1987.

Review of *Black Water, New Yorker,* August 10, 1992, p. 79.

Review of *Black Water, Publishers Weekly,* March 9, 1992, p. 47.

Clemons, Walter, "Joyce Carol Oates: Love and Violence," *Newsweek,* December 11, 1972, pp. 72-74.

Craig, Patricia, "Philosophical Tale of Gore," *New York Times Book Review,* February 12, 1984, p. 7.

DeRamus, Betty, "Peeking into the Very Private World of Joyce Carol Oates," *Detroit Free Press,* March 3, 1974.

Eder, Richard, "A Girl's Ballad," *Los Angeles Times Book Review,* May 10, 1992, p. 2, 15.

Flower, Dean, "Fables of Identity," *Hudson Review,* summer, 1986, pp. 309-21.

Franks, Lucinda, "The Emergence of Joyce Carol Oates," *New York Times Magazine,* July 27, 1980, pp. 22+.

Gardner, John, "The Strange Real World," *New York Times Book Review,* July 20, 1980, pp. 1, 21.

Glendinning, Victoria, "In Touch with God," *New York Times Book Review,* August 13, 1978, p. 10.

Gordon, Mary, "The Life and Hard Times of Cinderella," *New York Times Book Review,* March 2, 1986, pp. 7, 9.

Hunnewell, Susannah, "A Trusting Young Woman," *New York Times Book Review,* May 10, 1992, p. 29.

Johnson, Diane, "Balloons and Abductions," *New York Times Book Review,* September 5, 1982, pp. 1, 15-16.

Johnson, Greg, "Metaphysical Borders," *Southwest Review,* autumn, 1976, pp. 438-41.

Johnson, Greg, *Understanding Joyce Carol Oates,* University of South Carolina Press, 1987, 224 p.

Jong, Erica, "Uncanny States of East and West," *New York Times Book Review,* August 5, 1984, p. 7.

Joslin, Michael, "Joyce Carol Oates," *Dictionary of Literary Biography,* Volume 2: *American Novelists since World War II,* Gale, 1978, pp. 371-81.

Kakutani, Michiko, review of *You Must Remember This, New York Times,* August 10, 1987, p. C20.

Knowles, John, review of *With Shuddering Fall, New York Times Book Review,* October 25, 1964, p. 5.

Lehmann-Haupt, Christopher, review of *Marya: A Life, New York Times,* February 20, 1986, section III, p. 20.

Leonard, John, review of *Bellefleur, New York Times,* July 21, 1980, section III.

Marien, Mary Warner, review of *Heat, and Other Stories, Christian Science Monitor,* August 20, 1991, p. 14.

Oates, Joyce Carol, "Author's Preface," *them,* Vanguard Press, 1969.

Oates, "Why Is Your Writing So Violent?," *New York Times Book Review,* March 29, 1981, pp. 15, 35.

Oates, interview in *Michigan Quarterly Review,* spring, 1986.

Overbeck, S. K., "A Masterful Explorer in the Minefields of Emotion," *Washington Post Book World,* September 17, 1972, pp. 4, 10.

Parini, Jay, interview with Oates in *Boston Globe Magazine,* August 2, 1987.

Phillips, Robert, review of *You Must Remember This, America,* November 14, 1987, pp. 360, 362.

Ross, Jean W., interview with Oates for *Contemporary Authors New Revision Series,* Volume 25, Gale, 1989, pp. 343-53.

Sanborn, Sara, "Two Major Novelists All by Herself," *Nation,* January 5, 1974, pp. 20-21.

Shapiro, Charles, "Law and Love," *National Review,* October 27, 1973, pp. 26-27.

Straub, Peter, review of *Marriages and Infidelities, New Statesman,* August 23, 1974, p. 261.

Review of *them, Virginia Quarterly Review,* spring, 1970, p. xl.

Updike, John, "What You Deserve Is What You Get," *New Yorker,* December 28, 1987, pp. 119-23.

Urbanski, Marie Mitchell Olesen, "Existential Allegory: Joyce Carol Oates' 'Where Are You Going, Where Have You Been?,'" *Studies in Short Fiction,* spring, 1978, pp. 200-203.

Wagner, Linda W., "Oates: The Changing Shapes of her Realities," *Great Lakes Review,* winter, 1979.

Yardley, Jonathan, "Joyce Carol Oates on Automatic Pilot," *Washington Post Book World*, January 6, 1985, p. 3.

Zimmerman, Paul D., "Hunger for Dreams," *Newsweek*, March 23, 1970, pp. 108, 110.

■ **For More Information See**

BOOKS

Bastian, Katherine, *Joyce Carol Oates's Short Stories: Between Tradition and Innovation*, Verlag Peter Lang, 1983.

Bestsellers '89, Issue 2, Gale, 1989.

Contemporary Literary Criticism, Volume 1, 1973, Volume 2, 1974, Volume 3, 1975, Volume 6, 1976, Volume 9, 1978, Volume 11, 1979, Volume 15, 1980, Volume 19, 1981, Volume 33, 1985, Volume 52, 1989, pp. 328-40.

Creighton, Joanne V., *Joyce Carol Oates*, Twayne, 1979.

Dictionary of Literary Biography, Volume 5: *American Poets since World War I*, Gale, 1980, pp. 99-102.

Friedman, Ellen G., *Joyce Carol Oates*, Ungar, 1980.

Grant, Mary Kathryn, *The Tragic Vision of Joyce Carol Oates*, Duke University Press, 1978.

Lercangee, Francine and Bruce F. Michelson, *Joyce Carol Oates: An Annotated Bibliography*, Garland, 1986.

Oates, Joyce Carol, "The Nature of Short Fiction; or, The Nature of My Short Fiction," *Preface to Handbook of Short Story Writing*, edited by Frank A. Dickson and Sandra Smythe, Writer's Digest, 1973.

Wagner, Linda W., editor, *Critical Essays on Joyce Carol Oates*, G. K. Hall, 1979.

Waller, G. F., *Dreaming America: Obsession and Transcendence in the Fiction of Joyce Carol Oates*, Louisiana State University Press, 1979.

PERIODICALS

Commonweal, December 5, 1969, pp. 307-10.
Contemporary Literature, summer, 1982, pp. 267-84.
Ms., March, 1986, p. 44-50.
Nation, December 7, 1974, pp. 597-99.
New York Times Book Review, September 28, 1969, pp. 4-5; October 23, 1977, pp. 15, 18; August 16, 1981, pp. 1, 18; July 11, 1982, pp. 1, 15-16; January 20, 1985, p. 4; August 16, 1987, p. 3; January 3, 1988, p. 5.
Ohio Review, fall, 1973, pp. 50-61.
Paris Review, fall, 1979, pp. 199-226.
Publishers Weekly, June 26, 1978, pp. 12-13.
Saturday Review, October 26, 1968, pp. 34-35.
Studies in Short Fiction, winter, 1981, pp. 65-70.
Women and Literature, fall, 1977, pp. 17-28.

—*Sketch by Barbara A. Withers*

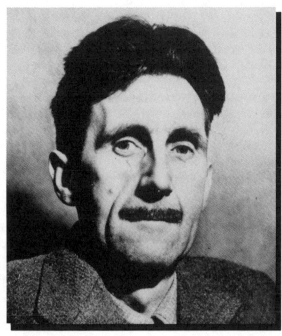

George Orwell

■ Personal

Has also written under real name; born Eric Arthur Blair, June 25, 1903, in Motihari, India (British citizen born abroad); died January 21, 1950, in London, England; son of Richard Walmesley (a colonial civil servant) and Ida Mabel (Limouzin) Blair; married Eileen O'Shaughnessy, June 9, 1936 (died, March 29, 1945); married Sonia Brownell, October 13, 1949; children: (first marriage) Richard Horatio (adopted). *Education:* Graduated from Eton College, 1921. *Hobbies and other interests:* Gardening and fishing.

■ Career

Writer. Served with Indian Imperial Police at Police Training School and as assistant superintendent of police in Burma, 1922–23; dishwasher in Paris, France, 1929; Evelyn's School (private school for boys), Hayes, Middlesex, England, teacher, 1932–33; Frays College (private co–educational school), Uxbridge, England, teacher, 1933; Booklovers' Corner (second–hand bookshop), London, England, clerk, 1934–35; "The Stores," Wallington, Hertfordshire, England, grocer, 1936–39; British Broadcasting Corp. (BBC), began as talks assistant, became talks producer, in Indian section of Eastern Service, 1941–43; *Tribune* (weekly newspaper), London, literary editor, 1943–45, author of "As I Please" column, 1943–47; *Observer*, London, correspondent in Germany, Austria, and France, 1945. *Military service:* Militia of Partido Obrero de Unificacion Marxista (POUM; "Workers' Party of Marxist Unity"), 1937; based in Catalonia, Spain, served on Aragon front during Spanish Civil War, became lieutenant; Local Defence Volunteers (became Home Guard), 1940–43; served in England during World War II, became sergeant.

■ Awards, Honors

First annual award for a distinguished body of work, *Partisan Review*, 1941.

■ Writings

NOVELS

Burmese Days, Harper, 1934.
A Clergyman's Daughter, Gollancz, 1935, Harper, 1936.
Keep the Aspidistra Flying, Gollancz, 1936, Harcourt, 1956.
Coming Up for Air, Gollancz, 1939, Harcourt, 1950.
Animal Farm (Book–of–the–Month Club selection), Secker & Warburg, 1945, Harcourt, 1946, published with illustrations by Joy Batchelor and John Halas, Harcourt, 1954.

Nineteen Eighty–Four (Book–of–the–Month Club selection), Harcourt, 1949.

The Penguin Complete Novels of George Orwell (omnibus volume), Penguin, 1983.

NONFICTION

Down and Out in Paris and London, Harper, 1933.

The Road to Wigan Pier, Gollancz, 1937, Harcourt, 1958.

Homage to Catalonia, Secker & Warburg, 1938, Harcourt, 1952.

Inside the Whale, and Other Essays, Gollancz, 1940.

(Contributor) Victor Gollancz, editor, *The Betrayal of the Left,* Gollancz, 1941.

The Lion and the Unicorn: Socialism and the English Genius (essays), Secker & Warburg, 1941, AMS Press, 1976.

Dickens, Dali and Others: Studies in Popular Culture, Reynal & Hitchcock, 1946, published in England as *Critical Essays,* Secker & Warburg, 1946.

John Burnham and the Managerial Revolution, Socialist Book Centre (London), 1946.

The English People, Collins, 1947, Haskell House, 1974.

Shooting and Elephant and Other Essays, Harcourt, 1950.

Such, Such Were the Joys (essays), Harcourt, 1953, abridged edition, substituting excerpts from *The Road to Wigan Pier* for "Such, Such Were the Joys," published in England as *England, Your England, and Other Essays,* Secker & Warburg, 1953.

A Collection of Essays, Doubleday, 1954.

The Collected Essays, Journalism and Letters of George Orwell, edited by wife, Sonia Orwell, and Ian Angus, Volume 1: *An Age Like This,* Volume 2: *My Country Right or Left,* Volume 3: *As I Please,* Volume 4: *In Front of Your Nose,* Harcourt, 1968.

Orwell: The Lost Writings, edited by W. J. West, Arbor House, 1985.

Orwell: The War Broadcasts, edited by W. J. West, Duckworth/British Broadcast Corp., 1985, published as *Orwell: The War Commentaries,* Pantheon, 1986.

Contributor, sometimes under name Eric A. Blair, of numerous articles and reviews to periodicals, including *Adelphi, New Leader, Manchester Evening News, New Statesman and Nation,* and *Horizon.* Author of "London Letters" column for *Partisan Review,* 1941–46.

OTHER

(Editor and author of introduction) *Talking to India: A Selection of English–Language Broadcasts to India,* Allen & Unwin, 1943.

(Editor with Reginald Reynolds, and author of introduction) *British Pamphleteers, Volume 1: From the Sixteenth Century to the French Revolution,* Wingate, 1948.

Editor, with T. R. Fyvel, *Searchlight Books* series, Secker & Warburg, 1941–42. Work included in numerous collections and anthologies, including *The Orwell Reader: Fiction, Essays, Reportage,* Harcourt, 1956.

■ Adaptations

Animal Farm was adapted as an animated film of the same title by Louis de Rochemont Associates, 1954, and for two filmstrips: *Animal Farm: A Review of the Novel of George Orwell,* Current Affairs Films, 1978, and *Animal Farm,* Ealing Films, 1979; *Nineteen Eighty–Four* was adapted as two films of the same title, by Holiday Film Productions, 1954, and another production in 1984; *Nineteen Eighty–Four* was adapted as a play of the same title, Dramatic Publishing Co., 1963; *Animal Farm* was adapted by Nelson Slade Bond for a play of the same title, Samuel French, 1964.

■ Sidelights

"There will be no loyalty, except loyalty to the Party. There will be no love, except the love of Big Brother. . . . There will be no curiosity, no employment of the process of life. All competing pleasures will be destroyed. But always—do not forget this, Winston—always there will be the intoxication of power, constantly increasing and constantly growing subtler. Always, at every moment, there will be the thrill of victory, the sensation of trampling on an enemy who is helpless. If you want a picture of the future, imagine a boot stamping on a human face—forever."

Unwary readers should be cautioned that they will find this disturbing image of the future—and many more like it—in British novelist and essayist George Orwell's *Nineteen Eighty–Four.* The scenes might be horrifying and the tension extreme, but that's the way Orwell (whose legal name was Eric Arthur Blair) intended them to be. Written as a brutal satire of Soviet leader Joseph

Stalin's politics of terror, Orwell hoped his novel would serve as a warning to complacent citizens that a similar dictatorship could be easily established anywhere in the world.

Orwell willfully wrote page after page of abject cruelty—typing out the final manuscript of his work while deathly ill—because of the importance he attached to his message. He labored so long over the manuscript that he collapsed as he reached its end and spent the last two years of his life bedridden. *Nineteen Eighty–Four*, the product of his heroic efforts, is considered a masterpiece of twentieth–century English literature. In the novel, Orwell brings together several recurring themes—individual freedom, the influence of language, the abuse of power, and others—that had commanded his personal and literary energies since the beginning of his career some twenty years earlier. *Nineteen Eighty–Four*, along with Orwell's satirical fable *Animal Farm*, propelled him to international literary prominence and remain eloquent reminders of his concern for his own and future generations.

Painful Beginnings

While known as the creator of a fictional world of the future, Orwell believed quite strongly in the importance of the past. For Orwell, the past meant the pre–1914 world of his childhood. Like Winston Smith, the main character of *Nineteen Eighty–Four*, Orwell longed to recapture an era before the horrors of war changed the face of his world. With World War I, many experienced for the first time the terrifying drone of warplanes and the vicious realities of trench warfare. "Men learned to accept as commonplace," Bertram D. Wolfe notes in *Marxism in the Modern World*, "the ruthless logic of mutual extermination. They learned to master their fear of death and the revulsion against inflicting it." While the war transformed the greater society in which Orwell lived, another event caused more immediate change in his own life. When he was eight his parents secured a scholarship for him to St. Cyprian's, an exclusive all–male preparatory school on the English Channel far from the family home. Many critics, such as Jeffrey Meyers and Anthony West, assert that the strict, repressive atmosphere of the school haunted Orwell's imagination throughout his life, influencing the themes and forms of his writings.

Orwell detailed his nightmare–like impressions of his early school years in the essay "Such, Such Were the Joys," published posthumously. All his feelings of guilt, humiliation, and rejection came back to him even as he wrote his reminiscences decades later: "This was the great lesson of my boyhood: that I was in a world where it was not possible for me to be good." Like many authors, Orwell would later turn adversity into material that appeared in his writings. "All Orwell's books," Meyers claims in *A Reader's Guide to George Orwell*, "are autobiographical and spring from his psychological need to work out the pattern and meaning of his personal experience; his great triumph is his ability to transform his early guilt and awareness of what it means to be a victim, described in 'Such, Such Were the Joys,' into a compassionate ethic of responsibility, a compulsive sharing in the suffering and degradation of others." Orwell was never allowed to forget that his parents were poorer than the sons of the very wealthy or members of the British upper class who made up the majority of his St. Cyprian's classmates. Even the school's staff would find occasion to remind the scholarship boys that they were different from the rest of the student body. "His awareness of having an ambivalent social position," writes David Morgan Zehr in *Dictionary of Literary Biography*, "and of money's extraordinary importance would become prominent themes in Orwell's first four books [*Down and Out in Paris and London, Burmese Days, A Clergyman's Daughter*, and *Keep the Aspidistra Flying*] and helped to shape his attitudes to what he came to see as the privileged intelligentsia."

After leaving St. Cyprian's, Orwell continued his education at prestigious Eton College, again on a scholarship. While he found the atmosphere at Eton more tolerant, instead of going on to university studies at Oxford or Cambridge with the rest of his class upon graduation, he decided to apply to the Indian Imperial Police. After passing the required examinations, he was sent to Burma, then a province of British–controlled India, and entered the Police Training School in Mandalay in 1922. He remained in Burma five years; during that time he learned to speak fluent Burmese, read unceasingly, and grew increasingly ill at ease with his authoritative role. After being ruled by the British since the mid–1800s, the desire for self–rule was strong amongst the native peoples with whom Orwell came in contact. As a member of the police, Orwell found himself uncomfortable in the position of furthering imperialism. He began to hate the very job he had come to Burma to carry out. "I was in the police," he explained in *The Road to Wigan Pier,* "which is to say that I was part of the actual machinery of despotism." Unable to ease his feelings of isolation, both from the distrustful native population and from his often cruel fellow officers, it was with a sense of relief that Orwell returned to England in 1927. Within a month he resigned his position and gave notice to his parents that he intended to become a writer.

Becoming Orwell

Although Orwell had had several poems published as an adolescent, up to this announcement he had done little to indicate that writing would be his chosen profession. His keen social conscience—developed during his school years and his stay in Burma—seemed to compel him to want to express his ideas on paper. In an essay entitled "Why I Write," Orwell traced the roots of his vocation to an even earlier time. He also admitted that no matter how hard he tried to avoid it, being an author seemed to be somehow inevitable. "From an early age," he wrote, "perhaps the age of five or six, I knew that when I grew up I should be a writer. Between the ages of about seventeen and twenty–four I tried to abandon this idea, but I did so with the consciousness that I was outraging my true nature and that sooner or later I should have to settle down and write books." Despite   his enthusiasm, Orwell's was not to be a story of overnight success. Peter Stansky and William Abrahams examine this part of the novelist's life in *Orwell: The Transformation.* "Between 1927 and 1932," they observe, "he would not take a regular job—he lived to write, a state made possible only by the generosity of his mother and his aunt Nellie Adam, who kept him in funds. It was an arduous apprenticeship, and his success in those five years was minimal." Stansky and Abrahams point out, however, that during this same period Orwell—writing as Eric A. Blair—saw a number of his essays, poems, reviews, and other pieces published in *New Statesman and Nation* and the *New English Weekly.* "The Hanging," considered one of his finest essays, appeared in the British journal *Adelphi* in 1931.

Having been unsuccessful in the roles of rich student and imperialist agent, Orwell's decision to be a writer opened to him the complete opposite world of the poor and oppressed. After moving to London, he purchased a set of second–hand clothes and set off to discover the roots of poverty among the city's vast number of unemployed. "My new clothes ... had put me instantly into a new world," he wrote in *Down and Out in Paris and London.* "Everyone's demeanour seemed to have changed abruptly. I helped a hawker pick up a barrow that he had upset. 'Thanks, mate,' he said with a grin. No one had called me mate before in my life—it was the clothes that had done it." Having trouble meeting expenses, he decided to move to Paris, where he could live more cheaply while continuing his writing and perhaps learn French at the same time. Still unable to make ends meet through his writing, he took a job as a dishwasher in a hotel restaurant. In 1929, nearly penniless and facing a pile of rejection letters from publishers, Orwell was forced to return to England.

During his travels he had gathered plenty of first–hand material for his writing, however, and he returned home full of plans for future projects. By October 1930 he finished a manuscript that told the story of his Parisian experiences in diary form. One publisher rejected the book saying it was too short, and then rejected it a second time even with the addition of a section on Orwell's London experiences. Another rejection notice arrived from the poet T. S. Eliot, who was then working as a reader at Faber and Faber. Discouraged and forced to look for another source of income, in April 1932 Orwell began teaching at a small private school for boys in Hayes, Middlesex, on the outskirts of London. Then, the good news came—*Down and Out in Paris and London* had been accepted for publication by Victor Gollancz and would be published the following year. Although Orwell was still using his real name professionally, in hopes of not disturbing his parents with the terrible living conditions described in the book, he requested it be published under a pseudonym. He suggested four possible names to the publisher, but left the final choice up to Gollancz. This was how he became George Orwell.

Down and Out in Paris and London was an uneven autobiographical piece in which the author wavered between storytelling and social criticism. "Poverty is what I am writing about," says the narrator as the book opens. According to Zehr the work embodied "Orwell's conflicting desires to

With the success of his novel *Animal Farm,* Orwell was able to rent Barnhill, a home on the isolated Scottish island of Jura where he finished his final novel and masterpiece, *Nineteen Eighty-Four.*

produce an imaginative work of art and to expound directly on social issues and conditions that he felt deeply about." His interest in language is also evident: a detailed description of slang used by London's lower class takes up three pages near the end of the book. Despite its irregularities, the book sold well; a second printing was ordered at the end of January, with a third following later in the year. Reviews appeared in prominent British periodicals, including the *Manchester Guardian* and the *Times Literary Supplement,* and most were favorable. Elated by his success, Orwell was all the more eager to finish the novel he was working on about his experiences in Burma. As the summer ended, he returned again to teaching, this time at a larger, more comfortable school. He taught French and other classes as well, devoting as much time as possible to finishing up the novel, *Burmese Days.* But in December, just after finishing the manuscript, he developed a bad case of pneumonia and was hospitalized. Under doctor's orders to recuperate for at least six months, Orwell resigned his teaching position and

moved back to the family home in Southwold on the east coast of England.

A Busy Decade

Burmese Days was published in 1934. After that Orwell managed to publish a new book in each of the remaining years of the thirties: *A Clergyman's Daughter* (1935), *Keep the Aspidistra Flying* (1936), *The Road to Wigan Pier* (1937), *Homage to Catalonia* (1938), and *Coming Up for Air* (1939). As Meyers notes, all the books focused on "two dominant themes—poverty and politics—or, as [Orwell] put it, 'the twin nightmares that beset nearly every modern man, the nightmare of unemployment and the nightmare of State interference.'" The element of moral instruction was so strong in Orwell's work that Robert L. Calder proposes in *Dictionary of Literary Biography* that he was "essentially a writer of essays who used fiction as a means of presenting an argument." Orwell's books poignantly reflect the depressed pre-war atmosphere of the thirties, when unemployment was a pressing concern worldwide and the jargon of totalitarianism—with the rise of Adolf Hitler's National Socialist (Nazi) party in Germany and General Francisco Franco's fascist state in Spain—was becoming familiar. The victimization that Orwell felt as a child in the hands of his persecutors at St. Cyprian's was replayed and intensified in these novels as one after another of his characters became swallowed up by their miserable surroundings. "In Orwell's earlier work, all society was a prison," declares Frederick R. Karl in *A Reader's Guide to the Contemporary English Novel,* "whether the prison of Flory's Burma, the prison of London and Paris, the prison of living on a pound a week in *Keep the Aspidistra Flying* [or] the prison of working in the coal mines in *The Road to Wigan Pier.*"

For much of the narrative material in these books, Orwell relied on his ability to convert his personal experiences into literary elements. With John Flory in *Burmese Days,* Orwell was able to rage against the imperialism he had seen first–hand in Burma. Like Orwell, Flory is repelled by the system he represents but unable to establish a true friendship with any of the natives he meets. As a member of the colonial class he finds he must conform or be destroyed. "Free speech is unthinkable. All other kinds of freedom are permitted. You are free to be a drunkard, an idler, a coward, a backbiter, a fornicator; but you are not free to think for yourself," Orwell declares in the novel. Flory's attempt at rebellion ends in failure and he commits suicide. Also like Orwell, Dorothy Hare in *A Clergyman's Daughter* goes hop–picking in the fields of Kent and teaches in a private school; Gordon Comstock in *Keep the Aspidistra Flying* is a struggling poet working as a clerk in a bookshop much like the Booklovers' Corner, where Orwell worked from 1934 to 1935. Both characters attempt to break out of their suffocating middle–class existences but fail in their efforts. However, Zehr finds signs in *Keep the Aspidistra Flying* of the beginning of Orwell's fierce patriotism, so notable during the war years, and repeated emphasis on the importance of traditional British values. "The novel is the first of Orwell's books," he notes, "in which we see the clear beginnings of his idealization of the ordinary in English life and of his commitment to traditional values." While both books reveal the author to be an astute social critic, neither worked well as a novel. Always a harsh self–critic, Orwell refused to have them reprinted during his lifetime.

Marriage, Coal Mines, and a Civil War

The year 1936 was significant for Orwell. By his own reckoning this was the year his writing became politically focused. It was also the year when he officially declared himself to be a socialist. In "Why I Write" he claimed, "Every line of serious work that I have written since 1936 has been written, directly and indirectly, against totalitarianism and for democratic socialism." Elsewhere in the same essay he characterized his non–political writing as "lifeless" and full of "purple passages, sentences without meaning, decorative adjectives and humbug generally." While his writing would embroil him in the political rhetoric of a world about to go to war, his personal life was happier than ever before. In June he married Eileen O'Shaughnessy and they set up a home

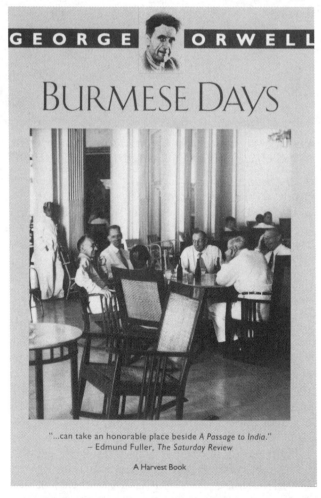

GEORGE ORWELL

BURMESE DAYS

"...can take an honorable place beside *A Passage to India*."
– Edmund Fuller, *The Saturday Review*

A Harvest Book

A complex portrait of a man who disapproves of, yet is isolated by, his involvement in British colonialism, this novel was based on the author's own experience as a policeman in Burma.

together in a 300–year–old house in the small village of Wallington, about twenty–four miles northeast of London. There the couple ran a small grocery store and kept busy collecting eggs from the hens they raised, milking their goats, and growing vegetables in their garden. For Orwell it was a chance to revel in the beauty of the English countryside that he had loved as a boy, and it also provided a perfect out–of–the–way retreat where he could work.

Two other events of 1936 kindled Orwell's political activism: his trip to investigate unemployment in England's industrialized north, and his participation in the Spanish Civil War. From January through March of that year he lived among the poor working class and unemployed laborers from England's coal mines. Emotionally stunned by the appalling working and living conditions of the coalminers, Orwell found he had to do more than just report on what he saw. "He came away from the mines and the North," note Stansky and Abrahams, "in a state of guilt, anger, and compassion, and with a new, untested belief in the necessity of a political resolution." Much to the dismay of his publisher, Victor Gollancz, who had commissioned the work for his planned Left Book Club, the book included more than just Orwell's intensely moving portrait of the poor. The reportage of the first section of the book was followed by Orwell's own story of his conversion to socialism, including his railing against British socialists. "Socialism, at least in this island," he wrote, "does not smell any longer of revolution and the overthrow of tyrants; it smells of crankishness, machine worship and the stupid cult of Russia." Gollancz felt obliged to publish *The Road to Wigan Pier* with his own foreword, stating his inability to agree with some of Orwell's statements.

In late December 1936, Orwell traveled to Spain, beginning a six–month saga that, according to Zehr, "provided the seminal experiences that would inform and structure *Animal Farm* and *1984*." Other foreigners were also coming to Spain at the same time, determined to defend the country's democratically elected government against the fascist takeover of Franco and his troops. While the purpose of Orwell's trip was to observe and to write about the war, he soon decided to join in the fighting. Since he had come to Spain as a correspondent for the British Independent Labour Party (ILP), Orwell enlisted in the militia of the ILP's sister organization in Spain,

Orwell earned popular and critical acclaim for this deceptively simple fable that satirizes the revolutions (particularly the Russian Revolution) and its repercussions.

the Partido Obrero de Unificacion Marxista (POUM—Worker's Party of Marxist Unity). *Homage to Catalonia* is Orwell's account of how the promise of the war was betrayed by infighting between the Communists and others on the Republican side. He was particularly outraged when, on leave in Barcelona after fighting on the Aragon front, he learned that the Communists were spreading false reports that the POUM were secretly supporting the fascists. Ten days after he returned to the front, Orwell was shot through the neck by sniper fire. He eventually made a full recovery, but was forced to flee from Spain with his wife—who had joined him there and was working as a secretary at the POUM office in Barcelona—when the POUM was declared illegal.

Homage to Catalonia was not well received at the time of its publication in 1938, but it eventually came to be looked upon as an essential part of the literature of the Spanish Civil War. Important not only for its honest portrait of war in general, it is also prized by critics who see in it the beginnings of Orwell's mature, unadorned writing style. Almost immediately upon finishing his Spanish reminiscences, Orwell began work on *Coming Up for Air,* his first novel to be published in three years. Like *Homage to Catalonia,* the novel looks back with nostalgia at a more innocent past while at the same time predicting a war–torn future. Orwell closes *Homage to Catalonia* by invoking the England of his childhood—"the railway–cuttings smothered in wild flowers"—and foreseeing a time when "the roar of bombs" would destroy it all. Orwell's protagonist in *Coming Up for Air,* George Bowling, is an insurance salesman who attempts to escape his drab middle–class existence by returning to his childhood home. Once there, he realizes the inaccessibility of the past when he discovers that the pristine beauty of the area has been destroyed by pollution and over–development. Bowling, like Orwell in *Homage to Catalonia,* predicts a bleak future: "It's all going to happen. All the things you've got at the back of your mind, the things that you're terrified of, the things you tell yourself are just a nightmare or only happen in foreign countries. The bombs, the food–queues, the rubber truncheons, the barbed wire, . . . It's all going to happen."

World War II began several months after *Coming Up for Air* was published, when Hitler invaded Poland, and France and England declared war on Germany. Eager to serve his country, Orwell—along with his wife—moved to London. After being turned down for military duty due to poor health, he found several other ways in which he could participate. He was an active member of the Home Guard, Britain's civilian defense force, and worked as a radio producer for the Indian Service of the British Broadcasting Corporation (BBC). After leaving the BBC, he became literary editor of the *Tribune,* a weekly socialist newspaper, and served as a war correspondent for the *London Observer.* He was in Germany, covering the closing months of the war in Europe, when he received word that his wife had died during an operation. Orwell's personal loss had come just

months before his biggest triumph as a writer: the publication of *Animal Farm* in August 1945. He had completed the book in early 1944, but because it was seen as an attack on Stalin—then Britain's ally—its publication was delayed until the end of the war. The first edition sold out within a matter of weeks and the book was a critical and popular success. In the United States it was a Book–of–the–Month Club selection and sold more than a half–million copies. It was quickly translated into nine foreign language editions that also sold well.

Animals in Revolt

Animal Farm is an allegory that can be enjoyed on two different levels by two distinct groups of readers. It can be read as an animal story, telling the fanciful tale of a group of barnyard animals who—after overthrowing Mr. Jones, their human master—begin their own republic based on the principles of Animalism. Critics often compare Orwell's animal story to the memorable Houyhnhnmland, inhabited by a race of horses, in eighteenth–century British satirist Jonathan Swift's *Gulliver's Travels.* While pigs lead the rebellion in *Animal Farm,* other creatures also figure importantly in the story, including a hard–working horse named Boxer, a skeptical donkey named Benjamin, and a raven named Moses who talks about eternal life in the Sugarcandy Mountain. On a deeper level, *Animal Farm* can also be read as a witty satire of Stalin's betrayal of the Russian Revolution of 1917, and other events in Soviet history. Reflecting on the book's dual purpose, critic Sant Singh Bal writes in *George Orwell: The Ethical Imagination:* "*Animal Farm* is more than a mere animal fable for the amusement of children. It is a novel in which the obvious satire against the Communist Russia is applicable to all revolutions at another level, and to human government in general." Similarly, Laurence Brander notes in *George Orwell* that while others of his time might have found various aspects of the Soviet government worthy of praise, Orwell "wrote a little story to remind people what Stalinism was really like. It was his most effective sermon; many preachers are most successful with the adults during the children's sermon."

Reviewers and readers alike delighted in discovering the different events and individuals from Soviet history that Orwell had skewered with his satire. The two pigs that emerge as leaders during the animals' revolt—Napoleon and Snowball—represent Joseph Stalin and Leon Trotsky, two important figures in the Russian Revolution. Snowball, the more intellectual of the pair, paints Seven Commandments of Animalism on the side of the barn. He also forms "the Egg Production Committee for the hens, the Clean Tails League for the cows, . . . the Whiter Wool Movement for the sheep, and various others." He acts courageously during the Battle of the Cowshed, helping the animals repel an attempted return by Jones, and is awarded an "Animal Hero, First Class" medal. Like Stalin and Trotsky, the two pigs have a falling out and Snowball is chased off the farm. Squealer, the pig who acts as Napoleon's spokesperson, makes it clear that Snowball is to blame for any disaster that might befall their community, and eventually convinces the others that Napoleon, not Snowball, was the hero of the Battle of the Cowshed.

Meanwhile, Napoleon, much like Stalin, has his enemies killed off after they "confess" to various crimes. Napoleon also makes a deal with Mr. Frederick of neighboring Pinchfield Farm, much like the one Stalin made with Hitler. Frederick reneges on the agreement and then attempts to take over Animal Farm. One by one the Seven Commandments of Animalism on the side of the barn appear to change to accommodate changes enacted by Napoleon. Finally, the last commandment, which had read "All animals are created equal," is changed to include the phrase "but some animals are more equal than others." The book ends with a scene much like the Teheran Conference of 1943, when the leaders of the Allied Countries met with Stalin. The pigs, who are wearing Mr. Jones's clothing and walking on two legs, sit down with their human neighbors. As the other animals gaze at the scene through a window: "[They] looked from pig to man, and from man to pig, and from pig to man again; but already it was impossible to say which was which."

While political satire is an integral part of the book's success, Orwell made it clear that *Animal*

The author's bleak vision of a totalitarian future, *1984* was dramatized in director Michael Radford's 1984 film adaptation featuring John Hurt and Richard Burton in his final screen performance.

Farm was meant to be more than just a criticism of Russia; it was critical of all totalitarian states. Critics agree that the book's worth will outlast the knowledge of the events it satirizes. Arthur M. Schlesinger, Jr., for example, in his *New York Times Book Review* critique of the novel, observes: "[Orwell] writes absolutely without coyness or whimsicality and with such gravity and charm that 'Animal Farm' becomes an independent creation, standing quite apart from the object of its comment. The qualities of pathos in the tale of the betrayal of the animals . . . would compel the attention of persons who never heard of the Russian Revolution." Or, as Stephen Greenblatt notes in *Three Modern Satirists: Waugh, Orwell, and Huxley,* "*Animal Farm* remains powerful satire even as the specific historical events it mocked recede into the past, because the book's major concern is not with these incidents but with the essential horror of the human condition. There have been, are, and always will be pigs in every society, Orwell states, and they will always grab for power." More than one reviewer summarized the book's theme with a famous maxim of one of Orwell's fellow countrymen, Lord Acton: "Power tends to corrupt; absolute power corrupts absolutely."

Power, and erasing memories, are two themes Orwell touches on in *Animal Farm* that are dealt with in more detail in *Nineteen Eighty–Four,* his last novel. Some critics, like Jenni Calder in *Chronicles of Conscience: A Study of George Orwell and Arthur Koestler,* maintain that *Nineteen Eighty–Four* covers material that had been important to Orwell for quite some time. "The emotions and attitudes of the book," she writes, "had been present for many years, certainly present in [*The Road to*] *Wigan Pier* and *Keep the Aspidistra Flying,* if not earlier." Most of the book was written on the island of Jura, in the Scottish Hebrides, to which Orwell had moved in May 1946. There, in the solitude of a rented farmhouse called Barnhill, he was able to complete the first draft of *Nineteen Eighty–Four* by October 1947. Then, worsening tuberculosis sent him to the hospital for seven months. When he was strong enough, he returned to Jura and finished the final draft of the novel in November 1948. Unfortunately, the effort of working on the book sent him back to the hospital. On October 13, 1949, he married Sonia Brownell in London's University College Hospital. He never recovered from his illness, however, and died January 21, 1950, at 46 years of age.

Big Brother, Newspeak, and Doublethink

Part one of *Nineteen Eighty–Four* introduces readers to the future world of 1984. The globe is divided into three superstates: Oceania, Eurasia, and Eastasia. Oceania includes the Americas, the British and other Atlantic islands, Australia, and South Africa. The superstates are always at war with each other, but while Oceania and Eurasia might be at war today, tomorrow they both might be fighting together against Eastasia. England, now called Airstrip One, is "the third most populous of the provinces of Oceania." Newspeak is the official language of Oceania, and its governing party is Ingsoc (Newspeak for English Socialism). In 1984, Newspeak is steadily replacing Old Speak (or standard English). The goal of Newspeak is to remove words from the common language that could be used to express feelings or thoughts in opposition to the Party. The leader of Ingsoc is a mysterious mustached fellow, Big Brother. His face appears everywhere on larger–than–life posters with the caption running beneath: "Big Brother is watching you." Other posters proclaim the three Party slogans: "War is peace," "Freedom is slavery," and "Ignorance is strength." The "sacred principles of Ingsoc" are: Newspeak, doublethink— the ability to hold as true two contradictory ideas or points of view at the same time—and "the mutability of the past."

The setting of the novel is London, capital of Oceania. The city is filled with bombed–out buildings and "vistas of rotting nineteenth–century houses." The main character is Winston Smith, a member of the Outer Party, who lives there in Victory Mansions. He works in the Records Department of the Ministry of Truth (Minitrue in Newspeak). As an Outer Party member he is required to follow the orders of the elite Inner Party members. While the Ministry of Truth oversees news, education, and the arts, the Ministry of Peace is involved in war activities, the Ministry of Love carries out the laws of the land, and the Ministry of Plenty is in charge of economic affairs. These governmental agencies employ the 15 percent of the population that belong to the Party. The remaining 85 percent are the proles. Proles are beyond consideration; they live in squalor and are "beneath suspicion." The elite of society are the Inner Party members; Outer Party members, like Smith, are kept under control by telescreens. These television–like inventions are installed in every residence to serve as surveillance devices.

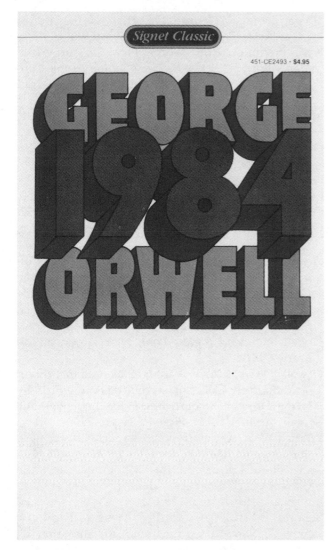

Signet Classic

451-CE2493 · $4.95

GEORGE 1984 ORWELL

Coining such phrases as "double-think," "unperson," and "Big Brother," Orwell's dystopian novel calculated the consequences of an all-powerful goverment; its unrelentingly grim vision was likely due to Orwell's losing battle with tuberculosis, which claimed him a year after the novel's publication.

They also broadcast patriotic music, morning exercise classes, and two–minutes hate sessions against Emmanuel Goldstein, the leader of opposition to the Party.

Part two of the novel begins when Julia, a female employee of the Ministry of Truth, secretly slips Smith a love note. Smith cautiously meets with her and discovers that she too hates their repressive society. Although the Party strictly forbids emotional attachment, the two fall in love. They arrange a trysting spot in the upper room of a prole antique shop. The room becomes a haven steeped in the past—on the wall is an old engraving of a long–destroyed London church—where the two meet as often as possible. While Smith continues to carry out his duties at the Ministry of Truth, including rewriting the past to conform with the present party line, he longs for the time he can barely recall from his childhood, when "an embrace, a tear, a word spoken to a dying man, could have value in itself." He mistakenly confides his rebellious thoughts to O'Brien, a member of the Inner Party. This section of the novel ends with the betrayal and arrest of Winston and Julia by the owner of the antique shop, who turns out to be a member of the dreaded Thought Police.

In part three, the shortest portion of the novel, Winston and Julia are imprisoned separately in the Ministry of Love. There, using physical and psychological torture, O'Brien "rehabilitates" Smith and explains to him the Party's theories of power and doublethink. After nine months, Winston is released back into society; when he and Julia meet again, they feel no love for one another. In the place of rebellion, Smith feels only love for Big Brother. An appendix at the end of the novel gives "the principles of Newspeak," including the revelation that in Newspeak most of the Declaration of Independence would be summarized in one word: "crimethink."

"It Depends on You"

Nineteen Eighty–Four was greeted with enthusiastic reviews. Critics were quick to point out the powerful emotional impact of Orwell's prose. In a 1949 *New York Times Book Review* essay, American critic and biographer Mark Schorer wrote: "No real reader can neglect this experience with impunity. . . . He will be asked to read through pages of sustained physical and psychological pain that have seldom been equaled and never in such quiet, sober prose." The same year, eminent British novelist V. S. Pritchett's response to the first British edition of *Nineteen Eighty–Four* appeared in *New Statesman and Nation*. "I do not think," the critic concluded, "I have ever read a novel more frightening and depressing; and yet, such are the originality, the suspense, the speed of writing and withering indignation that it is impossible to put the book down." Orwell responded negatively to early reviewers who saw *Nineteen Eighty–Four* as a critical attack on socialism or the British Labour Party. He also disagreed with those who saw his book as an attempt to predict the future. He issued a statement explaining the book's purpose, which Nigel Flynn quotes in *George Orwell,* "I think that, allowing for the book being after all a parody," Orwell asserted, "something like *Nineteen Eighty–Four* could happen. . . . The moral to be drawn from this dangerous nightmare situation is a simple one: Don't let it happen. It depends on you."

Even decades after *Nineteen Eighty–Four* was published, the impact of Orwell's novel is such that, according to John H. Barnsley in *Contemporary Review,* it "has become part of the common imaginative heritage of the Western world." The novel contributed a half–dozen or more words to our language, including Newspeak, Big Brother, and doublethink. It also gave us the term "Orwellian," used to refer to any governmental invasion of private life. The term seems ironic, since Orwell spent nearly his entire life exposing the truth about intrusive forms of government. To Orwell, of all the intolerable acts committed in the name of totalitarianism, the most offensive was the use of lies to change the past. According to John Strachey in *The Strangled Cry and Other Parliamentary Papers,* Orwell was convinced "it was forgery, even more than violence, which could destroy human reason." The truth was of utmost importance to Orwell, whether writing about the past, the present, or the future. In *Harper's,* Irving Howe praised the author as "the greatest moral force in English letters during the last several decades: craggy, fiercely polemical, sometimes mistaken, but an utterly free man."

■ Works Cited

Bal, Sant Singh, *George Orwell: The Ethical Imagination,* Arnold–Heinemann, 1981.

Barnsley, John H., "'The Last Man in Europe': A Comment on George Orwell's *1984,*" *Contemporary Review,* July, 1981, pp. 30–34.

Brander, Laurence, *George Orwell,* Longmans, 1954.

Calder, Jenni, *Chronicles of Conscience: A Study of George Orwell and Arthur Koestler,* University of Pittsburgh Press, 1968.

Calder, Robert L., "George Orwell," in *Dictionary of Literary Biography, First Series, Volume 98: Modern British Essayists,* Gale, 1990, pp. 254–260.

Flynn, Nigel, *George Orwell,* Rouke, 1990.

Greenblatt, Stephen, *Three Modern Satirists: Waugh, Orwell, and Huxley,* Yale University Press, 1965, pp. 37–73.

Howe, Irving, "George Orwell: 'As the Bones Know,'" *Harper's,* January, 1969, pp. 98–103.

Karl, Frederick R., "George Orwell: The White Man's Burden," in *A Reader's Guide to the Contemporary English Novel,* revised edition, Farrar, Straus, 1972, pp. 148–166.

Meyers, Jeffrey, *A Reader's Guide to George Orwell,* Thames & Hudson, 1975.

Orwell, George, *Down and Out in Paris and London,* Harper, 1933.

Orwell, *Burmese Days,* Harper, 1934.

Orwell, *Coming Up for Air,* Harcourt, Brace, 1950.

Orwell, *Homage to Catalonia,* Harcourt, Brace, 1952.

Orwell, *The Road to Wigan Pier,* Harcourt, Brace, 1958.

Orwell, "Such, Such Were the Joys," in *The Collected Essays: Journalism and Letters of George Orwell,* Volume 4: *In Front of Your Nose, 1945–1950,* edited by Sonia Orwell and Ian Angus, Harcourt, Brace, 1968.

Orwell, *Nineteen Eighty–Four,* New American Library, 1981.

Orwell, "Why I Write," in *Nineteen Eighty–Four: Text, Sources, Criticism,* second edition, edited by Irving Howe, Harcourt, Brace, 1982, pp. 243–248.

Orwell, *Animal Farm,* Signet Classic, 1990.

Pritchett, V. S., review of *Nineteen Eighty–Four, New Statesman and Nation,* June 18, 1949, pp. 646, 648.

Schlesinger, Arthur M., Jr., "Mr. Orwell and the Communists," *New York Times Book Review,* August 25, 1946, pp. 1, 28.

Schorer, Mark, "An Indignant and Prophetic Novel," *New York Times Book Review,* June 12, 1949, pp. 1, 16.

Stansky, Peter, and William Abrahams, *Orwell: The Transformation,* Knopf, 1980.

Strachey, John, *The Strangled Cry and Other Unparliamentary Papers,* William Sloane Associates, 1962.

Wolfe, Bertram D., "Leninism," in *Marxism in the Modern World,* edited by Milorad M. Drachkovitch, Stanford University Press, 1965, pp. 47–89.

Zehr, David Morgan, "George Orwell," *Dictionary of Literary Biography, Volume 15: British Novelists, 1930–1959,* Gale, 1983, pp. 407–423.

■ For More Information See

BOOKS

Bloom, Harold, editor, *Modern Critical Views: George Orwell* Chelsea House, 1987.

Crick, Bernard, *George Orwell: A Life,* Secker & Warburg, 1980.

Fyvel, T. R., *George Orwell: A Personal Memoir,* Macmillan, 1982.

Howe, Irving, editor, *"1984" Revisited: Totalitarianism in Our Century,* Harper, 1983.

Jensen, Ejner J., editor, *The Future of Nineteen Eighty–Four,* University of Michigan Press, 1984.

Lee, Robert A., *Orwell's Fiction,* University of Notre Dame Press, 1969.

Stansky, Peter, editor, *On "Nineteen Eighty–Four,"* W. H. Freeman, 1983.

Woodcock, George, *The Crystal Spirit: A Study of George Orwell,* new edition, enlarged, Schocken, 1984.

PERIODICALS

Canadian Forum, December, 1946; August, 1949.
College Literature (Orwell issue), winter, 1984.
Harper's, January, 1983.
Life, July 4, 1949.

Modern Fiction Studies, winter, 1968–69; spring, 1975 (Orwell issue); summer, 1980.
Nation, June 25, 1949.
New Republic, August 1, 1949.
New Yorker, September 7, 1946; June 18, 1949.
New York Herald Tribune Weekly Book Review, June 12, 1949; January 22, 1950; December 3, 1950.
New York Review of Books, June 14, 1984.
New York Times Book Review, June 12, 1949.
Time, February 4, 1946; June 20, 1949; November 13, 1950.

■ Obituaries

PERIODICALS

Newsweek, January 30, 1950.
New York Times, January 22, 1950.
Time, January 30, 1950.

—Sketch by Marion C. Gonsoir

Stella Pevsner

■ Personal

Born in Lincoln, IL; married a surgeon (deceased); children: Barbara, Stuart, Charles, Marian. *Education:* Attended Illinois University and Northwestern University.

■ Addresses

Home—Chicago, IL.

■ Career

Writer. Has worked as a teacher; has written advertising copy for a drugstore chain and for various advertising agencies; former promotion director, Dana Perfumes; free-lance writer of articles, commercial film strips, and reading texts. *Member:* Authors Guild, Society of Children's Book Writers, Society of Midland Authors.

■ Awards, Honors

Chicago Women in Publishing first annual award for children's literature, 1973, for *Call Me Heller, That's My Name;* Dorothy Canfield Fisher Award, Vermont Congress of Parents and Teachers, 1977, and Junior Literary Guild outstanding book, both for *A Smart Kid Like You;* Golden Kite Award, Society of Children's Book Writers, and Clara Ingram Judson Award, Society of Midland Authors, both 1978, both for *And You Give Me A Pain, Elaine;* Carl Sandburg Award, Friends of the Chicago Public Library, 1980, for *Cute Is a Four-Letter Word;* ALA/YASD Best Books for Young Adults Award, 1989, and Virginia Young Readers Award, Virginia State Reading Association, 1994, both for *How Could You Do It, Diane?;* Honor Book, Charlie May Simon Award, Arkansas Department of Education, 1994, Rebecca Caudill Young Readers' Book Award List, 1994–95, and Sunshine State master list of titles, Sequoyah Children's Book Award master list, all for *The Night the Whole Class Slept Over; Sister of the Quints* and *Jon, Flora, and the Odd-Eyed Cat* were Junior Library Guild selections.

■ Writings

JUVENILES

The Young Brontes (one-act play), Baker, 1967.
Break a Leg!, Crown, 1969, published as *New Girl,* Scholastic, Inc., 1983.
Footsteps on the Stairs, Crown, 1970.
Call Me Heller, That's My Name, Seabury, 1973.
A Smart Kid Like You, Seabury, 1975.
Keep Stompin' Till the Music Stops, Seabury, 1977.
And You Give Me a Pain, Elaine, Seabury, 1978.
Cute Is a Four-Letter Word, Houghton, 1980.

I'll Always Remember You . . . Maybe, Houghton, 1981.

Lindsay, Lindsay, Fly Away Home, Houghton, 1983.

Me, My Goat, and My Sister's Wedding, Houghton, 1985.

Sister of the Quints, Ticknor & Fields, 1987.

How Could You Do It, Diane?, Houghton, 1989.

The Night the Whole Class Slept Over, Houghton, 1991.

I'm Emma, I'm a Quint, Houghton, 1993.

Jon, Flora, and the Odd-Eyed Cat, Clarion Books, 1994.

■ Adaptations

A Smart Kid Like You was made into an ABC-TV *Afterschool Special* in 1976, under the title "Me and Dad's New Wife."

■ Sidelights

"When I was a child growing up in the small town of Lincoln, Illinois, the career choices for a girl were pretty well limited to teacher, secretary, nurse," wrote award-winning children's book author Stella Pevsner in an essay in *Something About the Author Autobiography Series (SAAS).* For those reasons, Pevsner didn't spend much time pondering a career as an author as a young child—she simply didn't think it was a possibility. Years later, she began writing for advertising agencies, for a perfume company, and then, freelance articles. It was not until one of her own children challenged her to write an entertaining book for kids that she decided to give it a try. That first book was published the following year. Since then, Pevsner has published many successful juvenile novels dealing with contemporary life.

Pevsner grew up in a large family in central Illinois. She had two older sisters whom she admired, and three brothers near her own age with whom she played. So, as a young girl she found herself acting like a tomboy to compete with her brothers, and at the same time admiring her sisters as they put on makeup and went out on dates. Her time off from school was filled with many of the traditional joys of childhood. She related in *SAAS,* "When I think of my childhood I often think of the summers. We would sit on the front porch and call out to the occasional acquaintance who walked by on the brick sidewalk. My three brothers and the neighborhood kids and I would play the childhood games of the era . . .

A childhood as an avid reader and a career in advertising eventually led Pevsner to writing contemporary books for teens, including this 1980 story of an eighth-grader determined to become popular.

hide-and-seek, Red Rover . . . and when it was dark, we'd dart around bushes, across stretches of grass, and capture lightning bugs to put into jars."

Another one of Pevsner's early loves was reading. In fact, she quickly became known as a bookworm in her family. Her mother, an accomplished needlepointer, often tried to get her daughter interested in embroidery. But Pevsner tried hard to get out of the assignments. At one time, her talented mother became interested in quilting and encouraged Pevsner to work at it. "The first time I stuck my finger hard enough to draw blood," she wrote in *SAAS.* "I thought I'd be excused and allowed to go back to my book. Wrong. Adhesive tape around the fingers kept the blood in me and off the quilt. If mothers of today want to drive their children into doing more reading, my advice to them is to put a quilt in a frame."

Housework was often seen by Pevsner as an annoying distraction from her reading. Her assignment was dusting, which was made more complicated by her mother's crocheted doilies covering every piece of furniture. But Pevsner found a way to relieve the tedium of the chore. "Saturday it was my job to take everything off the piano and the living room tables, dust and wax, and put it all back," she told *SAAS*. "To make all this bearable, I propped open a book in a hidden corner, and went back and forth, reading a few sentences before sending more dust flying. What could have been a simple task took me forever."

After cleaning, however, Pevsner was allowed to do all the reading she wanted. She made regular trips to the public library and brought home stacks of books. "Choosing books at the library was the highlight of my week. So many to choose from! I can still recall being in the cool shaded room set aside for children's books," she wrote in *SAAS*. When she got home, she sat under a big tree in the front yard and read for hours. Even though she read extensively as a child, Pevsner had little inkling that she herself would one day be a writer. "If someone had tapped me on the shoulder and whispered . . . 'Someday books you have written yourself will be on these very shelves,' I would probably have thought there was a lunatic at large," she commented in *SAAS*.

All Dolled Up

Dolls were also an obsession that Pevsner carried from childhood into adulthood. When she wasn't reading books, Pevsner was often sewing clothing for her collection of dolls. She wrote in *SAAS* that "at Christmas I can remember looking at my older sisters' gifts . . . compacts, clothes, fancy comb sets . . . and wishing I never had to grow up and get things like that and give up dolls. Well, I did, but I didn't." As an adult, with children in school, Pevsner once found herself attending an auction where many antique dolls were being offered for sale. Not being a connoisseur of dolls as collectibles, she bid on the ones that no one else wanted. Then she took them home and again

sewed clothes for them. "Partly to make these dolls legitimate, I used them in a book. In the narrative, it was the mother who kept the dolls. Her daughter referred to them, as did mine, as the 'glassy-eyed goons,'" she admitted in *SAAS*.

A high school English teacher helped push Pevsner towards her future career. He asked her to write a humor column for the school paper. "Although I had only a vague notion of what a humor column might be, I said sure, I would," she told *SAAS*. "He gave me a collection of essays by [James] Thurber and other humorists of the period for inspiration and suggested I write something clever on the subject of babysitting. . . . When my column appeared in print, I was amazed that the world didn't stop while everyone gaped at me and gasped, 'She writes!' Yet the

The mother of four children, the author has been both challenged and inspired to create entertaining stories of teen life such as *The Night the Whole Class Slept Over*, which includes weird parents, a silent sister, and an attempt to impress a female classmate.

fact that no one seemed shaken or more than mildly impressed didn't affect the new perception I had of myself. Indeed, I was a writer."

Further classes in creative writing were fun for Pevsner, and she continued to take writing classes in college. But her immediate goal was to be a teacher. She did teach for two years, but a summer spent in Chicago changed all that. While keeping a friend company who was signing up for a class in advertising, Pevsner decided to enroll also. She found out that she really loved the field. "It was such fun writing copy that didn't actually bend the truth, but certainly put the best possible view on the product," she wrote in *SAAS*. With the help of an employment agency, she landed that first crucial job in the field. It was working for a drugstore chain. She found it challenging, but not very stimulating. She discovered ways to increase her duties when a co-worker who wrote radio spots suddenly quit. Asked if she could write for radio, she said 'certainly,' and did it. Eventually she moved on to another job—writing copy for a department store. Then she began writing fashion copy for an advertising agency, moved on to agencies with varied products, and still later became the promotion director for a perfume house.

Suburban Stories

Pevsner's copywriting career came to an abrupt end when she got married. She quit her job and moved into a Chicago suburb that was a hour—and a world—away from the city. Her days were filled with the duties of a suburban housewife—cooking, cleaning, and taking care of her expanding family. However, she knew that she didn't quite fit in. While the other women were interested in home decor, she found herself thinking about her writing. Eventually, she began doing feature articles for a local paper. "I asked a friend to assess the general neighborhood opinion, and she said the women felt I was a bit eccentric, but generally okay," she explained in *SAAS*. Her house soon became the neighborhood play place, with her four children and their friends finding in Pevsner a permissive and fun mother. Pevsner got used to listening to dialogue and stories directly from the mouths of children, something that would be useful to her later in writing her stories. Still, writing novels for children was not in her plans. She continued to write for newspapers and finished a children's play and a reading program for children.

One of her sons first encouraged her to write for children. He had just written to his favorite author, asking her to write faster so he could have more books to read. When she politely answered that she was working as fast as she could, he informed his mother that she would have to write a book for children. She was dumbfounded at first, but soon decided that if her son had confidence in her abilities, she couldn't do anything but try. That summer she spent her time researching books that kids liked. She wanted to wait until the kids went back to school in the fall to actually begin writing. When the school bell rang again, she dove into writing *Break a Leg!*

"I'd never enjoyed writing so much," Pevsner declared in *SAAS*. "I was buoyed by my kids' interest in reading 'the next chapter' when they banged back into the house in what seemed to me just minutes after they'd left." *Break a Leg!* combines Pevsner's love of drama with her love of writing. The book centers around Fran, a sixth grader who joins a summer drama program. With her best friend away at camp, she must deal with the new personalities with which she is presented. A *Bulletin of the Center for Children's Books* critic said that "the theatrical background is appealing."

No sooner was this book finished than Pevsner was launching a new one. She was definitely hooked. This time, she started writing a mystery story. In *Footsteps on the Stairs,* Chip's interest with ESP and the occult causes him to become especially concerned about the apparent haunting of his friend Maury's house. "The book is well written, particularly in its dialogue," remarked a critic in *Bulletin of the Center for Children's Books. Call Me Heller, That's My Name* was Pevsner's first novel set in a different time period. Published in 1973, the book is about a young, spunky, orphaned girl of the 1920s. Heller gets her aunt Cornelia to come look after her, but she ends up feeling trapped by her aunt's control and her annoying habits, especially her insistence on calling Heller by her given name, Hildegarde. This book received the first annual Chicago Women in Publishing award in children's literature in 1973.

Pevsner delved in to deeper topics as she continued writing. *A Smart Kid Like You,* published in 1975, dealt with the issue of divorce. The main character, Nina, finds out that the teacher for her accelerated math class is her father's new wife. Not having adjusted to the divorce yet, she and

Being a kid sister is hard when there's trouble at home and nobody's got the answers...

Stella Pevsner
Winner of the Golden Kite Award

In this popular and award-winning 1978 book, a young girl's feelings of hostility toward her attention-grabbing sister are suddenly overshadowed by the unexpected death of her beloved older brother.

her classmates try hazing the teacher. In the end, she learns to accept what has happened and begins dating. Carol R. McIver wrote in *School Library Journal* that "the topic is highly relevant to many of today's young people." The book was made into an ABC-TV *Afterschool Special* under the title "Me and Dad's New Wife." Dyslexia is the subject of *Keep Stompin' Till the Music Stops*. Historic Galena, Illinois was the setting for this novel about Richard and his great-grandfather. The family tries to ship off the old man to a retirement village, but he manages to foil their plans. During this trauma, Richard accepts his learning disability and gains confidence.

And You Give Me a Pain, Elaine is one of Pevsner's most loved books. It chronicles the adventures of Andrea, a girl who feels ignored by her parents because her rebellious older sister Elaine is demanding so much time and attention. Much of her angst is washed away by the tragic death of her beloved older brother. Critics cited this novel as dealing well with the problems, both trivial and monumental, of the protagonist. Cyrisse Jaffee, writing in the *School Library Journal*, indicated that teens may enjoy it, due to its "realistic dialogue, likable protagonist, [and] humor." Pevsner wrote to *Contemporary Authors* (*CA*) about the impact of the book, claiming that "there must be many *Elaines* around, because since that book was published several girls have written to ask, 'Do you know my sister?' One of my favorite letters is from a girl who said, 'Your book is like a movie in my mind.'"

Travel had been a passion of Pevsner ever since she was a little girl. "I distinctly remember an art appreciation session in fifth grade where the painting was of Venice," Pevsner wrote in *SAAS*. "I told myself, *I'm going to go to Venice*. It didn't seem an extravagant notion, even though up to that age, the farthest away I'd ever been was Ohio. Through the years, I remembered that silent vow." As an adult, she ended up traveling quite frequently, to places as far away as Nepal, Iran, China, and India. These settings helped her write some of her books, including *Lindsay, Lindsay, Fly Away Home*, a story about a young American girl who is raised in India and who must return to America during high school. A goat Pevsner met in Katmandu helped inspire her to write *Me, My Goat, and My Sister's Wedding*. "When I asked my editor what he thought of my writing this book, he said cheerfully, 'Well, be sure the goat has an interesting personality,'" she wrote in *SAAS*. She drew upon her adventures with the far-away goat to liven up her narrative.

Dealing with Contemporary Problems

Once, when speaking before a group of eighth graders, Pevsner was asked by one of the girls to write a book about suicide. At first she demurred, saying it was too sad a subject. However, finding that she couldn't forget the girl's request, she did write a book called *How Could You Do It, Diane?* The story is told from the viewpoint of Bethany, who painfully tries to find out why her stepsister, a seemingly fun-loving girl, chose to end her life. A *Publishers Weekly* critic stated: "This book never answers that question [of why Diane committed suicide], which keeps the emotional bends of the story ringingly honest."

After the death of her husband, Pevsner spent a year helping manage his medical clinic. After it was finally sold, she decided to leave the suburbs and move to Chicago. Having received many requests from readers to write a sequel to the popular *Sister of the Quints,* a story of a thirteen-year-old girl who loses her identity when her stepmother has quintuplets, Pevsner wrote *I'm Emma, I'm a Quint.* This story is told from the viewpoint of one of the quintuplets, now an adolescent who

At first daunted, then haunted by a reader's request to write a book about suicide, Pevsner eventually created this 1989 tale of how the victim's friends and family try to deal with their loss.

is facing her own identity crisis. Next, desiring a change of scene from suburbia, Pevsner wrote *Jon, Flora, and the Odd-Eyed Cat,* a story which takes place in the South and centers around a boy's encounter with a mystical girl and her cat. This cat, who has one blue eye and one amber and wears a wreath of flowers, appears in the boy's room at night and involves him in strange summer solstice ceremonies.

"One of the reasons I find writing for children so satisfying is I know in advance my potential audience. Not *personally,* of course!," Pevsner told *CA.* "Yet I'm reasonably aware of what will amuse, intrigue, delight or create recognition in readers of a certain age range. . . . Although the lives of children today are a great deal different from earlier eras, emotions and feeling remain the same. Kids still hurt, they still struggle, and they still triumph." Pevsner's many books for adolescents are a testament to her ability to entertain and enlighten children. She concludes that "I hope my books help by saying, 'Yes, life is like this sometimes. It's not always easy. But you can make it if you just keep trying . . . and keep remembering to laugh.'"

■ Works Cited

Review of *Break a Leg!, Bulletin of the Center for Children's Books,* February, 1970, pp. 105.

Contemporary Authors New Revision Series, Gale, Volume 27, 1989.

Review of *Footsteps on the Stairs, Bulletin of the Center for Children's Books,* February, 1971, pp. 96.

Review of *How Could You Do It, Diane?, Publishers Weekly,* June 30, 1989.

Jaffee, Cyrisse, review of *And You Give Me a Pain, Elaine, School Library Journal,* November, 1978, pp. 77–78.

McIver, Carol R., review of *A Smart Kid Like You, School Library Journal,* May, 1975, pp. 58.

Pevsner, Stella, essay in *Something About the Author Autobiography Series,* Gale, Volume 14, 1992, pp. 183–93.

■ For More Information See

BOOKS

Speaking for Ourselves, NCTE, 1990.

—*Sketch by Nancy E. Rampson*

Chaim Potok

■ Personal

Original name, Herman Harold Potok; Hebrew given name, Chaim (pronounced "Hah–yim") Tzvi; born February 17, 1929; son of Benjamin Max (a businessman) and Mollie (Friedman) Potok; married Adena Sara Mosevitzky (a psychiatric social worker), June 8, 1958; children: Rena, Naama, Akiva. *Education:* Yeshiva University, B.A., (summa cum laude), 1950; Jewish Theological Seminary, ordination, M.H.L., 1954; University of Pennsylvania, Ph.D., 1965. *Religion:* Conservative Judaism. *Hobbies and other interests:* Painting and photography.

■ Addresses

Home—20 Berwick Street, Merion, PA 19066.

■ Career

Writer. Leaders Training Fellowship, Jewish Theological Seminary, national director, 1954–55; Camp Ramah, Los Angeles, CA, director, 1957–59; Har Zion Temple, Philadelphia, PA, scholar–in–resi-
dence, 1959–1963; Jewish Theological Seminary, member of faculty of Teachers' Institute, 1963–64; Conservative Judaism, New York City, managing editor, 1964–65; Jewish Publication Society, Philadelphia, associate editor, 1965–66, editor–in–chief, 1966–74, special projects editor, 1974—. Instructor, University of Judaism, Los Angeles, 1957– 59; visiting professor of philosophy, University of Pennsylvania, 1983, and Bryn Mawr College, 1985. Occasional commentator for National Public Radio. *Military service:* U. S. Army, chaplain in Korea, 1956–57; became first lieutenant. *Member:* Rabbinical Assembly, PEN, Authors Guild, Artists Equity.

■ Awards, Honors

National Book Award nomination for *The Chosen,* and Edward Lewis Wallant Prize, both 1967; Athenaeum Award, 1969, for *The Promise;* Professional and Scholarly Publishing Division special citation, AAP, 1984, for participating in the completion of the new translation of the Hebrew Bible; National Jewish Book Award, 1990, for *The Gift of Asher Lev.*

■ Writings

NOVELS

The Chosen, Simon & Schuster, 1967, anniversary edition with foreword by Potok, Knopf, 1992.
The Promise (sequel to *The Chosen*), Knopf, 1969.

My Name Is Asher Lev, Knopf, 1972.

In the Beginning, Knopf, 1975.

The Book of Lights, Knopf, 1981.

Davita's Harp, Knopf, 1985.

The Gift of Asher Lev (sequel to *My Name Is Asher Lev*), Knopf, 1990.

I Am the Clay, Knopf, 1992.

The Tree of Here (juvenile), illustrations by Tony Auth, Knopf, 1993.

The Sky of Now (juvenile) illustrations by Auth, Knopf, 1994.

NONFICTION

The Jew Confronts Himself in American Literature, Sacred Heart School of Theology, 1975.

Wanderings: Chaim Potok's History of the Jews, Knopf, 1978.

Ethical Living for a Modern World, Jewish Theological Seminary of America, 1985.

Tobiasse: Artist in Exile, Rizzoli, 1986.

PLAYS

The Chosen (musical), first produced on Broadway at the Second Avenue Theatre, July 7, 1988.

Also author of *Sins of the Fathers* (two, one-act plays), and *The Play of Lights,* both produced in Philadelphia at the Annenberg Theatre.

OTHER

Contributor to *Jewish Ethics* (pamphlet series), Leaders Training Fellowship, 1964–9. Also contributor to *May My Words Feed Others,* edited by Chayym Zeldis, Barnes, 1974; *Literature and the Urban Experience,* edited by Michael C. Jaye and Ann C. Watts, Rutgers University Press, 1981; *From the Corners of the Earth,* by Bill Aron, Jewish Publication Society, 1985; *The Jews in America,* edited by David C. Cohen, Collins, 1989; *Tales of the Hasidim,* by Martin Buber, Pantheon, 1991; *A Worthy Use of Summer,* edited by Jenna Weissman Joselitt with Karen S. Mittelman, National Museum of American Jewish History, 1993; *Graven Images,* by Arnold Schwartzman, Abrams, 1993; and *I Never Saw Another Butterfly,* edited by Hana Volavkova, Pantheon, 1993. Contributor to periodicals, including *Ladies Home Journal, Commentary, American Judaism, Saturday Review, New York Times Book Review,* and *New York Times Sunday Magazine.*

■ Adaptations

The Chosen, a movie based on Potok's novel starring Maximilian Schell, Robby Benson and Rod Steiger, was produced by Twentieth Century–Fox, 1982.

■ Sidelights

Ordained rabbi Chaim Potok never saw himself in a traditional religious role. He has worked as a writer, rabbi, and professor, often concerning himself with Orthodox and Hasidic Jews and how they merge their beliefs with twentieth–century life. Robert J. Milch wrote in the *Saturday Review:* "Judaism [is] at the center of all [Potok's] works. . . . [It motivates] his characters and provid[es] the basis for their way of looking at themselves, each other, and the world." Potok uses his rabbinical training to invent a believable world often populated by highly educated Jewish leaders and students. Above all, the writer's "primary concern is the spiritual and intellectual growth of his characters—how and what they come to believe," observed Hugh Nissenson in the *New York Times Book Review.*

Some critics compare Potok to Sholom Aleichem, the turn–of–the–century Russian Yiddish author of short stories and novels. The conflicts contained in Potok's books are cultural, religious, and scholarly. "That his novels have been best–sellers requires some explanation given the rather esoteric nature of his subject matter," commented Edward Abramson in *Chaim Potok.* "Many non–Jews think that the Jewish community is a homogeneous one with each member having substantially the same beliefs as the other." The critic further explained that "there is a wide divergence in the interpretation of law and ritual among Liberal, Reform, Conservative, Orthodox and Hasidic Jews."

Potok's father, Benjamin Max Potok, was born in Poland when tensions were rising between Jewish and Gentile residents. Benjamin Potok was a Hasidic Jew (Hasidism, a sect originating in Poland in the eighteenth century, arose in reaction to growing Jewish formalism and heavy empha-

Robby Benson and Barry Miller starred in the film version of *The Chosen,* the story of two Jewish boys who find common ground in the midst of great differences.

sis on scholarship. The Hasids formed tight communities that did not merge with the rest of society.) The elder Potok served in World War I, fighting in a Polish unit of the Austrian army despite the fact that most of the other soldiers were Gentiles. When his service was over, Benjamin Potok came home to find a pogrom—or organized massacre of Jewish residents—decimating his community. Fortunately, Potok was able to leave Poland for the United States, where he eventually married and settled in New York City.

Chaim Potok grew up in a close–knit Jewish community in the Bronx. Life in the city was frequently hard and sometimes violent, however, notably toward the immigrant Jews; the Potok family also had to deal with the economic difficulties brought on by the Depression. Young Potok found happiness, however, in a variety of things. "There were books and classes and teachers; there were friends with whom I invented street games limited only by the boundaries of the imagination," Potok once wrote.

Early Goals

Art appealed to Potok from childhood. One summer, Potok's parochial school hired an artist to teach a painting class. Potok's father and teachers dissuaded the boy from the idea of pursuing of art as a career (in large part because Hasids see art as a frivolous pursuit, or a rebellion towards God). While Potok's parents generally disregarded their son's artistic impulses, they nevertheless allowed him to write short pieces. Potok commented: "Scholarship—especially Talmudic scholarship—is the measure of an individual. Fiction, even serious fiction—as far as the religious Jewish tradition is concerned—is at best a frivolity, at worst a menace."

Potok attended an Orthodox Jewish day school, or yeshiva, where the studies included traditional Jewish writings. "This learning was largely restricted to discussion and study of the Talmud [which consists of civil, religious, and ethical laws based upon Jewish teaching and biblical interpretation that was originally oral and was passed down over the ages from Israel's earliest history], a collection of sixty–three books usually set out in eighteen folio volumes," explained Abramson.

Potok's high school teachers assigned such traditional reading matter as *Ivanhoe* and *Treasure Island.* In 1945, however, Potok read with great enthusiasm *Brideshead Revisited,* Evelyn Waugh's popular skory of early twentieth–century British upper–class life. After completing *Brideshead,* Potok decided to become a writer. "I remember finishing the book and marveling at the power of this kind of creativity," the author once wrote. As Potok told Abrams: "Somehow Evelyn Waugh reached across the chasm that separated my tight New York Jewish world from that of the upper–class British Catholics in his book From that time on, I not only read works of literature for enjoyment but also studied them with Talmudic intensity in order to teach myself how to create worlds out of words on paper. . . . In time I discovered that I had entered a tradition—modern literature."

Another important influence on Potok was James Joyce's *Portrait of the Artist as a Young Man.* The novel truly effected the young man's opinion of his place in the world. "Basic to [the novel] was . . . the iconoclast, the individual who grows up inside inherited systems of value and [will not tolerate] . . . the games, masks, arid hypocrisies he sees all around," Potok remarked.

As he grew older, Potok saw that his close religious community clashed with modern society in many areas. Potok wrote in *Literature and the Urban Experience* that he was "deep inside [the Jewish world], with a child's slowly increasing awareness of his own culture's richness and shortcomings. . . . [However] there was an echoing world that I longed to embrace. . . . It seemed to hold out at the same time the promise of worldly wisdom . . . and . . . the creations of the great minds of man."

Potok combined his interests in the religious and secular worlds by pursuing both Conservative Jewish and Gentile studies, receiving his bachelor's degree in English Literature from Orthodox Yeshiva University. Soon after, the author left Fundamentalist Judaism to adopt Conservatism—a decision he made with great difficulty. Nevertheless, Potok needed to find new fields of knowledge that could intertwine with his religious beliefs, and such knowledge turned up in the commentaries and methods of Gentile critics. "It was just this . . . that made it possible for him to achieve a reconciliation with Judaism," Abramson noted. Potok remarks in *Chaim Potok:* "The problems that troubled me [were] resolved by . . . the scientific approach to the sacred texts of Judaism. . . . They give the sources a form, a vitality which is impossible within a fundamentalist stance."

In this sequel to *The Chosen,* Reuven and Danny make some important choices about their respective futures.

Potok eventually attended the Jewish Theological Seminary in New York City. "I went to the seminary in order to study what it was I wanted to write about," he told Reed. Potok's seminary work led to his ordination as a Conservative rabbi in 1954. As a young rabbi, Potok traveled to the Far East immediately after the Korean War. Once there, he served in the United States Army with a medical and combat engineer's battalion. Potok's experiences in the Orient upset all his former convictions concerning civilization and religion. "In the shattered villages of Korea . . . in the teeming Chinese hovels of Hong Kong, in the vile back streets of Macao, all the neat antique coherence of my past came undone," he once explained. "It was not the anguish of my own people that sundered me . . . but the loveliness and the suffering 1 saw in the lives of pagans." Soon after, the author drew on his Korean experiences for his first novel.

In 1958, Potik married Adena Mosevitzky; he also finished and submitted his Korean novel, but publishers rejected it (most claimed the work lacked commercial value). Potok began a second novel despite the fate of the first. "We lived dollar to dollar in those days," Potok told Reed. "We didn't have a penny in the bank."

In 1962, Potok's daughter Rena was born. Soon after, the author and his family moved to Israel where Potok wrote his doctoral dissertation; he also worked on the first draft of his second novel. Upon returning to the States, the Potok family settled in Brooklyn, and Potok went back to the Jewish Theological Seminary, now as a member of the Teachers' Institute. At about the same time, he took a position at *Conservative Judaism,* work which ultimately led to his position as managing editor. In 1965, Potok's daughter Naama was born and the author received his doctorate in philosophy from the University of Pennsylvania; he also wrote a series of pamphlets under the umbrella title *Jewish Ethics* for the Leaders Training Fellowship and became editor at the Jewish Publication Society. (Much of Potok's long-term work with the Society involved the translation of the Hebrew Bible into English.)

The Chosen

It wasn't until 1965 that Potok completed his best-selling second novel, *The Chosen.* The book explores the conflict between the world of the Hasidim and that of Orthodox Jews. In the *Dictionary of Literary Biography,* S. Lillian Kremer explained that "The Crown Heights–Williamsburg section of Brooklyn, an area heavily populated by Jews, is the setting for a drama of reigious commitment. . . . Potok's descriptive and dramatic portrayal of scholarly endeavor brings new depth and breadth to American–Jewish fiction." Kremer also praised how the novel "captures the joy and intensity of Talmudic learning."

The two main characters in *The Chosen* are Reuven Halter, son of a progressive Talmudic scholar, and Danny Saunders, heir–apparent to the position of Zaddik, or spiritual leader, of the Hasidic community. A *Commentary* reviewer explained further: "Hasidism is hardly intelligible without . . . the Zaddik, the spiritual superman whose holy living not only provides . . . Inspiration for [his followers] lives' but who raises them aloft with him through [his] spiritual powers. . . . The Zaddik's prayer on behalf of his followers can achieve results far beyond the scope of their own puny efforts at prayer." Two forces run at odds in Danny's life: the encouragement of his Conservative tutor—Malter's father who guides the boy's intellectual growth—and Reb Saunders' tightly proscribed rules for his heir. Saunders has brought Danny up in a world of silence, where the only conversations occur during discussions of Scripture.

One of Potok's strong points in fashioning *The Chosen* is his explanation of Talmudic scholarship. "The elder Malter, patterned after the novelist's beloved father–in–law . . . is the idealized Jewish teacher," wrote Kremer. "Just as he fuses the best in Judaic scholarship with the best in secular culture, Reuven combines intellectual excellence in sacred and secular studies."

The Promise and My Name is Asher Lev

In 1969, the author completed *The Promise,* a sequel to *The Chosen.* Reuven prepares to become a rabbi, but butts heads with apostate scholar Abraham Gordon. Simultaneously Danny—now a student of clinical psychology—treats young Michael Gordon, the scholar's disturbed son. The family achieves unity, however, through Danny Saunders's betrothal and marriage to Rachel Gordon, his young patient's sister. The book's theme, said Kremer, focuses on how "each character defines himself, understands himself, and celebrates fines himself, understands himself, and celebrates himself as a twentieth–century Jew." In the *New York Times Book Review,* Nissenson lauded the novel by writing that "despite an occasional technical lapse, Potok has demonstrated his ability to deal with a more complex conception and to suffuse it with pertinence and vitality."

My Name Is Asher Lev concerns a Hasidic artist. As in his earlier books, Potok relates Asher's experiences in the first–person. Asher's story is "the mature artist's retrospective portrait of his childhood [and] a reexamination of his attitudes," wrote Kremer. Asher's parents dislike his interest in art, often scolding him for his apathy to Biblical scholarship. Asher often dreams of his deceased grandfather, a noted scholar. In the dreams, his grandfather condemns Asher for his devotion to art. Some members of the Hasidic community even consider Asher's gifts demonic, but the Rebbe—who leads the community and also employs Asher's father—unexpectedly champions the boy.

Asher's goal is "how to develop his aesthetic sense through painting," observed Abramson. Like Danny Saunders, Asher is born into the role of heir–apparent. In the latter case, Asher's future position entails working as an international emissary for the Rebbe. The tumult over Asher's studies increases when he begins to paint nudes and crucifixions. Although Asher sees the cross as a non–religious symbol, his father sees it as a figure for anti—Semitism. The crisis comes to a head in Asher's painting called the "Brooklyn Crucifixion." Eventually, Asher must choose between his community and his painting.

In the Beginning and More

During 1973, Potok left the United States with his family to live in Jerusalem. In 1975, he published his next work entitled *In the Beginning.* As with many of his other novels, *In the Beginning* deals with anti–Semitism. "Rarely has the rage of the Jew been so honestly portrayed," remarked Nissenson, who added that "by the power of his own intellect [Potok comes] to grips with the theme implicit in all of his previous work: the problem of sustaining religious faith in a meaningless world. . . . It successfully recreates a time and a place and the journey of a soul." The au-

thor goes beyond America's dislike of the Jews and looks at its historical precedence.

The author symbolizes theme through the relationship between David Lurie, a Jewish boy, and Eddie Kulanski, a Gentile. Other main themes in the work revolve around Biblical scholarship and the State of Israel. "The narrator here is a brilliantly gifted Orthodox Jewish boy who eventually accommodates himself to modern life," explained Nissenson. Through David, Potok uses stream–of–consciousness to depict the tragedies endured by the Jews in Europe. When David hears of the losses sustained by Jews during World War II, he enters a dreamland where an imaginary hero fights Nazi oppressors. David deeply loves the Torah, and sees it as a symbol of hope for all Jews. He alienates his family, however, when he adopts the shocking belief that using Gentile scholarship will bridge the gulf separating Jew and Gentile.

A *Time* reviewer writes that reading *In the Beginning* makes the reader "wholly aware of what it must have been like to belong to such a family and such a religion at such a time. Conveying vividly the exact feel of unfamiliar territory is a job almost exclusively performed by journalists. . . . That novels can accomplish that task superlatively is one of the reasons why they are still written— and read." Michael Irwin, writing in the *Times Literary Supplement,* noted that Potok "catches beautifully the atmosphere of a family party or a school quarrel. Rarer than this is the skill with which he shows how what a child learns and what it experiences are fused and transformed by the imagination." Finally, Daphne Merkin stated in *Commentary* that while Potok tends to stick to "fertile Jewish territory," he has hit "a formula for success . . . in which the only limits to artistic achievement are the limits of his own imagination." She did criticize, however, that "Potok's rendition of Orthodox life is entertaining and informative, but his work does not expand to the dimensions it reaches for."

In 1978, the author saw publication of the nonfiction work *Wanderings: Chaim Potok's History of the Jews.* In *The Christian Science Monitor,* Michael J.Bandler described the book: "Using hundreds of eminent sources and texts in several languages . . . [Potok] has fashioned an intelligent, thorough and credible one–volume chronicle that breathes with a passion that is more common to fiction than history. . . . It should be savored, scene by provocative scene, mulled over and retained." A *Maclean's* contributor mentioned a different consideration. "Behind Potok's account of the Jewish struggle to stay alive . . . is [his] own moral search: to understand how a people managed to survive both the seduction of comfort . . . [and] diabolical tortures . . . to remain Jews."

Three years later, Potok finished *The Book of Lights*. Steeped in the Jewish mysticism of the Kabbalah and full of moral decisions fraught with anguish, the work marked a new departure for the author. Johanna Kaplan, writing in the *New York Times Book Review,* called the novel, "The story of [a] dark and baffling inner journey." *The Book of Lights* tackles the subject of moral responsibility and the atom bomb, a dilemma epitomized by the characters Gershon Loran and Arthur Leiden. In the novel, Potok's characters work to incorporate their faith with a secular society. The book culminates in Jerusalem, where Loran works to resolve his spiritual dilemmas.

Davita's Harp and a Musical

Much of the impetus for the novelist's sixth work of fiction, *Davita's Harp,* was an experience of sexism his wife suffered while in her teens. The novel takes place in Depression–era New York. Both of Davita's parents—her WASP newspaperman father and Jewish mother—have abandoned religious beliefs for Communism. Seeking security, the girl explores Judaism and attends a yeshiva. Once there, Davita discovers a prejudice against female scholars; when she makes top marks, the young girl is denied the highly coveted school award because she is female. "Davita's commitment to patriarchal Judaism is deeply shaken at her graduation," explains Patty Campbell in the *Wilson Library Bulletin*. The school gives the Akiva award "to a boy to save the school the public shame of a girl as best student."

"That actually happened to my wife when she was a young girl in Brooklyn. I've known about it since we were married. Those things sit like a seed in the core of your being," Potok told Reed. "The harp got mixed in along the way and be-

The powerful bestseller by **Chaim Potok**

"Memorable...A book profound in its vision of humanity, of religion, and of art." The Wall Street Journal

MY NAME IS ASHER LEV

"A novel of finely articulated tragic power... Little short of a work of genius." The New York Times Book Review

Young Asher Lev's decision to pursue art instead of scholarship leads to conflict when one of his paintings is deemed highly controversial.

came the central metaphor." Critics praised the book for its use of commonplace items to establish the setting. "The idealistic underworld of American communism in the thirties leaps out in evocative details," remarked Campbell.

Toward the end of the decade, Potok himself rewrote *The Chosen* as a musical. Potok felt the time–consuming project was worthwhile, even though it took over a year. As he told Mervyn Rothstein of the *New York Times,* it appeared "that there was potentiality for seriousness here." Simultaneously, Potok felt that "it didn't have to be heavy–handed, because the novel itself is not heavy–handed." In theater script, Potok centered on "a sense of the way a particular core culture confronts the world outside, and the dimensions

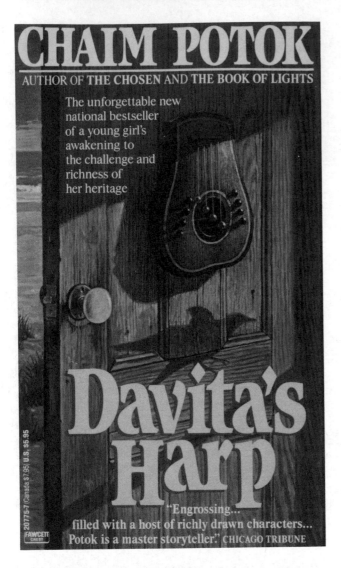

CHAIM POTOK

AUTHOR OF **THE CHOSEN** AND **THE BOOK OF LIGHTS**

The unforgettable new national bestseller of a young girl's awakening to the challenge and richness of her heritage

Davita's Harp

"Engrossing... filled with a host of richly drawn characters... Potok is a master storyteller." CHICAGO TRIBUNE

Potok based this novel on an incidence of sexism his wife experienced while in her teens

Matters become complicated when Lev's wife and son prefer the tight–knit Hasidic community to life on the Mediterranean. In the end, Lev's father resolves the conflict. As the elderly Rebbe's successor, Lev's father turns his attention to Asher's son, Avrumel. The older man decides that Avrumel shall take his father's place and continue the dynasty. The sad conclusion is that "the price of Lev's restoration to his people is his physical and personal exclusion. Much as Christ was a sacrificed `missing generation' between God and mankind, Lev's self–sacrificing art is a personal crucifixion. . . . [it also guarantees] that the tradition will pass on," described Brian Morton in the *Times Literary Supplement*.

The Tree of Here was Potok's first novel for young children. Jason—the book's main character—finds his life shaken when his parents plan to move. The boy believes he sees a face in the craggy bark of the large tree that grows in his backyard and concludes that the tree listens to him. In turn, Jason trusts the tree to whisper its own "secret feelings." Wanting to ease Jason's unhappiness, a gardener gives him a dogwood sapling to plant at his new home. While some critics lauded Potok's willingness to tackle a new audience, others opined that the final result lacked the author's usual insight and depth. A reviewer for *Publishers Weekly*, while acknowledging that the story "addresses the need for certain constants," concluded that the book ultimately "disappoints."

In her essay, Kremer summarized the general response to Potok's body of work by noting that the criticism "ranged from denunciation to acclaim." Some critics have called the author's approach, plots, and characters narrow and dry, pointing to a sometimes labored style and pompous narrative tone; these reviewers also write that Potok's brilliant theology students often seem too good to be true. Other assessors, however, note the author's deliberation of important issues with thought and care. Potok has likewise received praise for his piercing visions into Orthodox Jewish life and culture. (By comparison, many contemporary Jewish authors appear topical in their treatment of the variety of Jewish experience.)

Overall, Potok sees his mission as one that brings meaning to a nonsensical world. He once commented that doing this "specifically . . . is the task of the artist." In his interview with Rothstein,

of that confrontation," Rothstein reports. Many theater critics, however, found the production disappointing. *New York Times* contributor Mel Gussow noted that "the relationship between Reuven and Danny moves perilously close to a love that dare not speak its name . . . one that would clearly contradict the author's intent."

A Sequel and Children's Books

As a sequel to *My Name Is Asher Lev*, Potok wrote *The Gift of Asher Lev*. The author picks up the narrative many years after the first book. Lev has left New York and the Hasidic world to live with his family on the Cote d'Azur. A funeral brings the Lev family back to Asher's old home.

as much honesty as you can, and if you do it honestly and skillfully enough, somehow you're going to bridge the gap."

■ Works Cited

Abramson, Edward A., *Chaim Potok*, Twayne, 1986.

Bandler, Michael J., "Faith's Long Journey," *Christian Science Monitor*, December 16, 1969, p. 13.

Campbell, Patty, review of *Davita's Harp, Wilson Library Bulletin*, June, 1985, pp. 688–89.

Review of *The Chosen, Commentary*, September, 1967, p. 107.

Review of *In the Beginning, Time*, November 3, 1975, p. 94.

Gussow, Mel, "Theater: *The Chosen* As a Musical," *New York Times*, January 7, 1988.

Irwin, Michael, "A Full–Time Condition," *Times Literary Supplement*, April 9, 1976, p. 413.

Kaplan, Johanna, "Two Ways of Life," *New York Times Book Review*, October 11, 1981, pp. 14–15, 28.

Kremer, S. Lillian, "Chaim Potok," *Dictionary of Literary Biography*, Volume 28: *Twentieth-Century American–Jewish Fiction Writers*, Gale, 1984, pp. 232–43.

Merkin, Daphne, "Why Potok is Popular," *Commentary*, February, 1976, pp. 73–75.

Milch, Robert J., Review of *My Name Is Asher Lev, Saturday Review*, April 15, 1972, pp. 65–6.

Morton, Brian, "Banished and Banished Again," *Times Literary Supplement*, November 2, 1990.

Nissenson, Hugh, "The Spark and the Shell," *New York Times Book Review*, May 7, 1967, pp. 4–5, 34.

Nissenson, Hugh, review of *The Promise, New York Times Book Review*, September 14, 1969.

Nissenson, Hugh, "My Name Is David Lurie," *New York Times Book Review*, October 19, 1975.

Potok, Chaim, essay in *Literature and Urban Experience: Essays on the City and Literature*, edited by M.C. Jaye and A.C. Watts, Rutgers University Press, 1981.

Rothstein, Mervyn, "Crafting a Musical from *The Chosen*," *New York Times*, January 3, 1988.

Review of *The Tree of Here, Publishers Weekly*, August 30, 1993.

Review of *Wanderings, Maclean's*, January 1, 1979, p. 47.

■ For More Information See

BOOKS

Authors in the News, Gale, Volume 1, 1976, Volume 2, 1976.

Contemporary Literary Criticism, Gale, Volume 2, 1974, Volume 7, 1977, Volume 4, 1980, Volume 26, 1983.

Dictionary of Literary Biography Yearbook: 1984, Gale, 1985.

PERIODICALS

Chicago Tribune, December 1, 1987.
New York Times, November 2, 1986.
School Library Journal, October, 1993.
Studies in American Jewish Literature, spring, 1976.

—*Sketch by Jani Prescott*

Philip Pullman

■ Personal

Born October 19, 1946, in Norwich, England; son of Alfred Outram (an airman) and Audrey (Merrifield) Pullman; married Judith Speller (a therapist), August 15, 1970; children: James, Thomas. *Education:* Oxford University, B.A., 1968. *Politics:* Liberal. *Hobbies and other interests:* Drawing, music.

■ Addresses

Home and office—24 Templar Rd., Oxford OX2 8LT, England. *Agent*—Ellen Levine, 432 Park Ave. S., Suite 1205, New York, NY 10016; A. P. Watt, 20 John St., London WC1N 2DR, England.

■ Career

Teacher at Ivanhoe, Bishop Kirk, and Marston middle schools, Oxford, England, 1970–86; writer, 1986—. Lecturer at Westminster College, North Hinskey, Oxford.

■ Awards, Honors

Lancashire County Libraries/National and Provin-cial Children's Book Award, 1987, Best Books for Young Adults listing, *School Library Journal,* 1987, Children's Book Award, International Reading Association, 1988, Preis der Leseratten, ZDF Television (Germany), 1988, and Best Books for Young Adults listing, American Library Association (ALA), 1988, all for *The Ruby in the Smoke;* Best Books for Young Adults listing, ALA, 1988, and Edgar Allan Poe Award nomination, Mystery Writers of America, 1989, both for *Shadow in the North.*

■ Writings

YOUNG ADULT NOVELS

The Ruby in the Smoke (first novel in series), Oxford University Press, 1985, Knopf, 1987.

The Shadow in the Plate (second novel in series), Oxford University Press, 1987, published in United States as *Shadow in the North,* Knopf, 1988.

The Tiger in the Well (third novel in series), Viking (England), 1990, Knopf, 1990.

The Broken Bridge, Macmillan (England), 1990, Knopf, 1992.

The White Mercedes, Macmillan, 1992, Knopf, 1993.

The Tin Princess (fourth novel in series), Knopf, 1994.

CHILDREN'S BOOKS

Ancient Civilizations (nonfiction), illustrated by G. Long, Wheaton, 1978.

Count Karlstein, Chatto & Windus, 1982, edition

with pictures by Patrice Aggs, Doubleday (England), 1991.

How to Be Cool, Heinemann, 1987.

Spring-Heeled Jack, illustrated by David Mostyn, Doubleday (England), 1989.

PLAYS

Sherlock Holmes and the Adventure of the Sumatran Devil (produced at Polka Children's Theatre, Wimbledon, 1984), published as *Sherlock Holmes and the Adventure of the Limehouse Horror,* Nelson, 1993.

Three Musketeers (adapted from Alexandre Dumas' novel of the same title), produced at Polka Children's Theatre, Wimbledon, 1985.

Frankenstein (adapted from Mary Shelley's novel of the same title; produced at Polka Children's Theatre, Wimbledon, 1987), Oxford University Press, 1990.

ADULT NOVELS

Galatea, Gollancz, 1978, Dutton, 1979.

■ Adaptations

How to Be Cool was made into a television show by Granada in 1988.

■ Work In Progress

A picture book titled *The Firemaker's Daughter;* and *His Dark Materials,* the first book in what the author expects to be a science fiction trilogy.

■ Sidelights

Philip Pullman has likened his storytelling to the feeling a father has eating his own son. Unwittingly eating a stew made from the flesh of his son, a father declares, "I have a feeling this all belongs to me!" in a fairy tale called "The Juniper Tree." Similarly, Pullman feasts on his childhood as a storyteller, "consuming the experience I had as a child," he noted in *Something about the Author Autobiography Series (SAAS).* Best known for his young adult novels set in Victorian London that feature a clever young heroine named Sally Lockhart, Pullman has written books for children and adults, including a comic book mixed with a novel called *Spring-Heeled Jack.* Pullman's books are acclaimed for their compelling characters and atmospheric style and have been recognized on the American Library Association's Best Books for Young Adults listing.

Born in 1946 in Norwich, Norfolk, England, Pullman spent much of the first ten years of his life travelling the globe by ship. The son and then stepson of English airmen, Pullman followed their careers to Rhodesia, Australia, London, and Wales. He recalled that nothing was more exciting than coming into a new port, where he absorbed the strange sights and smells. Going through the Suez Canal Pullman saw palm trees and robed Arabs, and recalled in *SAAS* conjurers doing magic tricks with live chicks on the ship's deck in the evenings. When in Africa, the night air would fill with the smell of "roasting mealies (corn on the cob)," a smell he loved so much "that when years and years later I happened to smell it unexpectedly in a street market in London . . . I found tears springing to my eyes."

It was in Australia, however, that he made a great discovery: comic books. "I adored Superman, and Superboy, and Captain America, and Dick Tracy, but most of all I adored Batman. Those poorly printed stories on their cheap yellowing newsprint intoxicated me, enthralled me, made me dizzy with passion," he explained in *SAAS.* He wanted "to brood over the world of Batman and dream actively. It was the first stirring of the storytelling impulse."

The Servant of His Stories

In Australia, Pullman embarked on his life as a storyteller, making up stories to tell his brother each night in bed. He remembered in *SAAS* "the sense of diving into the dark as I began a story, with no idea at all what was going to happen." Pullman has followed his stories ever since. He once commented, "I am always the servant of the story that has chosen me to tell it and I have to discover the best way of doing that. I believe there's a pure line that goes through every story and the more closely the telling approaches that pure line, the better the story will be." He added that "I don't write stories to a plan or to make a political point. I've tried, and it doesn't work. The story must tell me."

Another influence on Pullman's storytelling was his grandfather. A clergyman in the Church of England, his grandfather spun stories to make mundane things livelier. Using terms from Western films, he romanticized a familiar road and stream calling them The Trail of the Lonesome Pine and Laughing Water, Pullman recalled in

Sixth Book of Junior Authors. Though his grandfather did not live to see Pullman's first children's book published, Pullman noted in *SAAS* that he and his stories are "still brightly alive to me."

After Pullman turned eleven, his family settled in North Wales, where he attended a school called Ysgol Ardudwy in Harlech. Though Pullman had stopped travelling he continued to indulge his curiosity. He fought back against bullies, held spitting contests, saw a dead man, and discovered art. It was poetry, however, that thrilled him; he committed a great deal to memory and adored writing in strict form. He noted in *SAAS* that although he would not consider himself a poet he thinks

SHE RISKED MURDER AND MAYHEM TO SOLVE THE MYSTERY OF HER FATHER'S DEATH AND FOUND—

THE RUBY IN THE SMOKE

PHILIP PULLMAN

The author wrote this 1985 novel—the first of three books about Sally Lockhart—after becoming intrigued by a picture on a postcard of a girl sitting on her father's lap.

that "the writing of verse in strict form is the best possible training for writing good prose."

The first in his family to attend a university, Pullman studied English at Exeter College in Oxford. Though he found his studies tedious, he obtained his degree in 1968. He had gone to school to learn how to write, but found the university unwilling to teach that. "So I didn't enjoy my English course, and I didn't get a good degree, but it wasn't entirely a waste of time. I got drunk; I played the guitar; I made some good friends, some of whom are still speaking to me." Pullman wrote in *SAAS* that he should have entered art school instead.

Planning a Rich and Famous Future

Upon graduation Pullman began writing his first book. His plan was to finish his first novel about a month after his final examinations, have it published within the year, and sell the film rights to become rich and famous. But after sitting down to write his first page, he realized he could not write a story because he had not decided on a point of view. Pullman noted in *SAAS,* "I learned more about the novel in a morning . . . than I'd learned in seven years or so of trying to write criticism."

Knowing he could not write full-time and earn enough to eat, Pullman worked in a men's clothing store and then a library. During these first years out of college, he worked by day and wrote three pages each night. Publication of his first novel, the name of which he will not reveal, taught him, as he related in *SAAS,* that "getting published wasn't either as difficult, or as important, as I'd thought." Although his first novel flopped, Pullman continued the tradition he started with his first book: he writes three pages a day whether or not he has anything to say.

After marrying and taking a teaching position in Oxford, Pullman continued to write. His first recognized book was an adult novel called *Galatea.* In *Galatea* flutist Martin Browning sets out to find his missing wife, Catherine, and finds himself on a series of surreal adventures. With $5,000 and friends he meets along the way, Browning's journey takes him to the Anderson Valley in Venezuela. Pullman deftly describes the make-believe portions of the landscape, but, as he noted in *SAAS,* he didn't know how to categorize the book and neither did the reviewers. A *Publishers Weekly* contributor hailed *Galatea* as "a virtuoso performance," and noted that "Browning's travels, taken as symbol, provide a provocative view of our lifestyles." And a *Times Literary Supplement* reviewer wrote that Browning was "clearly the toy of omniscient powers who regard him as inadequate and undeserving of the knowledge he seeks."

After writing *Galatea*, Pullman found that he enjoyed writing plays for his students. He relished telling his classes stories, and figured he had told *The Iliad* and *The Odyssey* each thirty-six times during his twelve-year teaching career. His first story for children was published after a student's father, who was also a publisher, complimented Pullman on his play and told him to consider writing books for children, according to a *Publishers Weekly* writer. Pullman turned his play, *Count Karlstein*, into his first children's book. Set in an early nineteenth century Swiss village encompassed by the estate of Count Karlstein, the story tells of the escape of young Lucy and Charlotte from their wicked uncle's plot. Count Karlstein had made a deal with Zamiel, the Demon Huntsman, ten years before Lucy and Charlotte, his orphaned nieces, came to live with him. The count had agreed to surrender a human soul to Zamiel on All Soul's Eve in exchange for an estate, wealth, and an honorable name. The count plans to offer his nieces to the demon, but his servant Hildi hears of the plan and tries to help the girls escape. Though the story is predictable, *Booklist* reviewer Karen Stang Haley noted that "the pleasure is all in the telling." *School Library Journal* reviewer Phyllis K. Kennemer maintained that the book would be a "good addition to horror story collections."

The Adventures of Sally Lockhart

Pullman found his storytelling voice in his next book, *The Ruby in the Smoke*. In this novel, he unravels the tale of young Sally Lockhart's mysterious adventure in nineteenth century London. Pullman thought of the idea for *The Ruby in the Smoke* while looking at the picture on a postcard he had bought while working at the library. "That was all I had to begin with," the Victorian picture of a girl sitting on her father's lap, Pullman recalled in *SAAS*. "An intriguing, puzzling picture,

like something out of a dream, with scraps of intense emotion still clinging that seem to have no reason for their intensity. I write to find out more about the picture." The tale proved so compelling that Pullman wove it into a trilogy, which includes *The Shadow in the North* and *The Tiger in the Well*.

The Ruby in the Smoke begins in October of 1872 as sixteen-year-old Sally Lockhart sets out to understand the warning in the letter her deceased father sent from Singapore. After innocently questioning one of her father's employees only to see him faint and die, Sally embarks on an adventure to find her legacy, a ruby with seemingly hypnotic powers, and to figure out the Seven Blessings. Aided only by her friends Rosa, Jim, and her new boyfriend Frederick, Sally thrusts herself into the vortex of an intrigue that includes murder, the opium trade, Chinese gangs, and the dangerous Mrs. Holland. Sally also confronts the truth behind a nightmare that has haunted her since childhood.

For the style of storytelling used in *The Ruby in the Smoke*, Pullman has been referred to as a modern day Charles Dickens. "This is a splendid book," asserted Peter Hollindale, reviewing the book for *British Book News Children's Books*, "full of memorable characters, furious action and heroic deeds in murky London settings." Brooke L. Dillon, writing in *Voice of Youth Advocates*, praised Pullman for respecting his teenage audience and "treating them to a complex, interwoven plot." She also added that his treatment of the British government's opium trade would make this book suitable for supplemental social studies reading. "There are not many books that offer such promise of satisfaction to so many children, of both sexes, of secondary age," noted David Churchill in *School Librarian*.

The sequel to *Ruby in the Smoke*, *Shadow in the North* picks up with Sally Lockhart six years later, when she is a Cambridge-educated, independent financial consultant. With her friends, including Frederick Garland, her boyfriend from the first book, Sally confronts the wealthiest man in Europe, Axel Bellmann, about shaky financial dealings that implicate the highest levels of government.

Though some reviewers found the second book in the trilogy of lesser quality than *The Ruby in the*

Smoke, most found it compelling. Hollindale maintained in *British Book News Children's Books* that the book "could mystify and distress young children who may have liked the earlier one. Older and tougher readers will relish it; but the effect is disturbing." Michael Cart wrote in *School Library Journal* that Pullman "demonstrates his mastery of atmosphere and style." But when taking into account Pullman's desire to struggle with the effects of the Industrial Revolution on men, Cart wondered "if the conventions of the mystery/adventure genre are not too fragile to bear the weight of Pullman's thematic ambition." Joanne Johnson similarly noted in *Voice of Youth Advocates* that the plot would have been more "interesting if there weren't quite so many different elements at play at once."

In the third book in the trilogy, *The Tiger in the Well,* Sally is pursued by an unknown man who has plotted to ruin her life. Living alone with her two-year-old daughter, Harriet, since the death of her lover, Frederick, Sally is surprised by the appearance of a man who claims to be her husband and sues her for divorce and custody of her daughter. As the story progresses, Sally struggles to find out who is treating her with such malice as she loses her home, her job, her daughter, and her sanity. Pullman draws parallels between the way Sally is being treated and the treatment of the Jewish immigrants and the poor.

Ilene Cooper, writing in *Booklist,* found the book "pulsing with life," and noted that "at first blush" the book may seem to contain topics too heady for young adults, "but not the way Pullman writes them." A *Publishers Weekly* contributor called the book "thought-provoking" and found it to be "as rich and captivating as a modern-day Dickens novel." Barbara Hutcheson declared in *Library School Journal* that "Pullman is fast becoming a modern-day Charles Dickens for young adults." As it is "never sordid or sensational," she noted that "this is a suspense novel with a conscience, and a most enjoyable one."

Pullman confessed, in *Sixth Book of Junior Authors,* that he can't explain why he writes his stories in a Victorian London setting, but offered the reason that he finds many parallels between that period and this, with "new technologies, nationalism, feminism," and "terrorism," and that he feels "at home" with the language. "It was a time

that was sort of balanced between the old and the new," he told *Publishers Weekly* contributor Bella Stander.

Pullman combined his interest in Victorian London and comic books to create *Spring-Heeled Jack,* the story of three orphans, Rose, Lily, and Ned, who run into trouble when trying to escape the Alderman Cawn-Plaster Memorial Orphanage. En route to a ship headed for America, the orphans are threatened by Mack the Knife and his sinister gang, and are tailed by Gasket and Killjoy, the orphanage's supervisors. The children find safety and their real father with the help of a stray dog, a sailor, and Spring-Heeled Jack, a superhero who wears a tophat, tights, and springy knee-high boots. A *Publishers Weekly* reviewer wrote that the

In this 1988 sequel to *The Ruby in the Smoke,* Sally is a financial consultant who suspects the wealthiest man in Europe of illegal financial dealings.

"classic spoof" of *Spring-Heeled Jack,* with its "zany" language, "is sure to engage even the most reluctant reader."

Pullman's Eclectic Writings

Pullman's story *The Broken Bridge* takes his readers to a new place, a modern-day Welsh village by the sea. His heroine, sixteen-year-old Ginny, is half-Haitian, half-English, and living with her father. Though she has never felt completely at home in her predominately white village, Ginny's life has been calm and happy until the summer her once open father suddenly becomes closed-mouthed. Ginny is surprised by the arrival of her white half-brother, Robert, who she discovers is her father's legitimate son while she is illegitimate. Between shifts at her two jobs and lengthy chats on the nature of sexiness with her best friend ("He was close enough for her to see the flecks of green in his eyes, and for a long confusing moment she couldn't tell whether he was kind, or sexy, or both," thinks Ginny), Ginny pieces together her bizarre past, finding her mother (who she believed was dead), her insane grandmother, and her father's connection to a gangster.

Barbara Hutcheson, writing in *School Library Journal,* maintained that "Pullman moves as comfortably in this contemporary small town setting as he did in Victorian London in his previous novels." Michael Dorris, reviewing the book in the *New York Times Book Review,* asserted that Ginny's life was "full of enough problems for a whole series of books." Although he felt that Pullman should learn that "less is more," Dorris wrote, "it's a credit to the storytelling skill of Philip Pullman that this contemporary novel succeeds as well as it does." But a *Publishers Weekly* contributor saw "the emotional truths that Pullman reveals" as being "so heartfelt and raw that they hardly read like fiction." Meg Engel of *Voice of Youth Advocates* noted that "the dialogue and portrayal of mixed-up teenage emotions are dead on."

After telling all he could about Sally Lockhart, Pullman continued the story of some of the characters he introduced in his trilogy with *The Tin Princess.* In *The Tin Princess* he elaborates on the life of Sally's protege, Jim, and his love, Adelaide, an orphan who disappeared in *The Ruby in the Smoke.* Pullman also continued writing in contemporary settings with *The White Mercedes,* a fast-reading tragedy of teenagers in contemporary Oxford.

Though Pullman is best known for his novels, he also writes plays and television scripts, and teaches two days each week at Westminster College near his home in Oxford. Pullman made enough money to devote himself to his writing when his satirical book *How to Be Cool* became a television show, but his teaching and projects in the theater and television give him contact with others. His involvement with the outside world is essential because, as he asserted in *SAAS,* "writing has to be solitary, but I don't want to be a hermit." Pullman lives with his wife, Jude, and raves about his talented sons, Jamie and Tom; he writes his three pages a day on his artificial-flower adorned computer in a shed he calls "the hut" in the corner of his garden.

This 1994 novel continues the stories of some of the minor characters Pullman introduced in his trilogy about Sally Lockhart.

■ Works Cited

Review of *The Broken Bridge, Publishers Weekly,* January 1, 1992, p. 56.

Cart, Michael, review of *Shadow in the North, School Library Journal,* May, 1988, p. 112.

Churchill, David, review of *The Ruby in the Smoke, School Librarian,* June, 1986, p. 174.

Cooper, Ilene, review of *The Ruby in the Smoke, Booklist,* March 1, 1987, p. 1009.

Cooper, review of *The Tiger in the Well, Booklist,* October 15, 1990, p. 439.

Dillon, Brooke L., review of *The Ruby in the Smoke, Voice of Youth Advocates,* October, 1987, p. 206.

Dorris, Michael, review of *The Broken Bridge, New York Times Book Review,* May 17, 1992, p. 24.

Engel, Meg, review of *The Broken Bridge, Voice of Youth Advocates,* October, 1992, p. 230.

Review of *Galatea, Publishers Weekly,* January 29, 1979, pp. 104-05.

Review of *Galatea, Times Literary Supplement,* December 1, 1978, p. 1385.

Haley, Karen Stang, review of *Count Karlstein, Booklist,* February 1, 1984, pp. 815-16.

Hollindale, Peter, review of *The Ruby in the Smoke, British Book News Children's Books,* March, 1986, pp. 33-34.

Hollindale, review of *The Shadow in the Plate, British Book News Children's Books,* December, 1986, pp. 30-31.

Hutcheson, Barbara, review of *The Broken Bridge, School Library Journal,* March, 1992, p. 259.

Hutcheson, review of *The Tiger in the Well, School Library Journal,* September, 1990.

Johnson, Joanne, review of *Shadow in the North, Voice of Youth Advocates,* December, 1988, p. 241.

Kennemer, Phyllis K., review of *Count Karlstein, School Library Journal,* March, 1984, p. 174.

Pullman, Philip, *The Broken Bridge,* Macmillan (England), 1990, Knopf, 1992.

Pullman, *Sixth Book of Junior Authors,* pp. 234-35.

Pullman, essay in *Something about the Author Autobiography Series,* Volume 17, Gale, pp. 297-312.

Review of *Spring-Heeled Jack, Publishers Weekly,* July 5, 1991.

Stander, Bella, interview with Philip Pullman in "Coming Attractions: A Variety of Authors and Artists Discuss Their Projects for the Fall Season," *Publishers Weekly,* July 27, 1990.

Review of *The Tiger in the Well, Publishers Weekly,* October 12, 1990.

■ For More Information See

PERIODICALS

Booklist, April 1, 1988, p. 1336; February 15, 1992, pp. 1099, 1102.

Publishers Weekly, May 30, 1994, pp. 24-25.

School Library Journal, December, 1991, pp. 117-18.

—Sketch by Sara Pendergast

Robert Redford

■ Personal

Born Charles Robert Redford, Jr., August 18, 1937, in Santa Monica, CA; son of Charles (an accountant) and Martha (Hart) Redford; married Lola Van Wagenen, September 12, 1958 (divorced); children: Shauna, David James, Amy Hart; three grandchildren. *Education:* Attended University of Colorado and Pratt Institute of Design; studied painting in Europe; studied acting at American Academy of Dramatic Arts. *Hobbies and other interests:* Skiing, horseback riding, mountain climbing, fishing, hunting, tennis, motorcycle racing, automobile racing.

■ Addresses

Home—Box 837, Provo Canyon, UT 84601. *Office*—Wildwood Enterprises, 100 Universal City Plaza, Universal City, CA 91608. *Agent*—Creative Artists Agency, 9830 Wilshire Blvd., Beverly Hills, CA 90212.

■ Career

Actor, director, and producer. Worked for International Business Machines, Inc. (IBM), and Standard Oil, 1950s. Owner of Wildwood Enterprises (motion picture production company), Universal City, CA, and Sundance (ski resort), Provo, UT; founder of Sundance Institute (for independent filmmakers); fundraiser for Institute for Resource Management; chairman of Provo Canyon Sewer District Committee, 1976—. *Member:* National Resources Defense Council, Environmental Defense Fund.

■ Awards, Honors

Emmy Award nomination, best supporting actor, National Academy of Television Arts and Sciences, 1962, for *Alcoa Premiere;* Golden Globe Award, new male film star of the year, Hollywood Foreign Press Association, 1966, for *Inside Daisy Clover;* British Academy Award, best leading actor, British Academy of Film and Television Arts, 1970, for *Butch Cassidy and the Sundance Kid* and *Tell Them Willie Boy Is Here;* Hasty Pudding Man of the Year Award, Hasty Pudding Theatricals, 1970; Academy Award (Oscar) nomination, best actor, Academy of Motion Picture Arts and Sciences, 1973, for *The Sting;* Golden Apple Award, male star of the year, Hollywood Women's Press Club, 1973; Golden Globe Awards, male world film favorite, 1975, 1977, and 1978; Academy Award nomination, best short feature, for *The Solar Film;* Academy Award, best director, Golden Globe Award, Outstanding Directorial Achievement Award for Feature Films, Directors Guild of America, and best director awards from the National Board of Review of Motion Pictures and the

New York Film Critics' Circle, all 1980, all for *Ordinary People*; L.H.D., University of Colorado, 1987; Audubon Medal, National Audubon Society, 1989, for "lifetime campaign for environmental protection"; Dartmouth Film Society award, 1990; D. Univ., University of Massachusetts, 1990; Golden Globe Award nomination, best director, 1993, for *A River Runs through It*; New York Film Critics' Circle Award for best picture, and Academy Award nominations, best director and best picture, both 1995, both for *Quiz Show*.

■ Films

ACTOR

War Hunt, T-D Enterprises/United Artists (UA), 1962.

Situation Hopeless—But Not Serious, Paramount, 1965.

Inside Daisy Clover, Warner Bros., 1966.

The Chase, Columbia, 1966.

This Property Is Condemned, Paramount, 1966.

Barefoot in the Park, Paramount, 1967.

(And producer) *Downhill Racer*, Paramount, 1967.

Butch Cassidy and the Sundance Kid, Twentieth Century-Fox, 1969.

Tell Them Willie Boy Is Here, Universal, 1970.

Little Fauss and Big Halsey, Paramount, 1970.

Jeremiah Johnson, Warner Bros., 1972.

The Hot Rock, Twentieth Century-Fox, 1972.

(And producer) *The Candidate*, Warner Bros., 1972.

The Way We Were, Columbia, 1973.

The Sting, Universal, 1973.

The Great Gatsby, Paramount, 1974.

The Great Waldo Pepper, Universal, 1974.

Three Days of the Condor, Paramount, 1975.

A Bridge Too Far, UA, 1975.

All the President's Men, Warner Bros., 1976.

The Electric Horseman, Columbia, 1979.

Brubaker, Twentieth Century-Fox, 1980.

(And producer) *The Natural*, Tri-Star, 1984.

Out of Africa, Universal, 1985.

Legal Eagles, Universal, 1986.

Havana, Universal, 1990.

Sneakers, Universal, 1992.

Indecent Proposal, Paramount, 1993.

DIRECTOR

Ordinary People (starring Mary Tyler Moore, Donald Sutherland, and Timothy Hutton), Paramount, 1980.

(And producer) *The Milagro Beanfield War* (starring Sonia Braga and Ruben Blades), Universal, 1988.

(And narrator and producer) *A River Runs through It* (starring Tom Skerritt, Craig Sheffer, and Brad Pitt), New Line Cinema, 1992.

Quiz Show (starring Ralph Fiennes, Rob Morrow, and John Turturro), Buena Vista, 1994.

EXECUTIVE PRODUCER

Promised Land, Vestron, 1987.

Some Girls, Metro-Goldwyn-Mayer/UA, 1988.

(And narrator) *Incident at Oglala* (also known as *Leonard Peltier: A True Story*), Miramax, 1992.

■ Television Appearances

"The Case of the Treacherous Toupee," *Perry Mason*, Columbia Broadcasting System (CBS), 1958.

"Iron Hand," *Maverick*, American Broadcasting Company (ABC), 1960.

"The Last Gunfight," *The Deputy*, National Broadcasting Company (NBC), 1960.

"In the Presence of Mine Enemies," *Playhouse 90*, CBS, 1960.

"Captain Brassbound's Conversion," *Hallmark Hall of Fame*, NBC, 1960.

"The Bounty Hunter," *Tate*, NBC, 1960.

"The Golden Deed," *Moment of Fear*, NBC, 1960.

"Comanche Scalps," *Tate*, NBC, 1960.

"The Iceman Cometh," *Play of the Week*, syndicated, 1960.

"Born a Giant," *Our American Heritage*, NBC, 1960.

"Black Monday," *Play of the Week*, syndicated, 1961.

"Tombstone for a Derelict," *Naked City*, ABC, 1961.

"The Coward," *Americans*, NBC, 1961.

"The Grudge," *Whispering Smith*, NBC, 1961.

"First Class Mouliak," *Route 66*, CBS, 1961.

"The Covering Darkness," *Bus Stop*, ABC, 1961.

"Lady Killer," *The New Breed*, ABC, 1961.

"The Right Kind of Medicine," *Alfred Hitchcock Presents*, NBC, 1961.

"A Piece of the Action," *The Alfred Hitchcock Hour*, CBS, 1962.

"The Burning Sky," *Dr. Kildare*, NBC, 1962.

"The Voice of Charlie Pont," *Alcoa Premiere*, ABC, 1962.

"Snowball," *The Untouchables*, ABC, 1963.

"A Tangled Web," *The Alfred Hitchcock Hour*, CBS, 1963.

"The Last of the Big Spenders," *The Dick Powell Show*, NBC, 1963.

"Bird and Snake," *Breaking Point*, ABC, 1963.

"The Evil that Men Do," *The Virginian,* NBC, 1963.

"The Siege," *The Defenders,* CBS, 1964.

(Narrator) "Condor," *National Audubon Society Specials,* Public Broadcasting System (PBS), 1986.

The Golden Eagle Awards (special), syndicated, 1987.

(Narrator) *Living Dangerously* (special), Arts and Entertainment, 1987.

Bill Moyers' World of Ideas (special), PBS, 1988.

(Narrator) "Grizzly and Man: Uneasy Truce," *National Audubon Society Specials,* PBS, 1988.

People Magazine on TV (special), CBS, 1989.

(Narrator, executive producer, and author of television play) "Yosemite: The Fate of Heaven," *The American Experience,* PBS, 1989.

Robert Redford and Sydney Pollack: The Men and Their Movies (special; also known as *Robert Redford: The Man, the Movies, and the Myth*), NBC, 1990.

The New Hollywood (special), NBC, 1990.

The Challenge to Wildlife: A Public Television Special Report (special), PBS, 1990.

(Narrator) *Three Flags over Everest* (special), PBS, 1990.

(Host and narrator) "Wolves," *National Audubon Society Specials,* PBS, 1990.

"Waldo Salt: A Screenwriter's Journey," *American Masters,* PBS, 1992.

Also appeared on episode of *The Twilight Zone,* CBS, early 1960s.

■ Stage Appearances

Tall Story, produced on Broadway, New York City, 1959.

The Highest Tree, produced on Broadway, 1960.

Sunday in New York, produced on Broadway, 1961.

Barefoot in the Park, produced on Broadway, 1963.

■ Writings

The Outlaw Trail (photographs by Jonathan Blair), Grosset, 1978.

(Editor and author of introduction) Richard Friedenberg, *A River Runs through It: Bringing a Classic to the Screen,* Clark City Press, 1992.

(Editor) *The Legacy of Wildness: The Photographs of Robert Glenn Ketchum,* Aperture Foundation, 1993.

Also author of the screenplay *The Solar Film.* Author of introductions for numerous books, including *Vanishing Creatures: A Series of Portraits,* by Dugald Stermer, Lancaster-Miller, 1981; *Greenhouse-Glasnost: The Crisis of Global Warming,* by Terrell J.

Minger, Ecco Press, 1990; *Outdoor Survival Skills,* by Larry D. Olsen, Chicago Review Press, 1990; *Save the Earth,* by Jonathon Porritt, Turner Publications, 1991; and *Exposure,* by *Outside* Magazine Editorial Staff, Simon & Schuster, 1992. Also author of forewords for *The Wind Power Book,* by Jack Park, Chesire, 1981; and *Cougar: The American Lion,* by Kevin Hansen, Northland, 1992. Contributor of articles to periodicals, including *Film Comment, American Film,* and *National Geographic.*

■ Work in Progress

Collaborating with Showtime to launch the Sundance Film Channel, a cable television network specializing in independent, foreign, documentary, and experimental films; acting in a Rob Reiner comedy about a lonely U.S. president seeking love in the White House.

■ Sidelights

"His image is that of the man to whom everything has come easily, the guy who always made captain of the team and got the girl," Philip Caputo described actor, director, and activist Robert Redford in *Esquire.* "The fact is, yeah, certain things did come easy to me in my life," Redford responded in an interview with Nicole Burdette for *Harper's Bazaar.* "The question isn't whether they came easy or not, it's what you did with what came easy."

Since he became a star in 1969 for his role in the blockbuster movie *Butch Cassidy and the Sundance Kid,* Redford has used his status to make a number of important contributions to film and to society. "Over the years, he has probably put his money, his mouth, his time, his energy, his intelligence, his expertise, and his muscle more fervently into the causes he believes in than any other Hollywood name-above-the-title. What's more, his commitment to the environment, to the dignity of American Indians, and to the artistic growth of independent film and new moviemakers through the work of his Sundance Institute has been carried out without any need for applause," Hal Rubenstein stated in *Interview.*

Redford has not always felt comfortable with stardom, especially when it impinged upon his personal life. "When you can't walk from here to there without 10 people stopping you, you lose moments of your life you didn't intend to. You begin to feel a slight panic that your time is not your own," he admitted to Frank Bruni in the *Detroit Free Press*. Rather than compromising his values, however, Redford built a ranch in Utah and found an acceptable balance. "It is a testament to the power of Redford's home-on-the-range aura that he seems to have slipped out of Hollywood without paying the requisite celebrity check that is normally handed to matinee idols. He retains a reputation for not making compromises, for maintaining his integrity, for not bowing to the craven demands of the Industry," Caputo noted. "Indeed, his filmography reads like the syllabus of a course on either the American identity or American manhood," Bruni declared. "To this day, when people say that someone looks like an all-American boy, what they mean is that he looks like Robert Redford."

A Rebellious Youth

Redford was born in Santa Monica, California, on August 18, 1937, the oldest of two sons in a family of Scotch-Irish descent. A few years later his family moved to Van Nuys, where they lived in a modest bungalow in a working class, mostly Hispanic neighborhood. In an interview for *Ladies' Home Journal*, Redford described himself to Myrna Blyth as "a funny-looking, freckle-faced kid with too many cowlicks." Redford remembered his mother as "joyous" and "affirmative," but she died when he was eighteen. His father, partly due to his own upbringing, tended to be strict and unemotional. "My father was angry, so upset with his life. He was a milkman, then an accountant at Standard Oil and unsuited for it. He should have been a sportswriter, but he was afraid to take a chance. He played it safe," Redford explained to Caputo. "The strongest connection I had with my dad came through baseball. He'd come home from work, all tired and pissed off. I'd wait for him, toss him a baseball glove, and we'd play catch."

Since his family did not have much money, reading became an important escape for Redford at a very young age. "My family couldn't afford to travel—the most they could afford was a movie on Saturday night in the neighborhood theater—and the library, which, by the way, had a greater impact on me then than I ever knew," Redford revealed to Burdette. "Every Wednesday night they would go to the public library, and I would go with them, because they couldn't afford a

baby-sitter. I was six years old, maybe seven . . . I fell in love with reading." "I dove into mythology, and that was the most important thing I ever did, for it was full of all these larger-than-life things, windows into greater possibilities, other realms," he recalled to Rubenstein. "And then in first or second grade, I had the benefit of a teacher who read us Laura Ingalls Wilder—*Farmer Boy* and *Little House on the Prairie*—in such a way that we were there. You could tell she really got off on it, but we did, too. Those two things led me into life with a tremendous respect for storytelling."

As Redford grew up, he became increasingly dissatisfied with his home life, school, and the overall social climate of the 1950s. During his teen years he rebelled by stealing hubcaps, climbing all the major buildings in town, and even breaking into a convent. "I had so many restraints on me as a kid, being told, 'Don't do this, don't do that.' I'd just go out and do it to show it ain't so. And I was aware of the fear you could generate in others through your behavior. . . . You know, going out to the edge," he admitted to Caputo. Later, sports provided a more acceptable outlet for his frustrations. "I obviously had some need to physicalize my life. I was born with a keen sense of nerves—not nervous tension, but there was a tension I needed to exhaust. And sports was it. I was fortunate enough to be good. Sports was a way out of the poor area of Los Angeles I grew up in, a neighborhood impoverished intellectually and culturally," Redford told Burdette. When he graduated from Van Nuys High School in 1955, Redford earned a baseball scholarship to the University of Colorado in Boulder.

At Colorado, Redford joined a fraternity and began taking art classes. He had enjoyed sketching and drawing from childhood, and he hoped to make a living as a painter. After a while, however, Redford became bored with school and started to resent the pressure he felt as a college athlete. This attitude led him to skip class and baseball practice and instead spend his time drinking. Eventually, he lost his scholarship and left the university. He then returned to California, where he worked in the oil fields in order to earn enough money to go to Europe and study painting. He took a freighter to Paris and then hitchhiked around Europe, but before long he got discouraged and returned home.

Redford won an Academy Award for directing his first film, *Ordinary People,* a movie about a mother who refuses to acknowledge that her son needs more from life than an upper-middle-class lifestyle.

Luckily, one of Redford's neighbors in his apartment building in Los Angeles was Lola Van Wagenen, a Mormon from Utah. After she helped him recover from his drinking problem and regain some focus in his life, the couple was married in 1958. They soon moved to New York, where Redford briefly studied art at the Pratt Institute of Design in Brooklyn. Since he was most interested in set design, however, he later decided to enroll in the American Academy of Dramatic Arts. He felt that acting could give him something to fall back on if he struggled as a painter, plus he could gain valuable contacts in theater. Redford settled in for two years at the academy and received positive reviews from his instructors.

Launched Acting Career

In 1959, Redford made his professional acting debut on Broadway in *Tall Story.* One of Redford's instructors was the stage manager and casting director for the show, and he recruited Redford to play a small role as a college basketball player. Later that year Redford went to Hollywood and landed several minor roles on television, but in 1960 he returned to New York. He won his first Broadway lead in 1961 in the romantic comedy *Sunday in New York,* which enjoyed a six-month run. In the early 1960s he also guest starred on many popular television shows, including *Route 66, The Twilight Zone,* and *Alfred Hitchcock Presents.* His movie debut came in 1963, when he played a young soldier in *War Hunt.*

At this time, director Mike Nichols noticed Redford's work and gave him his first big break. Nichols recruited Redford to star in Neil Simon's *Barefoot in the Park,* which became a huge success on Broadway. After appearing in eight shows per week for nearly a year, however, Redford got

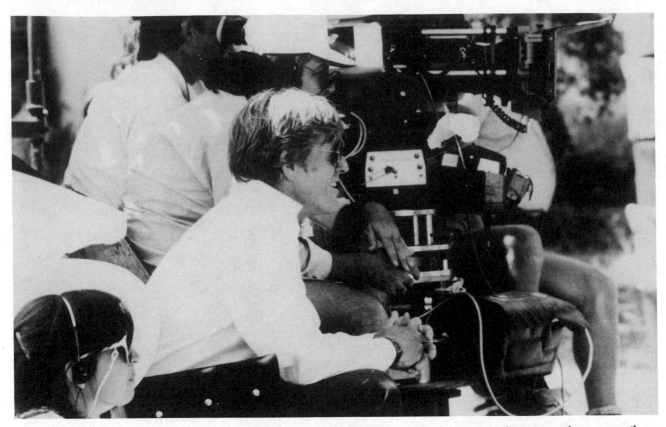

Redford's adaptation of *The Milagro Beanfield War* focused on a group of Hispanic Americans from a northern New Mexico village who join together to reclaim water rights from unscrupulous developers.

bored and finally resigned, never to return to the stage. Instead, he embarked on a long and illustrious film career. Although his first few movies did not fare particularly well at the box office, Redford still gained attention as a promising young actor. He appeared in *Situation Hopeless—But Not Serious* and *Inside Daisy Clover* in 1965, and then played a small but important role as an escaped convict in *The Chase* in 1966, which starred Marlon Brando and Jane Fonda. After his fourth major film, *This Property Is Condemned*, got terrible reviews, Redford decided to take some time off and moved first to Spain and later to the Greek island of Crete with his family.

In 1967 Redford agreed to come back to the United States to reprise his role in the movie version of *Barefoot in the Park*, opposite Jane Fonda. Critics claimed that the film was even better than the play, and it became a huge hit at the box office as well. Then, in 1969, Redford was truly elevated to star status following his performance opposite Paul Newman in one of the most successful Westerns ever made, *Butch Cassidy and the Sundance Kid*. The movie about the lives of two

clever and charismatic outlaws became a blockbuster and was nominated for six Academy Awards.

Success allowed Redford to pursue some film projects that held personal significance for him. He helped produce *Downhill Racer* in 1969, which was the "realization of his long-held desire to create an unflinchingly honest portrait of an athlete on screen," according to a writer in *Current Biography*. "I wanted to illustrate how we've been raised with this false legacy, that it doesn't matter whether you win or lose, it's how you play the game," Redford told Rubenstein. "It's bullshit. I learned that the hard way." In his next film, the Western *Tell Them Willie Boy Is Here*, Redford played a subdued lawman who has unusual sympathy for the young Indian he is forced to chase. Redford was named best actor in 1970 by the British Film Academy for these performances.

In 1972, Redford used his clout in the movie industry to produce *The Candidate*, a documentary-style satire about how politics can corrupt people. He played Bill McKay, a naive young lawyer who works on behalf of society's underdogs in community legal services. McKay undertakes what he thinks will be a hopeless campaign against a long-time senator, but ends up compromising his principles in order to win. In an interview with David Thomson for *Film Comment,* screenwriter Jeremy Larmer explained that the contradiction between a person's private convictions and public image was very relevant to Redford: "What happens, I think, is that the forces that play upon a public figure are much stronger than the person's ideas of who he is and what he's doing . . . some of McKay's experience is drawn from what happened to politicians I've known; some is taken from what happens every day with Redford."

Later that year, Redford played the title role in *Jeremiah Johnson,* which became his favorite among his films. It is based on the true story of a man who retreats from civilization to live alone in the wilderness. But when a group of soldiers need his help to locate a missing wagon train, he leads them through a sacred Indian burial ground with disastrous results. "Jeremiah was a man trying to make his way through life and still remain uncluttered by sophistication. But he discovers there is no place he can escape outside influences and codes," Redford told Caputo. Several years later, Redford obtained permission to remove Johnson's body from where it was buried next to a California freeway and take it to Wyoming for a fitting mountain man's funeral.

In 1973, after he and Barbra Streisand showed their sexual chemistry on screen in *The Way We Were,* Redford was labelled a "sex symbol." He was also nominated for a best actor Academy Award for his performance as a con man opposite Paul Newman in the prohibition-era comedy *The Sting.* In 1974, he played the title character in an ambitious film adaptation of F. Scott Fitzgerald's classic novel *The Great Gatsby.* In the 1975 thriller *Three Days of the Condor,* Redford played a simple man who reads spy novels for an obscure department of the CIA. When he returns from lunch one day to find everyone in his office dead, he goes underground and uses the tricks he has learned to foil a government plot.

The following year, as the country was still reeling from the Watergate scandal and President Nixon's resignation, Redford convinced *Washington Post* reporters Bob Woodward and Carl Bernstein to write a book about their role in exposing the coverup. Redford then played Woodward opposite Dustin Hoffman's Bernstein in the movie adaptation of *All the President's Men,* which won four Academy Awards and was named best picture of the year by the National Board of Review and the New York Film Critics. Like many of Redford's projects, this film focused on issues that were important to him personally but that studio executives doubted would appeal to large audiences. Over the years, Redford developed a reputation for going against conventional Hollywood wisdom and making "dangerous" career decisions that ended up being commercially and critically successful. In *The Electric Horseman,* for example, he played a cowboy who steals a million-dollar horse from a Las Vegas casino and rides off into the desert. And in *Brubaker,* released in 1980, he played a compassionate warden who fights to give his prisoners their basic human rights.

Redford's film appearances were more limited in the 1980s and early 1990s, and they included several "lighter" roles. As he explained to Bruni, "I periodically will take something that's different, just so I don't get stereotyped." In *Sneakers,* for example, Redford plays a radical from the 1960s who runs a company that breaks into buildings and computer systems in order to test their security systems. Ralph Novak, writing in *People,* said the movie featured "an energetic high-tech plot and a refreshingly playful performance by Redford." In 1993 he played a billionaire who offers a married woman one million dollars for a one-night stand in *Indecent Proposal.* The reason Redford spent less time acting during these years was that he kept extremely busy doing other things, like directing and producing films, running the Sundance Institute, and working on behalf of environmental and political causes.

A Life Outside Movies

In 1961, as he was just beginning his acting career, Redford bought two acres of isolated land in north central Utah from a sheepherder for $500. He intended it to provide an escape from the hectic pace of Hollywood and an antidote to the pressures of fame. "When *Butch Cassidy and the Sundance Kid* shot him into megastardom in 1968, Redford's private self no longer recognized his public self—the golden glamour boy. The house in the Utah mountains was the only place where those two halves could get reacquainted," Caputo explained. For the first few years, he and his wife had to walk to their property with snowshoes and melt snow for drinking water. Over time, however, Redford acquired 7,000 acres of land in the area, built a solar-powered home that was featured in *Architectural Digest,* and established a ski resort, a conference center, and even a clothing store.

Redford also created the Sundance Institute, which provides support for the work of independent filmmakers and sponsors an annual film festival. "The Sundance Institute is Robert Redford's deliberate and principled attempt to provide alternatives to Hollywood, set up in the pristine ecology of high-mountain Utah, as opposed to the smoggy L.A. where he was actually born," Thomson noted in *Film Comment.* "Sundance is movie production for bald eagles, liberals, and independents, and there is no Redford more earnestly in pursuit of integrity than the one who speaks for the Institute." The Sundance Institute celebrated its 25th anniversary in 1994, and Redford planned to expand its influence to cable television. He collaborated with Showtime to launch the Sundance Film Channel, a new cable network highlighting independent, foreign, documentary, and experimental films.

Redford fulfilled another of his personal dreams in 1978 when, during a three-year break in his acting career, he wrote a book. *The Outlaw Trail* tells the history of a rugged trail, leading south from Montana across Utah and Wyoming to the Mexican border, that many famous bandits used as an escape route between 1870 and 1910. Redford first learned about the trail when he filmed *Jeremiah Johnson* nearby. He was disgusted at how badly it was deteriorating, so he convinced *National Geographic* to let him write an article documenting its history. In preparation, he spent several weeks riding the route on horseback with a group of eight men. He also talked extensively with people who lived in the area and with descendants of the outlaws. Eventually he expanded the article into a coffee-table book, which a *Publishers Weekly* reviewer praised as "a keen adventure shared with an articulate, passionate, daring fellow who incidentally is the actor Robert Redford. . . . Redford's dismay at destructive progress is contagious, as is his marvelous euphoria that bubbles with the wonders of nature."

Redford also provided highly visible support to several environmental and political causes. His earliest victory came in 1970 when he led a group in protest against a proposed freeway that would have led through a canyon near his property in Utah. When construction of the freeway was halted, Redford told Dan Yakir and Jeffrey Wells of the *Saturday Evening Post* that the experience "taught me that one person can matter, that activism can make a difference." Redford also opposed the building of a nuclear power plant in Utah, which caused supporters to burn him in effigy. Although some people criticized him for using his position in the public eye for political purposes, Redford responded by telling Yakir and Wells: "Being an actor is not synonymous with giving up citizenship papers. I think I have the right." Over the years, Redford also narrated several television specials for the National Audubon Society, provided forewords for books about endangered species, and worked closely with the Environmental Defense Fund and the National Resources Defense Council.

Beginning with his production of *The Candidate,* and continuing in other films and in interviews, Redford has spoken out consistently about corruption in government. When asked by Blyth whether he would ever consider running for office, Redford responded with a stinging condemnation of the political system: "Politics, the highest calling in the land? It is *not* the highest calling in the land. It is completely stymied by compromise, corruption, weakness and ignorance that constipates the system almost to the point of grinding it to a halt. It barely moves. Thank God, it still does move, but it's not moving too well these days." In Redford's view, such corruption has affected society's values, as he explained to Rubenstein: "I think shame is pretty well gone out of our vocabulary. When I grew up, shame was used as a tool for check and balance. If you stood a chance of hearing someone say, 'Shame on you,' or, 'You should be ashamed of yourself,' you thought twice. It doesn't seem to be a factor today. You see [Senator] Bob Packwood, all those guys up there, Oliver North—you can just *feel* they're not telling the truth. And it's so *brazen.* If they have any shame, it's not for what they've done, but for getting caught at it. At one time, it might have been, Oh my God, what's going to happen to me? Now it's, Hey, you know how you deal with that? Treat it like nothing happened and people will respond the same way."

Another political issue of deep importance to Redford involved Native American rights. For example, he lobbied extensively in Washington, D.C., on behalf of Leonard Peltier, an American Indian Movement (AIM) activist who was convicted of murdering two FBI agents on a reservation in South Dakota in 1975. When these efforts were unsuccessful, Redford produced and narrated *Incident at Oglala,* a documentary that uses the Peltier case to expose the unfair treatment of Native Americans by the government. "It seemed pretty clear he was being railroaded," Redford explained to Joe Treen in *People.* "The issue of Leonard's guilt or innocence was too much of a fog. But what was emerging clearly was the issue of a fair trial. The case asks layers of questions about the double standard of our judicial system." The film shows the bleak conditions on the reservation, where a virtual civil war was taking place between AIM activists and government-backed Indian authorities. After the courts found four other activists innocent of the murders because their actions were justified by self-defense, the government used improper tactics—ranging from withholding evidence to coercing witnesses—to ensure Peltier's conviction. "*Incident at Oglala* never tries to whip us into a frenzy of indignation," Terrence Rafferty stated in the *New Yorker.* "It just shows us what life was like at Pine Ridge, and how determined the government was to keep Native Americans from asserting their rights; and by the time the picture is over we're seething."

Despite his cynicism about politics, on a personal level Redford remained optimistic. An avid outdoorsman for most of his life, he stayed in good physical shape well into his fifties by riding horses, skiing, hunting, and playing tennis. He also maintained a wry sense of humor and enjoyed playing practical jokes on his friends. Redford managed to raise his family in relative privacy in Utah, an apartment in Manhattan, and a home in the quiet suburbs of Westport, Connecticut. Although he and his wife divorced after thirty years of marriage, they maintained a friendly relationship. He was proud that his three

After unsuccessfully lobbying on behalf of activist Leonard Peltier, Redford produced and narrated *Incident at Oglala,* a documentary that uses the Peltier case to expose the unfair treatment of Native Americans by the government.

children turned out to be well-adjusted, artistic, and good parents for his grandchildren. "At the moment I have a funny kind of optimism having to do with this generation of parents, to use my own children as an example," he told Blyth. "I watch younger people, and there seems to be a lot of attention paid to child rearing, putting in time with the kids, expressing a lot of love and being really smart about it. Maybe I'm looking at a very small segment of society, but this generation of babies, when they grow up, they're going to grow up with a whole lot more of love that's been expressed. For the most part, that's pretty beneficial. And someday they'll be out there making decisions with a value system that might help turn around some things that have been so devalued in our society."

Continued Impact as Film Director

In 1980, Redford took his craft one step further by directing his first film, *Ordinary People*. Based on the novel by Judith Guest, it starred Donald Sutherland, Mary Tyler Moore, and Timothy Hutton as a family struggling to come to terms with the death of a son. Redford's directorial debut earned Academy Awards for best picture and best director, and also allowed him to reconnect with the artistic side of his nature. Since at first he was not familiar with the language of filmmaking, he drew pictures to show his camera operators how he wanted certain scenes to look. "I was so remorseful about giving up art that for years it made it hard to function happily as an actor. But now it's come full circle," Redford explained to Michael Rogers in *Rolling Stone*.

"I have no doubt that I'll phase out acting. I'm certain of it. Directing has given me a new surge of energy. It's a new beginning," he continued in a 1980 *People* article. "There's more art to it than acting. In acting, you're given a role, you fulfill it," Redford admitted to Caputo. "But in directing, you're putting something on the canvas. It's hard for me because I tend to live every moment for the actor. You have to learn how to hang back as a director, and that causes an inner tension." "Curiously, directing my own films has made me more tolerant and patient," he told Rubenstein. "I've always been an extremely impatient actor— you know, not too many takes, don't want to spend too much time on the set. Waiting around

Ralph Fiennes starred as ill–fated game-show contestant Charles Van Doren in Redford's Academy-Award nominated film *Quiz Show*.

drove me nuts. But now I'm much more sympathetic to a director's struggle."

After his highly successful first effort, Redford waited eight years before directing another film. But, true to form, his follow-up picture—*The Milagro Beanfield War*—was both personal and unconventional. The movie tells the story of a group of Hispanic Americans from a northern New Mexico village who join together to reclaim water rights from unscrupulous developers. Writing in *Newsweek*, David Ansen called it "a populist pipe dream of a movie, old-fashioned in its utter lack of cynicism and its wishful, team-spirit politics, and very up to date in its sly, underplayed texture and jumpy rhythms. Anyone allergic to whimsy in any form should beware; for the rest of us, *Milagro* provides plenty to smile about." "Redford leaves no doubt about which side he's on," Peter Travers continued in *People*. "The shots of the undeveloped landscape in sunlight or storm are breathtaking enough to make the blot of condos and tennis courts appear unbearable. But Redford is realist enough to know that so-called progress cannot be long held at bay. So he has turned his film into a fable in which even the bad guys eventually come to their senses."

Redford had to overcome several complications while filming *The Milagro Beanfield War.* Originally planning to shoot the movie on location in the town of Chimayo, New Mexico, Redford ended up facing a protest from townspeople similar to the one in his fictional story. Eventually he moved production to Truchas, but by then it was the rainy season and they had to delay filming outdoor scenes for nine months. Redford was also criticized by some who felt that an Anglo should not make an Hispanic movie, but several members of the cast defended him. For example, actor Ruben Blades told Ansen: "Redford made it possible for non-Anglo actors to have a good script, characters that weren't negative and, most important, to have the opportunity to work and collaborate. With this movie he proves that hearts don't require visas and emotions don't require subtitles."

Redford's third project as a director, *A River Runs through It,* was also considered risky by Hollywood standards. In fact, the idea was turned down by all the major studios, and Redford finally managed to get a minimal ten million dollars from Carolco only because of his status. Based upon a solemn, understated novel by Norman Maclean, *A River Runs through It* follows two very different sons of a stern minister as they come of age in rural Montana. Norman is bookish and responsible, while his brother Paul enjoys living dangerously—drinking, gambling, and running with a rough crowd. The family knows Paul is headed for disaster, but they are unable to communicate openly in order to save him. The only thing they all share is a love of fly-fishing.

Over the years, Maclean had refused many offers to buy the rights to his popular novel, but Redford was attracted to the theme of family communication and worked hard to convince him. "Redford's courtship of Maclean was conducted with the doggedness and delicacy of an international arms-control negotiation," Caputo noted in *Esquire.* "He invited the novelist to his Utah ranch, Sundance, for an introductory meeting. The two men then exchanged correspondence, each outlin-

ing his views of how the screen adaptation should be handled. Afterward, Redford made three trips to Chicago, trying to build trust." Finally, in an unusual arrangement, Redford allowed Maclean to look over the final script. If the author approved it, he agreed to step aside and let Redford make the film; but if he did not, Redford agreed to give up. Maclean was finally satisfied, though he died before the movie was completed.

Redford's adaptation, which starred Brad Pitt as Paul, Craig Sheffer as Norman, and Tom Skerritt as the father, was well-received at the box office as well as by critics. Writing in *Time,* Richard Schickel called it a "cool, quiet, allusive and, in the best sense, poetic movie, rich in unforced metaphors and unforced, indeed often unspoken, feelings." "It is hard to remember a serious work that has been more faithfully or more entrancingly turned into a movie," Schickel continued. "Partly it is because director Robert Redford has rigorously maintained the understated tone of a book that never plea-bargains, never asks outright for sympathy or understanding, yet ultimately, powerfully, elicits both."

Redford directed his fourth film, *Quiz Show,* in 1994. It is based on the true story of Charles Van Doren, an appealing young professor from a wealthy New England family who gained national attention during the 1950s by winning record amounts on the popular television program *Twenty-One.* Later, an investigation revealed that the show's producers fixed the outcome of games by giving Van Doren and other contestants the answers ahead of time. Redford again was drawn to the theme of an individual compromising his values for fame, as Blyth remarked in *Ladies' Home Journal:* "Van Doren is another, like the seemingly cool, seemingly confident heroes of *Downhill Racer* and *The Candidate,* who while succeeding spectacularly know deep inside they are also failing." Redford also viewed the story as an early indicator of what went wrong in American society: "I see the quiz-show scandals as really the first in a series of downward steps to the loss of our innocence. When it hit, the country was numbed by the shock. . . . But the shocks kept coming," he explained to Rubenstein. "I think people may look at this film and say, 'Well, as a scandal, big deal.' But in a historical context, it's very much a big deal. This was the beginning of our letting things go. And what did we do about it? Kind of nothing, as long as we kept being entertained." *Quiz Show* was named best picture by the New York Film Critics and also earned Academy Award nominations for best picture and best director.

Comments on Hollywood

Throughout his career, Redford has maintained a healthy perspective about Hollywood. "You know, I like films, acting, directing, being around creative people. It's all such a game, though. There are no ethics. It's all trade and barter: I'll entertain your lie if you entertain mine. The athlete in me likes the game, but you can't take it seriously," Redford told Caputo. "I think the film business has gone so low lately. It's tied to a fast-food, sound-bite, MTV, give-it-to-me-now mentality. Very little is asked of audiences now." He continued in the interview with Rubenstein, "The industry has become more centralized, more costly and more formulaic. It's so much about the opening weekend, about volume. You watch certain films and say, Why did that get made? How'd they spend that kind of money on that film? And you realize that there's an assembly line moving through the industry." But in addition to recognizing the perils of fame, Redford also recognized its benefits and used them to his advantage. "In Hollywood, all you have to do is make a success and then you can have terms that are pretty much your own," he explained to Blyth. "You have the opportunity to remain independent as long as you have success. Those are the odds I'd much rather play with."

■ Works Cited

Ansen, David, "Trouble in Miracle Valley," *Newsweek*, March 28, 1988, p. 67.

Blyth, Myrna, "The Way He Is," *Ladies' Home Journal*, October, 1994, p. 60.

Bruni, Frank, "The Price of Fame," *Detroit Free Press*, September 18, 1994, p. 1G.

Burdette, Nicole, "Weird Wild and Woolly: Welcome to the Offbeat World of Robert Redford," *Harper's Bazaar*, October, 1992, p. 164.

Caputo, Philip, "Robert Redford: Alone on the Range," *Esquire*, September, 1992, p. 166.

Current Biography, Wilson, 1982.

Novak, Ralph, review of *Sneakers*, *People*, September 14, 1992, p. 16.

Review of *The Outlaw Trail*, *Publishers Weekly*, July 3, 1978, p. 59.

People, December 15, 1980.

Rafferty, Terrence, "The Current Cinema," *New Yorker*, June 1, 1992, p. 59.

Rogers, Michael, *Rolling Stone*, October 2, 1980.

Rubenstein, Hal, "Robert Redford," *Interview*, September, 1994, p. 108.

Schickel, Richard, "Fishing for a Useful Life," *Time*, October 19, 1992.

Thomson, David, "Ordinary Bob: Can Robert Redford Ever Explode?," *Film Comment*, February, 1988, p. 32.

Travers, Peter, review of *The Milagro Beanfield War*, *People*, April 4, 1988, p. 10.

Treen, Joe, "A Question of Justice," *People*, May 4, 1992, p. 37.

Yakir, Dan, and Jeffrey Wells, *Saturday Evening Post*, November, 1980.

■ For More Information See

BOOKS

Contemporary Authors, Volume 107, Gale, 1984.

Downing, David, *Robert Redford*, St. Martin's Press, 1982.

Paige, David, *Robert Redford*, Creative Education, 1977.

Reed, Donald A., *Robert Redford: A Photographic Portrayal of the Man and His Films*, Popular Library, 1975.

Spada, James, *The Films of Robert Redford*, Citadel Press, 1977.

—Sketch by Laurie Collier Hillstrom

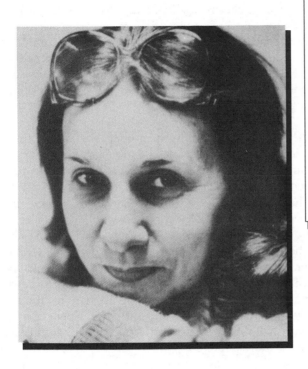

Ann Rinaldi

■ Personal

Born August 27, 1934, in New York, NY; daughter of Michael (a newspaperman) and Marcella (maiden name, Dumarest) Feis; married Ronald P. Rinaldi (a lineman), July, 1960; children: Ronald P., Jr., Marcella. *Education:* Attended high school in New Brunswick, NJ. *Hobbies and other interests:* Historical re-enactments, reading, writing, and studying American history.

■ Addresses

Home—302 Miller Ave., Somerville, NJ 08876. *Agent*—Rosalie Siegel, 1 Abbey Road, Pennington, NJ 08534.

■ Career

Writer. Somerset *Messenger Gazette,* Somerset, NJ, author of column, 1969–70; *Trentonian,* Trenton, NJ, feature writer and author of column, 1970–91. Member of the Brigade of the American Revolution.

■ Awards, Honors

New Jersey Press Awards from the New Jersey Press Association, first place, 1978 and 1989, and several second place awards in subsequent years, all for newspaper columns; *But in the Fall I'm Leaving* was deemed a Notable Children's Trade Book in the Field of Social Studies, National Council for Social Studies and the Children's Book Council, 1985; *Time Enough for Drums* was selected one of the American Library Association's Best Books for Young Adults, 1986, and was named a Junior Literary Guild selection; Best Book award, Pacific Northwest Library Association, 1994, for *Wolf by the Ears;* American Library Association Best Books for Young Adults citations for *The Last Silk Dress, Wolf by the Ears, In My Father's House,* and *A Break with Charity: A Stoy about the Salem Witch Trials; Wolf by the Ears* was also named to the American Library Association's "Best of the Best" in Young Adult Literature list; National History Award, Daughters of the American Revolution, for historical novels.

■ Writings

YOUNG ADULT NOVELS

Term Paper (also see below), Walker & Co., 1980.
Promises Are for Keeping (sequel to *Term Paper*), Walker & Co., 1982.
But in the Fall I'm Leaving, Holiday House, 1985.
Time Enough for Drums, Holiday House, 1986.
The Good Side of My Heart, Holiday House, 1987.

The Last Silk Dress, Holiday House, 1988.

A Ride into Morning: The Story of Tempe Wick, Harcourt, 1991.

Wolf by the Ears, Scholastic, 1991.

In My Father's House, Scholastic, 1992.

A Break with Charity: A Story about the Salem Witch Trials, Harcourt, 1992.

The Fifth of March: A Story of the Boston Massacre, Harcourt, 1993.

A Stitch in Time (first volume in the "Quilt" trilogy), Scholastic, 1994.

Finishing Becca: A Story about Peggy Shippen and Benedict Arnold, Harcourt, 1994.

Broken Days (second volume in the "Quilt" trilogy), Scholastic, 1995.

The Secret of Sarah Revere, Harcourt, 1995.

OTHER

Author of columns and editorials to the *Trentonian,* the *Philadelphia Inquirer,* and the New Jersey section of the *New York Times.*

■ Sidelights

One of the most prolific writers of historical fiction, Ann Rinaldi has been cited by several awards associations and has earned the praise of critics and the gratitude of her readers. Despite discouragement from her own father and from some of her teachers when she was young, Ann Rinaldi pursued a writing career as an adult. Her persistence survived through four initial manuscripts that failed to find a publisher. Then she looked at her work in a different way and recognized that it was simply not reaching the right audience. She expanded a short story into a full-length novel, targeted it at the young adult market, and sold it on the first try.

Rinaldi was the fifth and youngest child in her family. Her mother died when she was an infant. She spent the first two years of her life with an aunt and uncle who lived in Brooklyn, New York. Their home included several older teenage cousins who made a fuss over their young relative. Her aunt and uncle wanted to adopt her but one day her father came and collected Rinaldi, returning her to live with her real siblings and her stepmother. Looking back, Rinaldi stated in *Something about the Author* (SATA) that "the only happy part of my childhood ended" with this abrupt change. The reunited family lived in New Jersey, where her father worked as a newspaperman. He "did everything he could to prevent me from becom-

ing a writer," she declared in *SATA.* "At school they attempted to take out of me what spirit had eluded my stepmother." Rinaldi's father didn't believe in college for his daughters, so he pushed Rinaldi into business and a career as a secretary. She remained in a secretarial position until she married Ronald Rinaldi in 1960. She explained in *SATA* that her new husband was "middle-class and sane. I wanted sanity after my crazy upbringing."

Although she'd written poetry for some time, Rinaldi decided to become a novelist following the birth of her two children. She wrote four full-length novels that didn't find publishers. In 1969 she met with the editor of her local weekly paper, the Somerset *Messenger Gazette,* and suggested an idea for a column. He agreed to the idea and she soon syndicated the column to several weekly newspapers in New Jersey. A year later she called Gil Spencer, an editor at the daily *Trentonian* newspaper, and he hired her to write two columns a week. Rinaldi learned her craft from Spencer, who won a Pulitzer Prize, and from the others at this lively newspaper.

Rinaldi soon expanded her efforts to features and soft news while she continued to do the columns. She managed to place the columns in syndication, which meant her writing appeared throughout New Jersey. Rinaldi's column was selected for first place in the New Jersey Press Awards in 1978 and again in 1989. But she never stopped thinking about fiction. In 1979 she began reworking a ten-thousand-word short story she had been thinking about for many years. As Rinaldi poured over her own work, she realized that what she had was a young adult novel. She told *SATA* that her experience "in the newspaper and as a parent gave me so much more to bring to my fiction. The first publisher to read it, bought it."

Term Paper concerns Nicki, a teenager whose older brother is her substitute English teacher for a semester. When she writes about her father's death in her term paper, not only does she discuss her dislike for her father, but she also writes about the annoyance of her brother's new role as a surrogate dad. Rinaldi said in *SATA* that she wrote the book "because the characters had been part of me for years. Most of the motivation came from my own life. Family relationships, especially the tremendous influence older siblings have over younger ones, have always intrigued me." Describing *Term Paper* in the *School Library Journal,* Anna Biagioni Hart wrote: "A kind of junior *Dallas* in plot, this novel declares strongly for family obligations of love and forgiveness."

The sequel, *Promises Are for Keeping,* catches up with Nicki a year later. Her two brothers, Larry and Tony, now share the parenting responsibilities, but through a few blunders she manages to lose Larry's trust in her. Her struggles with her brothers involve regaining their trust while resisting their efforts to control her. In short, she's a typical teen. Will Manley of the *School Library Journal* praised the novel for the characters, especially the adults whom he found "more intersting and much better developed than in most books of this type." He noted that Rinaldi was "particularly adept at dealing with the perennial teen problem of peer pressure."

The Gradual Move to Historical Fiction

Rinaldi continued to work full time for the *Trentonian,* writing her books at night. Her assignments included covering bicentennial events in Trenton and Princeton and her son began to express an interest in history, especially the American Revolution. He joined a local re-enactment group and even crossed the river on Christmas Day with "Washington." Soon her daughter became intrigued as well. Rinaldi once commented to *Contemporary Authors (CA),* "We started following them all over the east on living history re-enactments of the Revolutionary War. My son, Ron, dragged us to every battlefield, monument, fort, battleground, north and south, from Saratoga to Yorktown. I began to see the history of my country as it was, from the bottom up, hands on, instead of out of a history book." She became as involved in the re-enactments as her children were, often learning the crafts, the dances, and the songs of the time, as well as recreating the foods that were eaten then. A 1981 re-enactment of the British surrender at Yorktown made her realize that she wanted to write about this period.

Before she tackled this subject, however, she wrote another novel set in the present, titled *But in the Fall I'm Leaving.* Brie, her teenage protagonist, lives with her newspaper publisher father and fantasizes that life would be grand if she could just live with her mother in distant California. Diane C. Donovan, who reviewed the book for *Best Sellers,* noted that "Rinaldi's ability to turn an ordi-

Rinaldi moved from contemporary young adult novels to historical fiction with works such as 1988's *The Last Silk Dress,* a story of the Civil War that finds a young Southern girl learning to question the double standards regarding sex and race that prevail in Confederate society.

nary theme into an engrossing, refreshing story makes this title anything but trite." A *Publishers Weekly* reviewer, found the book "disappointing and full of convoluted happenings that are mostly unbelievable." Nonetheless, Sherry D. Blakely wrote in *Voice of Youth Advocates* that "the character development is good and the lessons learned are valuable."

Because she was familiar with the town, she set her next novel, the Yorktown-inspired historical story, in Trenton. Rinaldi bolstered her re-enactments with library research, cramming sessions into her lunch hours and free time. *Time Enough for Drums* told the story of Jemima Emerson, a fifteen-year-old who bickers constantly with her tutor, an apparent Royalist. Devoted patriots, the Emersons survive the war in spite of Hessians, Redcoats, and deprivations. Jemima grows up to fall in love with her tutor, whose sympathies she may have been wrong about. *Booklist's* Hazel Rochman criticized the characters' lack of depth, but concluded that the book was a "light, enjoyable romance." A writer for *Publishers Weekly* forecast that readers would find the romance involving, but "may wish that Jem had a bit more substance."

Rinaldi reintroduced Brie, the protagonist of *But in the Fall I'm Leaving*, in *The Good Side of My Heart*. At sixteen, she falls for her best friend's brother with whom she would like to be more than just friends. She is stunned when he reveals his homosexuality to her. Conversations with her brother, a priest who is having his own crises, help her to come to terms with her disappointment. A critic writing in *Publishers Weekly* noted that "the issues of homosexuality, priesthood and illicit drugs bring an immediacy to the book, but a pat ending seems unrealistic." However, Clara G. Hoover, writing in *Voice of Youth Advocates*, lauded the novel as "well written" and found it "refreshing" to see the characters "work out their individual and collective problems, and through open discussion develop deeper understanding of, and love for, each other."

According to the legend, Tempe Wick, a young New Jersey farm girl, hid her horse in her house in order to keep him from being stolen by renegade soldiers. Tempe's fourteen-year-old cousin Mary, a supporter of the revolution, narrates the novel. As fierce British loyalists, her parents throw her out of the house and she seeks shelter at her aunt's farm. The Wick land has been temporarily given to the Continental Army for their camp. *Voice of Youth Advocates's* Marian Rafal praised the book for its "glimpse of a little known aspect of the American Revolution from the female perspective." In the *School Library Journal*, Lucinda Snyder Whitehurst remarked that Rinaldi "makes excellent use of her research into the period, establishing a believable army camp with such historical figures as General Anthony Wayne, as well as real soldiers whose letters provided details for the story." *A Ride Into Morning: The Story of Tempe Wick* also marked a new variation for Rinaldi: she began using little-known but real historical figures as the basis of her stories.

In *Wolf by the Ears*, Rinaldi again confronted the problems of slavery, prejudice, and racism in American history. She garnered praise from a *Publishers Weekly* contributor, who found the story "an intelligent yet earthy history that lends insight into the complex feelings surrounding race relations." *Wolf by the Ears* is told through the diary of Harriet Hemmings, a light-skinned slave in Thomas Jefferson's household who may also be his daughter. He has promised his slaves freedom at twenty-one, and the nineteen-year-old Harriet has yet to choose whether she will remain in Monticello or take her chances outside. Writing in the *School Library Journal*, Cathy Chaurette placed *Wolf by the Ears* in a new genre, the "docunovel" and remarked that Rinaldi's book "perfectly represents the promises and the pitfalls of these novels." She cautioned that "within the fictional world, Harriet does have special insight into the character of fictional Thomas Jefferson, and it is perhaps too much to ask young readers to remember that these do not necessarily translate into historical fact."

Fiery Historical Heroines

A running theme in Rinaldi's work is the headstrong protagonist who comes of age through her personal confrontations, often against a backdrop of national conflict. *In My Father's House* depicts the story of Osceola Mason, a Southern teenager whom a *Publishers Weekly* reviewer declared a "vibrant if sometimes unlikable heroine." Set between the years of 1852 to 1865, the novel portrays her difficulties with accepting her new stepfather and with her own romance, putting a personal stamp on her growing awareness of the issues at stake in the Civil War. *School Library Journal's* Whitehurst pointed out that the author "demonstrates that the North was not a human rights utopia" though she found the characters in possession of "too much 20th-century perspective in their easy acceptance that the War is a lost cause." A critic writing for *Kirkus Reviews* noted some of the same weaknesses that Whitehurst mentioned, but nonetheless deemed the book "a sweeping dramatic overview of the war, authentic and compelling."

For a new perspective on peer pressure, Rinaldi looked at the dilemma faced by a young woman on the fringes of the seventeenth-century Salem witch trials. Susannah English, the protagonist of *A Break with Charity: A Story about the Salem Witch*

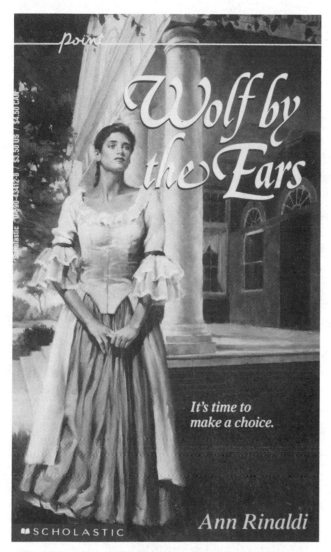

It's time to
make a choice.

Ann Rinaldi

■SCHOLASTIC

The author combines historical figures and fiction in this 1991 novel about Harriet Hemmings—who may have been the daughter of Thomas Jefferson by a slave—as she examines her feelings surrounding race, slavery, family, and independence.

Trials, finds herself torn between her attraction to the group of teenage girls who get up to all sorts of mischief in the small town and the repulsion their evil inspires in her. Writing in *School Library Journal,* Carolyn Noah said that "*A Break with Charity* portrays an excruciating era in American history from a unique perspective." A *Publishers Weekly* reviewer liked Rinaldi's "graceful blend of fiction and history" and found that the "factual style stands in a soothing contrast to her inherently shocking and histrionic subject matter." They concluded that it "ranks with Rinaldi's finest work."

Rachel Marsh, a fourteen-year-old orphan, is an indentured servant to lawyer John Adams and his wife Abigail in 1768 Boston. *The Fifth of March: A Story of the Boston Massacre* details her attempts to come to terms with conflicting emotions as the British soldier with whom she becomes involved is tried for murder following a riot on March 5, 1770. *Voice of Youth Advocates*'s Mary Hedge stated that "the romance in the book will appeal to many readers; however, the story is mainly for those who enjoy historical fiction." With some reservations, a critic writing for *Publishers Weekly* praised the book, pronouncing it "engrossing and educational reading." *Finishing Becca: A Story about Peggy Shippen and Benedict Arnold* is also about Revolutionary War times. Fourteen-year-old Becca, the protagonist, inadvertently becomes a witness to the events that led to General Benedict Arnold's betrayal during the Revolutionary War through her position as a maid in a wealthy Quaker home in Philadelphia. "Rinaldi," states a critic for *Kirkus Reviews,* " . . . takes her role as a historical novelist seriously, to which her long and informative endnote attests. This tale of treachery comes alive under her pen."

Returning to Salem for her next novel, Rinaldi set *A Stitch in Time* a century later than *A Break with Charity: A Story About the Salem Witch Trials.* Narrated by teenaged Hannah, the eldest daughter of the Chelmsford family, the story takes shape along with the quilt she is making and serves as the first volume the Quilt trilogy. Hannah tries to come to terms with her mother's early death, with her rebellious siblings and stern father, and even romance with a sea captain. Reviewing the book for *School Library Journal,* Beth Tegart remarked that "there is plenty of personal interest, adventure, humor, fear, and joy in this ambitious novel." *Broken Days,* the second Quilt trilogy volume, picks up Hannah's life in 1811. Now an adult, she lives in Salem with her 14-year-old niece, Ebie. The arrival of a half-Indian girl who asserts that she is the daughter of Hannah's sister Thankful throws the house into disarray. Aside from this, there is the looming threat of war with Great Britain.

Rinaldi has translated her own experiences with family upheaval and her interest in American history into a respectable body of young adult fiction. As Sutherland concluded in her review of *The Last Silk Dress* for *New York Times Book Review,* the book "is interesting not only for its theme and story, but for the evidence it gives of

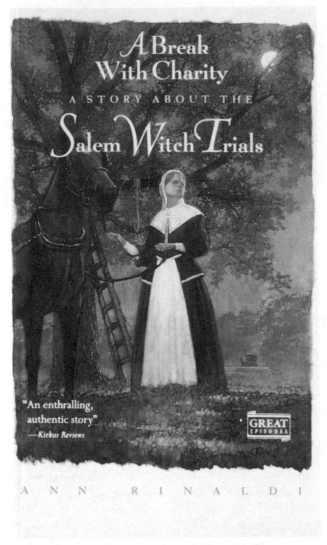

Peer pressure is not just a modern problem, as evidenced by the observations of one teenage girl in Rinaldi's 1992 novel about the seventeenth-century Salem witch trials.

Ms. Rinaldi's respect for her adolescent audience." For her own part, Rinaldi stated in *CA* that "I write young adult novels because I like writing them. But, as with my first book, I don't write for young people. I just write."

■ Works Cited

Beatty, Cynthia L., review of *The Last Silk Dress*, *Voice of Youth Advocates*, December, 1988, pp. 241–42.

Blakely, Sherry D., review of *But in the Fall I'm Leaving*, *Voice of Youth Advocates*, August, 1985, p. 189.

Review of *A Break with Charity: A Story about the Salem Witch Trials*, *Publishers Weekly*, August 3, 1992, p. 72.

Review of *But in the Fall I'm Leaving*, *Publishers Weekly*, June 27, 1986, p. 98.

Chaurette, Cathy, review of *Wolf by the Ears*, *School Library Journal*, June, 1992, p. 52.

Donovan, Diane C., review of *But in the Fall I'm Leaving*, *Best Sellers*, September, 1985, p. 240.

Review of *The Fifth of March: A Story of the Boston Massacre*, *Publishers Weekly*, November 8, 1993, p. 78.

Review of *Finishing Becca: A Story about Peggy Shippen and Benedict Arnold*, *Kirkus Reviews*, December 15, 1994.

Review of *The Good Side of My Heart*, *Publishers Weekly*, May 8, 1987, p. 72.

Hart, Anna Biagioni, review of *Term Paper*, *School Library Journal*, January, 1981, p. 72.

Hedge, Mary, review of *The Fifth of March: A Story of the Boston Massacre*, *Voice of Youth Advocates*, February, 1994, p. 372.

Hoover, Clara G., review of *The Good Side of My Heart*, *Voice of Youth Advocates*, August-September, 1987, pp. 122–23.

Review of *In My Father's House*, *Kirkus Reviews*, April 1, 1993, p. 463.

Review of *In My Father's House*, *Publishers Weekly*, April 26, 1993, p. 80.

Manley, Will, review of *Promises Are for Keeping*, *School Library Journal*, April, 1982, p. 84.

Noah, Carolyn, review of *A Break with Charity: A Story about the Salem Witch Trials*, *School Library Journal*, September, 1992, p. 279.

Rafal, Marian, review of *A Ride into Morning: The Story of Tempe Wick*, *Voice of Youth Advocates*, June, 1991, p. 101.

Rinaldi, Ann, comments in *Contemporary Authors*, Volume 111, Gale, 1984, pp. 391–92.

Rinaldi, Ann, comments in *Something about the Author*, Volume 51, Gale, 1988, pp. 149–51.

Rochman, Hazel, review of *Time Enough for Drums*, *Booklist*, May 1, 1986, p. 1304.

Sutherland, Zena, review of *The Last Silk Dress*, *New York Times Book Review*, April 10, 1988, p. 38.

Tegart, Beth, review of *A Stitch in Time*, *School Library Journal*, May, 1994, p. 132.

Review of *Time Enough for Drums*, *Publishers Weekly*, May 30, 1986, p. 69.

Whitehurst, Lucinda Snyder, review of *A Ride into Morning: The Story of Tempe Wick*, *School Library Journal*, May, 1991, p. 113.

Whitehurst, Lucinda Snyder, review of *In My Father's House*, *School Library Journal*, March, 1993, p. 224.

Review of *Wolf by the Ears*, *Publishers Weekly*, April 5, 1991, p. 146.

■ For More Information See

PERIODICALS

Booklist, March 15, 1992, p. 1365.

School Library Journal, May, 1986, pp. 108–09; August, 1987, p. 98; May, 1988, pp. 112–13; April, 1991, pp. 142–43.

Voice of Youth Advocates, February, 1981, pp. 32–33; August, 1982, p. 36; June, 1993, p. 94.

—Sketch by Megan Ratner

Zilpha Keatley Snyder

■ Personal

Born May 11, 1927, in Lemoore, CA; daughter of William Solon (a rancher and driller) and Dessa J. (a teacher; maiden name, Jepson) Keatley; married Larry Allan Snyder, June 18, 1950; children: Susan Melissa, Douglas, (adopted) Ben. *Education:* Whittier College, B.A., 1948; additional study at University of California—Berkeley, 1958–60. *Politics:* Democrat. *Religion:* Episcopalian. *Hobbies and other interests:* "My hobbies seem to change from time to time, but reading and travel remain among the top favorites. And of course writing which, besides being my occupation, is still and always will be my all-time favorite hobby."

■ Addresses

Home—52 Miller Ave., Mill Valley, CA 94941.

■ Career

Writer. Public school teacher at Washington School, Berkeley, CA, and in New York, Washington, and Alaska, 1948–62; University of California—Berkeley, master teacher and demonstrator for education classes, 1959–61; lecturer.

■ Awards, Honors

George G. Stone Recognition of Merit from Claremont Graduate School, Lewis Carroll Shelf Award, and Spring Book Festival first prize, all 1967, and Newbery honor book, 1968, all for *The Egypt Game;* Christopher Medal, 1970, for *The Changeling;* William Allen White Award, Newbery honor book, and Christopher Medal, all 1972, and Hans Christian Andersen International honor list of the International Board on Books for Young People, 1974, all for *The Headless Cupid; New York Times* Outstanding Book, 1972, National Book Award finalist, and Newbery honor book, both 1973, all for *The Witches of Worm; New York Times* Outstanding Book, 1981, for *A Fabulous Creature;* PEN Literary Award, 1983, and Parent's Choice Award, both for *The Birds of Summer;* Bay Area Book Reviewers Award, 1988, William Allen White Master Reading List, 1989–90, and Georgia Children's Book Award Master List, 1990–91, all for *And Condors Danced;* New Mexico State Award, 1989–90, and Notable Trade Books in the Language Arts list citation, National Council of Teachers of English, both for *The Changing Maze; Season of Ponies, The Egypt Game, The Headless Cupid, The Witches of Worm,* and *A Fabulous Creature* were all named American Library Association Notable Books; *The Velvet Room* and *The Egypt Game* were named to the *Horn Book* honor list; *The Velvet Room, The Changeling, The Headless Cupid, Below the Root, Until the Celebration,* and *Blair's Nightmare* were all Junior Literary Guild selections; *Blair's Nightmare* was included on state awards master lists in Missouri, Texas, Nebraska, the Pacific Northwest, and New Mexico; *Libby on Wednesday* was on the Virginia state award master list.

■ Writings

FOR CHILDREN

Season of Ponies, illustrated by Alton Raible, Atheneum, 1964.

The Velvet Room, illustrated by Raible, Atheneum, 1965.

Black and Blue Magic, illustrated by Gene Holtan, Atheneum, 1966.

The Egypt Game, illustrated by Raible, Atheneum, 1967.

Eyes in the Fishbowl, illustrated by Raible, Atheneum, 1968.

Today Is Saturday (poetry), photographs by John Arms, Atheneum, 1969.

The Changeling, illustrated by Raible, Atheneum, 1970.

The Headless Cupid, illustrated by Raible, Atheneum, 1971.

The Witches of Worm, illustrated by Raible, Atheneum, 1972.

The Princess and the Giants (picture book), illustrated by Beatrice Darwin, Atheneum, 1973.

The Truth about Stone Hollow, illustrated by Raible, Atheneum, 1974 (published in England as *The Ghosts of Stone Hollow,* Lutterworth, 1978).

Below the Root (first volume in the "Green-sky" trilogy), illustrated by Raible, Atheneum, 1975.

And All Between (second volume in the "Green-sky" trilogy), illustrated by Raible, Atheneum, 1976.

Until the Celebration (third volume in the "Green-sky" trilogy), illustrated by Raible, Atheneum, 1977.

The Famous Stanley Kidnapping Case, illustrated by Raible, Atheneum, 1979.

Come On, Patsy (picture book), illustrated by Margot Zemach, Atheneum, 1982.

Blair's Nightmare, Atheneum, 1984.

The Changing Maze (picture book), illustrated by Charles Mikolaycak, Atheneum, 1985.

The Three Men, Harper, 1986.

And Condors Danced, Delacorte, 1987.

Squeak Saves the Day and Other Tooley Tales, illustrated by Leslie Morrill, Delacorte, 1988.

Janie's Private Eyes, Delacorte, 1989.

Libby on Wednesday, Delacorte, 1990.

Song of the Gargoyle, Delacorte, 1991.

Fool's Gold, Delacorte, 1993.

The Trespassers, Delacorte, 1994.
Cat Running, Delacorte, 1994.

YOUNG ADULT NOVELS

A Fabulous Creature, Atheneum, 1981.
The Birds of Summer, Atheneum, 1983.

ADULT NOVELS

Heirs of Darkness, Atheneum, 1978.

OTHER

The Kerlan Collection at the University of Minnesota—Minneapolis houses a collection of Snyder's manuscripts.

■ Adaptations

Black and Blue Magic was adapted as a filmstrip with a tape, Pied Piper, 1975; *The Egypt Game* was adapted as a recording and cassette, Miller-Brody, 1975 and as a filmstrip and tape by Pied Piper; *The Headless Cupid* was adapted from *Newbery Award Cassette* stories as a recording and cassette, Miller-Brody, 1976, and as a filmstrip with a tape, Pied Piper, 1980; *The Witches of Worm* was adapted as a recording, Miller-Brody, 1978; *Below the Root* was adapted as a computer game, Spinnaker Software's Windham Classics, 1985.

■ Sidelights

"Growing up in a rather limited, narrow environment," Zilpha Keatley Snyder writes in *Innocence & Experience: Essays & Conversations on Children's Literature,* "I escaped through books and games into a much wider world. I loved almost any kind of story, any kind of imaginary world, but I loved best the kind that suggested that around any corner, no matter how unpromising, a free and boundless adventure might be waiting."

Snyder has drawn upon her own childhood experiences to create novels about lonely young girls who seek escape from their loneliness through imagination and games. In works such as *The Headless Cupid* and *The Witches of Worm,* Snyder demonstrates an affinity for the concerns of young people, growing up alone and isolated in an often hostile world. "I began by writing about a close, familiar world," she explains in *Innocence & Experience,* "but about a day that somehow turns out to be transformed into something strange and new and magical."

Come along for a summer of wonder and adventure.

Zilpha Keatley Snyder
Season of Ponies

Snyder wrote this 1964 tale after remembering a dream she had when she was twelve years old.

William Keatley and Dessa Jepson, Snyder's parents, married when he was in his forties and she in her mid-thirties. Keatley, with his younger brothers, had been placed in an orphanage by his father after his mother's death. Too old to be put up for adoption, Keatley was "farmed out" as a hired hand, working for families who sometimes abused him. As he grew older, he found work as a ranch hand and cowpuncher. Eventually he became a horse rancher in Wyoming. When he reached middle age he travelled to California to find his father's second family and there met Jepson, a second-generation Californian who taught in the town of Yorba Linda.

"It was a romance right out of Zane Grey—the bachelor rancher meets the lonely schoolteacher," Snyder explains in *Something about the Author Autobiography Series (SAAS)*. "My parents were living in Lemoore, California, when my older sister,

Elisabeth, and I were born, my father having accepted what he thought of as a temporary job until he could get back to ranching." The onset of the Great Depression, however, put a stop to William Keatley's dreams of returning to a pastoral life—as did the arrival of a younger sister, Ruth. "Although my father never lost his job," Snyder continues, "his salary was cut and cut again until he was finally unable to cover the mortgage payments and it was only the New Deal's mortgage relief legislation that enabled us to keep our home."

Storytelling Runs in the Family

Both of Snyder's parents were skilled storytellers. William Keatley had a store of yarns based on his years as a cowboy and a rancher—"wonderful stories," Snyder reports in *SAAS*, "about bronco-busting, roundups and stampedes and above all—HORSES." "As a child," she continues, "I knew all his horses through his stories including Old Washboard who had an iron mouth and a penchant for hunting wild horses." Dessa Jepson also displayed a talent for storytelling. "Mother's childhood was always very close to her and she had a tremendous memory for detail," Snyder recalls. "She made the people and events of rural California at the turn of the century as real to me as were those of my own childhood in the 1930s." Snyder soon showed that she had inherited her parents' gifts. "When I had something to tell," she explains, "I had an irresistible urge to make it worth telling, and without the rich and rather lengthy past that my parents had to draw on, I was forced to rely on the one commodity of which I had an adequate supply—imagination."

Snyder showed a literary bent in grade school. "At the age of eight I became, in my own eyes at least, a writer," she states in her *SAAS* essay. Her earliest writing was encouraged by a fourth-grade teacher, who typed and bound her work into a small book. But Snyder suffered from her lack of social skills when she entered the seventh grade in Ventura, California. "Too young for my grade, having been advanced by a first-grade teacher who didn't know what to do with me while she was teaching reading, and further handicapped by being raised by a mother who hadn't really faced up to the twentieth century," Snyder continues, "I was suddenly a terrible misfit. Still wearing long curls and playing secret games, I was too intimidated to make an effort to relate to girls who wore makeup and danced with boys. So I retreated further into books and daydreams." Still, "by the time I was in high school," she asserts, "my social skills had begun to improve, and I became a little less afraid of my peers."

Snyder attended Whittier College, a liberal arts school in southern California, where she improved her life intellectually, physically, and socially. While working as a waitress on campus, she met the man she later married: Larry Snyder, an athletic music major and "charismatic extrovert who was—and still is—a natural scholar, and a small-town boy who was born with a Ulysses-like yearning for new horizons," she explains in *SAAS*. After receiving her bachelor's degree in 1948, Snyder realized that her tentative plans to live and work in New York City were unrealistic and turned instead to teaching elementary school. "I

This 1965 children's book was based on a manuscript the author wrote when she was nineteen years old.

developed into what must have been a pretty good teacher," she states. "I taught in the upper elementary grades for a total of nine years, three of them as a master teacher for the University of California at Berkeley."

She married Larry Snyder in 1950, and the couple raised two children: Susan, born in 1954, and Douglas, born in 1956. In 1966, the couple also adopted a foster child, Ben, a native of Kowloon, China. The young family relocated often during the 1950s, partly because of the Korean War and Larry Snyder's connection with the U.S. Air Force. At various times they found themselves in California, Washington, Texas, New York, and Alaska.

Horses and Magic

It was not until the next decade, Snyder states, that her family life began to settle down and she turned again to writing. "Remembering a dream I'd had when I was twelve years old about some strange and wonderful horses," she recalls in *SAAS*, "I sat down and began to write." The resulting book, *Season of Ponies*, melds many elements from Snyder's past besides her dream, including the stories her father told her about his life. The protagonist, Pamela, is abandoned by her father the way Snyder's father left him, although Pamela's father leaves her with family: his two elderly, eccentric sisters living at Oak Farm. Pamela's loneliness is alleviated when she follows the sad sound of a flute and discovers an exotic herd of horses and their master, Ponyboy. Together Pamela and Ponyboy work to defeat the evil Pig Woman, and in the process Pamela grows and comes to understand herself better. "This wistful little story, combining elements of magic and practicality with touches of humor," writes Aileen Pippett in the *New York Times Book Review*, "should appeal to children who still retain a hope of crossing the border from everyday life to fairyland."

The Velvet Room, Snyder's second book, also uses the theme of retreat into fantasy from a harsh reality. It "evolved," the author declares in her *SAAS* essay, "from the remains of a manuscript written when I was nineteen years old." *The Velvet Room* tells the story of Robin, daughter of a poor sharecropper, who responds to pressures in her everyday life by withdrawing from it. Like Snyder herself in her preteen years, Robin seeks a quiet place of refuge where she can read and dream. Robin finds her place in the Velvet Room, a library on the property of the McCurdys, her father's employers. Yet the Velvet Room is not so much a place where Robin can hide as a cocoon in which she matures and prepares herself to face the world. She befriends young Grace McCurdy, saves the McCurdys' property from fire, and comes to realize, according to Patricia H. Allen in the *School Library Journal,* "that belonging to a place isn't as important as belonging to people you love and who also love you."

A family critic was responsible for the appearance of *Black and Blue Magic,* Snyder's third book. "On October 7, 1964," Jean Karl, Snyder's first editor, recalls in an essay for *Elementary English,* "Zil wrote, 'I have an anecdote about Dougie (my 8 year old) and *Black and Blue Magic.* He more or less ordered the book as he was "tired of sad stories about girls and wanted a funny one about a boy."'" The boy in the story, Harry Houdini Marco, lives in the San Francisco boarding house that his mother runs. Harry is a world-class klutz—until a kindly old man gives him a bottle of ointment that causes Harry to grow invisible wings. "'Recently I read [Dougie] the first 11 chapters,'" Snyder continued in her letter to Karl. "'I could see that he was entranced. . . . When I finished, he didn't say a word. He jumped up on his chair, stuck his arms out behind him, leaped off, and flapped out of the room. For a few minutes I heard him running through the house, apparently making occasional leaps from furniture (forbidden). Then he "flew" back into the room looking delighted, threw his arms around my neck and said, "That's great, Mom. I'll bet it wins the Blueberry Award!"'"

Shades of One's Own Life

The Egypt Game also draws on elements from Snyder's past. "A fifth-grade project on ancient Egypt," she explains in *SAAS,* led to an early fascination with the country and a time "in which I read, dreamed and played Egyptian. But my dream of Egypt was private and it was my daughter, many years later, who actually played a game very like the one in the story." *The Egypt Game,* however, uses less of the fantastic elements that characterize *Black and Blue Magic.* "April, an insecure sophisticate, and Melanie, a sensible Negro girl of comparable imagination," explains a reviewer for *Kirkus Service,* "transform a deserted back yard into the land of Egypt, and themselves into votaries of ancient rites." The girls' playing

is curtailed when a child in the area is mysteriously murdered, and the criminal eventually makes an attempt on April's life.

Again, Snyder stresses the positive effect that game-playing and imagination have on a child's life. At the beginning of the book, April's "outlandish dress, affected speech, and attempts to reveal how much better her earlier life was with her mother," declares Virginia L. Wolf in the *Wilson Library Bulletin,* "are all evidence that she is homesick and more than a little frightened that she does not belong anywhere." However, "in the playing of the game," states Marilyn Leathers Solt in *Newbery and Caldecott Medal and Honor Books,* "April has gained good friends, for the first time in her life. She has been searching for her iden-

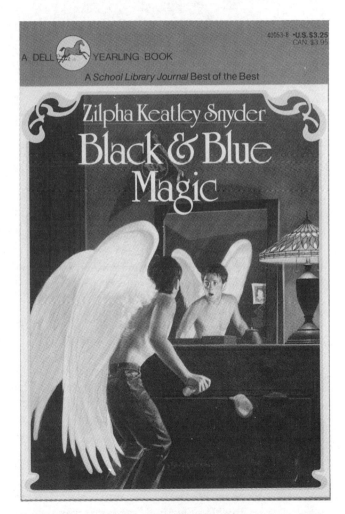

Snyder's son was bored with sad stories about girls, so when the author wrote this 1966 novel about a little boy named Harry who grows invisible wings, the author's son was thrilled. "I'll bet it wins the Blueberry Award!" he said.

LAUREL-LEAF CONTEMPORARY FICTION

Zilpha Keatley Snyder

What are the neighbors hiding behind closed doors?

DELL • 20154-3 •U.S. $2.95 CAN $3.95

The Birds of Summer

This winner of the PEN Literary Award is a novel for young adults who enjoy suspense.

tity and for improved personal relationships as well. Through the game she has gained both."

Similar to April in her sense of alienation is Ivy Carson, the self-proclaimed title character of *The Changeling.* Together with her friend Martha Abbott, Ivy creates a world of her own—"an ebullient and magical world," according to Jean Fritz in the *New York Times Book Review,* "inhabited by a secret sea monster, an aging horse, a baby who casts spells, a race of Tree People and a lady artist." Martha and Ivy play a game based on the story of the Tree People that "as time goes on . . . becomes [for Ivy] a defense against the unpredictable adult world and a consolation for Martha when the Carsons from time to time vanish strategically from the locality," declares Margery

Fisher in *Growing Point.* "When the girls have to admit that their plan never to grow up is unworkable, and Ivy goes to New York to fulfill her ambition to become a dancer, Martha realizes how far her life has been planned round the other girl's presence." Again, the imaginary game is the vehicle that allows the girls to mature.

In *The Headless Cupid,* the children involved are all members of a single family, and the imaginary game has more consequences than before. A widowed man with four children—David, Janice, Esther, and Blair Stanley—marries a divorced woman. The divorcee, Molly, brings into the family "her somewhat eccentric and unco-operative daughter Amanda," states Barbara Sherrard-Smith in *Children's Book Review,* "who arrives dressed in unorthodox garments which she claims are magical ceremonial robes, with a Centre-of-power sign stuck on her forehead, a case full of books about magic, and a large ill-tempered crow." "Every one of Amanda's actions," writes Fisher in *Growing Point,* "can be traced not to magic but to her laughable but passionate longing for power to offset her own immaturity." Amanda comes to be accepted by the other children after an adventure that involves a missing carved head from the banister. The Stanley children have figured in several other of Snyder's books, including *The Famous Stanley Kidnapping Case, Blair's Nightmare,* and *Janie's Private Eye.*

The Dark Side of Imagination

The Witches of Worm features a distinctly unhealthy use of the imagination: after reading about the Salem witch trials, young Jessica comes to believe that her cat, Worm, is a demon, forcing her to do wicked things. "Ivy [from *The Changeling*] and April [from *The Egypt Game*] both had the ability to transform life, as if they had found an octave higher than the normal range of experience," declares Jean Fritz in the *New York Times Book Review.* "Amanda, in *The Headless Cupid,* pursuing the darker side of the imagination, was able to take life to a lower-than-natural octave." Like Amanda, Jessica pursues a dark goal and, by blaming her cat for her own actions, is able to escape the pangs of conscience. Finally, however, she comes to understand the truth. "Jessica's tears, which prove that she's not a witch," says a reviewer for *Kirkus Reviews,* serve as "a form of self therapy." James Archer Fielding, hero of *A Fabulous Creature,* seemingly has very little of the fantastic

James Archer Fielding, hero of *A Fabulous Creature,* seemingly has very little of the fantastic about him. Dragged into the wilderness of the Sierra for a holiday, however, James encounters the fantastic in two forms: a large buck deer, and Griffin Donahue. Griffin is "an appealing 13-year-old," according to Patricia Lee Gauch in the *New York Times Book Review,* "who is both kooky kid and mystical creature, 'pure and free and beautiful.'" However, James also encounters the sexy-but-selfish Diane, who is staying at the nearby posh resort known as The Camp. Entranced by Diane's charms, James reveals the existence of the stag, betraying Griffin's trust. Diane and her father try to shoot the animal, but a series of accidents forces them to return to The Camp empty-handed. "I thought I was basing my story's antagonist on Greek mythology," Snyder reveals in her *SAAS* entry, "and only discovered after-the-fact that I'd been writing about someone I once knew—and feared; and my unconscious theme concerned the evil that arises when selfish and in-

The Stanley children—characters in some of Snyder's other books—are also featured in this 1989 story.

sensitive use is made of a naturally dominant personality."

In *And Condors Danced,* Snyder turns from contemporary fantasy to a historical setting: turn-of-the-century southern California. Faced with indifferent parents—an uncaring father and a dying mother—eleven-year-old Carly Hartwick finds support in the other members of her family, especially her Great-Aunt Mehitabel. Her best friend Matt and her Chinese housekeeper Woo Ying also care for her. But the family is beset by troubles, including a legal battle over the rights to water for their citrus farm. "Carly romanticizes, dramatizes, and fantasizes the events in her life," explains Susan H. Patron in the *School Library Journal,* "until two terrible things happen: her dog and her mother both die, and Carly's grief is more profoundly felt over the dog." Carly suffers under a huge burden of guilt until "her oldest sister breaks her silence about the mother who didn't love her youngest child and gave her away to be raised," declares Hanna B. Zeiger in *Horn Book,* then "Carly begins to understand her feelings."

Despite the pain that many of her protagonists undergo, Snyder's personal philosophy is rooted in optimism and joy. She states in *SAAS* that she takes joy in the composition of each of her works. "When Zil first began to write," Karl states, "her children were small, she was still teaching, and writing filled only a corner of her life." Now, "after a number of years as a full-time writer, she still finds the challenge and joy in it that she did initially. And this may be the secret of why each new book is fresh and different and full of joy for readers too."

■ Works Cited

Allen, Patricia H., review of *The Velvet Room, School Library Journal,* February, 1965, p. 30.

Fisher, Margery, review of *The Headless Cupid, Growing Point,* December, 1973, pp. 2287-88.

Fisher, review of *The Changeling, Growing Point,* September, 1976, p. 2939.

Fritz, Jean, review of *The Changeling, New York Times Book Review,* December 13, 1970, p. 26.

Fritz, review of *The Witches of Worm, New York Times Book Review,* December 10, 1972, pp. 8, 10.

Gauch, Patricia Lee, review of *A Fabulous Creature, New York Times Book Review,* March 5, 1981, p. 31.

Karl, Jean, "Zilpha Keatley Snyder," *Elementary English,* September, 1974, pp. 784-89.

Patron, Susan H., review of *And Condors Danced, School Library Journal,* December, 1987, p. 88.

Pippett, Aileen, review of *Season of Ponies, New York Times Book Review,* May 10, 1964, pp. 20, 22.

Review of *The Egypt Game, Kirkus Service,* February 15, 1967, pp. 200-1.

Sherrard-Smith, Barbara, review of *The Headless Cupid, Children's Book Review,* October, 1973, p. 146.

Snyder, Zilpha Keatley, *Something about the Author Autobiography Series,* Volume 2, Gale, 1986, pp. 215-226.

Snyder, "Alternate Worlds," *Innocence & Experience: Essays & Conversations on Children's Literature,* edited by Barbara Harrison and Gregory Maguire, Lothrop, Lee & Shepard, 1987, pp. 189-90.

Solt, Marilyn Leathers, "The Newbery Medal and Honor Books, 1922–1981: 'The Egypt Game,'" *Newbery and Caldecott Medal and Honor Books: An Annotated Bibliography,* by Linda Kauffman Peterson and Marilyn Leathers Solt, G. K. Hall, 1982, pp. 173-74.

Review of *The Witches of Worm, Kirkus Reviews,* July 15, 1972, p. 803.

Wolf, Virginia L., "The Root and Measure of Realism," *Wilson Library Bulletin,* December, 1969, pp. 409-15.

Zeiger, Hanna B., review of *And Condors Danced, Horn Book,* January-February, 1988, p. 66.

■ For More Information See

BOOKS

Children's Literature Review, Volume 31, Gale, 1994, pp. 149-70.

Contemporary Literary Criticism, Volume 17, Gale, 1981, pp. 469-75.

Hopkins, Lee Bennett, *More Books by More People,* Citation, 1974, pp. 318-22.

Something about the Author, Volume 75, Gale, 1994, pp. 190-94.

Twentieth-Century Young Adult Writers, St. James Press, 1995, pp. 598-600.

PERIODICALS

Book World, December 3, 1967.

Bulletin of the Center for Children's Books, June, 1974; December, 1979, p. 82; March, 1982; January, 1983; April, 1984; November, 1985; November, 1987; May, 1988.

Christian Science Monitor, February 29, 1968.

Horn Book, June, 1964, p. 284; April, 1965, p. 173; April, 1967, pp. 209-10; April, 1968, pp. 182-83; October, 1970, p. 479; October, 1971; December, 1972; October, 1973, p. 459; August, 1974, p. 380.

Junior Bookshelf, December, 1978, p. 324.

Junior Literary Guild, March, 1984.

Kirkus Reviews, March 1, 1974, p. 245; March 1, 1975, p. 239; February 1, 1977, p. 95; September 1, 1978, p. 973.

New York Times Book Review, May 9, 1965; July 24, 1966, p. 22; July 23, 1967; May 26, 1968; November 7, 1971, pp. 42-44; May 4, 1975, pp. 32, 34; May 23, 1976, p. 16; May 8, 1977, p. 41; July 8, 1984; December 27, 1987.

Saturday Review, May 13, 1967, pp. 55-56.

School Library Journal, April, 1990, p. 124.

—Sketch by Kenneth R. Shepherd

Oliver Stone

■ Personal

Born September 15, 1946, in New York, NY; son of Louis (a stockbroker) and Jacqueline (Goddet) Stone; married Najwa Sarkis (divorced); married Elizabeth Cox, June 7, 1981 (divorced); children (second marriage): Sean, Michael. *Education:* Attended Yale University, 1965; New York University, B.F.A., 1971.

■ Addresses

Agent—Marty Bauer, William Morris Agency, 151 El Camino Drive, Beverly Hills, CA 90211.

■ Career

Screenwriter and director of motion pictures; coproducer of television miniseries, *Wild Palms*, ABC–TV, 1993. Worked as a teacher in Cholon, South Vietnam, 1965–66; in Merchant Marines, 1966. *Military Service:* U.S. Army, 1967–68; served in Vietnam; received Purple Heart with Oak Leaf Cluster, Bronze Star. *Member:* Academy of Motion Picture Arts and Sciences, Writers Guild of America, Directors Guild of America.

■ Awards, Honors

Award for best dramatic adaptation, Writers Guild of America, Academy Award for best screenplay adapted from another medium, Academy of Motion Picture Arts and Sciences, and Golden Globe Award, all 1978, all for *Midnight Express;* Orson Welles Motion Picture Directorial Achievement Award for best writer–director of an English–language film, Academy Awards for best director, and for best picture, all 1987, all for *Platoon;* Academy Award for best director, 1990, for *Born on the Fourth of July.*

■ Writings

SCREENPLAYS

(And director) *Seizure,* Cinerama, 1973.
Midnight Express (adapted from the book by Billy Hayes), Columbia, 1978.
(And director) *The Hand* (adapted from the novel *The Lizard's Tail* by Marc Brandel), Orion, 1981.
(With John Milius) *Conan, the Barbarian* (adapted from tales by Robert E. Howard), Universal, 1982.
Scarface, Universal, 1983.
(With Richard Boyle; and director) *Salvador,* Hemdale, 1986.
(And director) *Platoon,* Orion, 1986.
(With Stanley Weiser; and director) *Wall Street,* Twentieth Century Fox, 1987.

(With Eric Bogosian; and director) *Talk Radio* (from the play by Bogosian), Universal, 1988.

(With Ron Kovic; and director and producer) *Born on the Fourth of July* (from the autobiography by Kovic), Universal, 1989.

(With J. Randal Johnson; and director) *The Doors,* Tri–Star, 1990.

(With Zachary Sklar; and director) *JFK* (from *On the Trail of the Assassins* by Jim Garrison, and *Crossfire* by Jim Marrs), Warner Bros., 1991.

(And director) *Heaven and Earth* (based on the autobiographies of Le Ly Hayslip), Warner Bros., 1994.

(And director) *Natural Born Killers* (based on an original screenplay by Quentin Tarantino), Warner Bros., 1994.

Also coauthor, with Michael Cimino, of *Year of the Dragon* (adapted from a novel by Robert Daly), 1985; and, with David Lee Henry, *Eight Million Ways to Die* (adapted from novel of same title by Lawrence Block), 1986.

OTHER

(With Boyle) *Oliver Stone's Platoon & Salvador* (original screenplays), Vintage Books, 1987.

(With Sklar) *JFK, the Book of the Film: A Documented Screenplay,* Applause Books, 1992.

(Editor) *Oliver Stone's Heaven and Earth* (text by Michael Singer from the screenplay by Stone), Tuttle, 1993.

Also contributor to books, including introductions to *JFK: The Last Dissenting Witness,* by Jean Hill, Pelican Publishing, 1992; *JFK: The CIA, Vietnam and the Plot to Assassinate John F. Kennedy,* by Fletcher L. Prouty, Carol Publishing, 1992; *Monkey Business: The Disturbing Case that Launched the American Animals Rights Movement,* by Kathy S. Guillermo, National Press Books, 1993; and *Shut Up, Fag!: Quotations from the Files of Congressman Bob Dornan,* edited by Nathan Callahan, Mainstreet Media, 1994.

■ Sidelights

"There is enough incense burning here to make you cough way out in the hall. There are also a meditation cushion, a stationary bicycle, and a shelf filled with . . . journals; he writes in them, he says, for at least twenty minutes every day. . . . The apartment walls are a jumble of paintings: a Warhol 'Last Supper'; a Francesco Clemente self–portrait; a fine, small Bierstadt; some awkward pieces by the Native American activist Leonard Peltier; and some even more awkward ones by . . . Sergio Premoli. The incense sticks on the mantel are surrounded by photographs: John F. Kennedy, Jim Garrison . . . , Jim Morrison. It is a kind of altar to Stone's dead," described Stephen Schiff in the *New Yorker.*

These photographs, and other objects in the apartment, also serve as an altar to several of the films created by writer/director Oliver Stone. One of the most controversial filmmakers working, Stone makes movies that assault the viewer at every turn as they tackle such ambitious topics as the Vietnam War, the assassination of President John F. Kennedy, the life of Jim Morrison and his band The Doors, the machinations of Wall Street, and the glamorization of serial killers and mass murderers by the media. "Stone's work tends to be loud and angry and fast, full of jagged politics and big emotions," maintained David Breskin in *Rolling Stone.* "Screen his movies in succession and you're left feeling you've survived a cinematic bar fight—a bit dented about the head and heart by the velvet fist of his vision."

Stone's strong vision is most often derived from personal experiences and personal obsessions. *Platoon, Born on the Fourth of July,* and *Heaven and Earth* stem from Stone's experiences in the U.S. Army during the Vietnam War; *Wall Street* explores morality in the high–finance world of Stone's stockbroker father; and *The Doors* and *JFK* delve deeply into the lives of two of the important icons from Stone's young adult life. Such ambitious subject matter, however, lends itself to a full range of critical and commercial reaction; both critics and moviegoers tend to either love or hate Stone's films. "These aren't wan little art films, enrobing noble themes in acute observation and good taste," pointed out Schiff in the *New Yorker.* "Stone's movies are pumped up, overbearing, action–packed, and loud—shot through with big emotion, big suffering, big stars. They court controversy, and not only in the ways that movies usually court controversy . . . but in the ways that political initiatives court controversy. Stone's movies grab your lapels and scream in your face: they bear messages; they raise issues; they make news."

The only child of a stockbroker father and French mother, Stone's childhood and early teenage years

Stone's 1986 film *Platoon* was lauded for its realistic portrayal of one young soldier's experiences during his tour of duty in the Vietnam War.

were very far removed from the politics and issues that later found their way into his movies. His parents met in 1945 when his father was serving in the U.S. Army during World War II; they were married in December of that same year and sailed for the United States. A year later Stone was born into a privileged life, splitting his time between homes in Manhattan and Connecticut and spending his summers with his maternal grandparents in France. Describing himself as a somewhat impetuous child and young adult, Stone sees himself as a mixture of his reserved father and sociable mother. "My dad was very loving," he remembered in his interview with Breskin for *Rolling Stone*. "That's a partial description of him. He was sarcastic and distant at times, but he was very loving—he was so proud of me, he admired me, I was the only child. He just didn't want me to get spoiled by my mom. He wanted to enforce discipline; he wanted me to learn discipline very early." Stone's mother, on the other hand, "is more outward, external, physical, in the world—not as abstracted as my dad. She never made enemies, she made friends. . . . Mom was a charming

woman: To me, she's a bit like a piece of Auntie Mame and a piece of Evita. Just larger than life."

Schooling was a serious part of Stone's early life; he attended an elite day school in Manhattan before beginning at Hill School, a college prep academy in Pennsylvania. It was during his junior year at Hill that Stone shockingly learned of the impending divorce of his parents. "I thought they were very contented and that I was rich and that we had it made," Stone told Breskin in *Rolling Stone*. "And basically my father said that they were unhappy and that they were betraying each other, that she was screwing around and he was screwing around, and that he was broke, in debt." The news was not even delivered in person; Stone's parents called the headmaster, who was then the one to convey the news. From that point on, Stone's world changed and the downward spiral that eventually led him to Vietnam was set in motion.

"I felt I was an outsider," Stone revealed to Breskin in his *Rolling Stone* interview. "The fam-

Michael Douglas won an Academy Award for playing greedy Gordon Gekko in the 1987 movie *Wall Street,* directed and cowritten by Stone.

ily was over. It just disintegrated. . . . The triangle splits, and we're three people in different places, and I'm sixteen, and all of a sudden I'm on my own. . . . I think that set up, basically, a period for me, from sixteen on, until thirty—I was going through a sort of adolescent thing. Especially from sixteen to twenty–two, a sort of revolution in my life. Everything was thrown topsy–turvy." Going on to college during this period, Stone spent only a year at Yale before dropping out in 1965 to join a teaching program that landed him in Vietnam; he wanted to experience things so he could write like Hemingway and Conrad. Teaching, like school, though, lacked something. Stone next joined the Merchant Marine. "I was seeing a side of the world I'd never seen," he related in his interview with Schiff in the *New Yorker.* "I did live a bit of Conrad. I was thinking I was getting material for a really big book."

This material did eventually end up in a book, but only after Stone quit the Merchant Marine and moved to Mexico to write it. The result was a fourteen–hundred–page autobiographical novel that Stone finished back at Yale, dropping out again

as soon as it was complete. "After the book was rejected by two or three publishers," Stone explained to Schiff in the *New Yorker,* "I took a blind drive up the East River Drive and I threw some of it in the East River, out the window. I felt like I was worthless. I had spent all this time looking inside and writing about myself, and I had just gone too far. I needed to get out of my head and back to reality, and Hemingway told me in his writings about going to war and being part of war. So I enlisted. I was ready to die."

Vietnam Volunteer

Along with Hemingway, patriotism and a desire to crush communism propelled Stone to enlist in the U.S. Army and request combat duty in Vietnam. "I was ready to die, but I didn't want to pull my own trigger," Stone observed in his *Rolling Stone* interview with Breskin. "Many a time I stood in the bathroom and looked in the mirror and had the razor out. . . . I went through all the computations of death in my head. I don't know how close I came. I certainly thought about it, and I emotionally identified with it, but I stopped myself." Unable to take his own life, Stone left it up to Vietnam to decide his fate. "I was either going to commit suicide in Vietnam or get killed there," he told Schiff in the *New Yorker,* adding: "I felt I couldn't be an honest human being until I knew what war and killing were."

Stone knew the meaning of war and killing by the time he finished his tour of duty, having been wounded twice and receiving a Bronze Star and a Purple Heart with an Oak Leaf Cluster for his courageous acts. Discharged from the Army in 1968, Stone returned home to a strained relationship with his father that only worsened when he was thrown in jail on a marijuana charge in San Diego; he stayed in jail for three weeks until his father could raise the bail. "Before that time," Stone told Schiff in the *New Yorker,* "I knew emotionally that Vietnam was rotten and corrupt, but politically I was not ready to question authority. I was a private—I was not an officer. I was not a leader. Seeing that prison—there were five thousand kids in it. Seeing that radicalized me."

The radical and rebellious streak that began in prison followed Stone as he moved back to New York City and eventually enrolled in film school at New York University (NYU). Stone continued his heavy drug use and his writing in a dumpy East Village apartment, while studying under Martin Scorsese, among others. "I had a broken window, with the snow drifting in the winter," Stone recalled in his interview with Breskin in *Rolling Stone.* "I'd wake up in the morning and there'd be a pile of snow in my room. I was writing, though. I wrote, it seems, for therapy: Between twenty–two and thirty, I wrote eleven screenplays. I never stopped writing. It was my only home. No matter how dissolute I got—and I took a lot of . . . drugs, booze, bad—I would get up each day, like my dad said: You do something every day you don't want to do. I felt an obligation to hold up my sanity, to write."

In the midst of all this writing activity, Stone married his first wife, Najwa Sarkis, a Lebanese woman who worked for the Moroccan Mission to the United Nations. She helped support him after he graduated from NYU in 1971 until he sold his first screenplay, *Seizure,* to a Canadian distribution company two years later. *Seizure* also marked Stone's directorial debut; this horror story of a fantasy writer whose fictions come to life went

virtually unnoticed, however. Although discouraged and angry, Stone continued to write. And in the summer of 1976, he faced the demons that haunted him and hammered out the script that would be used ten years later to make *Platoon.*

In the meantime, Stone made the move to Los Angeles, where he soon acquired both a divorce and an agent. Using his script for *Platoon* as his calling card, Stone discovered that the nation was still too close to the conflict to face the grim truth about Vietnam. The script did open doors for him, though, and a few short months after moving to Los Angeles, Stone jumped at the chance to adapt *Midnight Express,* Billy Hayes's tale of his imprisonment and escape.

In *Midnight Express,* Stone, who won an Academy Award for his screenplay, interprets the memoirs of Hayes. An American college student vacationing in Turkey, Hayes was arrested for trying to smuggle hashish out of the country. First sentenced to four years in prison, Hayes was then resentenced to thirty years before escaping to Greece. The extraordinarily brutal prison system is exposed in the film, as are the atrocities committed against Hayes. Many critics question the graphic violence that dominates *Midnight Express; Films in Review* contributor Rob Edelman, however, wrote that the director, Alan Parker, and the screenwriter, Oliver Stone, "put you right in [Hayes'] cell; they make you cry, make your stomach knot up, make you shiver at the needless brutality."

The controversy that surrounded *Midnight Express* served to make the film a commercial success and opened up even more doors for Stone. Still determined to relate a Vietnam story to audiences, and now a screenwriter in demand, Stone wrote *Born on the Fourth of July,* an adaptation of the memoir of the paraplegic Vietnam veteran Ron Kovic. When the financial side of this project fell apart, however, Stone contracted with Orion to direct and write another horror/suspense movie—*The Hand.* More successful than *Seizure,* this 1981 film focuses on Jon Lansdale, a cartoonist whose hand is severed in an accident. The hand comes to life, follows Jon around, and commits murders on his behalf. Vincent Canby, reviewing *The Hand* in the *New York Times,* maintained that the screenplay "is tightly written, precise and consistent in its methods," adding that the film suggested Stone to be "a director of very real talent."

The next few films Stone focused on, however, did not utilize these directorial skills. First came the screenplay for *Conan, the Barbarian,* an adventure fantasy starring Arnold Schwarzenegger in the title role. Next was *Scarface,* the saga of the rise and fall of Cuban refugee Tony Montana, who finds his American dream in the world of cocaine smuggling. Just escaping an "X" rating because of excessive violence, *Scarface,* starring Al Pacino, became a commercial hit in large part because of the notoriety surrounding it. Although writing that *Scarface* "lacks the generational sweep and moral ambiguity" of *The Godfather,* Richard Corliss concluded in *Time:* "The only X this movie deserves is the one in explosive." Canby similarly stated in the *New York Times* that "the dominant mood of the film is anything but funny. It is bleak and futile: What goes up must always come down. When it comes down in *Scarface,* the crash is as terrifying as it is vivid and arresting."

Stone began working as an independent writer/director in the mid–1980s. The first project he undertook was based on the experiences of his friend Richard Boyle (a freelance photojournalist) during the Civil War in El Salvador. The script Stone wrote with Boyle follows the photojournalist, and his friend Doctor Rock (a DJ), as their excessive lifestyle of drugs, alcohol, and women slowly fades away and they become involved in the Civil War surrounding them. The political indictment of U.S. policy in El Salvador made the script a hard sell, though, and Stone eventually directed the film for free in order to obtain financial help from the British film corporation Hemdale.

Salvador, released in 1986, was partially shot with a hand–held camera on a very low budget in some of the rougher areas of Mexico. The audience, and the distribution, were limited; critics cited Stone with manipulating history to serve his purpose and with creating two unlikable, farcical main characters. "A sprawling blend of gripping action and simplistic characters, of skillful photography and awkward editing, *Salvador* frustrates," pointed out Patricia Hluchy in *Maclean's,* concluding: "It is the victim of an artistic war—between repugnant farce and historical tragedy." David Denby, on the other hand, related in *New York,* "In everything he does, Stone pushes things to the limits. He puts mounds of corpses on the screen, and children with missing limbs, and he provides so little information and political context that the atrocities feel like high–minded exploitation, a way of showing off how bloody tough he is. Yet he has talent, and has made a disturbing movie."

Vietnam Revisited

The most important thing *Salvador* did for Stone's career was to bring him the money needed for *Platoon,* the script he had been trying to make since the beginning of his career. Hemdale agreed to produce the film, and Stone began shooting in the Philippines immediately, finishing just fifty-four days later. The first in Stone's trilogy concerning the Vietnam War, *Platoon* attacks the subject from a soldier's point of view, from Stone's view as a member of the 25th Infantry Division. "Vietnam messed a lot of guys up because it put us out of step with our own generation," explained Stone in an interview with Chuck Pfeifer for *Interview.* "There was such a dog–tired, don't-give–a–damn attitude over there, such anger and frustration and casual brutality. I remember being so tired that I wished the North Vietnamese Army would come up and shoot me, just to get this thing over with."

Authenticity, gleaned from these personal experiences, is what makes *Platoon* so gripping; numerous Vietnam veterans praised the film for its realistic portrayal of the conflict and all of its minute details. The young actors were even put through two weeks of boot camp by Stone and a former Marine drill instructor. The young hero of the film, Chris, is a college dropout who volunteers to go to Vietnam, much as Stone did. His thoughts and experiences are revealed through letters home that are read in voice–overs, a technic criticized by many reviewers. The war presents numerous moral decisions and ambiguities for Chris, who must in essence choose between two sergeants: Barnes, a ruthless killing machine, and Elias, an equally courageous fighter who maintains his values and morals at the same time.

"*Platoon* captures the crazy, adrenaline–rush chaos of battle better than any movie before," cited David Ansen and Peter McAlevey in *Newsweek,* adding: "Stone is ruthless in his deglamorization of war, but not at the expense of the men who fought there." Pat Aufderheide, writing in *CINEASTE,* also praised the film's grasp on reality. "It's brutally honest, a grunt's–eye, mud–level view," she asserted. "Part of its honesty is its unabashed romanticism—its reverence for ancient war cliches and heroic war archetypes, its vision of Vietnam as a staging ground in the war for America's soul." Stone himself told Ansen and McAlevey how important the authenticity of *Platoon* is to him: "I was under an obligation to show it as it was. If I didn't, I'd be a fraud." Ansen and McAlevey concluded: "After nine years of waiting, Stone has made one of the rare Hollywood movies that matter."

Picking up where he left off with *Platoon,* Stone tackles the story of Ron Kovic, a Vietnam vet, in his 1989 film *Born on the Fourth of July.* Coauthored by Kovic, the film begins with his youth and the events leading up to his Vietnam experience; from the beginning, he is primed with patriotism, war, and God to be the all–American hero. The war scenes seem horror–filled until Kovic returns home to a V.A. hospital in the Bronx. The atrocities here and his injuries—which leave Kovic paralyzed from the chest down at the age of twenty–one—begin the vet's descent. He goes from believing he did his duty, to a period of despair filled with drinking, and finally emerges as a writer and respected activist for his work with Vietnam Veterans against the War.

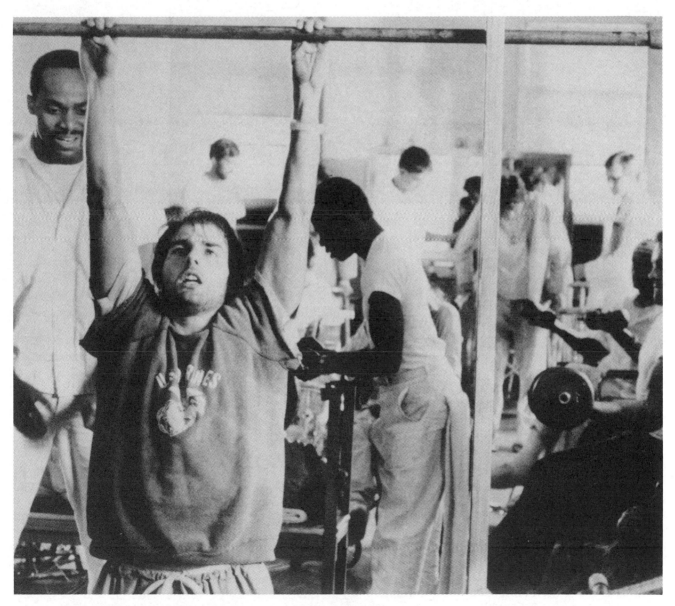

Stone won the 1990 best director Academy Award for *Born on the Fourth of July,* in which Tom Cruise stars as Ron Kovic, a paraplegic Vietnam veteran turned activist.

Tommy Lee Jones starred in *Heaven and Earth,* Stone's 1994 film based on the memoirs of Le Ly Hayslip, a Vietnamese woman whose life was torn apart by war.

"Oliver Stone has become as unrelenting as Kovic," stated Denby in his *New York* review. "From his earlier films, . . . we understood that he was enraged by the softness of American myth-making—the lies, the evasions, the Reaganite media scam that turned greed into public virtue and the disaster of Vietnam into an illusion of noble endeavor undermined by weak–hearted liberals. But *Platoon* was almost consoling in comparison with *Born on the Fourth of July.*" Although Stanley Kauffmann, writing in *New Republic,* found the screenplay "fuzzy" for failing to focus on the transformation of Kovic from patriotic volunteer to famed activist, he concluded that "the heat in the film is almost palpable as we sit before it. Stone, Kovic, . . . and all the others reached deep inside to make this picture, and it earns something more than respect." *Nation* contributor Stuart Klawans similarly described *Born on the Fourth of July* as a movie "which shoots off the screen like pressurized steam. Directed with furious, relentless energy by Oliver Stone, the film keeps hit-ting moments that feel like climaxes and then pushes them further."

The final film in the trilogy, *Heaven and Earth,* based on the memoirs of a Vietnamese woman, offers a different perspective. Released in 1994, this is Stone's first film to feature a female protagonist. Born in Central Vietnam in the early 1950s, Le Ly Hayslip leads a quiet life in her farming village until the war begins. She joins the Vietcong, only to be captured and tortured by the South Vietnamese. Upon returning home, she is greeted with hostility by the Vietcong and raped next to her own grave. It is while working as a bar girl in Saigon that Le Ly finally meets and marries Steve Butler, a U.S. Marine who takes her back to the States. This new country offers very little to Le Ly, who ends up with no identity, even when she returns home several years later. Received harshly by critics, *Heaven and Earth* was also less commercially successful than its predecessors. Pointing out that Stone attempts to use

Le Ly to lessen the guilt of the U.S., Jonathan Romney concluded in *New Statesman & Society:* "It's too much, as if an overeager Stone had pledged to his subject to use *all the resources* at his disposal to tell her story. The result is neither heaven nor earth but the big, dumb banging of purgatory."

In between his Vietnam films, Stone also focused on other important figures and events of the 1960s and 1970s; Jim Morrison's life and the story of his famous rock band are interpreted by Stone in his 1990 film *The Doors.* Beginning with Morrison's college experience, during which he studied film, the movie follows the young poet's epic rise to stardom and ends with his death of a drug overdose in 1971. The prominent drug abuse and other excesses in the film assault the viewer, as do Stone's interpretations of the myths surrounding the famous performer. "*The Doors* is an Oliver Stone movie all the way, big and brave and foolish," contended Robert Horton in *Film Comment.* "It's broad, juicy, cheerless, by turns exhilarating and embarrassing, always ready, indeed eager, to let passion eclipse good judgment," continued Horton, adding: "Morrison's story had bounced around Hollywood for years, and we are fortunate that it eventually rolled in Oliver Stone's direction. Both Stone and Morrison are/were unruly talents, not consistent or reliable or without their vulgar undersides, but good to have around. In some ways, Stone's *The Doors* may be the movie Morrison never lived long enough to make."

President John F. Kennedy, another icon whose life was cut short, and the events surrounding his death are the subject of Stone's *JFK,* released in 1991. The film is the director's most controversial; it offers a conspiracy theory that involves the CIA, the FBI, and the Pentagon in connection with the assassination. Based on books by Jim Marrs and Jim Garrison, a New Orleans district attorney who believes the Warren Report to be a lie, *JFK* is attacked by many critics because of its interpretation of history, not because of its actual qualities as a film. Mixing fact, through the use of newsreels and photos, with fiction, through reenactments among other things, Stone makes the line between what really happened and what did not very fuzzy. Garrison, the main character of the film, attacks the conclusion that Lee Harvey Oswald acted alone and sets out to prove his theory. The movie ends with the trial of Clay Shaw, a New Orleans businessman accused of conspiracy in connection with the murder. Garrison loses the case but is still convinced that powerful forces are keeping the truth hidden.

JFK "is a cunning, often mesmerizing piece of filmcraft and—make no mistake—it is propaganda, shot through with all the perils and pitfalls of that most troublesome genre," described *People* contributor Mark Goodman. Maintaining that all of Stone's films, no matter what the subject matter is, have something factually wrong in them, Peter Travers wrote in *Rolling Stone:* "Even when his intentions are worthy and backed with skilled technique—as they are in *JFK*—Stone will fudge any fact, hype any situation, pull any stunt to make his case. *JFK* is the best and worst of Stone in one volatile package." Also referring to Stone's manipulation of the truth, Ansen pointed out in *Newsweek:* "He manages to pack in an astonishing amount of information while maintaining suspense and narrative clarity. Quasi documentary in style, *JFK* shifts between color and black and white, fact and speculation, newsreel and staged re–creation, so that you can't always tell what's real footage and what's not, never mind what's true and what's not. . . ." Kauffmann in *New Republic* viewed *JFK* as much more than a mixture of fact and fiction. "Very few Hollywood people today make films primarily out of conviction, particularly political conviction. Admittedly, its easy to overvalue *JFK* because it's a rarity that way, but it's also easy to undervalue it cinematically because of its political and historical garishness." Kauffmann went on to conclude: "First, *JFK* is a fine piece of filmmaking. Second, it is a passionate work in an art that is mostly treated as an industry."

Murdering the Media

Bringing his passion into the 1990s, Stone assaults the media and all its excesses through the characters of mass murderers Mickey and Mallory Knox in *Natural Born Killers.* The couple begin their killing spree with Mallory's father, whose abusive behavior is satirically portrayed in the form of a 1950s sitcom, laugh track and all. The Knox couple suffer no remorse as they then proceed to travel across the country and kill fifty–two strangers for various, insignificant reasons. As the number of victims rise, so does the popularity of Mickey and Mallory, so much so that they are celebrities by the time they are captured. Once in jail, the media's exploitation of the couple reaches its high when Stone's most satirical character, Wayne Gale, sets up a live interview to be broadcast during halftime of the Super Bowl. The Australian host of the tabloid television show *American Maniacs,* Gale becomes a hostage when the Knox couple attempt to escape during the interview. The ensuing prison riot is broadcast live, as is Gale's death when the couple make it to freedom.

Stylistically, *Natural Born Killers* bursts with a barrage of almost every film technique available, including photos, grainy black and white film, slow motion and strobed motion, superquick close–ups, slide projection, and heavy–metal animation. Remarking upon the lack of emotion evinced by the acts of Mickey and Mallory, Owen Gleiberman observed in *Entertainment Weekly* that "what makes their lurid odyssey so mesmerizing is Stone's revolutionary cinematic style, a visual language at once lyrical, hallucinatory, and as deliriously assaultive as Mickey and Mallory themselves." Ansen asserted in *Newsweek* that Stone tries to place the blame for society's fascination with violence on the media, concluding that "what Stone can't acknowledge in his fitfully astonishing, ultimately numbing movie is that he and Wayne Gale are two sides of the same coin. Had he done so, *Natural Born Killers* might have gotten under the skin of the issues it tantalizingly raises." Gleiberman, however, sees Stone as accomplishing his purpose in *Natural Born Killers.* "Stone takes his characters right over the top," he concluded, "rubbing our noses in our own lust for excess, and some viewers are bound to say that he's gone too far. Yet this may be one case where too far is just far enough—where a gifted filmmaker has transformed his own attraction to violence into an art of depraved catharsis."

Over the course of his career, Stone has continuously used violence and other excesses to relate his messages to viewers. "The world is spinning much faster than my camera and myself," he explained to Breskin in his *Rolling Stone* interview. "I think movies have to break through the three dimensions, close as you can get. I think you go for every . . . thing you can to make it live. We're into new technology. Use everything you can. Make it breathe, make it coil, make it *live.*" And Stone's movies are alive, with controversy, debate, and criticism; the writer/director, however, explained to Schiff in the *New Yorker,* "I would

rather not seek out a controversy; I really would not. This is something that people don't understand. Controversy just categorizes you; it's boring. I've had so many categories in my life—fascist, bloody, conspiratorial, unsubtle, barbarian, ruffian. Sometimes I don't recognize myself." One thing Stone does recognize, though, is his contribution to the filmmaking industry. When asked by Breskin if he felt like a great artist, he responded with, "My true feelings? I never doubted it, from day one. When I was eighteen, I just felt like I had a call. Like I had a call. And living up to that call has been the hardest part. I've got a lot of work to do on myself, on what I'm doing, on my craft, but I never had a doubt."

■ Works Cited

Ansen, David, with Peter McAlevey, "A Ferocious Vietnam Elegy," *Newsweek,* January 5, 1987, p. 57.

Ansen, David, "A Troublemaker for Our Times," *Newsweek,* December 23, 1992, p. 50.

Ansen, David, "The Overkilling Fields," *Newsweek,* August 29, 1994, pp. 54–55.

Aufderheide, Pat, "Oliver Stone as Pulp Artist," *CINEASTE,* Volume 15, Number 4, 1987, p. 5.

Breskin, David, "The *Rolling Stone* Interview: Oliver Stone," *Rolling Stone,* April 4, 1991, pp. 37–40, 42–3, 62.

Canby, Vincent, "*The Hand,* Clever Horror Tale," *New York Times,* April 24, 1981, p. C8.

Canby, Vincent, "Al Pacino Stars in *Scarface,*" *New York Times,* December 9, 1983, p. C18.

Corliss, Richard, "Say Good Night to the Bad Guy," *Time,* December 5, 1983, pp. 96–97.

Denby, David, "In Another Country," *New York,* March 24, 1986, pp. 86, 88–89.

Denby, David, "Days of Rage," *New York,* December 18, 1989, pp. 101–02.

Edelman, Rob, review of *Midnight Express, Films in Review,* December, 1978, p. 635.

Gleiberman, Owen, "American Psychos," *Entertainment Weekly,* Fall Double Issue, September 2, 1994, pp. 90–92.

Goodman, Mark, review of *JFK, People,* January 13, 1992, pp. 15–16.

Hluchy, Patricia, "Rebels and Reprobates," *Maclean's,* July 21, 1986, p. 50.

Horton, Robert, "Riders on the Storm," *Film Comment,* May–June, 1991, pp. 57–61.

Kauffmann, Stanley, "The Battle after the War," *New Republic,* January 29, 1990, pp. 26–27.

Kauffmann, Stanley, "Dallas," *New Republic,* January 27, 1992, pp. 26, 28.

Klawans, Stuart, review of *Born on the Fourth of July, Nation,* January 1, 1990, pp. 28–30.

Pfeifer, Chuck, "Oliver Stone," *Interview,* February, 1987, p. 576.

Romney, Jonathan, "Promise Her Everything," *New Statesman & Society,* January 21, 1994, pp. 34–35.

Schiff, Stephen, "The Last Wild Man," *New Yorker,* August 8, 1994, pp. 40, 42–48, 50–53, 55.

Travers, Peter, "Oh, What a Tangled Web," *Rolling Stone,* January 23, 1992, pp. 48–49.

■ For More Information See

BOOKS

Contemporary Literary Criticism, Volume 73, Gale, 1993, pp. 361–88.

Current Biography Yearbook 1987, Gale, 1988, pp. 526–30.

PERIODICALS

Commonweal, January 16, 1987, pp. 17–18; January 13, 1989, pp. 20–21; February 14, 1992, pp. 17–18.

Nation, January 23, 1988, pp. 97–98; January 20, 1992, pp. 62–63; May 24, 1993, pp. 713–15; January 3/10, 1994, pp. 30–31.

National Review, March 24, 1989, pp. 48–49.

New Republic, January 19, 1987, pp. 24–25; January 4 & 11, 1988, pp. 24–25; June 14, 1993, pp. 32–35; February 7, 1994, pp. 26–27.

Newsweek, March 18, 1991, p. 57.

New York, January 19, 1987, pp. 78, 80; March 25, 1991, p. 68; May 17, 1993, p. 76.

New Yorker, January 12, 1987, pp. 94–96; December 6, 1993, pp. 46–47; January 17, 1994, pp. 87–88.

New York Times, August 16, 1994, pp. C15–16.

New York Times Magazine, August 30, 1987, pp. S34–35, S44.

Time, December 14, 1987, pp. 82–83; March 11, 1991, p. 73; May 17, 1993, pp. 60–61.*

—Sketch by Susan M. Reicha

William Wegman

Personal

Born William George Wegman, December 2, 1943, in Holyoke, MA; son of George W. (a factory worker) and Eleanor (a housewife; maiden name, Vezina) Wegman; married Gayle Schneider (an artist), in mid 1960s (divorced, 1978); married Laurie Jewell (a graphic designer; divorced, 1982). *Education:* Massachusetts College of Art, B.F.A., 1965; University of Illinois at Champaign–Urbana, M.F.A., 1967. *Religion:* Protestant.

Addresses

Home and office—431 East 6th St., New York, NY 10009–6305. *Agent*—Holly Solomon Gallery, 172 Mercer Street, New York, NY 10012.

Career

Artist, photographer, painter, illustrator, and author. Associate professor at University of Wisconsin, Madison, 1968–70, and at California State University, Long Beach, 1970. *Exhibitions:* One–man shows of photographs, videos, drawings, and paintings held in numerous cities throughout the United States and Europe, including Boston, Boulder, Chicago, Cleveland, Genoa, Hanover, Houston, London, Los Angeles, Miami, Milan, Naples, New York City, Paris, San Francisco, Scottsdale and Washington, DC. Wegman's work has also been included in group exhibitions in the Netherlands and Australia. Items held in permanent collections at the Brooklyn Museum, Museum of Modern Art, Whitney Museum of American Art, Chrysler Museum, Museum of Modern Art, Paris, Los Angeles County Museum of Art, International Museum of Photography, Rochester, NY, and the Honolulu Academy of Arts.

Awards, Honors

Guggenheim fellowships, 1975 and 1986; National Endowment of the Arts grants, 1975–76, and 1982; Creative Public Service Award, 1979.

Writings

Man's Best Friend: Photographs and Drawings, introduction by Laurence Wieder, Abrams, 1982.
Everyday Problems (drawings), Brightwaters Press, 1984.
Nineteen Dollars & Eighty–Four Cents, CEPA Gallery, 1984.
The History of Travel: The Catalogue of an Exhibition of Paintings by William Wegman, Taft Museum/ Butler Institute of American Art, 1990.
William Wegman: Paintings, Drawings, Photographs, Videotapes, edited by Martin Kunz, Abrams, 1990.

William Wegman Photographic Works, 1969–1976,
Fonds Regional d'Art Contemporain (Limousin,
France), 1991, Distributed Art Publishers, 1992.

(With Carole Kismaric and Marvin Heiferman)
Cinderella, Hyperion, 1993.

Little Red Riding Hood, Hyperion, 1993.

ABC, Hyperion, 1994.

OTHER

(Illustrator) Kathy Acker, *The Adult Life of Toulouse
Lautrec,* TVRT Press, 1978.

(Photographer) M. C. Escher, *M. C. Escher: Twenty-
Nine Master Prints,* Abrams, 1983.

Also creator of videos featuring himself, including *Deodorant* and *Rage & Depression,* and of several videos featuring Man Ray, including *Spelling
Lesson, Smoking,* and *New & Used Car Salesman.*
Contributor to magazines, including *Avalanche.*

■ Sidelights

Following the flip of a coin, William Wegman
bought a grey Weimaraner, taking the only male
from a litter of seven because, as he recalls in an
interview with Michael Gross for *New York,* it
looked to him "strange and distant." He did not
actually want a dog, but had decided that, if he
did own one, he would name it Bauhaus, a pun
on the minimalist German school of design popular during the 1920s. Unfortunately, the puppy did
not really suit the name, resembling instead a
"little old grey man." Pondering his dilemma, the
artist watched, he explains in his Gross interview,
as a "shaft of light like a ray blasted down," bathing the dog with an eerie brilliance. He recalls
thinking, "it was as if the God of Art were telling the dog, 'Your name is Man Ray'"—an ap-
propriately ironic form of homage to the American artist (Man Ray, 1890–1976) whose deft inno-
vations as a filmmaker and photographer would
anticipate Wegman's own innovative work in
video and photography.

Wegman's photographs and videos of Man Ray
(the dog), made between 1970 and 1982, won critical praise for their irony, deadpan humor, pathos
and clever commentaries on art and innocence.
Wegman and Man Ray also became popular with
television viewers, including the audiences of *Saturday Night Live, The Tonight Show,* and *Late Night
with David Letterman,* who greeted Wegman's curious, sensitive videos with enthusiasm.

Since 1986 Wegman's work with Ray's successors,
most notably Fay Ray, have continued to both
move and amuse audiences, most recently in
Wegman's parodies of the classic children's books,
Cinderella and *Little Red Riding Hood,* and in his
alphabet book, *ABC.* And in addition to his photographs and videos of dogs, Wegman has produced conceptual and altered (cut–up or drawn–
on) photographs, minimalist line drawings, and,
since 1986, paintings. However, the extraordinary
popularity and artistic success of his partnership
with Man Ray and Fay Ray have occasionally
tended to overshadow his other artistic accom-
plishments.

A Curious Painter Abandons Painting

Wegman was born in 1943 and grew up in a
small town in western Massachusetts, where, as a
precocious toddler, he started drawing and painting in watercolors. In 1949, Wegman contracted
Rocky Mountain spotted fever, a life–threatening
disease of extreme rarity east of the Rockies. He
recovered completely and became, he asserts in his
New York interview, "a good, normal kid." However, as he grew into his teen years Wegman's
endless curiosity about all kinds of activity made
it hard for him to fit in completely with any one
crowd: the car kids didn't trust him because he
played sports, and the athletes didn't trust him
because he toyed with cars. By the time he entered high–school Wegman had become a typical
loner: a guy with many skills and interests but
few friends. And he felt a little bit lost.

Direction entered Wegman's life in his senior year
when his art teacher recognized his gifts for drawing and painting, and encouraged his desire to be
an artist. "She saved my life in a way," he recalls to Gross, "because I would not have known
what to do with myself." Wegman enrolled in the
Massachusetts College of Art where, by his third
year, he had become well–known as "Willy
Wegman the artist." While forming passionate interests in philosophy, music, and literature, he
embraced rebellious or anti–art movements, like
Dada and Surrealism. Their playful and idiosyn-
cratic elements, as well as their mocking and socially satirical qualities, would both find new expression in Wegman's later, mature work.

Finishing college in 1965, Wegman enrolled in
graduate school at the University of Illinois, at
Champaign–Urbana, where he married an under-

Seen here with Fay and Battina—the successors to his first canine model, Man Ray—Wegman has turned his relationship with his pets into art that encompasses parody, irony, comedy, pathos, and social commentary.

graduate art student, Gayle Schneider. He also developed an interest in electrical–engineering which, as he relates in *New York*, he saw as a means of aligning himself with the "forefront of thinking—information theory." He had come to regard working in traditional mediums, such as painting and sculpture, as a retreat into the past: a "cop out."

Conceptual Art for the Common Man

Wegman earned his master's of fine arts degree in 1967. Moving to Wisconsin that year, where he would have jobs teaching art at the University of Wisconsin's Wausau campus and, later, in Waukesha, he developed a personal philosophy of never working "over his head." He found he worked best in a relaxed, amiable style and by focusing on what actually moved him, rather than on what he had been instructed ought to move him. For Wegman, artistry grew naturally out of his perceptions of the everyday world; instead of alluding to lofty notions about Art in order to push people around, he preferred to engage and delight people by having them look at unexceptional things in a new way.

The art world at the end of the 1960s was radicalized, reflecting the turmoil and seemingly irreconcilable conflicts that were shaking American society. As the decade passed through its final, convulsive, years, Wegman gravitated toward the new anti–art movement of Conceptual Art (or mind art), which de–emphasized the art object to concentrate on the idea or concept behind it. Arguing that creating paintings and sculptures merely served to flatter the affluent classes, the Conceptualists sought instead to invent original and unexpected presentations.

Wegman adapted the Conceptualist creed by working with surprisingly ordinary materials, such as cellophane, rubber, and household utensils. His choices intended to challenge complacent and hierarchical assumptions about what could constitute art. Departing from the mainstream of Conceptualism, however, Wegman infused his work with a strong element of humor, which tended to mask his intellectual ambitions. One piece he fashioned during this period wryly commented upon the consumerist approach to art, using inflatable rubber. While fixing up his home, Wegman attached a sculpture of his to the heating vent so that whenever the heat came up, the inflatable art work would slowly expand and, at the same time, snake upstairs. Eventually, as the house became warm, it also became filled with Wegman's giant balloon.

In another work, Wegman made eloquent use of Styrofoam by floating rows of Styrofoam commas down the Milwaukee River. Drifting into the medium of sound, he also composed a concerto for one hundred car horns. Sometimes Wegman used a camera to record or document the work, or included photographs within the work itself. It wasn't until 1969, however, commencing with "Cotto," a black and white photograph of the artist's hand, that he would come to consider a photograph as actual art in itself.

Wegman assumed the position of artist–in–residence at Wisconsin's Madison campus in 1969, where he added elements of Performance Art and Process Art to his now solid Conceptual base. He attached a Magic Marker to a plank of Styrofoam and stuck it in a pail of liquid solvent. As the plank dissolved, the marker left a wavy line on his studio wall. The finished "drawing," the wavy line, merely represented the completed process, or one haphazard effect of the process. No aesthetic object, in the accepted sense, its chief value was informational or documentary. The process itself, with its odd life caught and shaped by the flow of time and to a certain extent subject to the random intrusions of its surroundings, was the thing of paramount interest.

Conceptual Art Goes Video

It was during this period that Wegman began to make black–out video sketches which would become, according to Gross, "classics" of the genre. On a bare set, dressed simply, usually in jeans and a T–shirt, Wegman would face the camera and talk. In *Deodorant* he demonstrates a new underarm spray that he feels is an excellent product, although one has to spray it on for a couple of minutes for it to really work. While Wegman goes on talking monotonously about how functional it is, he seems to be untroubled that he is smothering his armpit under waves of billowing foam. In *Rage & Depression* he pretends to be a guy who has had to undergo shock therapy because he was always so angry at everyone. He explains that when the doctors put the electrodes on his chest he started to giggle and that silly, giggly, expression became forever frozen on his face. He tells us he's still miserable, but now, with his unchanging smile, everyone assumes he's happy—which makes everything weirder and worse. In these sketches Wegman enacted, according to Sanford Schwartz in the *New York Review of Books*, a

"somewhat unfocussed, fallible and physically inept character," a reinvention of the Modernist persona. The popularity of Wegman's videos attests to the universality of this comic figure, as well as the egalitarian ideals that underlie it.

Holly Solomon, who later became one of Wegman's dealers, maintains in her interview with Amy Hempel for the *New York Times Magazine*: "Video before Wegman was Andy Warhol recording a man sleeping for 24 hours. It was art about art. Billy [Wegman] felt a real responsibility to engage an audience, and not just art people." And art critic Bruce Boice remarks that Wegman's videotapes suggest the funniest television show he has ever seen.

Enter Man Ray

In 1970, Wegman moved to California to teach at a state college in Long Beach. There he came into contact with other Conceptual artists, including Ed Ruscha, John Baldessari, Allen Ruppersberg and

An acclaimed painter and filmmaker whose videos have been shown on *Sesame Street*, Wegman is perhaps best known for his Polaroid photographs of his pet Weimaraners, used here to tell the story of *Cinderella*.

Bruce Nauman, and entered an idyllic chapter of his life. He would fish, swim, and play on the beach with his new artist friends and the dog his wife had urged him to buy, Man Ray. Having been uninterested in owning a dog, Wegman originally had no thought of using him in his work. But Man Ray would not sit submissively by; he would howl when leashed in a corner, and gambol bothersomely onto the set in front of the camera when he was freed. By training the camera on him one day, Wegman discovered that, on video, Man Ray looked "absolutely gorgeous." At the same time he discovered that Man Ray liked the work. So, while it had been nearly impossible to work around Man Ray, it became increasingly appealing for Wegman to work with him.

The video works with Man Ray, made primarily between 1970 and 1977, evince droll parody, elaborating upon themes of Wegman's earlier work. In *Smoking,* the artist tries unsuccessfully to persuade the dog to smoke a cigarette; in *New & Used Car Salesman,* the duo spoof low–budget television commercials. *Milk/Floor* has Wegman crawling away from the camera, spitting a line of milk as he goes, disappearing around a corner. A moment later, Man Ray turns the corner, lapping up the trail of milk until his black nose runs smack into the camera lens. In *Spelling Lesson,* Wegman pretends to correct May Ray's spelling test, much to the dog's confusion; he pedantically points out that Ray has spelled the word "beach, the place" when what was called for was the word "beech, the tree."

Schwartz observes that, having established his video persona Wegman discovered in Man Ray a natural balance, a creature "of undiluted sinewy muscle . . . [who] was keener, leaner and sexier than his owner." Man Ray's discomfort in *Spelling Lesson* palpably conveys the dog's creatural vitality and displaced strength. Having surprised himself, Wegman's early videos of Man Ray surprised others as well. Art audiences, having grown used to Wegman's cool, ironic and disembodied work, did not expect to see a great big animal suddenly lunge around the corner.

Down East

While Wegman's California period was dreamy it was not perfect. Aside from some gallery interest in Europe, and the support of fellow artist, Ed Ruscha, collectors largely ignored him. While in-

tellectually engaging, Conceptual art, without its stock of beautiful or exotic art objects, was difficult to collect. After his teaching job ended, Wegman and his wife were forced to live on food stamps and the money Wegman took in through odd jobs.

In late 1972, the Wegmans left California for New York, where Wegman signed with the Sonnabend gallery, earning a monthly stipend of $500. He augmented his video performances with small drawings that would evolve over the next few years from scant, Minimalist sketches to parodies of contemporary attitudes about sex, mass media, class and art. These were made on regular 8½" x 11" typing paper using normal #2b pencils. In one of his drawings, a prisoner smugly asserts that even though he is a convicted felon, he will smoke only his brand of cigarettes. In another, Wegman has depicted eleven blocks of University buildings, the largest of which is labelled Administration, and the smallest, Art. Another drawing presents a romantic couple in classical Roman costumes embracing in a typically Hollywoodish clinch; Wegman's caption "I love you Elizopatra" facetiously alludes to the conceptual elevation of a film star, Elizabeth Taylor, into the legendary Cleopatra, and to the parallel reduction of the legendary Cleopatra into a banal, celluloid cliche.

While some critics felt his drawings to be stylistically similar to New Yorker cartoons, *New York Times* critic Roberta Smith commented on their offbeat charm and staying power. About the later drawings, Martin Kunz writes in his introduction to *William Wegman: Paintings, Drawings, Photographs, Videotapes,* "Wegman's references to the topics of sex, beautiful women, the hackneyed themes of the entertainment media and of society in general, are aligned with the central motif of his work, the transferral of the most banal, least artistically incriminated pictorial material to the domain of art without making noticeable changes."

At this time, influential collectors, such as Holly Solomon, started buying his work, and international celebrities, such as Mick Jagger and Andy Warhol, began to attend his openings. Still a shy, small–town boy at heart, with a penchant for the whimsical and the ordinary, Wegman wasn't ready for this caliber of attention. Instead of meeting success head on and enjoying it, though, Wegman tells Gross that he simply "freaked out and kind of hid." He became involved with alcohol and drugs as he began to feel increasingly isolated; work became nearly impossible. Wegman recalls in his *New York* interview: "I'd go into my video room and come out screaming."

Although Wegman's life gained some stability in 1978 when he married Laurie Jewell, a graphic designer, and moved into his third New York studio, on Thames Street near the Battery, dependence on alcohol and drugs continued to steadily destroy him. Becoming, in his own words, "a demon," Wegman was nevertheless heartbroken when a fire ravaged the building on Thames Street, consuming many of his oldest negatives, including his earliest pictures of Man Ray. Feeling himself mentally unable to produce art, Wegman's situation grew desperate when Sonnabend chose to cut off his monthly stipend. With the offer of a teaching position in hand Wegman fled alone to California late that year. Unfortunately, California had changed considerably since the early 1970s, and Wegman failed miserably to recapture the serenity for which he longed. He returned to New York immediately when Holly Solomon, a friend since 1975, offered to sign him up for her New York gallery.

Man's Best Friend

In 1979, Wegman began showing at Solomon and accepted Polaroid's invitation to use its new large–format camera, producing his first work in color since 1966. The Polaroids Wegman would produce over the next several years entailed a significant change from his previous photography. In addition to their larger size, (20 by 24 inches), Wegman's Polaroid photography demonstrates a marked degree of technical mastery and artistic control. Large–format Polaroid photography also requires trust and cooperation: Wegman learned to rely upon the expertise of skilled technicians who light the sets and run the camera, for $1,000 a day—a costly procedure compounded by the $30 the artist pays for each exposure. (On a typical day, Wegman estimates that he shoots about sixty frames, of which only five will be usable.) And Wegman has had to balance the competing claims of Conceptualism with the glamour of the medium, its rich, gorgeous, colors and striking visual appeal.

Although he had to considerably alter his method of working, one thing did stay the same: Man Ray remained his primary model. Having sulked

around the house during his friend's dry spell, Man Ray was delighted to return to work. In 1982, Wegman published his Polaroids of Man Ray under the doubly punning title *Man's Best Friend,* cited by Schwartz as the "most original book of photographs since Robert Frank's *The Americans* [1959]." Some of the most effective photographs from this collection include "Brooke," a parody of jean advertisements in general and the adolescent model, Brooke Shields, in particular, in which Ray seems to be wearing a droopy pair of jeans over his behind and fixing the camera with a 'come hither' stare; "Frog," in which Ray has been given a pair of fake bulging eyes and a pair of flippers for his back feet, and appears to be happily communicating with a plastic frog on a plastic lily pad placed before him; and "Dusted," in which Man Ray sits patiently, his body as articulate as a Rodin sculpture, as flour pours down over him and covers him.

Schwartz declares "Dusted" to be the "single most powerful image in *Man's Best Friend,*" in which Wegman expresses "the attachment he and Ray had for each other," the force that inspired Wegman "in one cycle after another, to release more of his talent." Schwartz concludes his praise for "Dusted" by observing that it also conveys Wegman's somber awareness of Man Ray's imminent death, invoking "the moment that Man Ray has died and is being taken up into the light." At the same time, "Dusted" also recalls the moment, a decade earlier, when the young California puppy found his rightful name.

The year *Man's Best Friend* appeared Wegman entered a rehabilitation clinic. Having determined once and for all to rid himself of his substance addictions, Wegman sought professional help and emerged, as he tells Gross, "liberated, healthy, spiritually awakened." Six months later Man Ray died. At the time of his death, Man Ray, Wegman's companion and model for almost 12 years, had become so widely known and loved that the *Village Voice,* parodying *Time* magazine, ran a full–cover photo of him as "Man of the Year."

Starting Over

With the passing of Man Ray, a hard–fought victory over drugs and alcohol, and a second divorce, Wegman recalls in his *New York* interview that he was ready to "leave my life and really start over." He has described the following period

The artist brought his unique style of photography to a new audience with his adaptations of traditional fairy tales, including this version of *Little Red Riding Hood*.

of his life as a kind of "renaissance," during which he began to meet people again and get invited places. Along with his social desirability, his stature as an artist increased with the success of *Man's Best Friend,* and, the following year, his first retrospective was mounted at the Walker Art Center in Minneapolis. No longer able to photograph Man Ray, he began drawing again and taking photographs of props, drawings, and people. The photographs he took of his girlfriend, Eve Darcy, lampooned the current fitness craze, comically probing its narcissism and self–importance. Despite the artist's productivity, Wegman's public experienced a gap in his work. "Everyone kept looking for the dog pictures, and they weren't getting them," he explains to Gross.

In 1986, four years after Man Ray died, Wegman acquired another Weimaraner puppy named Cinnamon Girl. He renamed her Fay Ray, in part a tribute to her predecessor and, within a year, he began using her as a new model. Comparing Man Ray with Fay Ray, Wegman relates in his interview with Hempel that "[Man] Ray was more of an equal. He had a sense of gamesmanship: if you do this to me, I can do this to *you.* Fay does things because I want her to."

Among Wegman's most unexpected uses of Fay have been the series of children's books he wrote and illustrated for Hyperion, the publisher owned by the Walt Disney Company, grouped under the series title "Fay's Fairy Tales." For his first children's publication, issued in early 1993, Wegman retold the classic fairy tale *Cinderella,* using seventeen Weimaraners. His casting decisions reveal the acuteness of his eye as well his relish of visual imagination. He explains in his interview with Gross: "I play with the specific character of the dogs. From below, Fay looks like Joan Crawford. She looks guilty. Fay can't be Cinderella. Batty can be Cinderella. . . . She's totally trusting and innocent. There's something eternally, everlastingly cute about her."

Some commentators have found his "adult sensibility" too sophisticated for this medium. While Kate McClelland, writing in the *School Library Journal,* deems his "urbane, tongue–in–cheek text" appropriate to the illustrations, and welcomes the "unique portraiture" of "elaborately dressed dogs" with "mournful countenances and . . . human hands," Lee Lorenz declares in the *New York Times Book Review* that *Cinderella* is betrayed by implau-

Wegman's distinctive style is on display here as Fay and Battina illustrate the alphabet in *ABC,* a work for children.

sibility. "Every child wants to know 'why?' and just too many why's are left hanging here."

Little Red Riding Hood, published later that year, was received more positively by critics. A *Publishers Weekly* reviewer points out instances of sublime irony, in which illustrations comically undermine the traditional text, such as when the wolf dissembles as grandmother. Since the image of dog–as–wolf–as–grandmother is exactly identical to that of dog–as–grandmother, the sequence beginning "what big ears you have!" produces tongue–in–cheek silliness instead of the customary thrill of foreboding. Rather than framing the act of discovery as a fearful and potentially disastrous experience, Wegman has pedagogically chosen to present it as a means of overcoming fright and finding pleasure.

Painting Again

In 1990, using the money he earned from the sale of his Polaroids, Wegman bought a large house in Maine where he was able to continue work on his newest artistic enterprize: painting. Although he had once spurned traditional forms of expression, in 1986, at age 43, Wegman "sheepishly" decided to start over as a painter. Of his turnabout decision, Angela Westwater, one of his dealers, remarks to Gross: "At this point, New York has lots of artists in mid–career repeating themselves ad infinitum. It is such a testimony to Bill that he's able to push himself into new work—and invest mediums he's used before with new energy and insight."

His first small, exploratory, paintings, done on birch bark, are colorful, textured versions of his cartoonish drawings, and brushy, abstract paintings traceable to the influence of Wegman's college friend, Neil Jenney. After 1990, with larger studio space now available, Wegman attempted larger and more involved canvasses. His bravado was immediately apparent in his thorough rejection of the prevailing orthodoxy, the Neo–Expressionism popularized by such dynamic contemporaries as Julian Schnabel and David Salle.

Employing a style he has whimsically deprecated as "sophomore surrealism," Wegman covers his paintings in a thin, nondistinct and mottled wash of acrylic, creating a surface texture that uses warmth, coolness, and density in such a way to remind some of J. M. Turner and Raoul Dufy. Upon this, he uses small brushes and oil paint to daub on simple, childlike figures like planes, ships, cowboys, Greek temples, and water sprinklers, culled from generic sources such as elementary readers and illustrated encyclopedias. What emerges has been defined as a stream–of–conscious, nationalistic tapestry, savoring of the optimism and innocence of the Eisenhower era—the period of Wegman's boyhood—but enlarged to epic scope and infused with wide–eyed wonder.

Working as a painter during the same period he produced Polaroid photographs of his Weimaraners has had interesting results. Wegman credits the relaxed personality of Fay Ray with having changed his heart rate, actually making him a better painter. Although he has been quoted as saying that as soon as he got funny he killed any majestic intentions in his work, Wegman's latest paintings have proven that majestic intentions can indeed be exceptionally durable.

Wegman's career has thus far been characterized by independence, prankish yet graceful irony, sensitivity to the process of making art, an extraor-

dinary range of emotional color, spanning cool detachment to poignant tenderness, and a complete investment in art's ability to communicate. Of this last characteristic of Wegman's work, Peter MacGill, his Polaroid dealer, insightfully remarks to Gross: "His videos are on *Sesame Street,* he's shown in the best galleries in the world, he's in the collection of virtually every museum, some of the most importance critics cherish his work, and so does my four–year–old. It's amazing to see his breadth of appeal without compromise."

■ Works Cited

Gross, Michael, "Pup Art," *New York,* March 30, 1992, pp. 44–50.

Hempel, Amy, "William Wegman: The Artist and His Dog," *New York Times Magazine,* November 29, 1987, pp. 40–44.

Kunz, Martin, "Drawings; Conceptual Pivot of Wegman's Artistic World," introduction for *William Wegman: Paintings, Drawings, Photographs, Videotapes,* edited by Kunz, Abrams, 1990.

Lacayo, Richard, "Bowwowing the Art World," *Time,* March 23, 1992, pp. 74–75.

Review of *Little Red Riding Hood, Publishers Weekly,* October 4, 1993, p. 77.

Lorenz, Lee, "Someday Her Weimaraner Will Come," *New York Times Book Review,* May 16, 1993, p. 22.

McClelland, Kate, review of *Cinderella, School Library Journal,* April, 1993, p. 138.

Schwartz, Sanford, "The Lovers," *New York Review of Books,* August 18, 1983, pp. 44–45.

■ For More Information See

PERIODICALS

ARTnews, January, 1990, pp. 150–55.

Los Angeles Times Book Review, November 25, 1990, p. 3.

New York Times Magazine, December 25, 1988, pp. 18–19.

People Weekly, September 9, 1991, pp. 105–08.

Time, May 3, 1993, p. 81.

—*Sketch by Michael Scott Joseph*

Acknowledgments

Acknowledgements

Grateful acknowledgement is made to the following publishers, authors, and artists for their kind permission to reproduce copyrighted material.

CHINUA ACHEBE. Cover of *Arrow of God*, by Chinua Achebe. Copyright © 1964, 1974 by Chinua Achebe. Cover by Paul Bacon. Reprinted by permission of Doubleday, a division of Bantam Doubleday Dell Publishing Group, Inc./ Cover of *Things Fall Apart*, by Chinua Achebe. Copyright © 1959 by Chinua Achebe. Reprinted by permission of Ballantine Books, a division of Random House, Inc./ Cover of *No Longer at Ease*, by Chinua Achebe. Copyright © 1960 by Chinua Achebe. Cover art by Leo and Diane Dillon. Reprinted by permission of Ballantine Books, a division of Random House, Inc./ Cover of *Anthills of the Savannah*, by Chinua Achebe. Copyright © 1987 by Chinua Achebe. Cover illustration by Joe Baker. Cover design by Service Station. Reprinted by permission of Doubleday, a division of Bantam Doubleday Dell Publishing Group, Inc./ Photograph courtesy of Chinua Achebe.

RAY BRADBURY. Cover of *Something Wicked This Way Comes*, by Ray Bradbury. Cover art copyright © 1990 by J.K. Potter. Reprinted by permission of Bantam Books, a division of Bantam Doubleday Dell Publishing Group, Inc./ Cover of *Fahrenheit 451*, by Ray Bradbury. Copyright © 1953 by Ray Bradbury. Cover art by Donna Diamond. Reprinted by permission of Ballantine Books, a division of Random House, Inc./ Cover of *The Illustrated Man*, by Ray Bradbury. Copyright © 1951 by Ray Bradbury. Cover art by Jim Burns. Reprinted by permission of Bantam Books, a division of Bantam Doubleday Dell Publishing Group, Inc./ Cover of *Dandelion Wine*, by Ray Bradbury. Copyright © 1946, 1947, 1950, 1951, 1952, 1953, 1954, 1955, 1957 by Ray Bradbury. Copyright © 1956, 1957 by The Curtis Publishing Company. Reprinted by permission of Bantam Books, a division of Bantam Doubleday Dell Publishing Group, Inc./ Cover of *The Martian Chronicles*, by Ray Bradbury. Copyright © 1946, 1948, 1950, 1958, by Ray Bradbury. Copyright © renewed 1977 by Ray Bradbury. Reprinted by permission of Bantam Books, a division of Bantam Doubleday Dell Publishing Group, Inc./ Photograph ©1986 Thomas Victor.

BROCK COLE. Cover of *Celine*, by Brock Cole. Cover art copyright © 1993 by Elaine Norman. Reprinted by permission of Farrar, Straus & Giroux, Inc./ Cover illustration by Brock Cole from his *The Goats*. Farrar, Straus & Giroux, Inc., 1987. Copyright © 1987 by Brock Cole. Reprinted by permission of Farrar, Straus & Giroux, Inc./ Cover by Brock Cole from *The Indian in the Cupboard*, by Lynne Reid Banks. Illustrations copyright © 1981 by Brock Cole. Reprinted by permission of Avon Books./ Illustration by Brock Cole from his *The Winter Wren*. Farrar, Straus & Giroux, Inc., 1984. Copyright © 1984 by Brock Cole. Reprinted by permission of Farrar, Straus & Giroux, Inc./ Photograph by Tobias Cole, courtesy of Farrar, Straus and Giroux, Inc.

ROALD DAHL. Cover of *Boy*, by Roald Dahl. Copyright © 1984 by Roald Dahl. Cover illustration by Quentin Blake. Reprinted by permission of A.P. Watt Ltd. on behalf of Quentin Blake./ Cover of *The BFG*, by Roald Dahl. Illustrations copyright © 1982 by Quentin Blake. Reprinted by permission of A.P. Watt Ltd. on behalf of Quentin Blake./ Cover of *The Witches*, by Roald Dahl. Illustrations copyright © 1983 by Quentin Blake. Reprinted by permission of A.P. Watt Ltd. on behalf of Quentin Blake./ Movie still from "The Witches" ©1990 Warner Bros. (All rights reserved)./ Dahl at 17, Courtesy of Repton School./ Dahl as older man, Photograph by Mark Gerson.

GENARO GONZALEZ. Cover of *Only Sons*, Genaro Gonzalez. Copyright © 1991 by Genaro Gonzalez. Cover design by Mark Pinon. Photograph by Evangelina Vigil-Pinon. Reprinted by permission of Arte Publico Press./ Cover of *Rainbow's End*, by Genaro Gonzalez. Copyright © 1988 by Genaro Gonzalez. Cover design by John E. Fleming. Reprinted by permission of Arte Publico Press.

PATRICIA HERMES. Jacket of *Nothing but Trouble, Trouble, Trouble*, by Patricia Hermes. Jacket painting copyright © 1994 by Jason Dowd. Reprinted by permission of Scholastic Inc./Cover of *Kevin Cortett Eats Flies*, by Patricia Hermes. Cover copyright © 1986 by Pocket Books. Cover illustration by Joanne L. Scribner. Reprinted by permission of Pocket Books, a division of Simon & Schuster Inc./ Jacket from *A Place for Jeremy*, by Patricia Hermes. Copyright © 1987 by Patricia Hermes. Jacket illustration by Leland Neff. Reprinted by permission of Leland Neff.

ZORA NEALE HURSTON. Cover of *Their Eyes Were Watching God*, by Zora Neale Hurston. Cover copyright © 1978 by the Board of Trustees of the University of Illinois. Reprinted by permission of the University of Illinois Press./ Cover of *Jonah's Gourd Vine*, by Zora Neale Hurston. Cover illustration copyright © 1990 by David Diaz. Cover design by Suzanne Noli. Reprinted by permission of HarperCollins Publishers Inc./ Cover of *Mules and Men*, by Zora Neale Hurston. Cover illustration copyright © 1990 by David Diaz. Cover design by Suzanne Noli. Reprinted by permission of HarperCollins Publishers Inc./ Cover of *Dust Tracks on a Road*, by Zora Neale Hurston. Cover illustration copyright © by David Diaz. Cover design by Suzanne Noli. Reprinted by permission of HarperCollins Publishers Inc./ Photograph of Hurston at Tuskegee Institute, courtesy of the Beinecke Rare Book and Manuscript Library, Yale University./ Photograph of Hurston's gravestone, courtesy of Georgia Curry./ Photograph of Hurston, courtesy of Clifford J. Hurston, Jr.

BARBARA KINGSOLVER. Cover of *Homeland and Other Stories,* by Barbara Kingsolver. Copyright © 1989 by Barbara Kingsolver. Cover design by Suzanne Noli. Cover illustration © by Lisa Desimini. Reprinted by permission of HarperCollins Publishers, Inc./ Cover of *Pigs In Heaven,* by Barbara Kingsolver. Cover design by Suzanne Noli. Cover illustration copyright © 1993 by Lisa Desimini. Reprinted by permission of HarperCollins Publishers, Inc./ Cover of *The Bean Trees,* by Barbara Kingsolver. Copyright © 1988 by Barbara Kingsolver. Cover design by Suzanne Noli. Cover illustration © by Lisa Desimini. Reprinted by permission of HarperCollins Publishers, Inc./ Photograph by Mark Taylor.

TANITH LEE. Cover of *Personal Darkness,* by Tanith Lee. Copyright © 1993 by Tanith Lee. Reprinted by permission of Dell Books, a division of Bantam Doubleday Dell Publishing Group, Inc./ Cover of *The Book of the Damned,* by Tanith Lee. Copyright © 1990 by Tanith Lee. Jacket art by Wayne Barlowe. Copyright © 1990 by Wayne Barlowe. Jacket design by Bagel Graphics. Copyright © 1990 by Bagel Graphics. Reprinted by permission of Overlook Press, Woodstock NY 12498./ Cover of *Heart Beast,* by Tanith Lee. Copyright © 1992 by Tanith Lee. Reprinted by permission of Dell Books, a division of Bantam Doubleday Dell Publishing Group, Inc./ Photograph ©Jerry Bauer.

LURLENE MCDANIEL. Cover of *So Much to Live For,* by Lurlene McDaniel. Copyright © 1991 by Lurlene McDaniel. Reprinted by permission of Willowisp Press./ Cover of *Too Young to Die,* by Lurlene McDaniel. Cover art copyright © 1989 by Karen Kolada. Reprinted by permission of Bantam Books, a division of Bantam Doubleday Dell Publishing Group, Inc./ Cover of *Time to Let Go,* by Lurlene McDaniel. Cover art copyright © 1990 by Ben Stahl. Reprinted by permission of Bantam Books, a division of Bantam Doubleday Dell Publishing Group, Inc./ Cover of *One Last Wish,* by Lurlene McDaniel. Cover art copyright © 1992 by Linda Benson. Reprinted by permission of Bantam Books, a division of Bantam Doubleday Dell Publishing Group, Inc./ Photograph courtesy of Lurlene McDaniel.

LARRY MCMURTRY. Cover of *Streets of Laredo,* by Larry McMurtry. Cover copyright © 1993 by Simon & Schuster Inc. Cover art by Tim Tanner. Reprinted by permission of Simon & Schuster Inc./ Cover of *The Last Picture Show,* by Larry McMurtry. Cover copyright © 1966 by Simon & Schuster Inc. Cover design by Jackie Seow. Cover illustration by Cathleen Toelke. Reprinted by permission of Simon & Schuster Inc./ Cover of *Horsemen Pass By,* by Larry McMurtry. Cover copyright © 1961 by Simon & Schuster Inc. Cover design by Jackie Seow. Cover illustration by Richard Mantel. Reprinted by permission of Simon & Schuster Inc./ Movie still from *The Last Picture Show,* as used in *The Art of Watching Films,* by Joseph M. Boggs. Copyright © 1991 by Mayfield Publishing Company. / Cover of *Leaving Cheyenne,* by Larry McMurtry. Cover copyright © 1991 by Simon & Schuster Inc. Reprinted by permission of Simon & Schuster Inc./ Photograph by Lee Marmon.

ARTHUR MILLER. Cover of *Death of a Salesman,* by Arthur Miller. Copyright © 1949 by Arthur Miller. Cover design by Gail Belenson. Photograph © Eileen Darby. Cover photograph reprint reprinted by permission of Eileen Darby./ Scene from "The Crucible" ©Mili Gjon./ Montgomery Cliff in "Misfits" ©Inge Morath/Magnum Photos./ Original cast of "All My Sons" ©Eileen Darby./ British production of "American Clock" Photograph by Robert Workman./ Photograph by Fred W. McDarrah.

JOYCE CAROL OATES. Jacket of *American Appetites,* by Joyce Carol Oates. Copyright © 1989 by The Ontario Review Inc. Jacket design © Vincent X. Kirsch. Reprinted by permission of Dutton Signet, a division of Penguin Books USA Inc./ Cover of *Them,* by Joyce Carol Oates. Copyright © 1969 by Joyce Carol Oates. Reprinted by permission of Ballantine Books, a division of Random House, Inc./ Cover of *Bellefleur,* by Joyce Carol Oates. Copyright © 1980 by Joyce Carol Oates, Inc. Cover photo by Bruce Katsiff. Hand tinting by Joanie Schwartz. Hand lettering by Iskra. Reprinted by permission of Dutton Signet, a division of Penguin Books USA, Inc./ Cover of *Foxfire: Confessions of a Girl Gang,* by Joyce Carol Oates. Copyright © 1993 by The Ontario Review, Inc. Jacket design by Roberto De Vicq De Cumptich. Jacket photograph by Roberto Dutesco. Reprinted by permission of Dutton Signet, a division of Penguin Books USA Inc./ Cover of *On Boxing,* by Joyce Carol Oates. Copyright © 1985 by The Ontario Review, Inc. Photographs copyright © 1987 by John Ranard. Cover reprinted by permission of John Hawkins & Associates, Inc. Cover photo reprinted by permission of John Ranard./ Photograph © Jerry Bauer.

GEORGE ORWELL. Cover of *Burmese Days,* by George Orwell. Copyright © 1934 by George Orwell. Copyright © renewed 1962 by Sonia Pitt-Rivers. Cover design by Eric Baker. Cover photo by Henri Cartier-Bresson/Magnum Photos, Inc. Cover design reprinted by permission of Eric Baker. Cover photo reprinted by permission of Cartier-Bresson/Magnum Photos, Inc./ Cover of *1984,* by George Orwell. Copyright © 1950 by New American Library on Cover. Reprinted by permission of Dutton Signet, a division of Penguin Books USA Inc./ Cover of *Animal Farm,* by George Orwell. Copyright © 1950 by New American Library on Cover. Reprinted by permission of Dutton Signet, a division of Penguin Books USA Inc./ Movie still from "Nineteen Eighty Four" Virginia Films./ "Barnhills", Orwell's home (1947) George Orwell Archive./ Photograph The Granger Collection, New York./

STELLA PEVSNER. Cover of *Cute Is a Four-Letter Word,* by Stella Pevsner. Cover copyright © 1980 by Pocket Books, a division of Simon & Schuster Inc. Reprinted by permission of Pocket Books, a division of Simon & Schuster Inc./ Cover of *And You Give Me a Pain, Elaine,* by Stella Pevsner. Cover art copyright © 1989 by Pocket Books, a division of Simon & Schuster Inc. Reprinted by permission of Pocket Books, a division of Simon & Schuster Inc./ Cover of *The Night the Whole Class Slept Over,* by Stella Pevsner. Cover copyright © 1991 by Pocket Books, a division of Simon & Schuster, Inc. Cover art by Craig Nelson. Reprinted by permission of Pocket Books, a division of Simon & Schuster Inc./ Cover of *How Could You Do It, Diane?,* by Stella Pevsner. Cover copyright © 1989 by

Pocket Books, a division of Simon & Schuster Inc. Cover art by Kim Milnazik. Reprinted by permission of Pocket Books, a division of Simon & Schuster, Inc./ Photograph courtesy of Stella Pevsner.

CHAIM POTOK. Cover of *The Promise*, by Chaim Potok. Copyright © 1969 by Chaim Potok. Reprinted by permission of Ballantine Books, a division of Random House, Inc./ Cover of *Davita's Harp*, by Chaim Potok. Copyright © 1985 by Chaim Potok. Reprinted by permission of Ballantine Books, a division of Random House, Inc./ Cover of *My Name Is Asher Lev*, by Chaim Potok. Copyright © 1972 by Chaim Potok. Cover art by Rhonda. Reprinted by permission of Ballantine Books, a division of Random House, Inc./ Movie still from *The Chosen*, copyright © 1982 Twentieth Century-Fox./ Photograph © Jerry Bauer.

PHILIP PULLMAN. Cover of *The Ruby in Smoke,* by Philip Pullman. Cover art copyright © 1987 by Linda Benson. Reprinted by permission of Random House, Inc./ Jacket of *The Tin Princess*, by Philip Pullman. Jacket illustration copyright © 1994 by Catherine Deeter. Reprinted by permission of Alfred A. Knopf, Inc./ Cover of *Shadow in the North*, by Philip Pullman. Cover art copyright © 1988 by Linda Benson. Reprinted by permission of Alfred A. Knopf, Inc./ Photograph by Robin Matthews.

ROBERT REDFORD. Ralph Finnes in *Quiz Show,* © 1994 Hollywood Pictures./ Movie still from *Ordinary People* Paramount Pictures./ Movie still from *The Milgro Beanfield War,* Photograph AP/Wide World Photos./ Press photo for *Incident at Oglala,* Photograph AP/Wide World Photos.

ANN RINALDI. Cover of *A Break with Charity: A Story about the Salem Witch Trials*, by Ann Rinaldi. Cover illustration copyright © 1992 by Bill Farnsworth. Cover design by Lisa Peters. Reprinted by permission of Bill Farnsworth./ Cover of *Wolf by the Ears*, by Ann Rinaldi. Text copyright © 1991 by Ann Rinaldi. Reprinted by permission of Scholastic Inc./ Cover of *The Last Silk Dress*, by Ann Rinaldi. Cover art copyright © 1990 by Lisa Falkenstern. Reprinted by permission of Bantam Books, a division of Bantam Doubleday Dell Publishing Group, Inc./ Photograph by Bill Philips.

ZILPHA KEATLEY SNYDER. Cover of *Season of Ponies*, by Zilpha Keatley Snyder. Copyright © 1964 by Zilpha Keatley Snyder. Cover illustration by Dave Henderson. Reprinted by permission of Dell Books, a division of Bantam Doubleday Dell Publishing Group, Inc./Cover of *Black & Blue Magic*, by Zilpha Keatley Snyder. Copyright © 1966 by Zilpha Keatley Snyder. Cover illustration by Dave Henderson. Reprinted by permission of Dell Books, a division of Bantam Doubleday Dell Publishing Group, Inc./ Jacket of *Janie's Private Eyes*, by Zilpha Keatley Snyder. Jacket illustration copyright © 1989 by Dave Henderson. Reprinted by permission of Delacorte Press, a division of Bantam Doubleday Dell Publishing Group, Inc./Cover of *The Velvet Room*, by Zilpha Keatley Snyder. Copyright © 1965 by Zilpha Keatley Snyder. Cover illustration by Dave Henderson. Reprinted by permission of Dell Books, a division of Bantam Doubleday Dell Publishing Group, Inc./ Cover of *The Birds of Summer*, by Zilpha Keatley Snyder. Copyright © 1983 by Zilpha Keatley Snyder. Reprinted by permission of Dell Books, a division of Bantam Doubleday Dell Publishing Group, Inc./ Photograph courtesy of Zilpha Keatley Snyder.

OLIVER STONE. Tommy Lee Jones prepares for scene in *Heaven and Earth*, Photograph by Mark Wexler./ Movie still from *Platoon*, Orion Pictures./ Movie still from *Wallstreet,* Twentieth Century Fox./ Movie still from *Born on the Fourth of July,* Universal Pictures./ Photograph AP/Wide World Photos.

WILLIAM WEGMAN. Illustration by William Wegman from his *ABC/William Wegman*. Copyright © 1994 by William Wegman. Reprinted by permission of Hyperion Books for Children./ Illustration by William Wegman from *Little Red Riding Hood*, retold by William Wegman with Carole Kismaric and Marvin Heiferman. Text and photographs copyright © 1993 by William Wegman. Reprinted by permission of Hyperion Books for Children./ Illustration by William Wegman from *Cinderella*, retold by William Wegman with Carole Kismaric and Marvin Heiferman. Text and photographs copyright © 1993 by William Wegman. Reprinted by permission of Hyperion Books for Children./ Photograph of Wegman with his dogs ©Madeleine de Sinety./ Photograph Benno Friedman/Outline.

Cumulative Index

Author/Artist Index

The following index gives the number of the volume in which an author/artist's biographical sketch appears.